PENGUIN HANDBOOKS
A GUIDE TO PROVENCE

Michael Jacobs was born in Italy and studied art history at the Courtauld Institute of Art in London, where he received a doctorate in 1982 for his research into eighteenth-century Italian art. In recent years he has taught at an American art school in Provence and has acted as a tour guide throughout Europe. He now works principally as a writer. Among his books are *The Phaidon Companion to Art and Artists in the British Isles* (1980, with Malcolm Warner), the volumes on *France* and *Britain and Ireland* in the Mitchell Beazley *Traveller's Guide to Art* series (1984, with Paul Stirton) and *The Good and Simple Life: Artists' Colonies in Europe and America* (1985).

He is based in London but spends half his year travelling, most recently to France, Mexico, Hungary, Spain and Brazil. At present he is writing a guide to Andalusia.

A Guide
to Provence

MICHAEL JACOBS

PENGUIN BOOKS

PENGUIN BOOKS

Published by the Penguin Group
27 Wrights Lane, London W8 5TZ, England
Viking Penguin Inc., 40 West 23rd Street, New York, New York 10010, USA
Penguin Books Australia Ltd, Ringwood, Victoria, Australia
Penguin Books Canada Ltd, 2801 John Street, Markham, Ontario, Canada L3R 1B4
Penguin Books (NZ) Ltd, 182–190 Wairau Road, Auckland 10, New Zealand

Penguin Books Ltd., Registered Offices: Harmondsworth, Middlesex, England

First published by Viking 1988
Published in Penguin Books 1989
1 3 5 7 9 10 8 6 4 2

Copyright © Michael Jacobs, 1988
All rights reserved.

Maps by Reginald Piggott

Made and printed in Great Britain by
Richard Clay Ltd, Bungay, Suffolk
Filmset in Sabon

To my friends in Lacoste

Contents

List of Illustrations

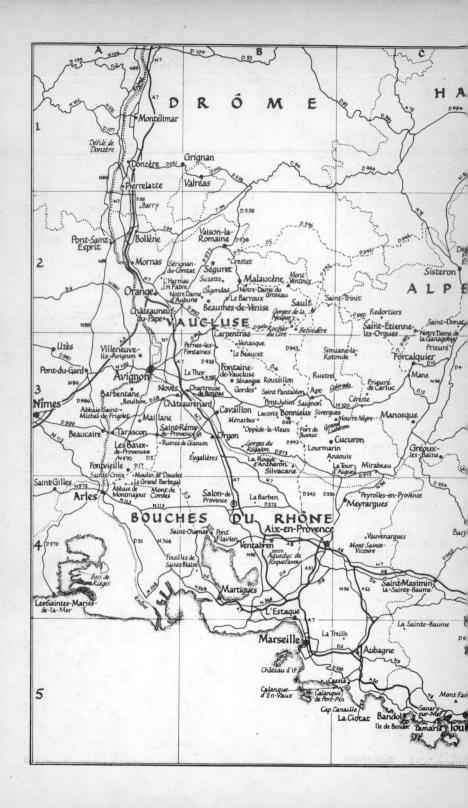

Preface and Acknowledgements

In the summer of 1981 I took up the post of art history teacher at an American art school in the south of France. The school was affiliated to the Cleveland Institute of Art, and was situated at Lacoste, a beautiful, isolated hill village between Aix-en-Provence and Avignon. Before going to Lacoste I had only a superficial knowledge of Provence. I had had family holidays on the coast, and had been to most of the famous tourist sights of the interior. But I was as yet unaware of the complexity of the region and the extraordinary variety of its scenery and monuments. From Lacoste I undertook longer and longer walking tours, and was also able to borrow the school moped, a twenty-five-year-old Peugeot which even accompanied me up to some of the highest passes in the Alps. In Lacoste itself I spent much of my time in people's homes and in the village's two cafés, where I picked up more information about Provençal life than would ever have been possible in libraries.

My greatest debt in the writing of this book must clearly be to the staff and students of the Cleveland Institute of Art at Lacoste, and to the villagers themselves. In particular I would like to thank Véronique Bienfait, Roddy O'Connor, Peter de Francia, Maurice Grau, Caroline Henne, Tina Mullen, Bernard Pfriem, Corinne Paquin, the Salva family, and Lilianne Ségura. Elsewhere in Provence I was generously helped by the staff of local tourist offices and town halls, shopkeepers, museum curators and others too numerous to be listed individually. However, specific mention should be made of the following: the staff of the Roumanille bookshop in Avignon, for their help with recently published books on the region; Marie-Madeleine Fulconis of the Association Stéphanois, for introducing me to the fascinating folklore and customs of the Tinée valley; Jean-Paul Clébert, for sharing with me his vast knowledge of Provence; John O'Keeffe, for his friendship and willingness to drive me to obscure places; and Sergio Kahn, Brigitte Perlès and their three children, for making my stay in Marseille so enjoyable.

Kyran O'Sullivan and Duncan and Nancy Caldwell acted as hosts during my various research trips to Paris, and Duncan freely lent me books from his impressive collection of esoteric travel literature. Yann Daniel, a former Breton resident of Lacoste now also living in Paris, has supplied me over the years with countless colourful stories about Provence. Friends and family from England came to see me in Provence and joined me on many of my trips around the region. Among these visitors were Des Brennan, Liz Burrett, Richard Cowan, Jeremy Galton, David, Francis and Mariagrazia Jacobs, Jennifer and Nicholas Johnson, Mark Jones, Paul and Janis Stirton, and Camilla Toulmin. Andrew Best, of Curtis Brown, first encouraged me to write this book, and kindly read through an early draft of the manuscript. Jackie Rae, as always, has provided constant advice and support.

M.J.

NOTE: For permission to use extracts from A. Bonner, *Songs of the Troubadours*, grateful thanks are due to Unwin Hyman Ltd.

1

Landscapes in History

In between Vienne and Valence, on the way south to Provence down the Rhône valley, stands a roadside monument marking the 45th parallel, the latitude equidistant from the North Pole and the Equator. From here, the Pont-de-l'Isère, the landscape begins to change. Mulberry bushes and other such flora of a northern climate give way to olive trees after Valence; the hills become drier and rockier; the first thyme appears at La Voulte-sur-Rhône. Making this journey in the middle of winter, the hero of Lawrence Durrell's novel *Monsieur* describes the pleasurable sensation of 'crawling out of winter into a nascent spring'. To Ford Madox Ford, who found Provence the only paradise on earth apart from the reading room of the British Museum, this stretch of the Rhône valley near Valence had a special significance: 'Somewhere between Vienne and Valence the South begins; somewhere between Valence and Montélimar . . . Eden!'

The first impression on arriving in Provence is invariably of being cut off from the rest of France, in a world which seems to have far more in common with countries to the south. Prosper Mérimée, stepping out of the Rhône ferry at Avignon, was surprised by the abruptness of the transition: ' . . . the language, the costumes, the appearance of the country, all seemed strange to someone coming from the centre of France'. He thought he was in the middle of a Spanish town. Stendhal, also arriving at Avignon from the north, was elated at being in a town which recalled his beloved Italy. Other enthusiastic visitors to Provence, such as Guy de Maupassant, were reminded elsewhere in the region of Greece. The poet Roy Campbell even considered the Provence which he had known in the 1920s to be the closest equivalent of the Africa of his childhood and adolescence.

This picture of Provence as an exotic land subject to a wide range of foreign influences is borne out by a glance at the region's complex history. Situated between Spain and Italy and at the foot of what was once Europe's major thoroughfare, the Rhône valley, Provence has acted not only as a vital commercial link between northern and southern Europe, but also, in the words of Ford Madox Ford, as a 'highway along which travelled continually the stream of the arts, of thought, of the traditions of life'.

Colonized by the Greeks, and invaded by the Celts and other peoples from northern Europe, Provence later became the first province which the Romans established outside of Italy. The Saracens from North Africa repeatedly invaded the region after the sixth century, and by the ninth century had occupied the whole of the mountainous district known as the Maures, which they referred to as Djabal Al Kilal. Provence, elevated into a kingdom by Charlemagne's son Lothare in 855, was joined to the Holy Roman Empire in the tenth century, but with its counts retaining a considerable independence. In the twelfth century Provence passed first to the Counts of Toulouse and then to the Counts of Barcelona: a reminder of the latter's former presence in the region is the name of the Alpine town of Barcelonnette, originally known as Barcelone. Italian influences came to supersede those of Spain in the following century, when the daughter of the Count of Barcelona married into the house of Anjou, which ruled the kingdoms of Sicily and Naples. The Italian connection was strengthened after 1274, when the papacy acquired the Comtat-Venaissin (a territory corresponding with the present-day Vaucluse) and later took up residence in the adjoining town of Avignon. Later in the century Nice and its surrounding region detached themselves from Provence and joined the earldom of Savoy in Italy.

Provence became incorporated into the kingdom of France in 1487, but even then its administrators enjoyed a high degree of autonomy. The Comtat-Venaissin meanwhile, though no longer used by the papacy as a residence after 1376, remained a papal possession ruled by an Italian viceregate until the French Revolution: passports were required to cross its borders, and it became a centre of refuge for Jews, criminals and other people escaping from French persecution. Another, if far smaller, foreign possession in Provence was the tiny principality of Orange, which became a possession of the Dutch house of Nassau in the sixteenth century and was only ceded to France in

1713 (a loss amply made up for by the accession of this same family to the throne of England).

The nineteenth century saw Provence acquiring more or less the shape it has today: the return to France of the Comtat-Venaissin in 1789 was to be followed by that of Nice in 1860, leaving only a small Alpine area north of Saorge in Savoy possession. Aix, the capital of Provence since the time of the Counts, was now replaced as capital by Marseille, a town rapidly rising to become Europe's leading port. At the same time the French government was pursuing a rigid policy of centralization, depriving Provence of much of its former administrative independence and strongly discouraging the use of the Provençal language in schools. It was against this background that the Provençal nationalist movement came of age. This movement, which had its origins in the writings of local eighteenth-century historians such as J.-P. Papon and Darluc, was essentially literary rather than political in motivation, and certainly was not inspired by any separatist ideals. At its forefront was a group of writers calling themselves the Félibres, who celebrated the wealth of Provence's native culture and aimed to preserve this now threatened culture for future generations. Above all the Félibres were dedicated to the cause of reviving the Provençal language, a language which had been little used by writers since the Middle Ages. By far the best known of the Félibres was the poet Frédéric Mistral, whose winning of the Nobel Prize in 1901 did much to draw world attention to Provence. It is impossible to travel in the region today without coming across some memorial to him or finding lines of his poetry engraved next to some famous beauty spot.

Ironically, Mistral and his followers were attempting to establish a strong cultural identity for Provence at a time when the region was becoming yet more varied socially. The rise of Marseille, and the development of industry elsewhere in Provence, contributed to the great increase in immigrants from Corsica and Piedmont, among whom was the grandfather of one of the most sentimentally Provençal writers of this century, Jean Giono. In more recent times the region has seen a considerable influx of workers from Morocco, Algeria and Spain, resulting in large African districts in the major coastal towns and a significant Spanish element in many of the villages of the interior. Tourism and the adoption of the region by artists and wealthy foreigners have further affected the character of Provence, in particular that of the coast. Poor, dangerous, and scarcely populated before the late eighteenth century, the coast was rapidly transformed the following century into the large cosmopolitan resort that most of it is today. Not a hint of this new culture is to be found in the work of Mistral, and only a curt dismissal in that of Giono, who considered that it had nothing to do with the 'real Provence'.

Present-day Provence comprises five of the administrative regions that are known today as *départements*: Bouche-du-Rhône, Vaucluse, Var, Alpes-de-Haute-Provence, and Alpes-Maritimes, the latter incorporating the Principality of Monaco, an independent state ever since the Grimaldi family acquired it from the Genoese in 1309. Put together, these five *départements* form a vast area of remarkable geographical diversity stretching from the east bank of the Rhône to the Alps. However, while all this area is officially Provence, the 'real', unofficial boundaries of the region are heavily disputed. Durrell tells a story of how he met an Arles man who in a homesick moment had had tattooed on his chest a map of the 'real Provence'. This map corresponded with what had been the heart of Roman Provence, an area extending not much further east than the Vaucluse town of Apt, but including also what is now the Languedoc *département* of the Gard on the western side of the Rhône. Mistral's Provence was concentrated on this same area. He too did not think of the Rhône as the dividing line between Provence and Languedoc, despite its having acted as such since the early Middle Ages. When describing once what he thought of as Provence, he wrote that it comprised all the land watered by the Rhône and swept by the infamous north wind which bore his name: and after all, he asked, could his friend and colleague Alphonse Daudet be called anything other than a Provençal writer even though he was born in the Gard town of Nîmes? On another occasion he defined the region in a more expansive way still: Provence, he then stated, went all the way 'from the Pyrenees to the Alps'.

Giono was less generous. For him the real Provence was the land to the north both of the river Durance and its tributary the Verdon, a largely desolate area of upper Provence which has received only partial coverage in guide-books. To most writers, however, the one real barrier within the official boundaries of Provence is the river Var. The area to the east of this river, the former County of Nice, is referred to less as Provence than as the Riviera or Côte d'Azur (a term coined in

1887 by the journalist Stéphen Liégeard). The *mistral* does not blow here, the food and architecture bear the strong imprint of the five centuries of Italian occupation, and the scenery is far lusher than anything to be found to the west. Yet perhaps the last word on this should be with the historical novelist Marcel Brion, who, in excusing himself from not including the Côte d'Azur in his own book on Provence, wrote that of course Provence did not stop at the Var, but it was just that on the other side of the river there began 'another Provence' deserving separate study.

'Naturally you love Provence,' says a character in Colette's novel *La Treille de muscat*, 'but which Provence? There are several.' It is vital to remember this when discussing any aspect of the region, beginning with the Provençals themselves. Any generalization about a people is suspect, but those made about the Provençals seem to be particularly so. The region's southern climate has led travellers to describe its people in the same hackneyed terms that are commonly applied to all those living in a Mediterranean climate. Thus to Victor Hugo the Provençals were hot-blooded and violent ('in Paris one quarrels, in Avignon one kills'); to Stendhal they were open, spontaneous and tolerant; to Durrell they were smiling, and delightfully unhurried. The two most stressed attributes of the Provençal character are undoubtedly laziness and whimsicality. The reputation for the former appears largely derived from the difficulties experienced by wealthy settlers on the Côte d'Azur in finding locals to work for them; the reputation for the latter was spread by the publication of Daudet's *Tartarin de Tarascon*, a story of an endearingly foolish man living in day-dreams. To Mistral's irritation the ridiculous figure of Tartarin became to most French readers the archetypal Provençal. His enormous popularity with the French has survived to this day, and only a few years ago an old house in Tarascon was chosen as the birthplace of this fictitious individual. The light-hearted, easy-going, indeed comic aspect of the Provençal people was given a further boost this century by the works of another Provençal author, Marcel Pagnol. Pagnol's immensely popular books, plays and films confirmed the Parisian view of Provence as an enormous playground, where people spent much of their time drinking *pastis*, playing *boules* and indulging in animated banter.

A number of recent Provençal authors have tried hard to refute this image of their people. One of these is Maurice Pézet, who wrote a study of popular uprisings in Provence (*La Provence des rebelles*, 1980) in the hope that the French reader would no longer think of the Provençal man as 'light-hearted, whimsical, lacking in seriousness, both in his work and in fighting, someone whose sole concern is to have a good time in the sun'. Giono took a harder line still. He thought that the stereotypical Provençal man of the open smile and gesticulating arms was in most cases just someone trying to live up to what others expected of him. At all events, he went on to say, such a type could only come from the rich fertile region of the Rhône valley. The lonely plateaux that Giono considered the real Provence produced in his view an altogether different type of person, silent and un-smiling.

'There is no single Provençal person,' suggested the chronicler of the Félibres, 'there are just Provençal people.' One could add that there is not even a unified Provençal language. The language which Mistral and his followers tried to revive was essentially the written language of the troubadours, and bears almost as little resemblance to Provençal as it is spoken as does the poetry of Robert Burns to the speech of the Scots. Spoken Provençal is difficult to transcribe, and like everything else to do with Provence, changes significantly from district to district.

The complexity of Provence, the impossibility of reaching any straightforward conclusion about its character, is illustrated above all in its geography. In many ways Provence has all the qualities of the earthly paradise invoked by Ford Madox Ford. Throughout history Provence has been praised for its natural abundance. The Romans gave the region the name of The Province because, in the words of the sixteenth-century Dutch botanist Thomas Platter, 'it is unrivalled not only in Europe, but also in Africa and Asia in its fertility, beauty, and the softness of its climate'. The seventeenth-century geographer Louis Coulon wrote that 'if we were living at the time of pagan gods, we would say that the Gods were competing with each other in granting Provence their favours'. Papon, in the following century, described Provence as this 'garden of the Hesperides, which under a beautiful sky, produces the perfumes of Arabia, the riches of the Orient, Spain and Africa'. An English traveller in 1701, Thomas Veryard, was no less complimentary: 'Nothing could have been more pleasant and diverting than our journey thro' Provence, where all our senses were ever cloyed with an immense variety of the most agreeable and charming objects. I fancied it to be one great Garden, where the Rival Products of Nature seemed to contend for the Masterdom. The fields and cultivated hills are stor'd with Vines, Almonds, Olives, Figs, Oranges and Pomegranates: and the Wast Ground (if I may so call it) is overspread with Rosemary, Time, Marjoram, Lavender, Myrtil, and divers other odiferous and medicinal Plants. In a word, it's the most fruitful and delectable Province on this side of the Alps, and justly stiled the Paradise of France.'

But, as Ford Madox Ford himself said, 'Every Paradise must have its Eve.' An English agriculturalist, Arthur Young, surveying Provence in the late eighteenth century, concluded that the Provençal environment was deceptively rich, and that in fact much of the land was unsuitable for farming: 'Good Heaven! – what an idea northern people have, like myself, before I knew better, of fine sun and a delicious climate, as it is called, that gives myrtles, oranges, lemons, pomegranates, odors in the hedges; yet are such countries, if irrigation be wanting, the veriest desert in the world. On the most miserable tracts of our heaths and moors, you will find butter, milk and cream; give me that that will feed a cow, and let oranges remain in Provence.'

The barrenness described by Young has been exacerbated by the notorious fires to which Provence has always been subject. Fires, in a dry region, incorporating the most forested *département* of France (the Var), have spread with great speed over vast areas. As recently as August 1986 a fire reduced to a charred wasteland much of the forested hill country in between the beautiful villages of Lucéram and Coaraze, thirty kilometres behind Nice.

Provence's traditional worst enemies, however, are neither droughts nor fires. 'The three curses of Provence,' goes a famous saying, 'are the *Mistral*, the Taxes and the Durance.' The Durance, and to a lesser extent the Rhône, had once the reputation of being two of France's most violent rivers. Before being tamed by the construction of irrigation and hydraulic works at the beginning of this century, they were notorious for flooding. Henry James visited Avignon in October 1882, and was almost present at one such flood: '. . . it was raining, as it rains in Provence,' he wrote shortly after arriving, thus reminding the reader that Provence is not just the land of the sun. The rain persisted for several days, reports came in that both the Durance and the Rhône were in danger of overflowing their banks, and eventually James curtailed his Provence trip and fled back north.

The *mistral* is the one enemy of the region that the visitor today is most likely to encounter. Described by Stendhal as 'le grand *drawback* de Provence', this biting, persistent and ferocious wind brings an element of wild unpredictability to the region's climate. The mild winters for which Provence is generally known can suddenly be transformed by its arrival, as Tobias Smollett found out while travelling between Montpellier and Nice. The wind ('the severest I've ever felt') started blowing after he had left Brignoles, and by the next day the ground had been covered by a thick layer of snow: 'This cannot be the South of France (I said to myself), it must be the highlands of Scotland!' Stranger still is when the wind strikes in the middle of summer, days of intense heat being abruptly interrupted by ones of considerable cold. At first the wind can be exciting, and indeed writers such as Mistral, Giono and Roy Campbell have described it as a powerful poetic force. But then, as it continues, and eyes become redder from persistent rubbing, it begins to wear a person down. Its persistence is remarkable. There is a saying in Provence that if the *mistral* blows for three days it will blow for six, if it blows for six it will blow for nine, and so on. In 1775, the wind was reputed to have blown without interruption for three months. No wonder the Marquise de Sévigné complained once to her son-in-law about the extreme character of the Provençal weather:

'How excessive you are in Provence! Everything is extreme, your heat waves, your calm days, your unseasonal rains, your autumnal thunderstorms! There is nothing temperate about you. Your rivers are overflowing, your fields are flooded and ruined, your Durance has always the devil inside it.'

Giono concluded that Provence was 'the land of contrasts'. He himself took a perverse pleasure in those dark elements in the region that so horrified the Marquise de Sévigné: in his novels he created a desolate picture of Provence which in its own way was no less romanticized than the sun-soaked paradise evoked by other authors. Yet it was also Giono who recognized, more than any other writer, the infinite variety of the region. 'Provence,' he wrote, 'has a thousand faces, a thousand aspects, a thousand characters, and it is false to describe it as a single and indivisible phenomenon.' According to Giono a day's journey by car through Provence would take the traveller across at least 500 landscapes, some reminiscent of Tuscany, others of Scotland, Lebanon, Rome and so on. Obviously no guide-book can hope to list all the region's natural attractions; and Giono himself confessed that after a lifetime of travelling in Provence he still could not truthfully say that he knew the region. But an awareness simply of the principal landscapes – which range from the spectacular mountain scenery behind Nice to the marshlands of the Camargue, from the arid wastes of the Crau to the endless forests of the Var – is surely proof enough that for variety alone Provençal scenery is unique in Europe.

Let us imagine now a journey through Provence, beginning where the opening paragraph of this chapter left off, somewhere along the Rhône valley south of Montélimar. Until the advent of the Paris to Avignon railway in 1855, the journey down the valley from Lyon would usually be undertaken by river, the roads being in a ruinous state, under constant threat of highwaymen, and much slower (at least six days instead of only two). A highpoint of the journey came just after Montélimar, when the Rhône cuts a narrow passage through the rock, with sheer walls rising to the east and jagged spikes to the west. The speed at which the Rhône once flowed created certain hazards, particularly further south, at Pont-Saint-Esprit, where the boats had to pass under one of the arches of a thirteenth-century bridge: disasters were common here, and timid passengers were allowed off at one side to be picked up at the other.

The beauty and excitement of this stretch of the Rhône – celebrated by Mistral in his last epic poem, *Le Chant du Rhône*, will probably not be appreciated by today's traveller. Though pleasure cruises still sail from Lyons, visitors to Provence are now more likely to approach the region either from the Autoroute du Soleil or by the world's fastest train service, the T.G.V. (Trains à Grande Vitesse), a service which reduces the whole journey from Paris to Avignon to just over three and a half hours. Both the motorway and the T.G.V. pass the more industrialized areas of a valley which now processes nearly half of France's nuclear energy. South of the Défilé de Donzère the Rhône is joined by a long canal which feeds the massive Bollène Hydro-Electric Station, alongside which is the Pierrelatte Atomic Energy Centre. These unprepossessing industrial works mark the boundary of present-day Provence. For a more sympathetic introduction to the region the car traveller should briefly leave the motorway at Bollène and follow the steep cul-de-sac which leads after a few kilometres to the ruins of Barry. Barry is one of Provence's many abandoned medieval hill villages, but a particularly extensive and evocative one. Overgrown, scented with herbs, and scarcely visited, it provides a most poignant contrast to the busy, modernized valley which it overlooks.

South of Bollène the valley opens up to turn eventually into the flat expanses of the Rhône delta. At Avignon, the traditional alighting point for boat travellers down the Rhône, the traveller faces a choice: either to leave the Vaucluse and go south down the valley to the sea, or to go east through upper Provence, a journey of near continuous mountain scenery. Let us take for a moment the latter alternative and begin by visiting the most celebrated of Provence's natural landmarks, Mont Ventoux.

Mont Ventoux, the highest mountain in France in between the Alps and the Pyrenees, dominates almost every vista in the Vaucluse. It first comes into view a few kilometres before Montélimar, but it is not until after Bollène – when it can be seen rising above the vineyards of the Côtes du Rhône and the bizarrely shaped peaks of the Dentelles de Montmirail – that its massive pyramidical form become fully apparent. It has the monumental look of a Mount Fiji or Kilimanjaro, and from a distance seems similarly covered in snow, though in fact its white crest is formed for much of the year purely of limestone. Apart from anything else the mountain is a geological and botanical curiosity, and one of the finest descriptions of it is by a naturalist, J.-H. Fabre. In his *Souvenirs entomologiques*, the work which established his enormous popularity as the 'Insects' Homer', Fabre likened the mountain to a heap of stones broken up for road-mending purposes, raised suddenly to a height of one and a quarter miles, and stained black with trees. Thanks to its height, Fabre continued, as well as to the isolated position which leaves it exposed on all sides to atmospheric influences, the mountain lends itself remarkably well to the study of the climatic distribution of plants. At its base grow olive trees, broom, aromatics, wild iris and other such plants dependent on a Mediterranean sun, while at its summit are to be found such sub-arctic flora as the Spitzbergen saxifrage and the Iceland poppy. Thus, as Fabre summed up, '. . . half a day's journey in an upward direction brings before our eyes a succession of the chief vegetable types we should find in the course of a long voyage from south to north along the same meridian'.

One can understand how such a strange and prominent mountain should have gained over the centuries a legendary, mystical character. Known since at least classical times as the 'windy mountain' on account of the constant winds that blow at its summit, it is a landmark which has inspired considerable awe and fascination. In 1327 the poet Petrarch, who had been observing the mountain ever since his childhood in Carpentras, felt finally compelled to climb it. Few of his contemporaries were bold enough to join him, and in the end he decided to have only his brother and two servants as companions. They set off from the village of Malaucène early in the morning, and were undeterred when, part of the way up, they came across an old shepherd who said that he too had been to the top many years before and had got nothing out of it except torn clothes and a firm resolution never to go there again. Though exhausted and having to pause many times for breath, the climbers reached their destination and were rewarded by an exceptionally clear view. Petrarch, sighing as he looked towards his native Italy, then sat down and took out a copy of Saint Augustine's *Confessions*, which happened to fall open at the following page: 'Men go far to observe the summits of mountains, the water of the sea, the beginnings and the courses of the rivers, the immensity of the ocean, but they neglect themselves.' The climbers returned to Malaucène after nightfall, and while his companions rested, Petrarch immediately wrote a long account of the day in Latin to a former teacher, thus turning the climb into the first recorded one in history. Some have questioned the truthfulness of this letter, thinking the climb to have been a purely imaginary one intended to have only a symbolic significance. None the less, there are details in Petrarch's account – such as his description of the gravel-like surface of Mont Ventoux, or the way the mountain casts a perfect conical shadow at sunrise and sunset – that could only have come from first-hand experience.

In the century after Petrarch had popularized the mountain, a small chapel dedicated to the True Cross was built at its summit, a relic of this cross placed inside it, and a hermit appointed as guardian. From then onwards a regular stream of pilgrims began making the ascent, as well as numerous scientists including the seventeenth-century Aix scholar and friend of Rubens, N. de Peiresc. The chapel was rebuilt in the eighteenth century, and shortly afterwards there began an annual pilgrimage to it on 14 September. One of those who later took part in this was the founder member of the Félibres, Joseph Roumanille. All the Félibres were in fact to make the ascent, for by then Mont Ventoux had not only a literary and religious importance, but had also come to be seen almost as a symbol of Provence. Mistral, for instance, describing his youthful aspirations as a poet, spoke about 'planting his standard on Mont Ventoux'.

The mountain's summit has changed considerably even since Mistral's day. The chapel, rebuilt yet again at the turn of the century, now shares the summit with a weather observatory, an air force radar station and a television mast. Viewing tables and souvenir stalls cater for the large number of tourists who come here, most of whom will have made the ascent by car. From 1902 to 1973 the road to the summit from Bédoin was used for motor-car hill trials, and today the summit is sometimes one of the stages in the Tour de France cycle race (a roadside monument marks the spot where the popular English cyclist Tom Simpson collapsed and died in the race of 1967). A visit to Mont Ventoux today might lack the romantic, mysterious qualities that it once had, but is certainly worth it for the magnificence of the view. In the intensely clear days that accompany a *mistral* the whole of Provence is spread out before you, from the Rhône delta to the snow-capped Alps: you can make out without difficulty most of the distinctive landmarks of Provence, such as the ranges of the Alpilles and the Sainte-Victoire, and even such tiny details as boats sailing on the sea near Marseille.

A remarkable feature of the view is the wild and unspoilt character of so much of the landscape. Directly in front of you to the south stretches the Vaucluse plateau, a broad wooded area intercut with empty valleys and such spectacular gorges as that of the Nesque. Giono wrote that there existed in upper Provence 'the civilization of the desert', and, appropriately, in the abbey of Sénanque, impressively hidden in one of these valleys, is a Centre for Sahara Studies.

Natural curiosities of all types abound in Provence. On the south-western edge of the Vaucluse plateau, just before reaching the long valley which divides the plateau from the range of the Lubéron, is the famous Fountain of Vaucluse. Once again it was Petrarch who made it famous, writing here many of his sonnets to his loved one, Laura. But it is not only the fountain's associations with Petrarch that have stirred the imagination of the many who have come here. The fountain takes the form of a dark, sinister cave at the foot of a sheer 700-foot cliff. Ominously silent for much of the year, it regularly erupts in winter and spring into a violent green torrent which rises above the cave to feed the exposed roots of a group of fig trees clinging to the cliff. The fountain is apparently fed by rainwater draining through the plateau into a vast labyrinth of underground tunnels; but the sheer violence of the torrent is more difficult to explain. In the summer of 1950 the underwater diver Jacques Cousteau tried with a team of colleagues to uncover the mystery; later he was to describe this attempt as 'our worst experience in 500 dives'. He and a companion were mysteriously overcome shortly after diving by the dangerous condition known as 'rapture of the deep', and almost died. They had reached a depth of nearly 200 feet, and the bottom of the fountain was still nowhere in sight.

Moving east along the southern edge of the plateau is Roussillon, and further east still Rustrel. Outside both these places the traveller will be surprised at coming across what seem like sections of the American desert. These are actually abandoned ochre quarries, the one at Rustrel being indeed called the 'Provençal Colorado'. The startlingly bright colouring of the ochre dust comprises a large range of orange, red and yellow tones, all brilliantly set off by the emerald green of the surrounding trees. The actor Jean Vilar described the quarry at Roussillon as 'the perfect setting for a tragedy: a red Delphi'.

At some point in between the Fontaine-de-Vaucluse and Roussillon, you enter the unofficial district known as the Lubéron. Its territory is not clearly defined, but falls roughly in between the southern edge of the Vaucluse plateau and the Durance river; its capital is Apt. Today the district has the reputation of being the most fashionable retreat in France, though the passing tourist is unlikely to be aware of this. The area has not been littered with new houses to the same extent as so many parts of the coast, but retains instead much of the secluded appearance that in the past made it a favourite place of refuge for all manner of heretics and recluses. As with Provence generally, however, it cannot be described as a unity. The Lubéron range itself, divided between the Petit and the rather wilder Grand Lubéron, changes radically between its northern and southern slopes. Should you, for instance, climb up the Petit Lubéron from the north, you will be struck by the transition from the deciduous wood on the one side to the landscape of aromatics on the other. The southern slopes, with their extensive views over the Durance valley towards the sea, have the open, Mediterranean character of much of lower Provence; the northern ones, in contrast, steep and scarred with ravines, belong more to the enclosed, isolated Provence so dear to Giono.

The heart of Giono's Provence lies in fact further east, in the *département* of Alpes-de-Haute-Provence. Though tourism is beginning to develop more rapidly here, inspired by articles describing this as 'the hidden Provence', much of it remains as little known as the Lubéron was up to the 1950s. Giono himself lived for most of his life around Manosque, which sits at the eastern foot of the Lubéron, overlooking the Durance as it turns sharply north towards Sisteron. The mountain range which fired his youthful imagination was not so much the Lubéron as the yet wilder Montagne de Lure, a continuation of the Ventoux range but far more inaccessible to the motorist. The name of one of its passes, Le Col de l'Homme Mort (the pass of the dead man) gives some idea of its forbidding character.

While the Lure framed Giono's horizon to the north, the vast plateau of Valensole, the setting too of many of his novels, confronted him to the east, on the other side of the Durance. Giono referred to this plain as a 'magnificent friend' of his, adding, however, that to the farmer it was a 'bad companion', 'the thrower of hail-stones, the creator of lightning, the great orchestrator of storms'. To the ordinary traveller the Valensole's greatest attraction is the blossoming, in March and July respectively, of its almond trees and lavender. The growing of almonds is a traditional source of Provençal economy, but that of lavender dates only from the late nineteenth century. The *département* of Alpes-de-Haute-Provence is the lavender capital of Provence, and some of the bleakest expanses here such as the plateau of Valensole are beautifully transformed in July into seas of vivid purple.

Beyond the Valensole is the one major tourist sight of the *département*, indeed one of the most impressive natural attractions in the whole of France, the Grand Canyon of the Verdon. As high in places as 1,500 metres and as wide as 700, the Grand Canyon stretches for twenty-one kilometres and is the most remarkable of a number of gorges cut by the Verdon river into the chalk plateaux of upper Provence. It was virtually unvisited before this century, for the simple reason that there were no roads and hardly any paths along it. Of the handful of peasants who made a meagre living by its sides, Papon wrote that they dressed in winter with furs, 'like the inhabitants of Greenland'.

The first successful attempt to sail down the canyon was not made until 1905. The expedition was led by the pioneering speleologist E.-A. Martel, who took three days to cover this wild and dangerous stretch of the Verdon. Today Martel is commemorated by a plaque placed at one of the canyon's most impressive viewpoints, the Point Sublime – which records that it was through his efforts that the opening up of the canyon for tourists became possible. In 1927 a footpath now named after him was laid out at the bottom of the gorge, in between the Chalet de la Maline and the Point Sublime. This is an exciting path which though followed today by numerous tourists still manages to fill the visitor with a great sense of adventure: considerable care is required to make the steep descent into the canyon, and you are strongly advised to bring extra clothing to deal with the sudden changes of temperature, and also a flashlight to use in the long dark tunnels built along the path near the Point Sublime. For those who are less energetic and are content simply to see the canyon from above, this was made possible by the daring construction in 1947 of the Corniche Sublime, followed twenty-six years later by the completion of the Route des Crêtes.

To the south and east of the Verdon Canyon lie respectively the coastal *départements* of Var and Alpes-Maritimes. Alpes-de-Haute-Provence extends far to the north of here, but after Sisteron, where the olive trees end, it takes on a rugged, Alpine character closer in spirit to Savoy or Dauphiné than to the rest of Provence. Barcelonnette, Provence's northernmost town, is squeezed into a narrow valley dominated by spectacularly high mountains. Such was once the poverty and isolation of this valley that from the early nineteenth century onwards, inspired by the successful example of three local brothers, there began a large-scale emigration movement to Mexico: some of the more successful emigrants eventually came back to their native valley, building on their return grand Mexican-style villas so totally incongruous in their Alpine surroundings.

It is high time to return to Avignon and from here go south, into a much more familiar Provence. Bouche-du-Rhône, which embraces most of the Rhône delta as well as Marseille and Aix-en-Provence, is the land not only of Mistral but also of Van Gogh, Cézanne and Pagnol. This is where the Romans left some of their greatest buildings outside Italy; where the troubadours reputedly held their Courts of Love; and where Provence was once ruled by its counts.

Frédéric Mistral was born and lived almost all his life in the village of Maillane, just south of the Durance. A small agricultural community hardly affected by tourism, Maillane is surrounded by the heavily fertile plain which covers much of the northern half of Bouche-du-Rhône. Always a prosperous area, its prosperity was increased in Mistral's day by the planting of long rows of trees to protect the crops from the region's cruel north wind: the cypresses made famous by Van Gogh, and the plane trees that today seem one of Provence's most characteristic features, nearly all date from this period. Bouche-du-Rhône remains to this day the market garden of France, and the town of Cavaillon, on the plain's eastern border, is reputedly the wealthiest town in the country.

Mistral came from what he described as 'a sort of peasant aristocracy', and spent much of his childhood and youth assisting his parents on the land. The farm where he was brought up survives, as does the so-called Lézard House in the middle of the village, where Mistral lived with his mother following the death of his father in 1855. Mistral had by then completed his law studies at Aix and was well embarked on the epic Provençal poem *Miréio*, which, on its publication in 1859, was to earn for the twenty-eight-year-old poet overnight fame. The second of his epic poems, *Calendau* (1868), was also written in the Lézard House, but then in 1876 he moved to the house next door, where he lived until his death in 1914, writing here his massive encyclopaedia of Provence, *Le Trésor de la Félibrige* (1878–86), and his posthumously edited *Le Chant du Rhône*. This house, with its heavy, bourgeois interior kept almost exactly as it was when Mistral was alive, is now a most evocative museum to his memory.

Miréio and *Calendau* provide perhaps the best introduction to the main landmarks of Bouche-du-Rhône. The *Chant du Rhône*, describing the highpoints of a river journey from Lyon, takes the reader only a short distance into the *département*. It ends with the poet sailing in between the twin castles of Beaucaire and Tarascon, a moment filled with a triumphant sense of arrival, inspiring the words, 'We are with God, and long live Provence.' The journey south from here is described in *Miréio*, which deals with a beautiful young girl brought up as a peasant's daughter among the wheat-fields of Mistral's childhood. She has many suitors, but falls in love with the only one of them who is not approved of by her father. Unable to marry him, she runs away dressed in the traditional costume of Arles to seek the help of the holy Marys at Les-Saintes-Maries-de-la-Mer, at the foot of the Rhône delta.

Mireille's anguished journey takes her first to the Alpilles, the small but distinctive mountain range which gives a savage indentation to the skyline south of Maillane. The gaunt, twisted peaks of scorched-white limestone, likened by an early nineteenth-century traveller to a 'frozen wave', were possibly the inspiration of a passage in Dante's *Inferno*. A narrow valley strewn with boulders called Le Val d'Enfer (the valley of hell) leads to the foot of the ruined town of Les Baux, the whitened walls of which are at first indistinguishable from the dramatic limestone spar on which they so perilously sit. In the early Middle Ages the seat of one of France's most powerful families, and the reputed scene of the troubadours' love tournaments, Les Baux declined in the fifteenth century and was largely destroyed in 1632 after having served as a refuge for Protestants. Regarded for years afterwards as a notorious bandits' lair, its fortunes improved in the early nineteenth century when there was discovered here the mineral which later came to be known as bauxite. From that point onwards it began also to develop as a major tourist attraction, impressing and sometimes depressing generations of travellers with its sinister, lunar-like setting.

Beyond the Alpilles the land stretches almost without interruption down to the Mediterranean. At one time this area was covered almost entirely by marshes and water, the small outcrops on which stand today the abbey of Montmajour and 'Daudet's Windmill' being originally two of a group of islands. The reclamation of the land was begun by the Romans and continued into the seventeenth century, much of the work being carried out by monks from Montmajour. Today the area has a parched look, and becomes increasingly so the further south you get, until eventually the agricultural plain dries up on its eastern side to turn into a bizarre desert strewn with stones, the Crau.

The Crau is a landscape which mirrors the torment in the heart of Mireille, who at this point in her journey is almost overcome with heat, exhaustion and grief. It is a landscape too which has intrigued travellers from ancient times. The Roman geographer Strabo tells the legend that the stones were provided by Jupiter as ammunition for Hercules, who had found his way to Spain barred by the Ligurians and had run out of arrows. In later centuries scientists provided scarcely more plausible explanations for the presence of these stones; finally, however, they were interpreted as having been deposited there by the Durance, which at one stage did not flow into the Rhône but went straight into the sea at this point.

Tourists do not stay long at the Crau, but they do at the adjoining Camargue, the wild expanse of marshy, sandy lagoons which constitutes the Rhône estuary. Mosquito-ridden, impossibly hot and humid during the summer, and subject at other times to some of the worst excesses of the *mistral*, the Camargue is the part of Provence whose charm is least readily apparent. And yet it has exerted a fascination perhaps greater than has any other area of the region. Its one indisputable feature of interest is its fauna and wildlife. Owing to its special atmospheric conditions you can find here species rarely found elsewhere in Europe: in July large areas of the marshland are turned bright pink by migrating flamingos from Africa. But above all there are its bulls and wild white horses, which, though hardly rare breeds of animal, encapsulate the romantic, mysterious qualities of the Carmargue. No one knows exactly when or from where they came, but they were certainly here at the time of the Greeks and might have been around much, much earlier: the local bull is of a type bearing a close resemblance to that painted in the prehistoric caves of Lascaux.

The appearance of the Carmargue has changed considerably over the centuries, thanks to such factors as the constant building of canals and irrigation schemes, the splitting up of the Rhône in the early eighteenth century into two branches, and, not least, the significant and unpredictable shifts of the alluvial soil on which it lies. Its heyday was under the Greeks and Romans, when the land was densely wooded and considered sufficiently salubrious for the construction of wealthy villas. The decline set in during the Middle Ages. Monks in the eleventh century exploited the salt banks on the eastern side of the estuary, but otherwise the land was little lived in apart from by fishermen and the odd hunter. The occasional traveller who came here described it as a primeval wasteland, Stendhal for instance writing that the area was how he imagined New Zealand would look.

By Stendhal's day the interior of the Camargue had in fact already begun to be repopulated. From the late eighteenth century onwards there started moving into the area a group of people who would later greatly contribute to its romantic appeal. These were the *gardians*, ranchers who made their living by herding bulls on horseback. They caught the imagination of Mistral and the Félibres, to whom their picturesque life-style, though so shortly established, seemed integral to the traditions of Provence and deserved to be saved for future generations. The task of protecting them fell to one of the younger and more eccentric of Mistral's followers, the Marquis Folco Baroncelli-Javon.

The Marquis's ancestors were Florentine merchants who had settled in Avignon in the fifteenth century and had built the magnificent Palais du Roure in the heart of the city. The palace still remained in the family's possession in the Marquis's time, but by this date the family had lost most of their money. The young Baroncelli-Javon struggled to live as a poet, but then in 1890, when he was twenty-one, he decided to leave his native Avignon, renounce what earthly possessions he still had left, and lead the life of a *gardian* in the Camargue; he was to do so for the next sixty years, fitting in, when time allowed, his literary activities. The Marquis's sympathies for his fellow ranchers, these so-called cowboys of France, extended to all oppressed minorities, including the Boers and the American Indians. His concern for the latter group led indirectly to one of the more bizarre episodes in the Camargue's history, when Wild Bill Hickok brought his famous Indian circus here. The Indians pitched their wigwams around the Marquis's house, and their famous chiefs such as Sitting-Bull decorated him with tomahawks and feathered head-dresses, and gave him the honorary name of 'Zind-Kala-Wasté', meaning faithful bird. This episode was entirely appropriate to an area which this century has been popularized by the tourist industry as the 'wild west of France'.

The *gardians* and their cowboy hats and leather breeches live on today, if only as a tourist attraction, but the threat to the environment remains constant. The attempts to exploit the land for its economic potential, in particular by the cultivation of rice, has led to serious ecological changes. The creation in 1928 of a Camargue National Park was at least recognition of these problems. The flora and fauna of an extensive area of the south Camargue are now protected by law, and the largest of the lagoons, the Étang de Vaccarès, is out of bounds to all but scientists. The ordinary tourist can today only dream of what is perhaps the most haunting place in the Camargue, the island of Rièges, on the southern edge of the Vaccarès lagoon. It was here, in the only part of the Camargue to retain its ancient wood, that a friend of Baroncelli-Javon, Joseph d'Arbaud, set his fantasy novel, *La Béstio d'ou Vaccarès* (1926). The book, a fable of man's destruction of the natural world, tells of a beast with a human face, the last survivor of a primitive species which had been chased everywhere by man and had eventually found in the Camargue the one place where it thought it could be safe from further oppression.

Mireille finished her journey in the Camargue, expiring on the beach at Les-Saintes-Maries-de-la-Mer. But a description of much of the coastal Provence which lies to the east is to be found in Mistral's later poem, *Calendau*, the story of a young fisherman from Cassis who travels all over the region to carry out exploits intended to prove himself to his loved one.

The French coast, having been flat for much of the way from the Spanish border, is joined shortly after the Camargue by the range of the Estaque, which divides the Mediterranean from the large inland sea of the Étang de Berre, now surrounded by petrol refineries. From here right into Italy, the coast remains impressively mountainous. The stretch from l'Estaque to beyond Cassis is characterized by its scorched limestone cliffs, the dazzling whiteness of which sets off the emerald green of the pines at their base, and the vivid purple of the sea below.

The publication of Mistral's *Calendau* did much to publicize the beauty of this landscape, which was later to be a major source of inspiration to the group of colourists called the Fauves. A special feature of this coast are the little inlets known in Provençal as *calanques*. The Calanques de Port-Pin and d'En-Vau – in between Cassis and Marseille, and accessible only by foot or boat – are particularly fine. The former, shaded on all sides by pines, makes a quiet, idyllic bathing place; the latter is less cosy, but more dramatic, being hemmed in by impressively tall cliffs and needles of limestone. But without doubt the most spectacular landmark on the coast lies on the other side of Cassis. This, the Cap Canaille, boasts cliffs of nearly 400 metres, a height which makes them some of the tallest cliffs to fall directly into the sea in Europe.

The landscape of arid limestone mountains sliced by cliffs continues inland from Cassis. Travelling north to Aix, you pass on your left Mount Garlaban, a mountain which loomed high in the imagination of the young Marcel Pagnol, who was later to build a film studio nearby. Further on, to the right, is the narrow, eastern end of the Massif de la Sainte-Baume, a range whose crowning limestone cliffs – compared by Stendhal to the fantastic barren shapes in the background of Leonardo da Vinci's paintings – provided a cave where Mary Magdalene is supposed to have lived for nearly twenty years. Further limestone cliffs, in this case stretching right across the horizon, come into view as you near Aix. These constitute the crest of Montagne Sainte-Victoire, a mountain made famous by Cézanne but which only assumes the familiar triangular shape which he painted when seen from the west.

The valley between Cassis and the Sainte-Victoire skirts the border of Bouche-du-Rhône, and marks the confines of the barren limestone landscape which characterizes the south-eastern corner of the *département*. To the east is the *département* of the Var, much of which is densely wooded. Those slopes of the Sainte-Baume which lie in the Var are covered at their base by a dense forest; further forests spread north and east from here to cover large areas of land in the little-spoilt northern half of the *département*. But above all there are the forests which extend to the south-east and shroud almost the entire coastal range of the Maures with what seems like an endless undulating blanket of dark green. The name of this range is in fact derived from

35

the Provençal word for a dark wood, *mauro*. It is tempting also to see
in the name a reference to the Moors, Saracens, Turks, Barbarians
and other invaders from North Africa and the Middle East who made
the area a centre for their incursions into Provence from the eighth
century right up to the eighteenth. However, these people were generally referred to by the Provençals under the generic term of Saracens
rather than Moors. As well as perpetrating terrible atrocities, the
Saracens taught the locals such skills as the extraction of cork and
resin from the trees of the Maures forest. To this day the making of
bottle corks is one of the area's principal industries, together with the
production of the delicious chestnut sweets known as marrons
glaçés.

The forests of the Maures come right down to the coast, and also
cover the beautiful islands of Hyères. Early travellers commented on
how wild and unpopulated this coast appeared, particularly when
seen after sailing from Italy. Today, of course, the coast is no longer
the same, but there none the less remain stretches of it that match the
wilderness of the Maures' interior. A delightfully secluded footpath
shaded by pines follows the Saint-Tropez peninsula from Cap Camarat
to Gigaro, and leads the visitor into an area little disturbed by tourists
(see page 322). As for the tree-lined beaches of what is now the nature
reserve of the Îles d'Hyères, these are suggestive of an unspoilt tropical
paradise.

Before the nineteenth century, travellers who journeyed between
Marseille and Nice generally preferred to go by boat rather than take
the slower and more dangerous coastal roads. A stretch particularly
notorious for its bandits was the Estérel, a range of red porphyry rock
immediately to the east of the Maures. At the time this too was
covered almost entirely in a dense forest of oaks, cork trees and pines,
though sadly these were largely burnt down in fires as recently as the
1960s and 70s. A great many of those early travellers who braved the
Estérel route came back with stories of skirmishes with highwaymen:
one of these travellers was the famous Swiss naturalist, Ferdinand de
Saussure, who contrary to all advice even did the journey on foot, and
narrowly escaped death in the process.

Alpes-Maritimes, the last of Provence's *départements*, was created
in 1860 out of the former County of Nice and an area to the west –
once belonging to the Var – in between the river Var and the Esterel.

The coastal district of this *département* has been praised over the centuries for its temperate winter climate (unaffected of course by the *mistral*) and the luxuriance of its vegetation, a luxuriance which helps give it a character far more redolent of Italy than of the rest of Provence. It is not surprising that this fragrant land of countless flowers and aromatics should have become from the sixteenth century onwards – when Catherine de Medici began patronizing the perfumers of Grasse – the perfume capital of the world. Thanks to a mid-nineteenth-century entrepreneur, the journalist Alphonse Karr, it was also here that the decorative possibilities of dried flowers were first realized on a large scale. Flowers of all sorts contributed to the attraction of the area for the English, who virtually took over the coast in the nineteenth century. The English were responsible for creating some of the finest gardens on the coast, and English naturalists such as Traherne Moggridge and Clarence Bicknell undertook some of the most important of the numerous botanical studies to be made here. As one Englishwoman put it: '. . . if they [the English] cannot get over their two great stumbling blocks, a foreign language and a different church, then they have at least admitted to their sympathies the insects and the flowers'.

The sub-tropical vegetation which falls vertiginously down to the sea from Nice to the Italian border spreads also for several miles into the mountainous hinterland. Then the Alps proper begin. Their gate is the dramatic Gorge of the Vésubie, into which Republican soldiers were thrown during the aftermath of the Revolution. The valley of the Tinée, to the north of here, has much in common with that of Barcelonnette, to which it is linked by the frighteningly bare pass of the Bonette: it is an isolated place, cut off from the rest of Provence, but with a fascinating culture all of its own. On the eastern border of Alpes-Maritimes is the equally idiosyncratic valley of the Roya, which connects on both sides with Italy and contains that section of Provence which served as the hunting ground of the kings of Savoy until as late as 1947. In this geographical and historical extremity of Provence is to be found one of the Alps' most mysterious mountains, Mont Bégo.

On clear days Mont Bégo can be seen from the Riviera, and it has been suggested that the name of the coastal town of Antibes (meaning in Greek the 'town which faces') is an obscure allusion to it, a mountain which appears to have been at the centre of an ancient cult.

To approach this mountain today you leave the Roya valley at Saint-Dalmas-de-Tende and follow a steep little road to the dam at Les Mesches (see page 334). From here it is a good four-hour uphill walk to the strange desolate valley which lies under the western slope of the mountain. This is the Valley of Marvels, over 2,500 metres high, and under snow between October and late June. During these three and a half months when the snow has melted, the rocks of the valley reveal, carved on their granite surface, an estimated 100,000 primitive engravings. The first mention of these is by one Pierre de Montfort, who visited the valley in 1460: 'It was an infernal place with figures of devils and a thousand demons carved all over the rocks.'

Who was responsible for these bizarre, remote works? Were they, as the handful of early visitors to the valley variously suggested, simply the doodles either of bored shepherds, or of Carthaginian soldiers taking a break on their way to Italy? The English botanist Clarence Bicknell stumbled across these carvings on a botanical expedition to the valley in 1879. Thereafter he was diverted from his initial vocation, and spent much of the rest of his life obsessively studying them, establishing beyond a doubt that they were prehistoric in origin and signs of the worship of Mont Bégo. How strange to think that this isolated, primeval-looking valley, revealed by Bicknell to be one of the largest prehistoric sites in Europe, should lie only a short distance away from the elegant Riviera. But such a contrast is simply one of a multitude of contrasts that make up this complex land of Provence.

2

Ancient Provence

'As if in answer to the insistent call of far-off Roman trumpets, I set out one early Autumn for Provence.' Many have shared the painter Augustus John's vision of Provence as a land dominated by its classical past. It is a vision which accords well with that of the wealthy, smiling and highly civilized country which features in so much of the literature on the region. Yet there is another Provence, which existed long before that of the Greeks and Romans and of which the extraordinary rock art of Mont Bégo acts as a powerful reminder. Provence is rich in prehistoric monuments, and the wild, primitive character of much of the countryside seems imbued with their presence.

The first traces of man in Provence are to be found where they are perhaps least expected – behind the elegant apartment blocks of cosmopolitan Monaco. The Grotte de l'Observatoire, one of the attractions of Monaco's Jardin Exotique, contains, in the chisel marks of its walls, evidence of the occupation of the cave by Cro-Magnon man, our direct ancestor. From 1884 onwards Cro-Magnon skeletons, covered in sea-shells, necklaces, and other such ornaments, were discovered in nearby caves; here also were found the earliest sculptures in Provence – female figurines which probably served as fertility symbols. But the most interesting discovery made in these so-called Grimaldi caves was of skeletons which are neither Cro-Magnon nor Neanderthal in type, but instead bear strong negroid features: this sign of early African infiltration into Europe has considerable implications for the study of how prehistoric man developed. These and the other Grimaldi findings are now tastefully displayed in the building alongside the Grotte de l'Observatoire, the Musée de l'Anthropologie

Préhistorique, the only one of its kind in Provence and one of the finest in France.

To find out more about the later history of prehistoric Provence you have to go into the interior, often to stray far from the beaten track. Some of the most impressive sites of the Neolithic period (sometimes clumsily referred to as the 'Polished Stone Age' to distinguish it from the 'Cut Stone Age' which preceded it) is the Mount of Cordes, one of the former wooded islands in the once marshy land north of Arles. In the middle of private property which requires special permission to visit, the hill is crowned by a remarkable burial chamber, the Grotte de Fées. This chamber, over forty-five metres long and two to three metres wide, is lined on all sides by massive blocks of stone covered with enigmatic carvings, some of which are thought to represent an ancient zodiac. Various other prehistoric remains encircle the hill, including the burial chambers of Coutinargues and Castellet, both of which contain the large stone plinths known as menhirs. 'Daudet's Windmill', with its regular stream of coach visitors, lies only two miles to the north, but the Mount of Cordes belongs to an altogether different world, empty and slightly sinister.

In between the Polished Stone Age and the Iron Age comes the megalithic period, the search for which takes you into the lost valleys, gorges and desolate plateaux of upper Provence. The wild look of the landscape is echoed in the conical stone huts called *bories*, which are particularly numerous in the Lubéron and the plateaux of the Ventoux. These huts bear a strong resemblance to the prehistoric *nuraghi* of Sardinia and the *orris* of the Pyrenees, and probably give a good idea of how megalithic man lived in Provence. None of the surviving *bories* in fact dates from before the eighteenth century, but archaeological evidence points to the existence of such huts in megalithic times: copied by generations of peasants, who have lived in them for much of the year so as to be near their flocks, the *bories* are an extraordinary example of the continuity of traditions over the centuries. The huts are generally isolated in the middle of fields, but in some cases clusters of them exist. One such case is the Village des Bories outside Gordes, now turned into a museum of rural life: these *bories* were possibly used to isolate victims of the Marseille plague of 1720, but they might also form a close approximation of a prehistoric village.

The caves that pock-mark the remarkable gorges of Provence's interior provide an inexhaustible source of material for the study of every period of prehistoric Provence. Comparatively recently there were found in the Verdon caves in between Quinson and the bridge of Aiguines some of the few examples of cave painting in the region. These works have been dated to the Iron Age, and are probably contemporary with the rock engravings of the Valley of Marvels (*c.* 1800 to 1500 B.C.) The predominance of bulls in the latter site, and the presence in both places of human figures wearing bull masks, suggests that the people who made them practised some bull cult, a cult which was still very active when the Greeks began arriving in Provence in the late seventh century B.C.

The people who inhabited Provence at the time of the Greeks' arrival are generally referred to as Ligurians, a name which was first used in the sixth century B.C. by one Heraclitus de Milet. The origins of the Ligurians – who were also among the earliest inhabitants of Italy – have been heavily disputed, some saying Greece, others even suggesting Jutland. In actual fact they were not so much a race as a collection of peoples of diverse ethnic origins. They appear to have populated much of Provence from the Iron Age onwards, and to have continued to practise their ancient rites long after the Greeks had colonized the coast. In about 224 B.C. a Greek sailor called Maarkos Sestios sailed from Greece to Provence, a journey which has been impressively documented thanks to underwater archaeology carried out by Jacques Cousteau. As Sestios' boat passed by Antibes, he was told about the Bégo mountain which stood out against the horizon, and about the Ligurians who worshipped by its sides.

Until the Romans tamed the greater part of Provence, the interior of the region must have inspired considerable awe and trepidation. The estuary of the Rhône, the main entry into Provence for those coming by sea, was described by early Greek sailors as the gates of hell: the land which lay upstream was full of mystery and potential danger. As it turned out the Ligurians were at first friendly with the Greeks, and were pleased to trade with them.

The first Greeks in Provence seem to have come from Rhodes, and it is possible that the name Rhône is a corruption of that of their country: to this day the plains of the Rhône valley are referred to as 'La Provence Rhodéenne'. However, it was Greeks from Phocis in Asia

Minor who played the most important part in colonizing Provence. The Phocians came here in search of salt, which was not so plentiful along the deeper shores of the eastern Mediterranean. They seem at first to have based themselves at the port of Saint-Blaise on the eastern edge of the Étang de Berre. Legend has it, though, that their first stop in Provence was at a deep inlet to the east of this. Immediately after dropping anchor, the captain of the Phocian fleet, Protis, went to pay his homage to the chief of a local Ligurian tribe and found himself invited to a banquet given in honour of the chief's daughter. At this banquet the daughter was to present a cup of wine to the Ligurian whom she was to choose as her husband. She decided instead to hand the cup to Protis, who was subsequently given as a dowry the stretch of coast on which Marseille was later built.

Marseille, founded according to legend in 600 B.C., rapidly became the main Phocian base in Provence. Its prosperity increased after 560 B.C. when wealthy Phocians immigrated here after Phocis itself had fallen to the Persians. From 535 B.C. Marseille suffered from its wars with the Etruscans and the Carthaginians, but it flourished once more after 474 B.C. and expanded its territory. The Phocians, who had already founded in the mid sixth century a trading post (called Thaliné Mamela) on the site of present-day Arles, now created further posts at the coastal towns of La Ciotat (Kitharista), Hyères (Olbia), Antibes (Antiopolis), Saint-Tropez (Athenopolis), Nice (Nikaia), and Monaco (Monoikos).

The narrator of Maupassant's short story, *Madame Parisse*, visits Antibes at sunset and cannot help thinking of the poetry of Homer. 'It's a town of the Odyssey,' she remarks. 'It's Troy.' Many have looked for signs of the former Greek presence in Provence, and some have even claimed that the women of Arles – who throughout history have been renowned for their beauty – retain the facial features of the ancient Greeks. More plausibly, the Greeks might have significantly altered the look of the Provençal countryside through their reputed planting here of the first olive trees.

Sadly the Greek legacy in Provence does not include many surviving ruins. Outside Marseille, the most extensive of these are at Saint-Blaise. The impressively sturdy defensive walls of this former port and trading post have been compared by at least one classical scholar to those at Mycenae, and might bring to mind lines from Homer were it not for the landscape of petrol refineries which they now overlook. Marseille itself had until this century virtually nothing to show from its Greek past. Then, in 1940, the destruction of the old port by the Germans brought to light a section of the Roman docks of the first century A.D., underneath which were later found the foundations of the original Greek docks: in 1975 this unusual archaeological site was converted into the fascinating Musée des Docks Romains. The remains of further docks, together with portions of the city's defensive walls, came to light in the mid 1960s and were afterwards incorporated into a public garden adjoining a large shopping centre.

Before the Romans arrived in Provence and built the classical monuments for which the region is so famous today, there came the Celts. Celtic tribes began descending on Provence from the fourth century B.C., entering the region by way of the Rhône valley. The Allobroges settled south of Vienne, and the Cavares in between Orange and Cavaillon. The tribes were welcomed by the Ligurians, with whom they soon intermarried. Of the Celto-Ligurian tribes the most notorious were the Salyans, who ruled much of the interior north of Phocian Marseille. Their capital was Entremont, on the northern outskirts of present-day Aix-en-Provence. Finds from this site and the nearby Salyan sanctuary of Roquepertuse can be seen in Aix's Musée Granet. These include a series of powerfully chiselled heads, testifying to the Salyan cult of decapitation. Another famous Salyan sculpture, found in the town of Noves and now in the lapidary museum at Avignon, portrays a monster holding in its grotesque paws two further human heads. This obsession with decapitation helped give the Salyans a reputation for violence. The Roman geographer Strabo noted their barbaric habit of adorning their architecture with the heads of their enemies, and in the Musée Borély in Marseille a portal from Roquepertuse complete with skulls has been reconstructed.

The violent nature of the Salyans is traditionally ascribed to their Celtic rather than their Ligurian blood. The Ligurian tribes who resisted Celtic influence apparently contented themselves with animal rather than human sacrifices. A probable sacrificial altar used by such Ligurians crowns one of Provence's most moving ancient sites, the Fort de Buoux. Lost in a narrow valley on the north side of the Grand Lubéron, the fort sits on a narrow rock escarpment overlooking a landscape of dense forest and sheer cliffs pitted with caves. It is a place which encapsulates many periods in Provence's history. Prehistoric in origin, it became in turn a Ligurian, a Roman, and finally a medieval citadel, which was destroyed in the seventeenth century by order of Cardinal Richelieu. The site, reached by steps carved into the rock by the Ligurians, is spread over an overgrown steeply-inclining stretch of land tapering to a pinnacle. The odd goat, the ruins of a church, some prehistoric silos, and a series of medieval walls and gates under which you have to pass, lead finally to the pinnacle, with its perilous drop and spectacular view embracing the whole sweep of the Grand and Petit Lubéron down to the distant Rhône valley. Carved into the rock is a duct and basin, which surely at this height and in this unlikely position could only have been used for sacrifices. Nearby is another flight of steps leading up from the valley, this one far steeper and clearly intended to be hidden. Archaeologists have imagined a procession of Ligurian priests slowly making their way up these steps to perform a sacrifice at the citadel's summit. This is a powerful image, evocative of what much of Provence might have looked like just before the coming of the Romans.

In 219 B.C. war was declared by Rome on the Carthaginians, and shortly afterwards Hannibal led his Carthaginian army from Spain to Italy. The exact route which Hannibal took on his march through Provence is not known, but he seems at any rate to have encouraged in the Celtic and Ligurian tribes that he came across an attitude of increased hostility towards the Phocians of Marseille. The Phocians, traditional allies of Rome, assisted the Romans in supervising the movements of Hannibal, and also put their navy at their disposal. It was thus natural that the Phocians should turn to Rome when, in the course of the second century B.C., it appeared that all the Celtic and Ligurian tribes were banding together to fight them. The Romans were anxious to help, but not for altogether altruistic reasons: their defeat of the Carthaginians had led to the possession of Spain, and by putting troops into Provence they hoped to create a bridge between Spain and Italy.

In 123 B.C. the Romans, led by Sextius Calvinus, captured the Salyan citadel at Entremont; two years later, a few kilometres away, they founded the first Roman settlement in Provence, Aquae Sextiae, the future Aix-en-Provence. Further Roman victories were followed by a far greater threat to the region than that posed by the Celts and the Ligurians. In around 103 B.C. an estimated million and a quarter Teutons and other peoples from northern Europe marched down the Rhône valley with the intention of settling in the promised land of the south. The tyrannical Roman general Marius, fresh from triumphs in Africa, was sent to intercede with them. He set up camps in between the Alpilles and the Étang de Berre, and while waiting he constructed across the plain, from the Durance valley to the sea, a series of canals known subsequently as the Fosses Mariennes. The tactics that Marius employed were compared by the English historian A. T. Cook to those used by Lord Kitchener at Omdurman: rather than attack the enemy immediately, he wished to direct them to a prearranged site. His hidden soldiers watched the enemy file past to the north of the Alpilles, eventually to raze the small Greek trading post of Glanum. Finally, when the enemy had gathered, as he had intended, in a field to the east of Aix, he sprang to the attack and surrounded the enemy on all sides. In the ensuing massacre, over 200,000 Teutons and others were left to rot on a site which became known as the Campi Putrendi ('the rotting fields'), a name later shortened in French to Pourrières. According to tradition, it was a prophetess named Martha (described variously as a Syrian or a Salyan turned traitress) who had directed Marius in the battle, and had later insisted that he (throw down 90,000 of his prisoners into the pit of the Garagai on Montagne Sainte-Victoire. It is also often said that the name of this mountain commemorates Marius' victory, though in fact this name, like that of Mont Ventoux, is probably derived from the Latin word for windy. At all events, Marius was to live on in the popular imagination of the Provençal people, and his name is still given to the sons of the region.

From the time of Marius' victory the Romans began consolidating their hold on the 'Province', which now extended north to Lyon and west to Narbonne, the latter city giving to this region its name of 'Gallia Narbonnensis'. Marseille and its dependencies remained initially an autonomous republic, but they made a disastrous choice of allegiance in the Roman civil war which had been sparked off by Marius' arrogance on his return to Rome. After taking the side of Pompey, the leader of the anti-Marian faction, the Phocians were laid siege to in 49 B.C. by Marius' nephew, Julius Caesar. Marseille lost its autonomy and thereafter entered a long period of decline, enjoying a reputation principally as a centre of Greek studies. In 46 B.C. the city's former trading post of Thaliné Mamela, which had been destroyed by the Ligurians, was turned by Caesar into a Roman colony, and many of Marseille's possessions were transferred here. Arles, whose importance as a port had been greatly increased by the construction of the Fosses Mariennes, became Caesar's favourite city in Provence.

The golden age of Roman Provence dates from the time of the Emperor Augustus, Caesar's great-nephew. Augustus created Roman colonies at Nîmes, Avignon, Carpentras, Vaison, Die, Digne and Riez; he turned Fréjus – a small port and market town founded by Caesar – into a major naval base; he set up a systematic and highly organized network of roads in the region; and in 14 B.C. he subdued the rebellious tribes of what is now the *département* of Alpes-Maritimes. The period of peace and prosperity which Augustus instigated was to last nearly 300 years, during which time were to be built the most outstanding series of Roman monuments outside Italy.

Roman remains can be seen throughout Provence, but the principal ones lie mainly along the three main roads built by the Romans. The road to the south, the Aurelian Way, stretches from the Italian border near Menton to the river Rhône at Tarascon, and is marked at its outset by one of Provence's many monuments associated with Augustus, the Trophy of La Turbie. Standing high above the coast between Nice and Menton, the Trophy commemorates Augustus' victory over the Alpine tribes, and records, in its restored inscription, that through Augustus 'all the people of the Alps, from the Adriatic to the Tyrrhenian sea, have been subjected to Roman rule'. Originally over 50 metres high, the monument comprised a massive square base, on top of which was placed a circular colonnade incorporating representations of the generals who had taken part in Augustus' campaigns; finally came a cupola crowned by a colossal statue of Augustus himself, flanked by two prisoners. Today only the base and the ruins of the colonnade are still standing, but even so the monument remains an eloquent testimony to the power of Rome.

La Turbie represented for the Roman traveller the entry into Gaul. The first town after that was Cememelum, which became, after the conquest of Alpes-Maritimes in 14 B.C., the military and administrative centre of the district. Situated above the Greek port of Nikaia, it forms today the fashionable Nice suburb of Cimiez. Its ruins surround a charming Italianate villa of the seventeenth century, now housing museums to Matisse and local archaeology. These ruins – including one misleadingly called the Temple of Apollo – are nearly all from the largest thermal complex as yet uncovered in Gaul.

Cimiez was repeatedly destroyed by the Saracens in the early Middle Ages, as was Fréjus, the next important stop on the Aurelian Way. Before then Fréjus had been a flourishing naval base of some 40,000 inhabitants. The remains of the Roman town, though very fragmentary and scattered around the uninspiring outskirts of medieval Fréjus, are notable for their variety. Put together, these fragments provide a telling picture of what the town was once like, with its amphitheatre, theatre, aqueduct, and well-defended port. The basin of the port has long been dry, but you can still see ruins of its surrounding walls and fortifications, and the stump of the lighthouse which stood at the opening of the canal linking the basin to the sea.

From Fréjus the Aurelian Way left the coast and went straight to Aix, the original Roman settlement in Provence but a town of which virtually nothing survives from its Roman past. An alternative route from here to Tarascon made a loop to the south, crossing, just north of the Étang de Berre, an extraordinary bridge of the first century A.D., the Pont Flavien. Formed of a single arch spanning a distance of over sixty feet, this well-preserved monument is magnificently flanked on either side by triumphal arches supporting crouching lions. No other Roman bridge of this type survives in Europe.

Few tourists make a special visit to the Pont Flavien but even fewer go and see the nearby Roman site of Barbegal, which lies to the south of the Aurelian Way as it passes in between the Alpilles and the Crau (see page 268). Hidden among fields of olive trees are the remains of an aqueduct which once fed water into Arles. A footpath alongside this leads the visitor to a point where a narrow channel is cut into a rock, after which the ground falls down abruptly to a scorched plain of wheat-fields. The steep slope of the hill is covered with the remains of no less than sixteen windmills, which were once made operative by water diverted from the aqueduct. This unique surviving example of an ancient hydraulics system, built probably in the third century A.D. and active until the fifth, is a magnificent example of the engineering sophistication of the Romans.

At the western end of the Alpilles, at a site called Eraginum (marked today by an important eleventh-century church), the Aurelian Way converged on the two other main roads of Roman Provence. Following the Rhône valley from Arles up to Lyon was the Agrippan Way, named after Augustus' childhood companion and the man who in fact directly supervised the building of Gaul's roadway network. Joining Eraginum from the north-east was the Domitian Way, a road which entered Gaul near the Alpine town of Briançon, eighty kilometres north of Barcelonnette. Descending from there down the Durance valley to past Sisteron, and then turning eastwards into the Lubéron, the Domitian Way thus took the traveller through the Provence later appropriated by Giono. Though Roman remains are relatively scanty here, the ones that you come across are often deeply impressive for being so unexpected. One such monument is at Riez, a small town in between the Domitian Way and the Canyon of the Verdon. This is the Temple of Apollo, the main surviving monument from the town's thriving Roman past. Its four remaining Corinthian columns stand elegantly in an overgrown field under the shadow of wild mountains. The slight uncanniness of their being there reflects a genuine archaeological puzzle: they are made of grey granite, a stone not found in the area and which must have been transported from at least 100 miles away.

To the west of Apt the Domitian Way crosses another of Provence's remarkable Roman bridges, the three-arched Pont Julien, built probably around 3 B.C. Standing isolated among fields and beautifully framing the range of the Petit Lubéron, the site is potentially a very romantic one, though unfortunately the strong smells of the polluted river Calavon make it not a place to linger. Further west, at Cavaillon, is a triumphal arch once thought to commemorate the victory of Domitius Enobarbus over the Cavares. This richly decorated monument is in fact of a later period, and may not even have any military significance at all, but might simply have been used as a town gate. Placed in its present position in the nineteenth century, it is the only Roman monument of a town which rose under Augustus to become the prosperous market town of today.

As it approached Eraginum the Domitian Way passed near to what is now one of Provence's most famous Roman sites, Glanum. Two extraordinary Roman monuments on the northern outskirts of Saint-Rémy precede the main site, and for many centuries these were Glanum's only visible remains. They were known to the locals of Saint-Rémy as the 'Antiques', and were a source of wonder to travellers such as the Englishman Nathaniel Wraxall, who wrote in 1786 that they 'forcibly recall the idea of Rome, the conquerors of the earth'. The earlier of the two, a triumphal arch, is the oldest such monument in Roman Provence and celebrates Caesar's victories over the Gauls and Greeks: a semi-naked Gallic warrior and a mournful woman in Greek costume are among the partially destroyed group of captives carved on either side of the arch. The other monument, known erroneously as the Mausoleum, is a memorial to Augustus' grandsons, Caius and Lucius Caesar, both of whom died young and to whom is also dedicated the Maison Carrée in Nîmes. This cenotaph, one of the best preserved examples of Roman architecture to be seen anywhere, is a tall, narrow construction comprising a stone podium on a stepped base, a four-way arch, and a colonnade surmounting a conical roof missing only its crowning pine cone. Carved reliefs of classical history and mythology surround the podium, and include scenes of the death of Adonis and of a young warrior falling from his horse, both of which were meant to allude to Caius and Lucius. The accentuation of the figures by a deeply cut outline – a technique described by Ruskin as 'sketching in sculpture' – is special to Roman sculpture in Provence, and gives to the works a crude vigour.

Up to the eighteenth century the presence of a town lying just a few hundred yards to the north of the 'Antiques' was unsuspected; then, encouraged by allusions to Glanum in classical literature, archaeologists began making important finds on the site. However, it was not until 1921 that a systematic excavation of the place was undertaken. Slowly there was revealed a settlement which dated back to about the sixth century B.C., had been razed to the ground twice in its history, and had finally been covered after the third century A.D. by alluvium shifted by the blocking of the town's water courses. The original Glanum was founded by a Ligurian tribe called the Glanici, who built it around a sanctuary dedicated to a water divinity. From about the fourth century B.C., Greek merchants from Marseille began trading with the Glanici, and many of them even settled here; though the Greeks were never to colonize the town, their example encouraged the building of numerous Greek-style houses. Marius' legions moved into Glanum following its destruction by the Teutons in 102 B.C.; it was completely Romanized after Caesar had conquered Marseille in 49 B.C. In its later years it seems to have developed the character of a hill station and health resort, but none the less it still remained important as a sanctuary; interestingly, both the Romans and the Greeks before them were apparently quite happy to adopt to their own purpose the Ligurian gods.

The site is squeezed into a fold of the Alpilles. At its furthest and narrowest end is the sacred spring around which the settlement grew. This is encased by a Hellenistic basin (restored in the second century B.C.), from which steps lead down to a pool still filled by water from the spring. Opposite are steps climbing up to the cave which contained the original Ligurian sanctuary. Elsewhere in the site can be found the ruins of several temples, a forum, a large thermal complex complete with mosaics, and some wealthy villas. The different periods of Glanum can to a certain extent be told from the masonry: the Hellenistic buildings are of large stone blocks, those put up by the first wave of Roman settlers employ small, irregular stones, while the buildings dating from after Caesar's colonization are of regularly cut quarry stones firmly held together by mortar.

The only other Roman site in Provence which compares with Glanum in the extent of its excavations is that of Vaison, the town which has come to be known as Vaison-la-Romaine. Vaison lies in a wooded setting to the north of Mont Ventoux and to the east of the third main road of Roman Provence, the Agrippan Way. A settlement had existed by the banks of the Ouvèze since Ligurian times, but it was not until after the Romans came here in the twelfth century B.C. that the town developed into an exceptionally prosperous community. Rich merchants and retired legionary officers purchased villas here, and by 40 A.D. Vaison had been described as 'Urbs Opulentissima' and ranked among the wealthiest towns of Roman Gaul. It remained as such until the late fifth century, when it was destroyed by Franks. Later its inhabitants moved to a more defensible position on top of the steep hill on the other side of the Ouvèze. The ruins of the Roman town lay buried and largely forgotten until the early nineteenth century, when a new town began to be built on the site of the Roman one and many chance discoveries were made. A systematic excavation of the site was finally carried out after a dedicated local archaeologist – the Abbé Martel – discovered fragments of an amphitheatre in 1907. Today the Roman remains at Vaison are divided between two adjoining areas, the Villasse and the Puymin quarters, the latter containing an excellent modern museum displaying finds from the site.

The ruins of Roman Vaison, this ancient Beverly Hills, have certain similarities with those of Pompei. The views over the ruins are dominated by Mont Ventoux just as those at Pompei are by Vesuvius. More importantly, the ruins forcibly convey what life must have been like in a Roman town. Running south from the entrance to the Villasse quarter is a main street, with pedestrian pavement, covered gutter and a shopping arcade. To the left are the scanty remains of the town's administrative and judicial centre, while to the right are the complete foundations of a large house belonging to a wealthy patrician. This splendid building, known as the House of the Silver Bust after a portrait of the owner now in the museum, has a pillared entrance hall, a living-room adorned with a reproduction of the Emperor Hadrian in armour, and two colonnaded gardens with pools. Among the attractions of the more extensive Puymin quarter are a group of public latrines recalling those of Pompei, and rare examples of Roman houses built to be rented. Above all there is the theatre, which was built into the hollow of a hill and is still reached by a tunnel cut into this: because the stage was actually carved into the rock, you can still see features such as the trench into which the curtain was lowered, and the pits that held the stage props.

One of the finest and best-preserved Roman theatres in the world is to be seen to the south of Vaison, at Orange, an important stop on the Agrippan Way. Orange, the ancient capital of the Cavares, was colonized by Roman legionaries at the beginning of Augustus' reign and soon numbered around 85,000 inhabitants (about three times its present population). Those travelling south to Orange down the Agrippan Way would enter the town through what is today the third largest triumphal arch in existence. Built, like the theatre, shortly after the town was founded, this was the first such monument in Gaul in the new triple-arched style, a style which was later adopted in the nineteenth century for the Arc de Triomphe in Paris: it is encrusted with carvings, most of which are of army and naval trophies symbolizing Rome's victories over the Gauls and the Greeks. The scale of the arch is striking, but is paltry in comparison with that of the theatre in the centre of present-day Orange. The first glimpse of this is of the massive façade wall, a wall which Louis XIV described as 'the largest wall in my kingdom'. This façade of Piranesi-like grandeur shields one of the few surviving stage walls from antiquity: though today this has lost its marble facing, and most of its columns and statuary, it still proudly displays in its central niche a monumental statue of Augustus, recently reconstructed from fragments. The auditorium – originally covered by an awning supported by poles attached to large blocks projecting from the theatre's façade – is ingeniously scooped out of the hill.

Arles, at the southernmost end of the Agrippan Way, and near the intersection of the Julian and Domitian Ways, is a town which has been compared by generations of travellers to Rome itself. This 'Gallic Rome', as the poet Ausonius termed it in the fourth century, is similar to the Italian city in the way in which its ancient monuments form an integral part of the Arles of today. Thus, looking up from one of the coffee tables of the delightful Place du Forum – the square which from the time of Mistral has been popularized by artists and writers – you will see attached to the old-fashioned Hotel du Nord the columns and pediment of a Roman temple.

The one inescapable element of the Arles skyline is its amphitheatre, which in its day was even higher than it is now, having originally had a third storey. Probably constructed at the end of the first century A.D., it once held up to 25,000 spectators. The greatest care was taken to ensure the audience's comfort: an awning protected them from the sun and rain, while leaving room for air to circulate; fountains scented with herbs helped further to purify the atmosphere. In addition, this luxurious establishment had mosaic floors, gilded porticoes, marble-clad walls, and – to segregate the different areas of the auditorium – cords studded with precious stones. All this care for detail seems curiously at odds with the brutality of the gladiatorial and animal combats that took place within. Something of the spirit of the old amphitheatre lives on today: on Sunday afternoons in the summer this venerable building is transformed into a packed and animated bull-ring.

The imposing bulk of the amphitheatre contrasts with the sparser, more peaceful ruins of the adjoining theatre, now enclosed in a walled garden. Henry James came here by moonlight and found the place 'one of the most charming and touching ruins I had ever beheld'. He likened the two solitary columns of the otherwise destroyed stage wall to 'silent actors', and seems fortunately to have been unaware that they were used in the seventeenth and eighteenth centuries as gibbets from which to hang prisoners. It was here too, in 1681, that there was discovered the best-known statue from Roman Provence, the Venus of Arles. The town retains only a copy of this (in the vestibule of the town hall), for the original was presented shortly after its discovery to Louis XIV, who had it 'restored' by the sculptor Girardon; the work, with its two arms added by Girardon, is now in the Louvre in Paris.

If there is one other Roman monument in Arles which the visitor should see, this must surely be the subterranean monument or Cryptoporticus lying underneath the no less remarkable Museum of Early Christian Art. This vast space – the dating of which has varied as widely as from the first century B.C. to the third century A.D. – was a municipal depot, used largely to store grain. It consists of two barrel-vaulted galleries, subtly lit by lamps hidden in the original ventilation shafts. The sound of dripping water permeates the empty gloom, contributing to an atmosphere redolent of the catacombs of Rome.

To complete a tour of Roman Provence, you have to cross the present-day boundaries of the region. Nîmes, on the other side of the Rhône valley from Arles, competes with this city in the number of its Roman monuments and has also been called the French Rome. Named after a spring which the Romans called Nemausus, Nîmes was a Celto-Ligurian settlement turned by Augustus into a colony for veterans of his Egyptian campaign; the enchained crocodile in the Nîmes city arms is a reference to Augustus' defeat of Antony on the Nile. Augustus provided the town – an important stage on the road between Italy and Spain – with the most extensive ramparts in Gaul. Two of the city's gates (the gates of Augustus and France) survive, as do some scanty remains of the original defensive walls. As with Arles, the largest Roman monument in the city is the amphitheatre. Slightly smaller than that of Arles – which was built by the same architect, T. Crispius Reburrus – it is none the less in even better condition, and would be even more so had not the Frank leader, Charles Martel, taken his revenge on Rome by filling it with wood in the eighth century and setting fire to it. But Nîmes' most special Roman feature is the small temple known obscurely as the Maison Carrée. Few other buildings in the whole Roman world are in quite such an extraordinary state of preservation. The impression which this building made on travellers in the past was an unforgettable one: Thomas Jefferson had it copied as the model for the Virginia State Capitol, while the agriculturalist Arthur Young revisited it continually during his stay in Nîmes in 1787 and concluded that it was 'beyond all comparison the most light, elegant and pleasing building I ever beheld'.

To the west of the old town of Nîmes, but still within the confines of the former Roman walls, is the Jardin de la Fontaine, a delightful, shaded park built in the eighteenth century to accommodate a number of Roman remains. On the summit of the wooded hill on which the park is laid out is the Tour Magne, a tower which formed part of the original ramparts. This monument, thought by many to be a commemorative tower such as those at Glanum and La Turbie, is only a shadow of its former self. Described by Henry James as a 'dateless cube', its appeal has been primarily the extensive view to be had from its top, a view which extends to the walled town of Aigues-Mortes on the western edge of the Camargue. At the bottom of the hill, enclosed by eighteenth-century balustrades, is the spring of Nemausus, and by the sides of this are the ruins of the Temple of Diana. This is a richly decorated building which was possibly not a temple at all but rather a place which lodged those faithful to the god Nemausus. Its architect was one M. Vispanius Agrippa, who may also have designed the Maison Carrée. He was certainly responsible for another of the outstanding monuments of Roman Provence, the Pont du Gard.

The city of Nîmes was provided with water from the Nemausus to begin with, but this supply soon proved inadequate. The situation was remedied by the difficult engineering feat of building an aqueduct from the town of Uzès, thirty-five miles away. The round basin, or castellum, to which the water was led still survives in Nîmes, and you can see around it the holes of the ten lead pipes which distributed the water from here to different parts of the city. The course of the aqueduct from Nîmes to Uzès is marked by other remains, such as bridges and underground channels. The crossing of the river Gardon provided the architect with his greatest technical challenge: though the Gardon is a quiet, insignificant river in summer, it swells dangerously in winter, and as late as 1958 destroyed the modern suspension bridge at Remoulins.

The Pont du Gard, the section of the aqueduct spanning the

Gardon, has survived to this day virtually intact, an enormous structure comprising three tiers of arches curved slightly on one side to resist better the pressure of the water. The excitement which this monument inspires is partly connected with its being splendidly isolated in the middle of the most beautiful countryside. A particular thrill is reserved for those who decide to walk across the aqueduct on the narrow, unprotected path above its covered channel. This route can only be recommended to those who are sure of foot and do not suffer from vertigo: notices at either end of the bridge warn the prospective pedestrian that people have been blown off in times of strong wind. Standing on top of the Pont du Gard and looking down to the river fifty metres below is certainly a stomach-churning experience, and one which fills the visitor with that sense of the Sublime which generations of visitors here have rarely failed to note. Jean-Jacques Rousseau, for instance, described the sensation of 'vanishing like an insect in this boundless edifice'. 'As I humbled myself,' he continued, 'I could vaguely feel something which raised my soul, and I said to myself: "I wish I were a Roman!"' The ever-grumbling Tobias Smollett paid the monument what was for him the highest possible accolade of comparing it to Westminster Bridge in London. He also thought it would be an excellent spot for a picnic, a challenge which was taken up over a century and a half later by the family of Marcel Pagnol. Idyllic descriptions of Sunday lunches by the Pont du Gard feature in Pagnol's charming book of childhood reminiscences, *La Gloire de mon père*. Not even the crowds who throng to the place today detract significantly from the nobility of the monument or the bucolic calm of its surroundings.

The Pont du Gard, the Maison Carrée, the amphitheatres at Nîmes and Arles, the 'Antiques' of Glanum – these and the many other great Roman monuments of Provence were the main reasons why tourists lingered in the region up to the early nineteenth century. Yet their history up to then had been one of neglect and violation on the part of the Provençal people. Each of these monuments has a sad story to tell about the uses to which it was put after the Fall of the Roman Empire. Thus the amphitheatres of Nîmes and Arles were completely covered with ramshackle houses notorious for their harbouring of germs and criminals; Orange's theatre was partly transformed into a prison, and its triumphal arch into a small castle, before being used as

a firing-range for members of an archery club; the Maison Carrée
served in turn as a town hall, a private house, a stable, a church, a
granary, a public market, and finally, after 1823, a museum. The
praise which travellers always bestowed on these and other Roman
monuments was invariably matched by anger and sadness at what
had become of them. 'I blush,' wrote Nathaniel Wraxall of the Maison
Carrée, 'for the bigotry and mean superstition which has converted
this small temple into a chapel of the virgin, decked out with crucifixes,
gilding and catholic pageantry.' The eighteenth-century Polish traveller Count Moszynski was furious with indignation at the way in
which the amphitheatres at Arles and Nîmes had been so heavily built
over that it was difficult to see anything of the original architecture.
Aubin-Louis Millin, a French traveller of the early nineteenth century,
lamented the fate of Orange's theatre, which had in addition to its
prison a group of filthy, disease-ridden hovels lining the very stage on
which 'were surely once played the comedies of Plautus and Terence
and the tragedies of Seneca'. As for the Maison Carrée, Millin found
it so surrounded by rubbish and excrement that he would not have
been surprised 'had the temple been consecrated to the goddess of the
Cesspool'.

Stranger still to understand was the wilful demolition of a number
of Provence's Roman buildings. The most notorious example of this
was the pulling down as late as 1779 of a large and famous mausoleum
attached to the former palace of the Counts of Provence at Aix: this
whole historic complex was demolished to make way for a Palace of
Justice. E. Garçin devoted a long section of his *Géographie de la
Provence* (1787) to this unforgivable act of vandalism. He emphasized
the irony of how a monument which had managed to survive for over
eighteen centuries, withstanding even the ravages of the Dark Ages,
should have been destroyed in 'this century of taste, philosophy and
letters'. He suggested that the only possible act of contrition for this
was to erect in front of the new Palace of Justice a monument recording
that on this spot once stood the last remains of the first Roman
settlement in Provence, the last remains of a glorious city which came
to be known as 'the City of Towers'. Needless to say, no such
monument was erected and the mausoleum has vanished almost
completely from the memory of the Aix people.

The story of neglect and violation of Provence's Roman past is by no means over. I went recently to visit the remains of a Roman aqueduct at Meyrargues, to the north of Aix. Meyrargues itself is an unpromising place, a town which has kept little of its past but has instead numerous characterless modern villas. I was thus pleasantly surprised to find that just beyond Meyrargues' rapidly expanding suburbia was a stretch of untouched countryside, in the middle of which stood – like a fragment of a Claude painting – the remaining arches of the aqueduct. Approaching closer, however, I noticed that a fence of barbed wire surrounded it, and there were notices telling the visitor to keep out. A man came up to me and proudly introduced himself as the owner of the ruin. He seemed deeply concerned about the poor state of the monument, and only later did I realize that his concern stemmed from his longing for it to fall down completely. 'It must have been beautiful once,' he said, 'but now it no longer works it's of no use to anyone.' He had already applied to the Aix authorities for planning permission to demolish the aqueduct and build in its stead two villas. To his surprise permission had not been granted, but he was confident that one day it would.

3

A Second Palestine

In 1614 César de Nostredame, son of the famous prophet and astrologer Nostradamus, published one of the first detailed histories of Provence. In his introduction he praised his native region not just as 'the cherished province of the Romans', but also as 'a second Palestine, a holy and sacred land, happily enriched by most of the venerable and holy relics of the family of God'.

Pontius Pilate, after serving in Jerusalem, came to Vienne. Much of the remaining cast of the New Testament followed him across the Mediterranean and settled in Provence, at least according to legend. This legend has become so integral to Provençal history that – as the Jesuit geographer Louis Coulon noted in 1670 – to deny it would almost be considered 'blasphemous' by the Provençal people. The story goes that the Jews of Palestine put to sea without oars or sails a boat carrying Mary Jacobé (the Virgin's sister); Mary Salomé (the mother of the apostles James and John); Mary Magdalene and her sister Martha and brother Lazarus; Saint Sidonius (the blind man whose sight had been restored by Jesus); and Saint Maximinus. Sarah, the black servant of the first two Marys, was left behind on the shore, but wept so much after the boat had been abandoned by the Jews to the waters that Mary Salomé threw her mantle over the sea so that she could walk over it to join them. Another miracle landed the boat safely at the foot of the Camargue, at a place now known as Les-Saintes-Maries-de-la-Mer.

After erecting an oratory on the site of an ancient temple, the group divided. Mary Salomé, Mary Jacobé and Sarah remained at Les-Saintes-Maries-de-la-Mer; the others went in different directions, intending to spread the word of Christ as widely as possible. Maximinus and Sidonius journeyed to Aix, while Martha ended up at

Tarascon, where she held up a cross to tame the Tarasque, a monster which had terrified the neighbourhood. Mary Magdalene, together with Lazarus, preached at Marseille in front of a Roman temple which was later pulled down to make way for the city's cathedral. The Magdalene moved on subsequently to the range of the Sainte-Baume, and lived there for thirty-three years in a damp cave which faced north and was rarely penetrated by the sun. At the end of this period of solitary penance she made her way to a place east of Aix now named Saint-Maximin, where Saint Maximinus was waiting to give her the last rites.

The story of the Magdalene and her companions on the so-called Boat of the Bethany is curiously linked to traditions going back to pre-Christian times, in particular to the cult of the Roman general Marius. A classical *stele* at Les Baux commemorates Marius, his wife Julia, and Martha, the Syrian or Salyan prophetess who advised him before and after the battle of Pourrières: it bears the inscription 'Tres Marii imagines' (three images of Marius) which later was interpreted as 'Les Trois Maries' (the three Marys). Furthermore the prophetess Martha was confused elsewhere with the Saint Martha who killed the Tarasque; and the site on which the oratory was built at Les-Saintes-Maries-de-la-Mer was originally a temple dedicated to a trinity of mother goddesses. Such correspondences between classical and Christian culture abound in the early history of Provence. It has even been suggested that the shadowy Saint Mitre – whose name was given to many early Provençal churches – was none other than a Christian transformation of Mithras, a pagan god whose cult was very widespread in this region.

Whether or not the Magdalene and her fellow disciples were ever in Provence, the legend that they were was fully exploited by the medieval Church. The supposed discovery in 1187 of the body of Saint Martha turned the collegiate church dedicated to her in Tarascon into one of the most celebrated sanctuaries of France; a major pilgrimage centre was also established at Les-Saintes-Maries-de-la-Mer after the finding there in 1448 of bones claimed to be those of Saints Sarah, Mary Jacobé and Mary Salomé. The skull of the Magdalene, together with relics of Saints Maximinus and Sidonius, and of some of the babies from the massacre of the innocents, were in the possession of the Cassianites (followers of Saint John Cassien) from the fifth century onwards, but were later hidden to avoid being taken by the Saracens. They were hidden so successfully that they could not be found again until 1279, in a burial vault belonging to a former Roman villa at Saint-Maximin. By this date another skull attributed to the Magdalene had been in the possession of the Burgundian abbey of Vézelay for nearly 200 years. The pope, asked to decide which of the two skulls was the authentic one, opted for that at Saint-Maximin, thus ending Vézelay's days as an important pilgrimage centre and encouraging the construction at Saint-Maximin of the grandest gothic church in Provence.

Of all the many holy sites in Provence, the one most likely to capture the imagination of the non-believer is the Magdalene's cave in the Sainte-Baume. The wood which lies underneath this was a spot sacred to the Ligurians, the Romans, and the Gauls. Prehistoric paintings have been found in a cave near to that of the Magdalene, and it is possible that the two caves had a religious significance long before the Magdalene's supposed stay here. A flight of 150 steps carved into the rock leads today from the wood to the Magdalene's dramatically positioned cave. The original steps were built in the fifth century by Saint John Cassien, who created a hermitage here towards the end of his life. Pope Stephen IV made the steep ascent to the cave in 816, and in his footsteps came a long succession of popes, kings, and other dignitaries. Together with the reliquary at Saint-Maximin, the place had become one of the most venerated Christian sites after the Holy Sepulchre in Jerusalem. People have continued to come here up to the present day, and on 21 July each year the caves serve as an impressive setting for a candlelit mass attracting large numbers of people.

The sanctuary of the Sainte-Baume was vandalized during the Revolution, and the cave's present furnishings and small adjoining hostelry date mainly from the nineteenth century. The extensive cave, with its gloomy lighting and sounds of dripping water, is certainly atmospheric, and boasts a fine example of religious kitsch in the form of a white marble statue of the Magdalene, a work for which a celebrated actress called Mlle Clairon is thought to have posed. But what makes a visit to the cave so memorable is its view over the wood below to the barren limestone peaks behind Marseille. I once came here at the end of a *mistral*, when few people were around and the wind had cleared the sky of all clouds and haze. The extensiveness of the view, combined with the silence and loneliness of the place, created a most powerful impression. One of the nuns who take it in turn to reside at the hostelry told me that the feeling of serenity which she had experienced while staying here in the middle of winter was greater than she had ever known.

From the cave you should walk up to the top of the mountain, a walk which the portly Stendhal did, puffing all the time and lagging behind his younger companions but ultimately judging the extra climb to have been worthwhile. The panorama from the ridge is yet more magnificent and takes in also the forest of the Esterel and the coast towards Saint-Tropez. On top of the sheer cliff which falls down to the cave is a chapel marking the site of a column (the '*saint pilon*') which in turn commemorated the spot to where the Mary Magdalene was lifted up seven times a day by angels. Once there she listened in ecstasy to the music of the heavens.

Legend surrounds the lives of many of the other saints associated with the Christianization of Provence. One of the most important of these figures was Saint Trophimus, the cousin of the first Christian martyr Saint Stephen. Born in Ephesus in Asia Minor, Saint Trophimus became a disciple of Paul and accompanied him to Rome, from where he was sent on a mission to Gaul. Most of what is known about his life from this point is derived from tenth-century accounts, which apparently confused him with an early Bishop of Arles who had the same name but who was certainly not preaching in Arles before the late second century. The Saint Trophimus of medieval fame came to this city by 46, conveniently just in time for the arrival in Provence of the Boat of the Bethany. He gathered his disciples on the outskirts of the town, at the cemetery of the Alyscamps, an out-of-the-way meeting place analogous to the catacombs of Rome. To escape the hostility of pagan priests he hid afterwards in a grotto under the nearby hill, on which the abbey of Montmajour was later founded. Visitors to the abbey today should ask to see the small chapel of Saint-Pierre, which is built into the rock underneath the main abbey buildings and is reached from them by an old flight of steps. At the back of this eleventh-century building – the dilapidated architecture of which perfectly complements the rocky, overgrown setting – is a tiny hermitage marking the supposed hiding-place of Saint Trophimus and featuring his rock seat and confessional.

On his return to Arles, Saint Trophimus stopped a public sacrifice and in so doing converted to Christianity the prefect of the town, who gave him a room in his palace in which to practise, a site occupied today by the twelfth-century church of Saint-Trophime. Towards the end of his life Saint Trophimus decided to bless the cemetery of the Alyscamps, which by now allowed Christian sarcophagi. Christ himself made an appearance at the ceremony, and, kneeling down on a rock, left the imprint of his knee.

The Alyscamps, one of the greatest necropoli of the Roman world, became after Trophimus' death a major Christian cemetery and place of pilgrimage. It once contained not only the tomb of Saint Trophimus himself, but also that of the patron saint of Arles, Saint Genesius, a writer and clerk who according to legend was martyred after refusing to take down a decree against the local Christians. In addition it had a chapel erected around Christ's knee-print, and a church reputedly built by Saint Trophimus and dedicated to the Virgin when she was still alive (this was later replaced by Notre-Dame-des-Grâces, a building amalgamated in turn into the twelfth-century abbey of Saint-Honorat-des-Alyscamps). The fame of the cemetery began to decline somewhat after the tenth century, when Saint Trophimus' relics were transferred to a church in the centre of Arles, eventually to be taken from there to the cathedral bearing his name. The Alyscamps today is a fraction of its former size, much of it having been destroyed with the building in the nineteenth century of the adjoining railway works. Moreover, its finest sarcophagi have nearly all gone: some were transferred to the town's Musée d'Art Païen, many more were given away from the Renaissance onwards as presents to visiting dignitaries. None the less, the Alyscamps is well worth a visit and should perhaps be a starting-point for anyone interested in the early Christian history of Provence. The remaining sarcophagi have been arranged in rows alongside a shaded avenue leading to the twelfth-century church of Saint-Honorat. A notice half-way down this avenue records that 'Van Gogh, moved by the beauty of the site, took out his easel'. A painter who generally shunned conventional beauty, Van Gogh was attracted by the derelict, abandoned look of the Alyscamps. Distant from the main tourist sights of Arles, and in unprepossessing suburban and industrial surroundings, the place still retains the little-visited character that so touched Van Gogh.

Arles, the Rome of ancient Provence, was to an even greater extent the Rome of Christian Provence. When the Roman emperor Constantine moved to Arles in the third century B.C. and was converted to Christianity, the town emerged as one of the leading Christian centres in Europe. Its importance as such increased in the fifth century, when Provence played a pioneering role in the introduction into Europe of the monastic movement which had begun in North Africa and Asia Minor.

The key figures in this movement were Saint John Cassien and Saint Honoratus. The former, who ended his life in the Sainte-Baume, arrived in Marseille around 415 after having spent time in Constantinople, Rome and Palestine. In 416 he founded in this city Provence's first important monastery, the abbey of Saint-Victor, named after the patron saint of sailors and millers who was martyred in Marseille in the third century by being slowly ground between two millstones. Saint Honoratus was a converted Gaul who studied in Greece and Italy before leading a hermit's life in a grotto in the Estérel. From here he moved to one of a group of islands named the Lérins off the coast of Cannes. The peaceful, wooded Îles de Lérins today form a striking contrast to the international metropolis of Cannes, just half an hour's boat ride away. On the Île Sainte-Marguerite the notorious Man in the Iron Mask was imprisoned in the seventeenth century; on the adjoining Île Saint-Honorat, Saint Honoratus founded before 426 what was to be with the abbey of Saint-Victor at Marseille one of the great monastic institutions of Europe. The latter island, a centre of learning and missionary activity, was later known as the Île des Saints because of all the renowned holy men and future bishops who stayed here, among whom was the young Saint Patrick.

In 426 Saint Honoratus came to Arles to become bishop here and brought with him a monk from the Lérins, Saint Hilarius, who was to succeed him in the bishopric. Saint Cesarius, also from the Lérins, became Bishop of Arles in 530. All three saints had monasteries built around the town, and established the place as a monastic centre superseding Marseille and the Lérins. A monk in Arles in the eighth century was Saint Gilles, a man who according to legend had given all his money to the poor and had then set sail from Greece in a raft which had miraculously borne him to Provence. After leaving Arles the saint saved a hind by snatching a huntsman's arrow in mid-flight.

The amazed huntsman, who came from a rich and noble family, commemorated the event by founding, just north of the Camargue, the abbey of Saint-Gilles, soon to become another of Provence's famous pilgrimage centres.

Lesser saints whose names crop up again and again in the early history of Provence include Saint Donatus, Saint Véran and Saint Siffrein. The first of these entered Provence by the Domitian Way around 500, and, after taking a side road, ended up high in the lonely forests of the Lure. By a fountain where he loved to rest he founded a priory, the small church of which – one of the remotest in Provence – still inspires a bi-annual pilgrimage (on 15 August and 8 September). Saint Véran, a monk at Lérins before being made Bishop of Cavaillon in the early seventh century, belongs to the line of Provençal saints who from the time of Saint Martha and the Tarasque have been reputed to have killed monsters and other troublesome beasts. Thus the Magdalene cleared her cave of vipers, Saint Honoratus rid the Lérins of a population of ravenous lizards, Saint Victor defeated a dragon at Marseille, and Saint Véran saved the village of Vaucluse from the claws of the Coulobre, a hideous beast who lurked deep in the waters of the village's mysterious fountain. The tomb of the saint is to be found in Vaucluse's romanesque church, a pleasantly quiet place to visit in the middle of what is otherwise a village brimming with tourists.

Saint Siffrein came to the Îles de Lérins at the age of ten, brought there by his wealthy father, who retired to the monastery after being widowed. Later becoming a monk there himself, Saint Siffrein soon acquired such a fame for his holy deeds and character that he was invited in *c.* 555 to become bishop of Venasque. Venasque, imposingly situated on top of a rocky escarpment on the foothills of the Ventoux, is one of a number of former Provençal bishoprics (Riez is another) which grew around important Roman settlements but were later reduced to insignificant small towns or villages. Today it is difficult to believe that this small, isolated community gave its name to the papal possession of the Comtat-Venaissin. In 557 its bishopric was annexed with that of the low-lying Carpentras: Saint Siffrein was made bishop of the two towns, but remained in Venasque, a place whose later decline went in tandem with Carpentras's rise to become capital of the Comtat and the thriving commercial centre of today.

Bankrupted in the late Middle Ages, Venasque's population gradually fell to about twenty families in the 1950s. In recent years a growing number of tourists have been coming here, attracted by the charm of the situation, its romanesque church (where Saint Siffrein is buried), and the adjoining eleventh-century 'baptistery', the foundations of which are all that are left of the cathedral complex built by Saint Siffrein in the sixth century.

While Provence is rich in the relics and memories of its early saints, relatively few examples of Christian art and architecture survive here from before the eleventh century. Among the principal survivals are the third- to sixth-century sarcophagi, which appear to have been produced mainly in the large sculptural workshops established by the Romans in Arles and Marseille. The biggest collection of these works in Provence is in the Musée d'Art Païen in Arles, but a single outstanding sarcophagus can be seen in the delightfully old-fashioned museum housed in the former palace of the Counts of Provence in Brignoles. This work, known as 'La Gayole', might date from as early as the second century, and at first glance appears to have nothing specifically Christian about it: only after a more careful look does it become clear that alongside a figure of Apollo is one of Christ as a shepherd. The sculptural sophistication and pronounced Roman character of this and other early sarcophagi dies out after the sixth century. The few sculptural works known from between the sixth and the eleventh centuries – for instance the eighth-century tomb of Bishop Bohetius in the chapel of Notre-Dame-de-Vie outside Venasque – reveal an impoverished art reduced to the carving of crude geometrical patterns.

A combination of later building campaigns and the devastating raids first of the Barbarians and then of the Saracens did away with most Provençal buildings of the early Christian period. Of the original monasteries of Saint-Victor and the Îles de Lérins all that remains are the crypt of the twelfth-century abbey church of Saint-Victor and a few heavily reconstructed chapels around the Île Saint-Honorat: both monasteries were razed by the Saracens in the ninth century. Nothing whatsoever is left of the monastic buildings put up in Arles by Honoratus, Hilarius and Cesarius. The best idea of what early Christian architecture was like in Provence is given by the remarkable baptisteries at Aix, Venasque, Riez and Fréjus. The one at Venasque is now generally thought to have been heavily rebuilt in the twelfth century, and the other two have elements (for instance the cupolas) that are probably of this same date. However, even if the actual fabric of these buildings is not entirely of the fifth and sixth centuries, their architecture is certainly closely modelled on the originals. Quatrefoil structures centred around a large circular font in which new Christians were once completely submerged, these baptisteries appear to have been erected on the site of pagan temples, the columns and capitals of which they often incorporated.

The beginings of a renaissance in Provençal art and architecture following years of decline and destruction date from the late tenth century. Motivated to a large extent by Saint Mayeul, there was a renewed impulse to found monasteries. Saint Mayeul came from Valensole in upper Provence, and though he later became abbot of the Burgundian abbey of Cluny, he never forgot his Provençal upbringing. Apart from reconstructing the bishoprics of Apt, Fréjus, Senez and Glandève, re-erecting Apt cathedral, compensating the abbey of Saint-Victor in Marseille for its loss of treasures, and putting up numerous rural churches throughout Provence, he and his wealthy family created, endowed or rebuilt the monasteries and abbeys of Montmajour, Salagon, Carluc and Ganagobie. It was the capture of Saint Mayeul in 964 that incited the Provençal people more than any other event to repel the North African invaders. In 973 the main Saracen stronghold in the Maures was taken. Though there were to be coastal raids from North Africa up to the thirteenth century, the Provençal victory at La Garde-Freinet led in the eleventh century to a period of increasing stability conducive to the building campaign started by Saint Mayeul.

Provence's important pilgrimage centres, and its critical position on the pilgrimage routes to both Rome and the Spanish town of Santiago de Compostela, brought vast numbers of pilgrims and consequently vast wealth into the region after the eleventh century. Moreover, Provence became in the Middle Ages a major base of the Crusaders. The perfectly preserved walls of the Camargue town of Aigues-Mortes – from where Saint Louis of France set out in 1248 on his crusade to Palestine – are today the most forceful reminder of this episode in Provence's history. But one should remember too that the Crusaders created a significant renewal of activity in the ports of Marseille and

Arles. Arles indeed experienced in the twelfth century one of the greatest periods in its history. It was a period of prosperity dominated by two of the century's most celebrated religious and political occasions: the transference in 1152 of the relics of Saint Trophimus to the town's recently rebuilt cathedral, and the coronation there twenty-four years later of the Holy Roman Emperor Barbarossa.

The twelfth century saw a vast amount of building activity in Provence. There must be more romanesque churches and monasteries in the region than in any other part of Europe; furthermore, the romanesque style lingered longer here than in most other places and strongly influenced the character of later Provençal architecture. For all the great cultural diversity of Provence, there is a striking sameness about its churches: the first impression on entering them is that they are dark, heavy and extremely austere. The romanesque buildings of the region set the pattern by generally having restrained decoration, squat proportions, solidly cut masonry scarcely relieved by windows or other such breaks, and very simple plans, often without an ambulatory, sometimes without side-aisles, and hardly ever with radiating chapels in the apse. Every corner of Provence is filled with such buildings – they turn up in the remotest, most unlikely places, and many of them do not even rate a mention in all but the most specialist publications. They are one of the region's most appealing features, yet up to the early nineteenth century travellers invariably turned a blind eye on them, considering them for the most part sad examples of the decline of Provençal architecture after the departure of the Romans. Later in the century, at the height of the gothic revival, the medieval church architecture of Provence continued to be neglected because of its predominantly romanesque character. Even up to recent times, scholars have studied the medieval churches of Provence less than those of any other French region: Provençal romanesque is thought to be charming but backward, and therefore less worthy of study.

Not surprisingly, given the troubled history of Provence between the sixth and tenth centuries, the rebuilding of churches and monasteries from the eleventh century onwards took defensive considerations seriously into account. The rebuilt monasteries of the Îles de Lérins and Saint-Victor, for instance, both look more like fortresses than religious institutions. The former building, dating from 1073, was described by Maupassant as 'a castle straight from Walter Scott'. It is certainly a most romantic place, a tall crenellated block dominating a shaded bay on the island's southern coast. Inside the building, abandoned since the Revolution, is a first-floor cloister and, above this, two chapels; from the top is a wonderful view of the coast from the Cap d'Antibes to the Esterel. Of the abbey of Saint-Victor, only the church still functions. Rebuilt in around 1040 over the fifth-century crypt, it was remodelled in the thirteenth century. With its battlemented towers and exceptionally solid walls, it appears to stand guard over Marseille's harbour. Another outstanding fortified church is that of Les-Saintes-Maries-de-la-Mer, which was built in the twelfth century as a replacement for a ninth-century structure which had actually been incorporated into the town's ramparts. The present building, a cross between a boat and a toy castle, seems to float like some strange apparition in the middle of the town's central square.

The renaissance of Provençal architecture during the romanesque period was accompanied by a renewal of interest in classical forms. Provençal sculptors and architects had the advantage over other regional artists of France in belonging to a land particularly rich in classical remains, and it was perhaps inevitable that they should one day begin seriously to study these. Characteristic Roman forms such as gabled pediments began to be incorporated into Provençal churches after the twelfth century; the crude geometrical doodles of the Dark Ages gave way to sophisticated acanthus, egg-and-dart moulding, and other such classical ornamentation; the figurative style of Roman and early Christian art was revived.

A jewel of the Provençal romanesque is the isolated church of Saint-Gabriel, the main façade of which features a massive arch enclosing a door and tympanum flanked by Corinthian columns supporting a gabled pediment. The sculpture on the tympanum resembles an early Christian sarcophagus, while the source of inspiration for the whole is undoubtedly a triumphal arch such as those at Orange and at nearby Glanum: the strong classical character of this church is especially appropriate for a building which marks the important Roman crossroads at Eraginum. Less well known is the chapel of Saint-Quenin at Valréas on the outskirts of another major Roman site, Vaison-la-Romaine. Prosper Mérimée was not unreasonable in mistaking the curious triangular apse of this for a surviving Roman temple. As with so many other romanesque buildings in Provence, the fluted

Corinthian pilasters which articulate the apse's exterior give to an otherwise simple structure a quality of elegant sophistication. An equally modest building is the church of Notre-Dame-de-Sainte-Aubune, under the Dentelles de Montmirail near Beaumes-de-Venise: its bell-tower would be indistinguishable from those of countless other romanesque churches were it not for its delicate pilasters, which lend to the structure the grace of some Roman memorial.

The only enthusiasm which early travellers showed towards Provence's romanesque buildings was frequently reserved for such classical detailing. Thus Stendhal, who abhorred the stylized vigour of the romanesque sculpture at Autun in Burgundy, managed to find praise for the acanthus and other ornamentation which enlivens the beautiful church of Le Thor on the banks of the Sorgue: '. . . the west portal of this church displays all the delicate ornamentation that can be found in sculpture of the late twelfth century'. Stendhal's response to the famous sculpted portal of Saint-Trophime at Arles is not recorded, but one suspects that he would have reacted to it in the same way as he did to that at Autun. Henry James praised the portal for its 'primitive vigour', but thought this out of place in a town which was 'delightfully pagan'. The west portal at Arles, together with that at Saint-Gilles, are the main examples of architectural sculpture in Provence, a region where twelfth-century sculpture on a large scale is rare. Though neither of the portals meets with strictly classical criteria of taste, they are far more classical in character than are those of Burgundy or of other areas of France. The overall design for both of them is taken from the triumphal arches of the region, and – among a number of direct quotes from classical art – there is even a figure of Hercules incongruously appearing among the saints at Arles.

The sculptural richness of the Arles portal is continued in the remarkable cloister of this building. Provence boasts one of the greatest series of romanesque cloisters in Europe. These range from that at Saint-Trophime – sculpturally the finest in the region – to the grand, austerely beautiful cloisters at the abbeys of Montmajour, Sénanque, Silvacane and Le Thoronet. In between are the intimate flower-filled cloisters of Saint-Véran in Cavaillon (remodelled in the fourteenth century) and Saint-Paul-du-Mausole near the 'Antiques' of Glanum. The latter, ornamented with sculptured capitals now in a sadly crumbling condition, belongs to an institution which from the seventeenth century has been known for the care of mental patients. The peaceful, neglected charm of the cloister had an appeal to Van Gogh similar to that of the Alyscamps in Arles: in this case, however, the place was forced upon him, as he was confined in the hospital shortly after he cut off his ear in the autumn of 1888.

The appreciation of architecture is connected to a large extent with its setting, and in few other parts of Europe are the settings so dis-tractingly beautiful as are those of Provence's rural churches and monasteries. The church at Saint-Trinit, which once formed part of a medieval priory dependent on the Benedictine abbey at Villeneuve-lès-Avignon, is a modest romanesque structure made memorable through its being attached to a half-deserted hamlet in the middle of the wild plateau of Valensole in Alpes-de-Haute-Provence. Carluc and Saint-Donat, also in this *département*, are abandoned monasteries with particularly evocative settings. Both places have undergone restoration to save them from further ruin, but fortunately they have been spared the treatment they would have received had they been in Britain – the statutory green fence, neatly mown grass, and prominent information panels with which the Department of the Environment succeeds in diminishing the romantic appeal of most of this country's monu-ments.

Carluc lies at the end of a tiny side road off the Domitian Way in between Forcalquier and Apt. The setting is quite Virgilian – a large group of oak trees, a fast-running stream crossed by an old bridge, a field with sheep, and a large beehive clinging to the abbey's main sur-viving relic, the apse of the twelfth-century church. Saint-Donat, in the foothills of the Lure range above the Durance valley, marks another lonely spot chosen for meditation by the reclusive Saint Donatus. As you drive down the D101 towards the valley, catching the occasion-al view of the bizarre rock formations aptly named Les Mées (the fairies), the ruined abbey appears suddenly to your right, unmarked and solitary. The abbey church, though abandoned and scarcely visited, is in a remarkable state of preservation, and is one of the rare surviving examples of the first flowering of the Provençal romanesque in the eleventh century.

Directly overlooking the Durance valley, a few kilometres further south, is the priory of Ganagobie, which has recently been reclaimed by a religious order and is in the process of being extensively restored and rebuilt. The *Christ in Majesty* above the church's west door ranks after the tympanum of Saint-Gilles and Saint-Trophime as one of the best sculptural groups in Provence. Inside the building is another very important and unusual feature – a group of polychrome floor mosaics dating from the mid twelfth century and including ornamental patterns that are oriental in inspiration. But yet again it is the setting which ultimately makes a visit here so special. The abbey clings to the edge of a high plateau, from which there is an almost aerial view over the Durance valley towards Les Mées and the snow-capped backcloth of the Alps.

Purity of architectural style and an unspoilt setting come together in three of Provence's best-known romanesque monasteries, the so-called 'Cistercian Sisters' of Le Thoronet, Silvacane and Sénanque. The Cistercian order was founded by Saint Bernard, abbot of Cîteaux in Burgundy, in the early twelfth century. Attacking the taste for luxury and ostentatiousness which had come to characterize the life-style and architecture of the Benedictines of Cluny, Bernard advocated a severe type of monastic building, unornamented and rigorously simple in plan. His beliefs had a wide following, and in his lifetime no less than 354 Cistercian foundations were set up around Europe.

The Cistercian ideals of austerity in architecture were perfectly suited to the Provençal romanesque, and it could be said that the three main abbeys that the order founded here represented the apogee of this style. In contrast to so many other Provençal abbeys, built often over a very long period of time, the three 'sisters' are characterized by a striking unity of conception: the impression of intimidating severity that you receive on entering their churches is rigorously kept up as you wander around the cloisters and excellently maintained surrounding buildings. None of the buildings have monks any more, but that of Sénanque has – in addition to its Centre for Sahara Studies – a school for Gregorian chant. A concert in the church here is an extraordinary experience – the simple and penetratingly clear sounds of plainsong ideally complement the vast gaunt space in which they are heard.

As for the landscape settings of the three abbeys, they are all very different. Le Thoronet is hidden in low-lying, densely wooded countryside just north of Les Maures: the abbey buildings stick out of the forest like Mayan temples in the Yucatan. Silvacane occupies a rather English-style setting, with oaks and ploughed fields, along an otherwise much-built-over stretch of the Durance valley south of the Lubéron. Sénanque, in the foothills of the Ventoux, has the most spectacular position of them all. It is best approached from the narrow, winding and unprotected road which leads from Gordes and, before descending, hovers high above the abbey, which from here has the perfect regularity of an architect's drawing-plan. A field of cultivated lavender in front of this provides in July the main note of colour in this wild, cliff-lined valley. Two Benedictine monks, touring France in 1717 to find out about the state of religion in the country, came to Sénanque and described the place as in the middle of a 'terrifying solitude, hemmed in by savage and arid mountains of an extraordinary height'.

The teachings of Saint Bernard made a profound impression on his contemporary Saint Bruno. The order of hermits which the latter founded, the Carthusians, were later to maintain the most spartan of life-styles at a time when the Cistercians themselves had fallen prey to the love of luxury which they had once criticized in the Benedictines. One of the great Carthusian monasteries in Provence, the Chartreuse de la Verne, has a setting which makes even that of Sénanque seem intimate by comparison. High up in the Maures, overlooking a forested landscape stretching in all directions as far as the eye can see, its remoteness is accentuated by its being at the end of a steep and stony forest track, the drive along which can be done only at a very slow speed. The Charterhouse was built in 1170, but was considerably altered following two fires later in its history; abandoned after the Revolution, it entered a long period of decline from which it has been saved by its recent acquisition by a small group of nuns. Built in the reddish-brown schist of the Maures, with doors and windows high-lighted in bluish-grey serpentine, the buildings take on at sunset an unforgettable hue of pink tinged with a sinister purple. A visit to the place in 1875, when the building was used as a farmyard, makes up one of the best chapters of Maupassant's travelogue on Provence, *Sur l'eau*. Never, Maupassant wrote, had he experienced such an oppressive sadness as he did when walking in the Charterhouse cloister: '. . . the man who built this retreat must have been a desperate person to have known how to create such a walkway of desolation'.

After the great flowering of churches and monasteries in the

romanesque period, Provençal ecclesiastical architecture began generally to decline. Not only was the gothic style slow to develop here,
but also it produced few religious buildings of major importance. The
basilica of Saint-Maximin, built largely during the fourteenth and
fifteenth centuries, is the most famous gothic church in the region, yet
it lacks the elegance and lightness characteristic of the gothic cathedrals of the north of France. Paradoxically, however, the fourteenth
century saw another major chapter in the religious history of Provence,
a chapter in which the hitherto insignificant town of Avignon was
turned into the capital of Christianity. The papacy established itself
here in 1309 and remained until 1377. If Provence lagged behind the
rest of Europe in its architecture, it became, thanks to the popes, a
vital centre of humanism and painting.

The first pope to settle here was Clement V, who had left Rome to
escape from the factionalism which had led to the assassination of his
predecessor, Boniface VI. The French king, Philip IV (Philippe le Bel),
had greatly encouraged him to make the move. The reasons why
Avignon itself was chosen were various. The town was near Vienne,
where an important Church council was shortly to take place; it
occupied a strategic position on the north–south axis of Europe,
equidistant from Italy and Spain, and at the gates of the French
kingdom. Above all, it adjoined the Comtat-Venaissin, a territory
which – for reasons that will later be given – had been ceded to the
papacy in 1274. During the early years of the popes' residency in
Avignon, the town remained the property of the Counts of Provence,
vassals of the Holy See, but in 1348 it was bought from them by Pope
John XXII.

The coming of the papacy transformed Avignon almost overnight
into an international meeting-place of pilgrims, diplomats, ecclesiastics and courtiers. The new arrivals included numerous painters,
the most influential of whom were from Italy to begin with. Italy's
fame as a centre of painting had already spread widely: in 1294 Philippe
le Bel had sent his own painter, Étienne d'Auxerre, to study in Rome,
and in the following decade had invited three Roman artists to come
to the French court. In the building-up of Avignon as a papal capital,
it was natural that the popes should try to enlist the services of the
leading Italian artists of the day. The Renaissance art historian Vasari
claimed that Giotto was among the Italians who came to Avignon

during this period, and though there is no evidence to prove this, there is equally no reason to dismiss the claim as most later art historians have done. Giotto's great Sienese rival, Simone Martini, was certainly here, as was another outstanding painter from Siena, Matteo Giovannetti. The style which they and their followers evolved here, refined, decorative and full of playful and carefully observed details, became known afterwards as the 'International Gothic' because of the speed at which it was transmitted from such an international centre as Avignon to the main courts of Europe.

The glamorous image which Avignon conveyed as a thriving centre of the arts was a mask to the sordid reality of everyday life there. The crowds that converged on the town in the fourteenth century contained a large criminal element, attracted by the place's reputation as a safe haven. The taverns of Avignon became notorious throughout Europe for crime and debauchery. Dirt and disease were endemic, encouraging plagues savagely to sweep through the town at regular intervals. Further havoc was wreaked by the so-called *routiers*, private armies who, when not engaged in mercenary activities, lived by pillage and would descend on Avignon, refusing to leave until the Pope had paid them handsome sums of money. Petrarch, the best-known humanist in the papal entourage, had every right to hate the town, which he described once as the 'unholy Babylon, the hell of living people, the thoroughfare of vice, the sewers of the earth'. 'Of all the towns that I know,' he went on to say, 'it is the most rotten . . . how shameful to see it suddenly become the capital of the world.'

The vitality and some of the squalor of papal Avignon are to be found in the town of today. Of all the towns of Provence's interior, Avignon is the most animated, the least parochial and the least conservative. Crowded with tourists and young people at most times of the year, Avignon becomes during its celebrated international theatre festival in the summer a veritable tower of Babel spilling over with street players, clowns, drug-addicts and buskers. Away from the bustling thoroughfare leading from the station to the Papal Palace, you will find a place which in its dark and dirty streets, small, decrepit squares and maze of hidden churches even has much of the physical character of the medieval town, made picturesque through time.

The imposing bulk of the Papal Palace, dominating a large traffic-free square, is Avignon's major tourist attraction today, though this was not always the case. Count Moszynski, writing in 1785, considered it a 'confused collection of buildings' and, fifty years later, Prosper Mérimée echoed the views of many of his time (Dickens, for instance) by saying that it looked 'less like a home of the representative of a peace-loving God than the citadel of an ancient tyrant'. The palace is in fact not one but two palaces, the first built by Benedict XII between 1334 and 1342, and the second by Clement VI between 1342 and 1352. Benedict was a Cistercian, which explains the austerity of much of the architecture. Moreover, by the time Mérimée was writing, the building not only looked like the grim barracks which he and many others compared it to, but actually was one: the soldiers garrisoned here did much damage to the interior, and Stendhal even claimed that there had been reports of soldiers leaving the building carrying fragments of frescoes by Giotto (*sic*) under their arms. Despite the popularity of the Papal Palace today, a visit here remains an interesting but not especially enjoyable experience. The compulsory guided tour takes you through an interminable series of empty rooms relieved only by the occasional frescoes. In the Banqueting Hall are detached frescoes and *sinopie* (underdrawings) executed by Simone Martini for the porch of the adjoining romanesque cathedral of Notre-Dame-des-Doms; in the chapel of Saint-Martial are some lively scenes by Matteo Giovannetti from the life of Saint Martial, who came from the same village as Benedict XII. The most popular of the palace's frescoes are those by an unknown artist decorating all four walls of the Stag Room. These scenes of stag-hunting, fishing, falconry and ferreting are amusing, decorative works which have sadly lost much of their colouring. For a more representative selection of works by the so-called Avignon School you should visit the museum recently installed in the nearby Petit Palais, which was built in 1317 as a home for the Grand Penitentiary of Clement V, Cardinal Bérenger Frédol, but then radically remodelled during the Renaissance.

The buildings put up by the popes and their retinue were not just restricted to Avignon itself. Villeneuve-lès-Avignon, on the other side of the Rhône and thus in French territory, developed as an exclusive residential district for members of the papal court. Churches and other religious institutions were also built here, including most notably the vast Chartreuse du Val de Bénédiction, founded by Innocent VI to commemorate the General of the Carthusian Order's modest refusal of the papacy. The visitor to Villeneuve should not fail to see the musty, highly atmospheric local museum housed in a seventeenth-century palace. This contains Enguerrand Quarton's *Coronation of the Virgin*, a work which might possibly have been painted for the Charterhouse. It is perhaps the most remarkable achievement of the Avignon School, though it dates from a period when Italian influences were on the wane and the popes themselves had long since departed.

The last of the Avignon popes, Gregory XI, left for Rome in 1376. The papacy had been responsible for many commendable achievements during the course of its residency here: the complex bureaucracy of the clergy had been skilfully reorganized by John XXII, university education had been promoted, and various attempts had been made to intercede in royal rivalries and establish peace. None the less, the presence of the papacy so near to French soil had always made the Avignon popes subject to much hostile criticism, particularly from England and Germany. Their departure in 1377 was met with widespread relief, not least from Petrarch. But the story does not end here. A group of thirteen French cardinals refused to accept the elected successor to Gregory XI and chose instead Robert de Genève, who styled himself Clement VII. While the true popes remained in Rome, the 'anti-Pope' Clement VII took up residency in Avignon. He died in 1394 but, despite general hostility to the idea of two popes ruling, he was replaced by another 'anti-pope', Benedict XIII from Catalonia. Under Benedict XIII Avignon turned into an enormous military arsenal, until eventually the 'anti-pope' began to lose more and more of his supporters. The 'schism' in the Church was resolved in 1417, and Benedict died a lonely death in Spain five years later.

Thanks to the strong cultural identity which Avignon had established during the fourteenth century, artists continued to flock here both during the period of the 'anti-popes' and also afterwards, when the town was ruled by cardinal delegates from Italy. They came here from all over Europe, finding work both in Avignon and in neighbouring towns, especially Aix-en-Provence, which the Counts of Provence had made their capital in 1189. An important Italian artist active in Provence during this later period was the sculptor Francesco Laurana, who worked in Avignon, Tarascon and Marseille. For the altarpiece of the Célestins in Avignon, he produced his last known work (now in the church of Saint-Didier). In this, a scene of *The Carrying of the Cross*, Laurana contrasted a group of mourners in an idealized Italianate style with a group of soldiers depicted with all the brutal realism characteristic more of northern than Italian Renaissance art.

Flemish influences in particular came to dominate Avignon tastes in the fifteenth century. These influences were brought to Avignon not just by artists from northern France and Flanders itself, but by those whom Benedict XIII encouraged to come from his native Catalonia: Catalan art of the period combined strong Flemish inspiration with Spanish coarseness and love of the grotesque. Two of the great masterpieces of the late Avignon School are the *Annunciation* by the Master of King René, and Nicolas Froment's *Burning Bush*. Both these works, respectively in the Aix churches of the Madeleine and Saint-Sauveur, are in the new Flemish medium of oils: the former is very Flemish in the way in which it sets the religious scene in a carefully observed domestic interior of the time; the latter displays a typically Flemish obsession with minutely realistic landscape and portraiture. Enguerrand Quarton (Charenton), a native of Laon in northern France, was in Arles at the time when the *Annunciation* was painted and is likely to have seen and been deeply impressed by it. His *Coronation of the Virgin* was painted shortly after his move to Avignon in 1454 and is virtually his only documented work. The Flemish-style realism of the faces is matched by the realistic detail of the landscape, which features unmistakable representations of Mont Ventoux and the Mediterranean coast at L'Estaque. The *Avignon Pietà* in the Louvre, also originating from Villeneuve-lès-Avignon, has generally been attributed to him. One of the most moving religious paintings of the whole fifteenth century, this work sets large-scale and strikingly life-like figures against a stark gold background. It has two qualities which we can perhaps identify as common to the greatest examples of Provençal art and architecture – simplicity and robust vigour.

The Avignon School was not the only school of painting in Provence in the late Middle Ages. There were many artists active in those easternmost districts of Provence then belonging to Italy. In fifteenth-century Nice the Bréa family and their large workshop mechanically turned out altarpieces for churches in Nice itself and in the surrounding hinterland. These works, decorative, charming, and rather old-fashioned, are exactly what one would have expected froman out-of-the-way school of Italian painting of this period. Even more provincial, though somehow more memorable in their impact, are the fourteenth- and fifteenth-century frescoes that decorate numerous chapels and churches in remote Alpine villages such as those along the valleys of Tinée and Roya. The extensive decoration of these buildings comes as a surprise after the bare austerity of so many of the churches of Provence proper. One of the largest and best-preserved fresco cycles in the Alpine district is by one Giovanni Canavesio and is in the isolated chapel of Notre-Dame-des-Fontaines near La Brigue. The style is naïve but lively, and suggests that as well as a north Italian training, the painter had some knowledge of German art: grotesque details such as the exposed entrails of the hanging Judas are very Germanic.

The annexation of Provence to the French kingdom in 1487 had considerable implications for the development of art here. The Avignon School declined rapidly in importance, and artists who might once have gravitated to Avignon and Aix now found more profitable employment at the French court at Fontainebleau near Paris. In terms of its art and architecture Provence became a backwater of France, rather than remaining an important centre in its own right. As for Nice and the Alpes-Maritimes, these districts, still belonging to Italy, understandably continued to follow Italian rather than French fashions, which is why the baroque style made far greater headway here than it did in the rest of Provence. Many of the churches in Nice and the Alpes-Maritimes mirror in their own modest way the colour, ornamental exuberance and dynamic movement of those of seventeenth- and eighteenth-century Italy.

· The Italian baroque, anathema to French tastes in general, had also to contend in Provence proper with a deep-rooted love of simplicity and the unornate. With one or two exceptions, such as the profusely decorated parish church of L'Isle-sur-la-Sorgue, the churches of Provence's interior remained as simple in their ground plans and ornamentation as they had been during the romanesque period. Only in Marseille and Toulon – both of which had close naval and mercantile links with Italy – did the Italian baroque style make any significant impact. This was due largely to one of the great individualists of

French art, Pierre Puget, who worked as a sculptor, architect and painter and divided much of his life between the two cities.

Puget, unquestionably one of Provence's grea˚ ˙t native artists, falls outside the mainstream of both French and Provençal art. His genius was recognized at the French court but he enjoyed only a limited success there, owing to the unclassical character of his work and his unruly, romantic temperament. In his native Provence, where he was thus forced to live, he towered over his conservative artist contemporaries and also experienced difficulties with the equally reactionary authorities. Puget's roots lie essentially in the Roman baroque: he was trained in Rome under the painter and architect Pietro da Cortona, and fell also under the influence of Gianlorenzo Bernini, a man whose versatile talents were much to his own heart. Puget painted many altarpieces for churches in Marseille and Toulon, but though these were sought out and described by eighteenth- and nineteenth-century travellers, they are not among his most successful or original works. A far greater achievement is his extraordinary hospice complex in Marseille, Notre-Dame-de-la-Charité (begun 1640), one of the few architectural projects which the timid city authorities allowed him to construct. Comprising a large quadrangle centred on a domed oval church, it is a conception of considerable dynamism and power. Abandoned after the Revolution, it was used first as a barracks and then degenerated into a place of refuge for dangerous criminals and vagabonds; in the last few years it has been startlingly restored and whitewashed, and now forms a most imaginative setting for ambitious art exhibitions.

But Puget is best remembered as a sculptor, and in this field he was unrivalled by his contemporaries anywhere in France. Unfortunately, few of his religious sculptures can be seen in Provence. The Musée des Beaux Arts in Marseille contains a highly theatrical bas-relief of *Saint Charles Borromeo in the Plague of Milan* (this, his last work, executed between 1692 and 1694, was turned down by Louis XIV). It has also dramatically lit copies of his four saints decorating the niches in the crossing piers of Santa Maria di Carignano in Genoa (c. 1661–5). These massive, twisting figures are the closest equivalent by a French artist to the virtuoso, emotionally compelling art of Bernini.

So far this chapter has looked exclusively at the Catholic contribution to the culture of Provence. Yet two of the most appealing religious monuments of the eighteenth century are not churches but synagogues. The synagogues at Cavaillon and Carpentras are reminders of the important role played by Judaism in the history of the region.

No one knows when or why the Jews first came to Provence. Possibly they were here as early as the fourth century B.C., but more likely they came in the first century A.D. At any rate, by the twelfth century they formed a sizeable community in Avignon. In 1349 the Jews were expelled from France, and from then up to the Revolution they were not officially permitted to live in the country. A great many of them took refuge in the County of Nice and above all in the papal possessions of Avignon and the Comtat-Venaissin, an influx which significantly increased after the rest of Provence was joined to France in 1487. While Jews were persecuted throughout France and Europe, they remained relatively safe in the papal states. To the papacy these people had a considerable historical and curiosity value. They were a vestige of the Old Testament, and indeed the ghetto at Avignon came to be known as the 'Jerusalem of Provence'. To ensure the survival of such a people was to maintain a living proof of the existence of the Old Testament, and in so doing to emphasize the truth and triumph of the Christian religion.

The main ghettos in Provence were at Nice, Avignon, Cavaillon, Carpentras, and L'Isle-sur-la-Sorgue. Originally the ghettos were formed by the Jews themselves for their own safety, and not every Jew was forced to belong to them (many rich Jews preferred to live outside). However, between the fifteenth and seventeenth centuries, fear that too many Jews would descend upon Avignon and the Comtat led to increasingly severe restrictions being put on them until eventually, after 1646, they were rigidly confined to the ghettos and allowed out only during the daytime. Known as *'carrières'* after the Provençal word for street, *carriero*, these ghettos consisted of a single street tightly packed with overcrowded houses. Walls surrounded the ridiculously small areas that were granted for use as ghettos; windows had to face inwards, or, if this was not possible, had to be heavily barred. The Jews, made to wear yellow hats after 1525, were punished if they were outside the gates of the ghetto at nightfall; during the terrible plague of 1721, they were kept in the ghettos both day and night. There was at first much poverty in the ghettos, which was not really surprising considering that the only trades that the Jews were allowed were usury and the selling of second-hand clothes. The severest penalties were imposed on those accused of committing crimes against Christians. In 1341 a professor at Avignon University noted the mutilated testicles of a Jew castrated after having been accused of robbing a Christian woman.

Inevitably these people, made to live in such strange conditions, exerted a strong fascination on outsiders. The oriental beauty of the Jewish women became legendary outside the ghetto walls, and young Christian men would often brave the strict segregation laws to sneak into the ghetto at night and sleep with them. Conversely Jewish men would take the even braver step of staying outside the ghetto walls and sleeping with Christian women, whose pleasure in such relationships was reputedly heightened by the thought of tasting forbidden fruit. By the eighteenth century the ghettos had developed as one of Provence's major tourist attractions. To French people in general the Jew was a rare animal, and the prospect of visiting a whole community of them was rather like going to a zoo. As with a zoo, the ghettos tended to smell and be very dirty. Travellers usually commented on this with feelings ranging from a sense of bravery at having gone into such places to outright disgust, but never with compassion. A typical reaction was that of Darluc, the author of *L'Histoire naturelle de Provence* (1782): 'The Jewish quarter is so contaminated as to revolt even those least concerned with cleanliness. It is surprising how the police, whose first duty should be to look after public health, should allow in the middle of a town so many breeding-grounds of disease, and do not force the filthy Jews to keep their streets and houses cleaner.'

Despite the lingering appearance of poverty, the Jews of Provence had made considerable material progress by the eighteenth century and many now took a leading part in the commercial life of their towns. An indication of the new-found wealth of the Jewish communities are the sumptuously ornate synagogues at Carpentras and Cavaillon, both of which were rebuilt in the late eighteenth century on sites dating back to the fifteenth. The former, the more important of the two, served a much larger community and is still in use; the latter is now a show-piece attached to a Jewish museum housed in the bakery which once provided the unleavened bread. A visit to the synagogue and museum at Cavaillon takes up a chapter in Judith Krantz's 'pulp' novel, *Mistral's Daughter*. In this the eponymous heroine surprises her first lover by driving him after their first kiss not to a renowned beauty spot such as Arles but to dreary Cavaillon. She is an American in search of her French-Jewish roots, and has read about the synagogue in the Michelin Green Guide, where, she wrongly claims, it is listed under 'Other Curiosities'. At the door she and her friend buy the entrance tickets and purchase a copy of André Dumoulin's slim guide to Cavaillon's museums and monuments (it is still on sale here). They enter and are amazed by what they see; their journey has been worth it even in their present heightened amorous state. 'They found themselves in an almost empty room that nevertheless gave an immediate impression of the most gracious harmony of spirit. It could have been a perfect small salon from some abandoned palace built in the style and at the time of Versailles.'

The ghettos were abandoned during the Revolution and the Jews were soon scattered throughout France. The Revolution saw also the closing of yet another important chapter in the religious history of Provence: it brought to an end the conflict between Catholics and Protestants, a conflict which had been particularly heated here and which had its origins in the twelfth century when the region had become a major base for the heretical sect of the Cathars. The Counts of Provence had tolerated this sect, and had taken their side during the wars directed against them by the French kings backed by the papacy. Avignon, a Cathar stronghold in the thirteenth century, was stormed by French troops in 1226 and again in 1274. It was as a punishment for supporting them that Count Raymond Bérenger III of Provence had been forced to hand over to the papacy the Comtat-Venaissin.

The Cathars held similar beliefs to those of a sect founded in 1184 by a Lyonnais lay preacher called Jean Valdo. The Vaudois, as this sect was named, were opposed to the extravagance and ostentatiousness of the Catholic Church, preached the virtues of poverty, and did away with all religious ritual. Chased away from the Lyon area, the sect spread to the remote Alpine valleys of Piedmont and then came back to France, finding a home in the Lubéron, an area which from then on was always to be associated with heretics. One of the places where they settled here was the high and beautifully situated village of Sivergues, which remains to this day the Lubéron's remotest community. Other Vaudois villages in the area included Lourmarin, Cabrières, La Motte, Puget, Lacoste and Ménerbes; the name of the 'Valmanasque', the valley in between Lacoste and Ménerbes, means the 'Valley of the Sorcerers' and is thought to be a reference to this sect. But the greatest concentration of Vaudois in the Lubéron was at Mérindol, a town whose name was given to the notorious Decree which led to one of the bloodiest incidents in the area's history.

The Vaudois were hard-working and peace-loving people who never forced their beliefs on others. None the less this did not stop them from being constantly persecuted, even in the Lubéron: in 1532 seven of the heretics were condemned by the Parliament at Aix to be burnt at the stake, and two years later many more were imprisoned on the orders of the Bishop of Apt. Finally, in 1540, Francis I of France issued the Decree of Mérindol, which threatened them with massacre unless they capitulated with the Church. He revoked the Decree the following year, but by then Baron Maynier of Oppède had formulated a cruel plan from which he was not going to be deterred. Inspired less by Catholic fanaticism than by the desire to increase his own lands, the Baron set about carrying out the Decree in as literal and ferocious way as possible: each village in the Lubéron suspected of harbouring the Vaudois was besieged and then set fire to. Many of the Vaudois who escaped sought the protection of the Simiane family, the then owners of the castle at Lacoste. The Simianes were pleased to grant them their protection, but the walls of their castle were not strong enough to withstand the vicious onslaught of the Baron's troops. Here, in this castle which would one day be the scene of the orgies of the Marquis de Sade, an estimated 350 Vaudois were tortured, raped and killed. The Baron was not brought to trial until 1551, by which date news of his atrocities had scandalized Europe. To everyone's surprise he was acquitted, but he had not long to live. He died in mysterious circumstances in 1558, murdered probably by a Protestant doctor.

In the course of the sixteenth century the Vaudois sect was amalgamated with Protestantism, and many of the Vaudois villages such as Sivergues and Lacoste became centres of the new religion. Protestantism had a remarkable success in Provence, which was why the region was so strongly affected by those waves of religious repression that periodically swept through France right up to the Edict of Tolerance of 1787. Not all the violence was on the part of the Catholics.

The Protestants committed numerous atrocities themselves, and were responsible for destroying or greatly damaging many of Provence's finest church monuments, including the abbey at Sénanque and the churches in Orange. The principality of Orange, under Dutch rule until 1713, was particularly affected by the Wars of Religion. Describing Orange in 1670, the Jesuit priest Louis Coulon referred to the Protestants 'ruining the most beautiful buildings, demolishing the altars, chasing away the priests, and profaning the holy places through the poison of their teaching'.

Protestant temples are found throughout Provence today, but these are little used as places of worship. The same holds true of most of the Catholic churches, the doors of which are almost always locked. The Temple at Lacoste serves exclusively as a venue for civic receptions, films and art exhibitions; meanwhile the Catholic church here celebrates mass only at Christmas, and opens its doors at other times of the year simply for the occasional concert or lecture given by the local art school. In the Lubéron the Vaudois sect gave way to Protestantism, which in turn gave way to communism.

Up to the Revolution the Provençal people were considered as among the most fervently religious people of France, and their religious behaviour reminded many travellers of the fanatacism of the Spaniards and the southern Italians. Surveys conducted by the Church after the Revolution showed the Provençals to be among the least religious in the country. This dramatic change of attitude is reflected in the region's popular festivities, the subject of a lively and highly stimulating book by the Marxist art historian Michel Vovelle, *Les Métamorphoses de la fête en Provence de 1750 à 1820* (1976). These festivities and other popular manifestations of religious culture deserve to be taken seriously. Fascinating and revealing in their blending of the sacred and the secular, they have also been Provence's liveliest and most original contribution to Christian culture in recent times.

Certainly few religious paintings in Provence since the time of the Avignon School have the charm or interest of such popular works as the ex-votos that enliven many of the region's pilgrimage chapels. Painted to commemorate the recovery from some accident or illness, these are naïve works illustrating the hazards of everyday life. The tradition goes back to classical times, but the first painted ones that survive are from fifteenth-century Italy. The ex-voto makes its first appearance in Provence around 1600 and reaches the height of its fashion in the nineteenth century: the tradition caught on here more than in any other region in France. A particularly extensive group of ex-votos is in the pilgrimage church of Notre-Dame-de-Lumières near Apt; the largest collection in a museum is in the Musée Ziem at Martigues.

Cribs are another Provençal speciality and indeed furnish some of the liveliest examples of sculpture in the region. Tradition has it that Saint Francis of Assisi invented this popular art form in the thirteenth century by wrapping up a live child in swaddling clothes and placing him in a rustic setting. The fashion for cribs was at any rate not widespread until after the Counter-Reformation, when the Church sought ever simpler and more attractive ways of promoting the Christian message. Begun in Italy and enjoying a particular success in Naples, the fashion soon caught on in Spain, Austria and southern Germany. In France it was widely resisted except in Provence, where there was a long history of popular devotional traditions at Christmas-time. Among the greatest examples of poetry written in Provençal between the thirteenth and nineteenth centuries are the Christmas hymns of the seventeenth-century priest Nicolas Saboly. These unpretentious, movingly simple works, greatly admired by the Félibres and still sung today, are the direct oral equivalent of the crib, and their enormous popularity with the Provençal people helps to explain why cribs too were so much loved here.

One of the earliest examples of a Provençal crib is the group of carved figures in gilded wood in the church of Saint-Maximin. Over the years such figures became less sophisticated but more realistic: an impression of flesh was given by making the hands and faces in wax or terracotta while covering the rest of the bodies in real fabric. An even more popular type of crib figure was developed during the Revolution. As the churches were now inaccessible, a church statue maker from Marseille named Jean-Louis Lagnel had the idea of producing cheap terracotta figurines that could be purchased by families for their own homes. Since 1803 these figurines, known as *santons*, have been sold at an annual fair held in the centre of Marseille between late November and early January. The colourfully painted *santons* were originally in contemporary dress, but most of the ones to be seen today are in Provençal costume of the 1820s and 30s, which

was when the craft for these figurines reached its peak. In the early
nineteenth century a mechanical crib figure was also invented, which
is still very popular today: carpenters were made to saw, drummers to
drum, old women to sway in rocking chairs. *Santons* of all types fill
many of Provence's museums today, though one of the finest of the
cribs is at the delightful museum at Brignoles which houses the famous
Mayoles sarcophagus. This crib, dating from the late nineteenth
century, is activated by pressing a switch: slowly the story of Christ's
birth is re-enacted with the aid both of changing lighting (turning
from dawn to night and back to dawn again) and moving figures,
including a group of traditional Provençal dancers.

With the invention of mechanized figures the religious element in
the cribs became increasingly disguised, so that by the 1840s the three
kings were made to travel to Bethlehem by train and the birth of
Christ was announced on another occasion by a delegation from the
Marseille sanitary commission. It was in reaction to such vulgar
transformations of the Christ story that in 1844 a Marseille worker
called Antoine Maurel got together with a group of his colleagues to
perform a simple version of the Nativity in Provençal. Every person
was played by a man, except for the Virgin and the Christ child, who
were represented by life-sized statues. The so-called 'Pastorale Maurel'
enjoyed an immediate success and soon inspired numerous imitations,
generally involving the inhabitants of a Provençal village coming to
Bethlehem for the Nativity. Mistral and the Félibres did much to
encourage such popular Provençal entertainments. In 1888 Van Gogh
attended a 'pastorale' performed at a variety theatre in Arles, and
thought how overjoyed the Félibres would have been at what he saw:
for him the spectacle was something out of an etching by Rembrandt.

It is not just Christmas which is celebrated in Provence with such
fervour and enthusiasm. Throughout its history the region has been
especially rich in religious festivities, some of which even have their
origins in pagan traditions. This is the case with many of the rain
ceremonies once held in this land so often beset by drought: statues of
saints were submerged in water, virgins bathed, and even representations of pagan gods carried in a procession together with Christ's
effigy. But the most bizarre of these ceremonies was undoubtedly that
of the Jouviers at Grasse: every year a group of boys would assemble
on the field next to the chapel of Saint Hilary and compete as to

who could urinate the highest and furthest; the winner, after having received a prize, would be carried in triumph down the main street. Sadly this ceremony was brought to an end following the intervention of Monsignor de Verjus, the Bishop of Grasse.

Two of Provence's best-known religious festivities are those of the Tarasque at Tarascon and the Fête Dieu at Aix-en-Provence. The former, held every year on Saint Martha's day, featured a large representation of the monster of Celto-Ligurian origin being paraded around the town's streets. In the eighteenth century the beast held a very real danger for those watching the parade: with its tail made out of a wooden beam, it was sometimes made to charge at the spectators, a number of whom would end up with broken arms and legs, much to the others' amusement. A milder form of the parade has lasted up to the present day, and the processional beast used on these later occasions can be seen at the castle at Tarascon. The Fête Dieu – the feast of Corpus Christi – was instigated by Urban IV in the thirteenth century and was celebrated by festivities throughout Provence. In the fifteenth century King René turned those at Aix into by far the grandest in the region, and gave over five whole days of public holiday to them. At the centre of the festivities was a long procession containing numerous costumed groups. The people masquerading as Jews had an unfortunate role: placed behind the lepers and others representing sufferers from contagious diseases, they were constantly spat at by the jubilant crowd. The Fête Dieu celebrations at Aix were abandoned after the Revolution, but there have been several attempts to revive them since the early nineteenth century.

The fun-fair atmosphere characteristic of the Tarasque and Fête Dieu festivities lives on today in such occasions as the Mardi Gras carnival at Nice or the famous *bravades* at Saint-Tropez (held on 16 and 17 May), in which soldiers in seventeenth-century costume fire salvoes in honour of the town's patron saints – a ceremony dating back to the time when religious festivities had to be protected by militia.

Pilgrimages provide Provence with some of its other great surviving spectacles. In May each year a nocturnal candlelit procession is made down a valley behind Venasque to the chapel of Saint-Gens near near Le Beaucet. Saint Gens was a twelfth-century saint whose miracles included taming and befriending a wolf who had eaten two cows, saving Le Beaucet from drought, and creating a spring near the solitary site where he lived as a hermit. The scanty remains of the twelfth-century chapel marking this site are incorporated within a large nineteenth-century structure. The annual procession to the chapel ends by the spring behind this, where the pilgrims anoint themselves with water. Because Saint Gens is not a figure widely accepted by the Church, the procession has more a popular than a religious character. This is why it made such a strong impression on the twelve-year-old Mistral, who claimed also that after anointing himself with the spring water he never suffered again from fever.

Christianity, mixed with far larger portions of the secular and the pagan, make up one of Provence's most popular tourist attractions, the pilgrimage to Les-Saintes-Maries-de-la-Mer on 24 and 25 May. A major pilgrimage to this place has existed since the discovery of the Marys' remains in the thirteenth century. However, the occasion has changed radically in character since the middle of the last century and is now thought of principally as a gathering of gypsies, who have always adopted the Marys' Egyptian slave Sarah as their patron saint. The first mention of gypsies at the festival is an article of 1852 in the *Illustration parisienne*. A sizeable number of gypsies was present also at the pilgrimage a few years later, when Mistral paid his first visit to Les-Saintes-Maries-de-la-Mer. He wrote about them with considerable enthusiasm, and in so doing seems to have encouraged a growing number of them to come here, aware perhaps of the great potential of being a tourist attraction. In 1935, following the intervention of the Marquis Folco de Baroncelli-Javon and his fellow Félibre Joseph d'Arbaud (author of *La Béstio d'ou Vaccarès*), the pilgrimage was made officially open to them and a special day (24 May) set aside exclusively to the cult of Saint Sarah.

Today gypsies from all over the world descend upon the town in their now mechanized and often luxurious caravans, accompanied by equal numbers of tourists, journalists, and film-directors anxious to witness the traditions and life-style of a quaint ethnic group. On 24 May the saints' shrines in the church are lowered by rope and pulley down to the altar; this is followed by an all-night vigil during which the gypsies (up to 1955) used to remove an item of their clothing in deference to Sarah's act of taking off her cloak on arriving at Provence. The next day the shrines, together with sculpted representations of the saints on their boat, are taken down to the sea; the sculptures were at one stage dipped in the sea, as in medieval rain ceremonies. Bull-fighting, dancing and fairs fill up the rest of the two days.

When Mistral came here in 1857, he had already been planning for several years his first epic poem of Provençal life and culture, the one which would establish him as the region's greatest writer and would serve as a guiding light to the renaissance of Provençal literature in the second half of the nineteenth century. Among his fellow passengers in the horse-drawn carriage which took him and his friend Anselme Mathieu from Arles to Les-Saintes-Maries-de-la-Mer was a young girl of dazzling beauty. She had a sad and distracted face, and Mistral found out from another passenger that she had recently been abandoned by her fiancée and had afterwards shown signs of madness, to help cure her of which her mother had taken her on this pilgrimage. When the carriage became stuck on the muddy, rain-soaked road and the passengers were forced to walk, Mistral and Mathieu took it in turns to carry the girl, reputedly the most beautiful girl in Beaucaire. Later that day, during the service at Les-Saintes-Maries-de-la-Mer, just at the point when the shrines were being lowered, a girl with long fair hair falling about her rushed from out of the crowd and threw herself at the altar. Many of those present thought that this stunning apparition was the Magdalene herself come to visit her sisters, but Mistral and Mathieu immediately recognized that it was the Beaucaire girl. 'Oh great Saints,' she shouted, 'in pity give me back the love of my betrothed.'

The memory of this incident remained with Mistral, and almost certainly inspired the subsequent development of his poem *Miréio*, whose heroine, it will be remembered, visits Les-Saintes-Maries-de-la-Mer to seek solace after being rejected by her lover and later expires from love on the town's beach. Out of a pilgrimage based on the legend which established Provence as 'a second Palestine', Mistral fashioned a tale which played on that other reputation which Provence had acquired over the centuries — as the 'Land of Love'.

4

The Castles of Courtly Love

Generations of travellers have come to Provence with a very romantic image of the region. Tourists today are sometimes lured here by a vision of a sensual, indolent land blessed by a warm climate. In the past, lines from Petrarch's love poetry or half-formed notions of the troubadours and their chivalric ideals have similarly determined the expectations of travellers. For many Provence has always been a land where love flourishes.

The young narrator of Mario Vargas Llosa's novel, *Aunt Julia and the Scriptwriter*, taunts his romantic aunt – with whom he himself is shortly to become involved – by explaining that 'love didn't exist', that it was purely a chemical reaction disguised by poetry, 'an invention of an Italian named Petrarch and the Provençal troubadours'. He has actually little belief in what he is saying, but none the less there is a certain element of truth in his professed views. The courtly love tradition, with which he confuses all romantic love, was first developed by the troubadours and later taken up by Petrarch, whose poems to Laura remained for centuries afterwards the most read outpourings of love in a western language.

The troubadours were poets who recited or sang their works from court to court. To begin with, in the twelfth century, they found their audiences mainly in the south of France or Occitania, which was ruled by a series of noble families rather than by a single monarch as in the north of the country. Some of the troubadours, such as Marcabrun and Bernart de Ventadour, were from poor, humble backgrounds, others were kings themselves; but the great majority of them came from the middle classes. They all wrote in what we now always know as Provençal, but which should really be called Occitan, as it was the language not just of Provence but of the whole of the south of France, with the exception of Roussillon and Gascony. Provençal is a Romance language having much in common with Italian, Spanish and French, but being particularly close to Catalan, the language spoken both in Catalonia and in the adjoining territory of Roussillon. The Provençal as used by the troubadours was a highly refined form of Provençal which scarcely changed over the years and took into no account the numerous variations that made up the spoken language. It was, in other words, more of a literary means of expression than a language of the people, and moreover was learnt by many of the most cultivated minds of Europe.

The origins of troubadour verse – effectively the origins of all western lyric poetry – have been endlessly debated, some seeing them in the popular poetry of the time, others in the Latin culture of the Church, and yet others in the culture of the Arabs in Spain. Whatever the answer, the poetry which the troubadours evolved was one in which form was far more important than subject-matter. Indeed, the subject-matter was nearly always the same – love, and in particular the love which came to be known as 'courtly love'. This form of love was governed by certain strict requirements: the poet could never call the loved one by her real name; he had to refer to himself in such feudal terms as his lady's 'serf' or 'vassal'; his hopes of requited love had to be based on making himself worthy of his lady and not on personal charm or good looks; lastly and most important, his love could not be addressed to an unmarried woman or to his own wife, for it was a love which thrived on the knowledge that it was an impossible one. Contrary to what is sometimes thought, 'courtly love' was by no means synonymous with 'platonic love'. The beauty which the poet saw in his lady was not just a spiritual one, and the favours which he so hopelessly craved from her were often quite specific: for instance, all that the troubadour Cercamon wanted of his lady was to have her next to him, 'naked to kiss and embrace within a curtained room'. By no means should the troubadours be regarded as wistful dreamers living in a state of constant sexual frustration. William IX of Aquitaine claimed in one poem to have made love to two women 188 times in one week (two manuscript variations admittedly record a more modest figure of only 88).

William IX, who was born in 1071 and was also one of the most powerful feudal lords in France, was the first but not the most subtle of the troubadour poets, and his works are read today largely for their historical and humorously erotic value. The greatest period in troubadour literature was the second half of the twelfth century, a period which produced Guirault de Bornelh and Arnaut Daniel. The former, the most successful troubadour of his day, was later superseded in critical esteem by the latter, whom Dante considered the greater of the two and a craftsman of incomparable virtuosity; his exceptionally complex rhymes and metrical schemes were a great influence on Ezra Pound, a poet who did much to revive an interest in troubadour poetry in recent times.

In the course of the thirteenth century Occitania suffered a series of major political setbacks: chaos ensued, and courts which once had glorified their image by their active encouragement of the troubadours now concerned themselves more with their survival. Occitania declined, while the French kings became ever more powerful. The latter, after a century of struggle with the English kings for the soil of France, gradually recaptured the lands north of the Loire. They also set off to the south on a crusade against the Cathars, whose faith was widely tolerated here. The Counts of Toulouse and Aragon, after having spent much of the previous century quarrelling over the domination of Languedoc and Provence, were sufficiently worried by the crusade's ruthless and brilliant leader, Simon de Montfort, to join forces and help the Cathars. In the battle held at Muret near Toulouse in 1214, Simon de Montfort emerged as the overwhelming victor and King Alfonso of Aragon was killed. Eventually much of Occitania came under the rule of the French kings, leaving only a greatly diminished Provence as an independent territory. The Counts of Provence, the Lords of Les Baux, and other members of the Provençal nobility continued to be patrons of the troubadours, but otherwise these poets had to seek employment outside the south of France, in places such as the courts of Aragon and northern Italy. Guirault Riquier, who was born in Narbonne but worked for much of his life in Aragon, is generally called the last of the troubadours, a reputation which reflects the nostalgic nature of his verse. In his last known poem, written in 1292, he laments being 'born too late' and records the passing of an era:

In noble courts no calling is now
less appreciated than the fine art
of poetry.

Though some of the greatest patrons of troubadour verse came
from Provence, and the region has been perennially associated by
travellers with these poets, very few of the troubadours were actually
native to the place. Most of the best poets to have worked here were
from outside the region, men such as the Mantovan poet Sordello and
the Toulouse-born Peire Vidal, who were supported respectively
by Count Raymond Bérenger IV of Provence and the Viscount En
Barral of Marseille. Sordello, the subject of a famous poem by Robert
Browning, was featured in Dante's *Purgatorio* as the spirit who guides
Dante and Virgil through the Ante-Purgatory. Vidal, who enjoyed a
reputation as a great eccentric, developed an enormous love for
Provence not entirely unconnected with his passion for En Barral's
wife, N'Alazais.

With each breath I draw in the air
I feel coming from Provence;
I so love everything from there
that when people speak well of it,
I listen smiling, and with each
word ask for a hundred more,
so much does the hearing please me.

For there is no greater dwelling than that
which lies between the Rhône and Vence,
enclosed by the sea and the Durance,
nor any place where shines such joy.
For among those noble people – with
a lady who turns sorrow to laughter –
I have left my joyous heart.

En Barral knew perfectly well that Vidal was courting his wife, but
as he had a great fondness for the mad poet he apparently did not
mind about this. He remained completely unperturbed when one
morning Vidal crept into N'Alazais's room and kissed the sleeping
woman on the mouth. N'Alazais's own reaction to this was rather
different to her husband's. Blissfully happy to be woken up in such a

way, her laughter turned immediately to tears and screams as soon as she realized that it was Vidal and not En Barral who had kissed her. Vidal rushed out of the town and fled the country, returning only after En Barral had persuaded N'Alazais to forgive the poet and grant him the kiss as a gift.

One of the few important troubadours native to Provence was Raimbault d'Orange. He had a line in caustic humour and self-mockery. In one of his most celebrated poems he tells all husbands that they have no need to fear him, because not only has he become impotent but also he has personal qualities which leave much to be desired.

> Though I seem likeable and pleasant,
> I'm really thin, nasty and cowardly
> (with or without my armour),
> leprous and foul-smelling,
> a vile, niggardly host, and the worst
> soldier you have ever seen.

All this did not stop the Countess of Die – the beautiful wife of William of Poitiers – from loving him. The Countess was a troubadour herself and indeed, on the strength of her four surviving works, one of the finest of the four known women poets of the Middle Ages. Her poems, according to tradition, were all inspired by her love for Raimbault.

Along with Raimbault, the other great troubadour of Provence was Folquet de Marseille. Like Vidal, he too had the support of Viscount En Barral and fell in love with the obstinately chaste N'Alazais. It was reputedly out of sadness caused by her untimely death that in 1195 Folquet renounced his career as a troubadour and entered the monastery of Le Thoronet. Elected abbot of this place in 1201, he was later made Bishop of Toulouse. During the crusade against the Cathars he sided with Simon de Montfort, and in so doing had to turn against his own people and his former patrons. Dante (and later Mistral) referred to him as 'the abominable' for this act of treachery, but none the less, like all Italians, admired him for his support of Catholicism; the people of southern France never forgave him.

The lives of the troubadours – together with the legends with which these lives are so often intertwined – are sometimes more interesting than their works. Such is the case with the unfortunate Guilhem de

Cabestangh. The story told of him has no documentary evidence to support it and has also been told of several other medieval figures, including the Breton harper called Guiron, the German *Minnesinger* Reinmar von Brennenberg, and the French *trouvère* the Châtelain of Courcy. To confuse matters further there are two versions of the story, one having de Cabestangh falling in love with a woman from the region of Roussillon, another (quoted by Stendhal in his treatise *On Love*) saying that she came instead from the village of Roussillon in the Vaucluse. At all events the woman's husband, whoever he may have been, was so jealous of de Cabestangh that he had him killed and made his wife unwittingly eat her lover's heart flavoured with pepper. After finishing what she thought a good and very tasty dish, she was told what it consisted of. Horrified, to say the least, she threw herself out of the castle window, at which point of the story the version which has it that the Roussillon in question was the one in the Vaucluse provides the finest sequel. Though not a single stone of the castle survives here, the memory of the fair victim is traditionally preserved in the famous bright red ochre dust which permeates the village: this is of course the blood which the poor woman so abundantly shed after her fall and which will never be wiped away.

Real traces of troubadour Provence are more hard to come by. While there are countless churches that have come down to us from the period, the castles where the troubadours sang and found the women to inspire them have for the most part either completely disappeared or else survived only as ruins. The most tragic loss was the thirteenth-century castle of the Counts of Provence at Aix, so shamefully pulled down in 1779 together with the remains of the Roman forum. Of the Counts' other residences in Provence there remains principally the thirteenth-century palace at Brignoles, today forming part of the local museum, and – thanks to heavy rebuilding and restoration – projecting more a nineteenth-century than a medieval character.

The imagination of tourists chasing after the troubadours is unlikely to be stirred by the scanty remains of the castle at Romanin, which sits uneasily alongside a hang-gliding centre outside Saint-Rémy. For all its unprepossessing present-day appearance, it is none the less a place closely associated with the courtly love tradition. Jean de Nostredame, in his *Lives of the Provençal Poets* (1575), relates that one Estephanette de Gantelme lived here in the late thirteenth century and held in the building 'an open and plenary court of Love'. The 'Courts of Love' were an institution which has figured prominently in most people's conceptions of medieval Provence. Yet more myth than fact surrounds them, and rarely is any clear picture given of what they were actually like. They are described sometimes as poetry competitions addressed to young women and rewarded by a kiss and a feather, and at other times literally as courts in which a panel of women discussed and passed judgement on matters concerning love. According to Nostredame, the 'Courts of Love' at Romanin belonged to the latter category. One of the burning issues which Estephanette and her team had supposedly to resolve was 'Which is the more worthy to be loved; he who gives liberally or he who gives against his will in order to be regarded as liberal?'

The one place which immediately comes to mind at the mention of the 'Courts of Love' is Les Baux. Of all the relics of troubadour Provence, this is by far the most evocative and the best known: it is principally through Les Baux that Provence today is invariably thought of as the land of the troubadours. Its popularity dates from the early nineteenth century, when a taste for the Middle Ages came to rival the nostalgia for classical antiquity and when the romantic appeal of ruins began to be widely recognized. The novelist Rose Macaulay has a long section on Les Baux in her book *The Pleasure of Ruins* (1957): '. . . it had everything that the ruin-tasters could desire – antiquity, abandonment, decay, a magnificent and forbidding site. It was indeed "an awful pile . . . /Waste, desolate, where Ruin dreary dwells", with, in addition, the romance of troubadour Provence, Courts of Love, and all the rest of the medieval feudal trappings beloved of the public.'

Romantic accounts of Les Baux are coloured as much by tales of bloodshed and political intrigue as they are by ones of love and poetry. The nineteenth-century historian John Addington Symonds wrote that 'There is nothing terrible and savage belonging to feudal history of which an example may not be found in the annals of Les Baux.' Throughout the twelfth and early thirteenth centuries the Lords of Les Baux fought to gain possession of Provence, and – after the Counts of Provence had taken the side of the Cathars – found allies in the papacy and the French kings. The Angevin succession proved favourable to them, but this did not stop them from profiting from the confusion in which the region was left during the rule of Queen Jeanne I in the early fourteenth century. From then until 1420, when the territory passed finally into the hands of the Counts of Provence, they terrorized the region and had no hesitation in enlisting the services of the dreaded mercenaries, the *routiers*. The last of their number, Raymond-Louis de Beaufort, Viscount of Turenne, was little more than a brigand chief.

Guides at Les Baux delight in telling stories of Raymond forcing his victims to jump off the castle walls and laughing at their fear. But, as Rose Macaulay observed, the guides will tell you mainly about the 'Courts of Love'. To her these were the 'least interesting phenomena of Les Baux's romantic history, though apparently regarded as the greatest pleasure for tourists'. They are also historically the most questionable aspect of Les Baux's past. It is known that the blood-thirsty barons were patrons to such illustrious troubadours as Pierre d'Auvergne, Guirault de Bornelh and Raimbault de Vaquières, and that the women of Les Baux really did figure in their works. However, the idea of troubadours competing for the favours of a line-up of court beauties, as the guides would have us believe, has more basis in the works of romantic novelists such as Sir Walter Scott than in fact.

The historically-minded tourist will actually find less of interest in the Les Baux of the troubadours than in the place as it later developed. In the sixteenth century the settlement at the castle's foot became a Protestant town of about 6,000 inhabitants. Though by the mid nineteenth century this had been reduced to what one traveller described as a 'squalid little village' full of beggars, a number of fine sixteenth-century palaces survived, buildings which constitute today the greatest architectural joys of Les Baux. The medieval stronghold at the top of the hill was devastated by Cardinal Richelieu and is now a particularly bleak sight. Only the outer walls of the thirteenth-century keep are still standing, and these are worth a visit largely for the vertiginous views to be had from the top of them.

Of course not all the famous tales of love associated with twelfth- and thirteenth-century Provence were linked with the troubadours. A romantically inclined medieval traveller would almost certainly rather have caught a glimpse of the castle of Beaucaire than of that of Les Baux. This was the setting of what was perhaps the best known of all medieval love stories, Aucassin and Nicolette. The original version of this often repeated story comprises an unusual mixture of prose and verse. Its anonymous author came from the north of France and had probably never been to the south; but his tale was soon appropriated by the Provençal people and turned into a ballad of the region. The story concerns the old and feeble Count Garin of Beaucaire, his love-stricken and slightly foolish son, Aucassin, and the resourceful Carthaginian slave-girl Nicolette. The father desperately tries to prevent his son from marrying the socially inferior Nicolette, and eventually has them both locked up in different parts of his castle; the ending is a happy one. The triangular-shaped keep, clinging to a cliff-face over the Rhône, can still be seen, and some might doubtless like to imagine that this is where the dungeon was into which Aucassin was thrown. Nicolette herself was put in a high tower in the castle proper, but of this there is no trace: the medieval structure, heavily rebuilt at a later period, was almost all dismantled by Richelieu and only a thirteenth-century chapel was spared.

The castle at Ansouis, to the south of the Lubéron, gives a better idea than most other castles in Provence of what a noble residence was like in the Middle Ages. The main block of the building is of the seventeenth century, but attached to this is an extensive twelfth- to fourteenth-century fortress. Apart from a short period after the Revolution, the castle has belonged to this day to the same family, the Sabrans, which perhaps partly accounts for its very special atmosphere. Like Beaucaire, it too is associated with a famous couple whom Fate kept apart, if for admittedly rather different reasons. The story of the love of Elzéar and Delphine offers an excellent corrective to the tales of fatal passion and unrequited sexual yearning of which the Middle Ages is so full.

In 1298 it was arranged that the thirteen-year-old Elzéar de Sabran should marry the fifteen-year-old Delphine de Puy Michel, a wealthy descendant of the Viscount of Marseille. Unfortunately the girl had already pledged her love to someone else – God. From an early age she had resolved to live like a nun, and nothing was going to make her give up her virginity. The potentially embarrassing dilemma in which the girl placed her family was finally resolved on the intervention of a monk, who hinted that it was possible to be chaste and married at the same time. The marriage thus went ahead, and when Elzéar made his first approaches to his new wife she told him of her resolution, which he happily accepted. They maintained their chaste relationship until Elzéar's death in 1327, after which Delphine gave up all her earthly goods and lived a life of poverty and good deeds. Both were later sanctified, and have always been greatly venerated in Provence.

The lives of Elzéar and Delphine coincided with the last years of the troubadours and the emergence of Petrarch as Europe's greatest lyric poet. Petrarch, like Dante before him, found enormous inspiration in the verse of the troubadours. Dante was already in his thirties when the troubadour tradition began to die out, but Petrarch was born a good ten years after the death of the last troubadour, Guirault Riquier. Thus while Dante continued in a tradition, Petrarch revived one, and did so at a time when the age of the troubadours and their ideals of courtly love must have been looked back on with enormous nostalgia.

Petrarch was born in Florence in 1304, but his notary father was exiled from the city when the future poet was only eight. The family took refuge in Avignon, and Petrarch was educated in Carpentras. He entered a minor Church order in his twenties, and thereafter devoted as much time to classical scholarship and the writing of treatises and letters as to poetry. Up to 1353 he was based mainly in Avignon and the Comtat-Venaissin, but he made extended visits to Italy, on the first of which, in 1341, he was elected poet laureate in Rome. The one event in his life best remembered by future generations of his readers was when he first set eyes on Laura, on Good Friday, 1327, outside the convent church of Sainte-Claire in Avignon. She was to remain his constant muse, even after her death, and the subject of most of his greatest poems. As with some ideal lady of the troubadours, Petrarch's love for her was never requited. It was in fact six years before he even declared himself to her, a period marked by sudden transitions from joy to grief depending on whether he believed she had smiled or been angry with him. After he had finally made his bold declaration, she replied, not surprisingly, 'I am not, Petrarch, the women you think I am.' This did not prevent Petrarch from continuing to pester her for the next fifteen years, during which time he would come periodically to say goodbye to her for ever. She died in 1348, probably of the Black Death, but continued to haunt the poet. In 1358 he wrote that he had spent twenty-one years burning with love for her, and ten years crying for her. It should be noted that throughout this period he never as much as mentioned the Avignon woman by whom he had two illegitimate children.

Did Laura exist, or had Petrarch simply invented her to emulate the courtly love tradition of the troubadours? Her name has certainly a suspicious ring to it, the laurel having been after all the symbol of poetry ever since Daphne was turned into the tree after being chased by Apollo, the god of poetry. Was Petrarch, in chasing Laura, likening himself to Apollo? Doubts about Laura's existence were expressed even in Petrarch's lifetime. The Bishop of Lambez, one of the poet's closest friends, told him once that 'your Laura is only a ghost built up out of your imagination . . . if there is any reality in all this, it is your passion, not for your fictitious Laura, but for the Laurel that is the crown of poets and that, as your works and studies demonstrate, you are hastening after'. To this Petrarch indignantly replied: 'Would to God that my Laura was an imaginary person and that my passion for her was only a game! Alas! It is a frenzy!' Furthermore, he claimed in his *Dialogues with Saint Augustine* (begun in 1342) that many of his readers had actually gone to Avignon to see Laura and had been disappointed by her because she had seemed to them too much of a 'real woman'.

Speculation as to who this putative person could have been has been rife. We know from Petrarch the date of her death, that she was married, and that she was buried in the convent church of the Franciscans in Avignon. The one Laura of this time who most closely fits these clues is one Laura de Noves, who married when very young into the noble Sade family and who, by an extraordinary coincidence, was instructed in the joys of poetry by her aunt, Estephanette de Gantelme of 'courtly love' fame. The tradition that she was the Laura immortalized by Petrarch is the oldest there is and goes back to at least the early sixteenth century. In 1533 a Lyon poet called Maurice Scève caused considerable excitement by claiming to have found the remains of Laura de Sade in the church of the Franciscans. They were enclosed in a small lead box, together with a sonnet and a medal bearing the inscription 'M.L.M.J.' The sonnet was immediately ascribed to Petrarch and the inscription read as *Madonna Laura Mortua Jacet* (Here Lies the Dead Lady Laura). Francis I of France was sufficiently impressed by this to visit Avignon and to order the construction of a

mausoleum in the church. Few seemed to take much notice of Petrarch's first biographer, Alessandro Vellutello, who came to Avignon
two years after the supposed discovery and found that the tomb
which Scève had thought was Laura's was so worn that its inscription
was completely illegible. The medal eventually ended up in an English
collection, where it was redated to the fifteenth century and reinter-
preted as an amulet worn for protection against the plague, the initials
now being read as those of the Four Evangelists. During the Revolution
the sonnet was lost and the church of the Franciscans largely destroyed. The mausoleum was never built. None the less, a visit to the
site of 'Laura's tomb' remained well into the nineteenth century an
essential part of any tourist's itinerary around Avignon.

A visit to this church would invariably be followed by an excursion
to the most famous place associated with Petrarch, the village and
fountain of Vaucluse. This was the once tranquil spot – the 'val
chiusa' of the sonnets – where Petrarch would escape the squalor and
noise of Avignon and, while watching the Sorgue frolic its way down
the narrow, shaded valley leading from the spring, try, without success, to forget his beloved Laura. Generations of tourists have been
misled into thinking that the romantically-perched castle high above
the spring was Petrarch's castle, though in fact it belonged to a friend
of Petrarch, Philippe de Cabassole, Bishop of Cavaillon, who would
sometimes come to Vaucluse to interrupt the solitary, near monastic
life-style which the poet generally led here. Petrarch's own home was
in the village itself, and has long since disappeared.

Since the time of Petrarch's death an ever growing number of travellers have come to disturb the peace of the Vaucluse. By the seventeenth
century it had become a tourist attraction rivalling the classical
buildings of Provence, and indeed a major reason for visiting the
region. Its fame was given an additional boost with the publication in
1754 of Voltaire's popular epic poem, *L'Henriade*, in which the God
of Love and his cortège leave ancient Italy and fly towards Vaucluse,
'A haven yet sweeter, a place which in its heyday,/ Saw Petrarch sigh
his verses and his love'. M. Bérenger, the romantic author of *Les
Soirées provençales* (1786), remembered Voltaire as he stood by the
side of the Sorgue reciting out loud from his copy of Petrarch the
sonnet which begins, '*Chiare, fresche, dolci acque . . .*' Another
French traveller, Millin, came to the place several years later and

reported how by now every tourist who visited the fountain would inscribe their name or some lines of poetry on the rocks. He himself did the same, and contemplated picking some plants from around the fountain to bring back as sentimental gifts to his friends. In the nineteenth century souvenir shops proliferated, and the first hotels, bars and restaurants bearing the name of Petrarch and Laura were opened. Henry James visited the place in 1882, reluctantly:

> I had a prejudice against Vaucluse, against Petrarch, even against the incomparable Laura. I was sure that the place was cockneyfied and threadbare, and I had never been able to take an interest in the poet and the lady. I was sure that I had known many women as charming and as handsome as she, about whom much less noise had been made; and I was convinced that her singer was factitious and literary, and that there are half a dozen stanzas in Wordsworth that speak more to the soul than the whole collection of his *fioriture*.

After the visit, James concluded that the place was 'indeed cockneyfied' but that he would have been foolish not to have come here, for its charms and fascination were undeniable. James's verdict holds true even today, when the place has become more popularized than ever and by a generation to whom Petrarch means relatively little. With the crowds and without a knowledge of Petrarch, it is still possible to become immersed in the strange beauty of the site.

The troubadours and Petrarch were not the only people to have contributed to the romantic image of Provence which so often features in histories of the region. That this image greatly distorts the truth is illustrated by the case of Jeanne I, the ruler of Provence during Petrarch's time. She was actually in Provence for only one year, 1348, coming here from her throne at Naples to escape the repercussions of the murder of her young husband, Andrew of Hungary. In 1348 she sold Avignon to Clement VI, thereby earning absolution from her crime and enough money to buy back her Italian throne. Her other contributions to Provence's history were also negative: her ruling of the region from afar led to much civic disorder and confusion, as did her later decision to side with the anti-popes at Avignon. Yet for all this she has always been known as 'La Belle Reine Jeanne', a glamorous, persecuted figure whom one nineteenth-century English writer described as 'the most dangerous and the most dazzling woman of the fourteenth century'. Mistral did his best to further this image in his play, *La Reino Jaino*, which when first put on in Paris was poorly received by an audience who did not understand what an important place this queen held in the hearts of the Provençal people.

A legendary image also surrounds the man who was effectively the last ruler of medieval, independent Provence, René of Anjou. To this day René is referred to as 'le Bon Roi René' ('Good King René'), and the period of his rule is regarded as one of the most glorious in Provençal history. Walter Scott, in his historical novel *Anne of Geierstein*, popularized René's Provence as an idyllic place little disturbed by crime, and described René himself as a 'romantic old monarch with the universal tastes for music and poetry'. Unlike Queen Jeanne, René did spend much of his time in Provence, particularly in the second half of his life, after he had lost his throne at Naples and was King of Sicily only in title. It is certainly true that under René Provence knew a greater period of peace than did any other part of France; furthermore, René was undeniably a cultivated man, someone who patronized the arts, revived an interest in the poetry of the troubadours, and composed works himself, including much love poetry and a treatise on courtly love. However, to maintain his rule he had to impose the heaviest taxes that the Provençal people had yet known; it was also through his incompetence that Provence passed to Louis XI of France after the one-year rule of his successor, Charles of Anjou. Ford Madox Ford curtly noted that René was 'good' because he was hard up and substituted fines for executions. Stendhal was rather harsher in his judgement. 'This king René was a good man without character or talent. For the pleasure of a few motets and some mediocre pictures, he allowed all his territories to be swept from under him by the wily Louis XI; Provence is indebted to him for having lost its nationality.'

Though lack of funds considerably curbed building activity during René's rule, there are a number of places here which preserve his fabled memory. The least visited of these is the castle named after him at Peyrolles, near Aix-en-Provence. Romanesque in origin and owned for over 250 years by the Archbishops of Aix, the castle was purchased by René after 1475 and greatly enlarged by him. In 1481 the castle came into the possession of the French kings, who kept it until 1668; after the Revolution it became the property of the town and is now used partially as a town hall. The present-day appearance of this massive building owes much to seventeenth-century remodelling, but elements of the fifteenth-century structure peep through in the garden façade and terraces. The condition of the whole place is unfortunately the worst of any major building in Provence: much of the crudely modernized interior is an empty crumbling shell, and no attempt has even been made to remove from one of its walls an S.S. symbol and other German graffiti from the Second World War.

The magnificent if heavily restored castle at La Barben near Salon, given by René to his daughter Yolande in 1453, lives up more to romantic notions of René's Provence. It is a crenellated structure thrust high on a rock above a wooded ravine. The homely interior, which has been looked after since 1474 by the Forbin family, has charming medieval and Renaissance furnishings, as well as delicate decorations from the seventeeth and eighteenth centuries. An additional attraction is its small seventeenth-century garden by Le Nôtre, in the middle of which is a pool where Pauline Bonaparte used to bathe naked, protected from prying eyes by sheets held by black servants.

For a castle more firmly rooted in the fifteenth century than those at Peyrolles or La Barben, the visitor has to go to Tarascon, where René often stayed during his last years. Work was begun on the building in the twelfth century, but the construction dates mainly from the first half of the fifteenth. The castle is one of the most unified and best preserved in medieval Provence. The romantic appeal of the building, with its crenellated towers magically reflected in the waters of the Rhône, must have been heightened for eighteenth and nineteenth-century travellers by the place's inaccessibility. During the whole of this period the castle was used as a prison, access to which was extremely limited for visitors. There are various reports from the late nineteenth century of scholars bearing official letters being turned away by an unflinching, toothless gaoler. Today, like so many castles looked after by the French state, the interior is bare and disappointing and makes one almost wish that one had stayed outside and preserved one's illusions. Its principal interest lies in its views across the Rhône to Beaucaire, and in its small inner courtyard, adorned on one wall with a fifteenth-century monument to René and his second wife Jeanne de Laval.

Jeanne de Laval, a plain and unremarkable woman to judge from contemporary accounts and pictures, has been as much romanticized as her husband and has frequently been described as a great beauty. The castle at Les Baux was presented to her as a gift, and in the valley underneath the village is a small building which has been known for centuries as the Pavilion of Queen Jeanne. This classical-style building, one of the gems of Provençal Renaissance architecture, epitomized for future generations the glories of independent Provence, so much so that Mistral had it copied for his tomb at Maillane. One wonders whether he and many other romantic nationalists like him would have made the building such an object of veneration had they known that it had nothing to do with Jeanne de Laval but had in fact been built in 1581 by the Protestant Baroness of Les Baux, Jeanne de Quiqueran.

The works of Mistral and countless other Provençal writers from the sixteenth century onwards are suffused with a nostalgia for the Provence of the troubadours, Petrarch and King René. In their attempts to emulate this golden age, they have tried to maintain both the Provençal language and the tradition in Provence for love poetry, which they have considered as the region's greatest contribution to world literature. 'No other literature', wrote the author of a nine-teenth-century anthology of Provençal verse, 'has given such a place to love as has that of Provence.' One of the earliest important writers in Provençal after the troubadours was Bellaud de Bellaudière, who was born in Grasse in 1532 and later settled in Aix. His major work, *Obros et rimos*, is a posthumously published collection of sonnets reflecting the loves and adventures of Bellaudière's picturesque Bohem-ian life.

Between Bellaudière and the Félibres there were numerous other authors of secular Provençal verse, though none of more than local significance. The Félibres represented the culmination of nationalist tendencies in Provençal literature since the Middle Ages and have rarely been rivalled by any subsequent writers in the language. The original group consisted of seven friends – Frédéric Mistral, Joseph Roumanille, Théodore Aubanel, Alphonse Tavan, Anselme Mathieu, Jean Brunet, and Paul Giéra – who would meet most Sundays in and around Avignon to eat, drink and recite poetry. A favourite meeting-place was Giéra's nineteenth-century mansion at Fontségugne near Châteauneuf-de-Gadagne, a village a few kilometres away from the

Fontaine-de-Vaucluse and within sight of Mont Ventoux. Today the area has been much built up and industrialized, but to Mistral it was a countryside full of idyllic memories. In his autobiography he quotes the peasant poet Tavan's description of the shaded spring after which Giéra's house was named:

> It is the favourite trysting-spot of the village lovers on Sundays, for there they find a grateful shade, solitude, quiet nooks, little stone benches covered with ivy, winding paths among the trees, a lovely view. The song of birds, the rustling of leaves, the rippling of brooks! Where better than in such a spot can the solitary wander and dream of love, or the happy pair resort, and love?

It was at Fontségugne, on 21 May 1854, that Mistral and his friends decided to call themselves the Félibres and dedicate their lives to bringing about a renaissance of Provençal culture comparable to that of the Middle Ages.

Undoubtedly the Félibres saw themselves as latter-day troubadours, and in some of their meetings at Fontségugne they serenaded the ladies of the house in conscious imitation of what they imagined the 'Courts of Love' to have been like. The most amorous of the Félibres was Anselme Mathieu, who soon won the nickname of 'Le Félibre des Baisers' (the Félibre of the Kisses). Mistral, who related in his *Memoirs* many of Mathieu's inventive amorous ploys, described him as 'someone lost in visions of a reawakened Provence, and . . . the gallant squire of all fair damsels'.

A finer poet than Mathieu was Aubanel, a member of a leading Avignon publishing family, the premises of which today are a delightful family museum (see page 242). Aubanel too was a great romantic who devoted much of his work to extolling the beauty of women. The great love of his life was Jenny Marivel ('Zani'), whom he first met at Fontségugne. She was wearing a dress the colour of pomegranate, and from then onwards the pomegranate was always to be the symbol of love in his verse. In 1854 'Zani' retired to a convent, and the distraught Aubanel had to console himself with a pilgrimage to Notre-Dame-de-Lure. Years after her departure (they were never to meet again), Aubanel was to recall the happy days spent with her at Fontségugne: 'Dost thou remember, behind the convent walls, thou with thy Spanish face, how we chased each other, running, racing like mad among the trees . . .? And ah, how sweet it was when my arm stole round thy slender waist, and to the song of the nightingales we danced together while thou didst mingle thy fresh young voice with the notes of the birds.' The departure inspired Aubanel's *Miagrauno Entreduberto* of 1860; but a far more robust group of poems was his *Les Filles d'Avignon* of 1885, regarded at the time as one of the most audacious groups of love poems written by the Félibres. In one of these works he implores the Venus of Arles to remove her garments:

> Show us thy naked arms, thy naked breasts, thy naked thighs
> Disrobe completely, oh divine Venus!
> Beauty covers thee better than thy white robe
> Throw to thy feet that whole robe which around thy hips
> Is draped, encircling all that is most beautiful about thee
> Abandon thy stomach to the kisses of the sun!

Though addressed only to a statue, this poem is exceptional among the work of the Félibres in having a strong sexual element. Sexual explicitness might have characterized much of the verse of the troubadours, but is rarely to be found in later Provençal poets. To Mistral the three essential ingredients of love were Simplicity, Truth and Chastity, qualities which inform most of his insipid heroines from Mireille onwards. He and his fellow Félibres differed from the troubadours, too, in their belief in simplicity of expression: while the troubadours wrote complex verse for the aristocracy, the Félibres wrote simple verse for the Provençal people as a whole. One of their disciples of whom they were most proud was Charloun Rieu, a peasant who lived a life of solitude and simplicity near Les Baux. While continuing to work as a peasant, Rieu produced some of the most touching Provençal love poems in recent times. His inspiration goes back to the troubadours, and he is even commemorated by a monument on top of the citadel of Les Baux. But he derives from these poets only their obsession with unrequited love and not their sophisticated and often humorous means of expressing it.

The glamorous view of medieval Provence which has usually been upheld by writers will doubtless continue to sustain the region's reputation as the land of romantic love. But the land which inspired the troubadours, Petrarch and the Félibres also produced a man whose life and work was the very antithesis of romantic love – the Marquis de Sade. The Marquis belongs to the end of a long period in Provençal history – in between the annexation to France in 1487 and the Revolution – which has been neglected equally by historians and tourists. He was no isolated phenomenon. His taste for sodomy, which so horrified his French contemporaries, was apparently widespread in the Provence of his day, as it was in other Mediterranean countries. More importantly, the particular part of Provence where his activities were centred, the Lubéron, had been known for its dissolutes and free-thinkers ever since it had harboured the Vaudois. In the castle at Ménerbes lived Count Rantzau, a Danish nobleman who had run away from Denmark in 1766 after being implicated in the murder of the Queen's lover and confidant, Frederick Struensee; at Ménerbes he lived openly with an actress mistress and led a notorious life of debauchery. The castle at Mirabeau, on the other side of the Lubéron, was the family home of G. H. Riquetti, Count of Mirabeau, the famous orator and thinker of the French Revolution. Before immersing himself in politics he had led a dissolute youth, and had been imprisoned and disowned after eloping with the wife of another aristocrat. His reputation was first made as the author of a number of pornographic works written while in prison. He was incarcerated in the Bastille at the same time as the Marquis de Sade.

The Marquis de Sade believed, like Voltaire, that 'Love is the fabric of Nature embroidered by the imagination'. 'A man who falls in love with a woman,' he once wrote, 'is no different from one who desires her body. He is deceiving himself if he wants her heart.' There is thus a wonderful irony in the fact that his family were the direct descendants of the muse who traditionally inspired Petrarch's sonnets, Laura de Sade. It was a connection which the perverse Marquis was to savour all his life.

The Sades were one of the oldest and most respected families in Provence. At the time of the Marquis's birth the family had two major properties in the Vaucluse. One was the now ruined castle at Lacoste, which they had acquired in the late seventeenth century from the Simianes: this was the same castle where many of the Vaudois had been savagely massacred in the mid sixteenth century. The other was the castle at Saumane, an imposing thirteenth- to seventeenth-century pile (still in private possession and closed to visitors) on top of a wooded hill near the Fontaine-de-Vaucluse. The first of the castles was owned by the Marquis's parents, who were based mainly in Paris where the mother was a lady-in-waiting at the court. The Marquis was born in Paris in 1740, but when only five was entrusted to the care of his uncle at Saumane.

The uncle was abbot of the Benedictine monastery of Saint-Léger-d'Ébreuil but lived at Saumane for much of the year. He was not the holiest of men, and his taking up of religious orders in 1734 had inspired the cynical reaction from Voltaire, 'What a lot of Holiness all at once in one family! So that's why you tell me you are going to give up making love.' Far from giving it up, the abbot was to maintain a mistress or two at Saumane for the rest of his life, and in 1754, when his nephew was twelve, he was even briefly imprisoned on a charge of debauchery after a police raid on a brothel. The abbot's influence on his nephew was a profound one, and not just in terms of inspiring a life-long loathing of the Church and all its hypocritical morality. The abbot devoted as much time to his scholarly pursuits as to his amorous ones, and for most of his nephew's youth was engaged in research on Petrarch. As both the descendant of Laura de Sade and the owner of the poem which had been found in Laura's supposed tomb, he naturally had a vested interest in trying to prove that this woman had been the Laura of the sonnets. His work on Petrarch and Laura was eventually turned into the most successful biography of the poet as yet written. His enthusiasm for the subject was communicated to his nephew, who was later to write, when in prison, that reading Petrarch was his only consolation. Perhaps it was not entirely coincidental that the first important love of his life was for an Avignon girl named Laura de Lauris.

The Marquis met Laura while engaged in a brief career as a drinking, gambling and womanizing soldier in the King's guard. His father was opposed to the relationship, not on the grounds that Laura was socially unsuitable (she was in fact a fellow aristocrat) but because he had planned to marry his son to one Renée-Pélagie de Montreuil, the elder daughter of a wealthy Parisian banking family. The Sades' financial fortunes were then at a low ebb, and it was hoped that this match would save them from dwindling further. On hearing of his father's plans, the Marquis rushed to Avignon to try and marry Laura instead. She refused, having recently taken another lover. In the short period in which he had known her, he had been inflicted with his first (and, some say, last) real taste of sexual happiness, as well as a heavy dose of syphilis. In May of 1763 he obeyed his father's wishes and married Renée-Pélagie.

Two years later he made his first protracted stay in Lacoste, bringing with him not Renée-Pélagie but an actress friend whom he passed off as his wife. He was to return regularly to the castle until his imprisonment in 1778. He had no particular affection for Provence, disliked the villagers of Lacoste, and abhorred nature and rural life; yet he appears to have developed an obsession with this castle. Much of what money he had was spent on a lavish embellishment of the building, and at one time he even planned in the park an elaborate temple to the arts. To satisfy an enormous passion which he had for the theatre, he adapted a room within the castle for the production of plays written mainly by himself and performed by some of the best available actors in France. To these spectacles he invited all the gentry of the region, but with his growing ill-repute these people came increasingly to shun his house, and he was forced to rely on the audience support of the villagers.

The castle is best remembered today as the scene of orgies, flagellations, acts of sodomy, and other such activities inspired by the Marquis's insatiable sexual appetite. Already in 1765, when the Marquis was living openly at Lacoste with his actress mistress, the castle had earned the reputation of an 'accursed place'. By then the Marquis had already had a brief spell in prison as a result of his treatment of a girl prostitute in Paris (sodomy and heresy, of which he was accused by her, were both acts punishable by death). That time he had managed to be released because of his noble birth; but when in 1767 he became involved in a similar incident in Marseille, he sensed that this time he would not be so lucky and escaped briefly to Italy with his sister-in-law, with whom he was then having an affair. After a suitable lapse of time he returned to France and made straight for Lacoste, where he attempted to maintain a discreet presence. Throughout all his troubles Renée-Pélagie had remained totally devoted to him (masochistically one might say), and though she knew that she would never be able to reform his sexual ways, she at least tried to ensure that his activities in this field should be contained within the castle so as to avoid further scandal outside the area. For this purpose she employed ostensibly as domestic staff a number of young women sworn to secrecy. Inevitably, however, new allegations were made against the Marquis, forcing him to flee the country once more and leading this time to his being imprisoned almost immediately on his return to Lacoste in 1778.

After several months in prison, the Marquis wrote to Renée-Pélagie telling her of a dream he had had in which Laura de Sade had come to visit him. 'Suddenly she appeared to me . . . I saw her! The horrors of the tomb had not altered the splendour of her charms, and her eyes had as much fire as when Petrarch praised them.' She was covered entirely in black crape and her beautiful blonde hair hung loosely above this. 'Why do you lie groaning on the floor?' she asked the Marquis. 'Come and rejoin me. No more evils, no more sorrows, no more care in the limbless space where I dwell. Take courage and follow me there.' Hearing this, the Marquis fell in tears at her feet. 'Oh my Mother!' he shouted. She held out her hand to him, which he covered in tears, bringing tears to her eyes too. 'When I lived in this world that you detest,' she continued, 'I amused myself by looking into the future; I imagined my descendants down to you, *but I did not see you so wretched*.' Full of despair and affection, the Marquis threw his arms around her neck, to plead with her either to stay or to take him with her; but she vanished, leaving him with only his sorrow.

In all the Marquis spent twelve years in prison, being transferred during his last years from Vincennes to the notorious Bastille. Released after the Revolution, he managed to convince his contemporaries of his revolutionary zeal (he had in fact as much contempt for the republicans as he had for the aristocracy) and served for a while on a revolutionary tribunal. By now Renée-Pélagie had finally left him and he was living in a state of near poverty with an actress friend in Paris. During the Terror his castle at Lacoste was partially pulled down by the locals, and in 1797 he paid his last visit to Provence to sell what was left of the building. From this decade are the first of his writings which would establish his reputation for future generations, though which would also have the more immediate effect of incarcerating him in 1801 in the mental hospital of Charenton, where he was to die in 1814. His interest in the theatre during these years at Charenton remained as strong as ever, and he had his plays enacted there by his fellow inmates. He retained also his affection for his castle at Lacoste, a place which features as the main setting of most of his writings, including *Justine* and *120 Days of Sodom*. In a letter of 1805 to his notary at Apt, he pathetically inquired after the state of his castle and asked also if something of his 'own character' could still be felt in its 'poor park'.

After the sale of the castle in 1797, the standing parts of the building were used first as a modest domestic habitation and then as a shelter for the farm animals of the community. In the first half of this century a growing number of Sade's devotees, including the surrealist poet André Breton, came to Lacoste to pay their respects to the master and to sign their names on the castle's crumbling walls. Then in the 1960s the ruin was purchased by a local teacher called André Bouer, a man from an old Vaudois family who boasted also an ancestor who had been Mayor of Lacoste during the Marquis's time. With the aid of a grant from the French government, Bouer embarked on what had been a life-long dream; he began to rebuild the castle with the intention of returning it to the state in which it had been left by the Marquis. To aid him in the reconstruction he has undertaken extensive archival work, and has come up with much new material about Lacoste and the Marquis, including the revealing fact that the Marquis had a passion for the candied fruit of Apt. The reconstruction of the castle is still going on, twelve years later, though Bouer's impossible dream remains as far from being realized as ever. In the village it is widely rumoured that Bouer sees himself as the Marquis's reincarnation.

The story of Bouer and his obsession with the castle is just one of many strange and scurrilous tales associated with Lacoste, a place as far removed from traditional conceptions of village life as the life and works of the Marquis are from traditional tales of love.

5

Village Life

The heroine of Mistral's *Miréio* is not just a love-stricken girl, she is also an embodiment of rural Provence threatened by the spectres of change and industrialization. Mistral saw the preservation of rural life and its traditions as vital to the renewal of his native land. This life always remained an essential inspiration to him, as it did to other great Provençal writers and artists of recent times such as Alphonse Daudet, Jean Giono, Henri Bosco, and Marcel Pagnol. Tourists in Provence today, wary of the coast and its spoilt resorts, escape often to the villages of the interior, where they hope to find what is left of the 'real Provence'.

Agriculture prospered throughout the Provence of Mistral's childhood. The traditional sources of the region's economy, such as its silkworms, vines, olives, almonds and abundant fruits and vegetables, were exploited more successfully than ever before. Old enemies such as floods, droughts, and the *mistral* were partially contained through the creation of canals and irrigation schemes and the planting of vines and rows of trees to act as windbreaks. A plant producing a highly popular red dye (used by soldiers in both the French and English armies) was introduced into the Vaucluse. Rice culture was established in the Camargue.

The second half of the nineteenth century, the period of Mistral's maturity, saw fundamental changes to the Provençal economy and the breakdown of numerous agricultural communities. In the 1870s and 80s exceptionally severe frosts created permanent damage to many of the olive groves; vines were destroyed by the terrible scourge of phylloxera; the dye extracted from the plant known as the *garance* was superseded by an artificial dye; disease and increased competition from elsewhere brought silk production to a virtual halt.

Industrialization took root mainly in and around Marseille and Toulon and at first made relatively little headway in the interior. The coming of the railway did little to alter this imbalance, and in fact made it worse: rather than bring potential new sources of wealth to the interior, it tended to encourage numerous country-folk to abandon their threatened lands and try to find employment in the main coastal towns. Large areas of the Var and upper Provence became seriously depopulated.

Mistral looked back to the rural Provence of his childhood with enormous nostalgia, and described it as some idyllic biblical world unaffected by modern civilization. As late as 1885 the English traveller Charlotte Dempster could be struck by how antiquated much of the countryside still was: 'Machinery for agricultural purposes is unknown, and broad-footed oxen tread out the grain on a paved threshing-floor, to which not even the authority of a scripture could reconcile a Scottish bailiff.' However, to Mistral the countryside had by this date already begun to be spoilt. Those parts of it that had survived relatively unscathed the agricultural crises of the 1870s and 80s (most notably the ever prosperous Rhône valley) were for him now under a far greater threat – 'Progress, the fatal Reaper, against whom it is useless to contend . . .' 'In the present day,' he wrote, 'when machinery has almost obliterated agriculture, the cultivation of the soil is losing more and more the noble aspect of that sacred art and of its idyllic character.' He described with horror a modern harvest: 'All this is done in the latest American style, a dull matter of business, with never a song to make toil a gladness, amid a whirl of noise, dust and hideous smoke . . .'

One of the greatest tributes ever paid to the disappearing rural world of nineteenth-century Provence was written by Mistral's friend, Alphonse Daudet. Daudet's *Letters from My Windmill* (1866) is a book which is still extraordinarily popular, and the mill at Fontvieille from where the author pretended to tell his stories continues to attract a never-ending succession of tourists. The lower half of this building contains souvenirs of Daudet; the upper half comprises the original working mechanism of the mill and a display relating to Provençal mills in general.

Daudet's mill is one of many such buildings in the Fontvieille area which were abandoned around the middle of the last century. The story of their abandonment is the subject of the first of Daudet's tales, 'The Secret of Master Cornille'. Shortly after Daudet has moved into the mill, he is approached by an old man who tells him that the surrounding countryside has not always been 'the dead and soulless place which it is today'. At one time, he goes on to say, there were working windmills on every hill – everywhere you looked you could see sails turning in the *mistral*, and rows of donkeys carrying to the mills sacks of grain to be ground. 'These mills,' he sums up, 'constituted the joy and the wealth of our land.' But then one day 'some French men from Paris' had the idea of building a large steam-operated flour-mill on the Tarascon road. From that time onwards everyone in the neighbourhood had brought their grain to this modern establishment, and the old mills had had to close down. Only one of the millers, Master Cornille, had continued to work as before . . .

No one understood how this man could keep up in this way, for no one went to him any more with their grain. Furthermore, his behaviour had become very strange from the moment the modern flour mill had begun functioning. His fifteen-year-old granddaughter, whom he clearly loved and had looked after in the mill ever since her parents had died, was suddenly sent away to live on her own. He had taken to going around like a tramp and at church he stood at the back with the paupers. He allowed no one to visit him at the mill and always kept the place securely locked. However, one day his daughter and her boy-friend managed to climb through a window, and the secret of Master Cornille was finally revealed – all around were sacks filled not with flour or grain but with white earth. He had only been pretending to mill flour, and now that his secret was finally out, all his remaining self-respect had gone. His neighbours immediately came to the rescue by carrying to him in a procession all the grain that they could lay hold of, a sight which brought tears to the old man's eyes. Thereafter he was never to lack work again, but after his death there was no one left to succeed him. 'Everything comes to an end in this world,' the tale concludes.

Daudet's tales are written with an engaging simplicity and sense of fantasy. They can be funny and also very touching, but never have the cloying sentimentality which often creeps into the writings of Mistral. Daudet's attitude towards rural nostalgia was refreshingly down-to-earth. He loved the Provençal countryside but needed the excitement of the city. The last story in *Letters from My Windmill* is entitled 'Nostalgie de caserne' ('Barracks Nostalgia'), and deals with a Provençal soldier on leave at his home village. 'Oh! What good Provençals we make! Over there, in the barracks of Paris, we miss our blue Alpilles and the wild smell of lavender; now, here, right in the middle of Provence, all we can think of is Paris, every memory of which is precious to us!' The tale (and the book) ends with the soldier still dreaming of Paris. 'Oh Paris! . . . Paris . . . Always Paris!'

Elsewhere in the book Daudet describes a visit to Mistral at his home in Maillane. The poet recites passages from his epic work *Calendau*, which he has only just brought to completion. Daudet is so impressed by the poem that he exclaims in an aside: 'And now lay out the railway tracks, put up the telegraph poles, throw out the Provençal language from the schools! Provence will always live on in *Miréio* and *Calendau*.'

Unlike Daudet, Mistral did not so easily resign himself to the disappearance of traditions, and throughout his life he tried to ensure that the Provence of his childhood would not just be remembered through his poems. He actively defended the teaching of the Provençal language in schools, supported and even revived many traditional festivities, encouraged a greater wearing of folk costumes, and compiled over the years a massive encyclopaedia of Provençal culture, *Le Trésor de la Félibrige*. In 1896 he founded a museum devoted exclusively to the folklore of Provence, and in 1904 he gave to this all the money which he had earned that year after winning the Nobel Prize for Literature.

The Museon Arlaten, housed in a sixteenth-century palace in the centre of Arles, is a place so strong in atmosphere that it repays a visit even if you give the most cursory glance to its exhibits. Costumed waxwork figures in reconstructed interiors contribute to an impression of stepping back in time, as you wander from room to room in this dusty, sombrely lit treasure trove of relics and photographs of Provence's pre-industrial past. The museum is situated in Arles because Arles and its district has always been the part of Provence with the most distinctive folk culture. For instance, the finest examples of traditional furniture in the region are in the so-called Arles style, which originated in the district in the eighteenth century and is characterized by its elegant rococo swirls. This style, so different from the heavier furniture style associated with upper Provence, was imitated by craftsmen right up to recent times and enjoyed a popularity which extended well beyond the region. Some of the most intricate works by the Arles craftsmen are the bread containers known as *panetières*. These are perhaps the most typically Provençal of all items of furniture and are almost always found on the kitchen walls of old Provençal houses. They had almost the status of a domestic reliquary, and were indeed often decorated with religious images.

Arles's greatest contribution to the folk art of Provence were the costumes worn by its women. In the past there was little consensus of opinion as to which other European costumes they were most similar to. Count Moszynski was adamant that the blouses were in a 'Circassian' style, a fashion later adapted in Poland and called in Paris 'La Hongreline'. Arthur Young, Stendhal and A. Thiers were reminded respectively of the costume of women in England, the Roman Campagna and Catalonia. Bérenger – influenced by the romantic notion that the Arles women had retained the beautiful profiles of their Greek forebears – stated without any evidence whatsoever that the costume was 'the costume of the ancient Greeks'. Like the furniture of Arles, the costume was in fact an adaptation of bourgeois Parisian fashions of the period of Louis XV, but, unlike the furniture, it was an adaptation which was always being modified slightly to meet the latest Parisian whims. Thus, after the Revolution, necks were bared, and hair, previously tightly contained within a bonnet, was allowed to hang outside this (a sight which had previously been thought of as obscene and was still considered so in Brittany).

The 'traditional' costume of Arles survived to a much later date than did the traditional folk costumes of most other areas of France. None the less, by the late nineteenth century it was no longer in common everyday use as it was in Brittany, and was kept more for special occasions. Mistral helped to ensure that it has been worn to this day by women appearing in carnival processions and other such festivals. As with so many aspects of present-day Provençal folk culture, such as music and dancing, the costume is no longer part of a vital tradition but is rather little more than a masquerade. It has continued to be modified, but with results that have horrified traditionalists. The Félibres' disciple, Joseph d'Arbaud, was reduced almost to apoplexy by the sight of a young girl wearing the Arles bonnet over short hair: 'I would prefer the costume to die out completely than to see it degraded in this way.'

Before founding his museum at Arles, Mistral wondered whether to found instead an outdoor museum, to be a national park of the Camargue. In the end he hoped that the Marquis Baroncelli-Javon would create such a park, and that it would be the perfect complement to his Arles museum. Mistral was not so much interested in the remarkable wildlife of the area as in its ranchers or *gardians*, whose life-style remained more exotic than did that of all other country people in late nineteenth-century Provence. Baroncelli-Javon not only took up this life-style himself but also reinstated and sometimes even invented traditions and costumes that made it seem yet more picturesque. Reports of his activities encouraged a number of like-minded individuals from outside the area to come and ride with him. One such person was René Baranger, the author of *Un An de gardianage en Camargue*. The fourteen-year-old René, searching for a life-style which satisfied his passion for horses and the open air, turned up one day at the Marquis's Camargue estate or *mas* to be greeted by the Marquis's daughter wearing the traditional Arlesienne costume. He stayed a year with the Marquis, sometimes taking part in bull-herding expeditions which lasted up to several days. 'For an instant,' he wrote, remembering the moment when he and his companions mounted their horses to set off into the wilds, 'I had the illusion that I was present at one of those pioneering wagon trails which struggled bravely with the unknown deserts of America's West, half a century ago.'

The exotic appeal of the Camargue and its *gardians* was furthered in 1951 by the appearance of the film *Crin blanc*, which deals with the relationship between a *gardian*'s young son and a wild horse which refuses to be tamed. The image of the Camargue which this film conveyed was of a wild land peopled with cowboys living in whitewashed mud houses roofed with straw. Tourism has capitalized on this image with the creation of corrals, rodeos, and luxurious hotels and holiday homes built in a 'traditional' Camargue style. Those wishing to maintain their romantic illusions about the life-style of the *gardians* should perhaps go no further than the excellently arranged ethnographic museum at Pont de Rousty, on the northern edge of the park.

You should also go to a Provençal bull-fight. While the habitat and life-style of the *gardians* have been glamorized for the tourist trade, the fights for which the bulls are raised still inspire an intense popular fervour and are one of the few genuine survivals of Provençal folk culture. The squeamish should not be put off, for the bulls are not killed in these fights, the object of the game being simply to wrest a ring from one of the animal's horns. Only at one time in history has a serious attempt been made to stop the sport, and once again it was Mistral who came to the rescue. Towards the end of the last century the French government insisted for a while that the arenas at Arles and Nîmes should be closed for all bull-fights. The people of Nîmes defied the order and arranged a fight, which Mistral attended, thereby risking a fine. On the arrival of the poet, the assembled 20,000 spectators got up to applaud him. 'In the south,' he told them, 'the passion for bull-fighting is more deeply rooted than in Spain itself.'

Fortunately Mistral did not live long into the twentieth century. Progress might have spared his bull-fights, but otherwise it showed little concern for the traditional Provence which he so loved. The old world receded as fast as the modern one advanced. In the early years of this century the depopulation of much of upper Provence continued unchecked. With more and more people leaving for the cities, the character of many of the villages changed significantly. The remaining inhabitants of these places moved down to the lower half of the village so as to be nearer the fields and main lines of communication with the outside world. Unable to sell the houses in the upper part of the village, and unwilling to pay taxes on them, the owners would usually destroy the roofs of these buildings. Whole villages were sometimes abandoned in this way. By the 1930s Provence had become a graveyard of villages.

The death of the village was the principal theme in the work of the two outstanding novelists of Provence who rose to fame in the 1930s, Henri Bosco and Jean Giono. 'To abandon the dry hills for the humid plain,' Bosco wrote in one of the most powerful of his novels, *Barboche*, 'is always saddening for those who love bare spaces, bracing winds and lonely plateaux.' The story of this novel is that of a woman who takes her young nephew to see the village where she was brought up. It is a long journey, and they arrive at their destination at nightfall. They put up at a house just outside the village, and the aunt decides to wait till the next day before showing her nephew around. As soon as she thinks he is asleep she creeps out of the house and walks into her native village, unable any longer to restrain her curiosity to see the place again. Her nephew, who has silently followed her, watches as she bursts into tears. The village of her childhood is little more than a heap of ruined buildings.

The story has a strong autobiographical element, and represents Bosco's attempt to recapture the Provence of his childhood. It ends on a wistful note. After a series of fantastic adventures the aunt and her nephew arrive back home. They tell the story of their journey, which by now has sentimental memories of its own. A journey undertaken out of nostalgia has ended up by being itself an object of nostalgia.

Giono's Provence, like Bosco's, is a compound of reality and fantasy. His novels have their basis in the dying Provence of the 1920s and 30s, and many of them are set in the abandoned or semi-abandoned communities under the Lure mountain (while Bosco found his inspiration in the villages of the Lubéron). *Colline*, the first of the trilogy of novels which established Giono's reputation (the other two are *Un de Baumugnes* and *Regain*), is one such book. The oldest man in the isolated hamlet of Les Bastides Blanches is dying. As he lies paralysed on his bed, he talks ceaselessly; his stream of words is at first ignored by the other inhabitants of the hamlet but then inspires increasing fear as soon as strange events begin to happen. The spring which has unfailingly supplied the hamlet with water over the years inexplicably runs dry. A group of men go to the well of the nearest village, a place which has been deserted since the 1880s and which gives an eerie foretaste of what the hamlet itself might one day become. 'The houses are half caved in. In the streets overgrown with nettles, the wind roars, bellows, bawls out its music through the holes of shutterless windows and open doors.' A girl mysteriously falls ill on the men's return to Les Bastides; later a fire sweeps over the surrounding countryside and narrowly avoids the village. The dying old man is now thought to be an evil sorcerer, and his death seems the only solution to everyone's problems; in the end he dies naturally. The book closes with a wild boar being killed and the blood from the animal's carcass dripping into the soil. Attempts have been made to locate Les Bastides Blanches and other dead or dying communities featured in Giono's novels; but though he took his inspiration from real places, he tended to amalgamate them all and create a Provence which was entirely his own. It has been argued that he is the least regionalist of writers.

Marcel Pagnol was the man who perhaps did most to influence the way we look at Provence today. The son of a schoolteacher who in turn was the son of a stonemason, Pagnol was born in 1905 in Aubagne, a small town which is now little more than a suburb of Marseille. Soon the family moved into Marseille itself, where Marcel's father got a job at one of the city's most prestigious schools, the Chartreux. Marcel studied here himself, and in later life recalled how any attempt to speak Provençal – the language most commonly used in Aubagne in the late nineteenth century – was rigorously suppressed by the school authorities. His most treasured childhood memories were of his weekends and holidays spent in the home which his family owned at the village of La Treille, just outside Aubagne. The house, called La Bastide Neuve, still survives and is marked by a plaque.

Pagnol moved to Paris as a young man and made his name here with a trilogy of plays set in and around Marseille; these plays, *Marius*, *Fanny* and *César*, were turned in the 1930s into successful films, the last one by Pagnol himself. By 1931 Pagnol had already begun serving his apprenticeship as a film-maker and was dreaming of setting up a film studio in Provence. The first film which he wrote, produced and directed was *Angèle* (1934), which, like a number of his finest films, was based on a work by Giono. The relationship between the two men was a strange one. They had in common a fascination with village life and a passionate love of nature, but otherwise their outlook on life was radically different. While Giono's Provence was tinged with a deep pessimism, Pagnol's had a fundamental optimism and gaiety. Even in adapting Giono's works, Pagnol was often able to find humour and high spirits. His cheerful view of Provence was no less romanticized than Giono's morbid one, but it was a view of the region which was more easily accepted by the public.

Angèle, adapted from *Un de Baumugnes*, is the story of a farmer's daughter who follows her lover to Marseille, where she is forced by him to prostitute herself; her family kills him, and she returns to her farm. The farm in question was specially built for the film in a bleak valley under the picturesque Barres de Saint-Esprit and within sight of the Garlaban, the mountain which featured heavily in Pagnol's childhood memories of La Treille. In 1935 Pagnol bought a large area of countryside around the farm and applied unsuccessfully to build his studios there; they were later installed in a large nineteenth-century house outside Cannes. He was none the less able to use the property which he bought under the Barres de Saint-Esprit when in 1937 he decided to film Giono's *Regain*. This novel is set in a dying village called Aubignane, whose inhabitants in the end are reduced to a semi-savage by the name of Panturle and a sorceress of Piedmontese origin, La Zia Manèche. Through the wiles of the latter, two women are made to pass through the village, one of whom is a former singer at Manosque who has been raped by a group of lavender pickers. She and Panturle fall in love, and she manages to civilize him. The village will survive. Giono told Pagnol that Aubignane was based loosely on Redortiers, an abandoned collection of houses near the Lure village of Banon (the place is still deserted and makes a most impressive sight). There were practical difficulties in filming at Redortiers, and so Pagnol instructed a mason friend from his childhood, Marius Brouquier, to construct the fictional village next to the farm used in the film *Angèle*. Brouquier had three months to put up the house of Panturle, a forge, a bakery, a windmill and a street of ruined houses. Angèle's farm and Brouquier's village are still standing, and are so convincing that un-suspecting walkers might easily believe that they have stumbled on the ruins of a real community rather than on some figment of Giono's and Pagnol's imagination.

An episode from Giono's *Jean le bleu* provided Pagnol with the plot of the most popular film he ever did, *La Femme du boulanger* (The Baker's Wife, 1939). The story is as usual a simple one, and concerns a beautiful young woman leaving her worthy and older baker husband for an equally young and beautiful shepherd. The baker – played by the much-loved Provençal actor Raimu in one of the great perform-ances of his career – is so distraught that he takes to drinking absinthe and in the end gives up baking altogether. At this point the villagers decide that the situation is an urgent one, and form a Committee for Public Safety. Four of them, whose families have been divided by feuds for years, go out and search for the young couple, and in their search make up their quarrels and become good friends. They abandon the search to shouts of 'long live the baker's horns', and on their return to the village they present some actual horns to the baker. A new search party is sent out, and eventually the couple are found on an island in the middle of a swamp. The couple's situation is potentially an idyllic one, but the young woman already has doubts about how long such an idyll can last. She is persuaded to return home and to reality. The baker is encouraged to give her a beating, but he gives her instead a piece of bread shaped like a heart. 'I put the dough in the oven and it just turned out like that. It's odd.'

After the war, Pagnol gave up film-making, settled at La Treille, and devoted himself to full-time writing. His autobiographical trilogy – *La Gloire de mon père* (1957), *Le Château de ma mère* (1958), and *Le Temps des secrets* (1960) – are some of the most enchanting and amusing childhood memories by any recent author. The tone in which he describes the landscape around La Treille, which he endlessly explored as a child, and where his brother later became a goatherd, is quite bucolic. Appropriately, in 1958, he brought out a verse translation of Virgil's *Bucolics*, a work which he prefaced with another memory of this landscape: 'Et Ego in Arcadia ... On the hills of Provence, in the ravines of the Baume Sourne, at the bottom of the Gorges of Passe-temps, I have often followed my brother Paul, who was the last goatherd of the area.' Pagnol died in 1974 and was buried with other members of his family in the cemetery of La Treille. Admirers of Pagnol who come to La Treille expecting some miniature Arcadia will certainly be disappointed. Like Aubagne, the place has been swallowed up by Marseille, and though a short walk takes you to unspoilt parts, it is difficult to feel far from the city's ugly presence. The beauty of the remaining countryside is a fragile one.

The character of rural Provence has changed as much since the Second World War as it did in the first half of the century. This time though, writers and artists have themselves played a major role in the story of this transformation. By moving into parts of the countryside which they have considered quaint and 'undiscovered', they have encouraged countless tourists to follow in their footsteps. The pattern is a familiar one, and one which even before the war had led to the spoiling of a number of villages and towns in the interior behind the Côte d'Azur. By 1950 much of upper Provence had still to be 'discovered', but it was not long before writers, artists and tourists began moving into the area in ever increasing numbers. It was in the summer of that year that an American sociologist called Laurence Wylie settled with his family in the Vaucluse village of Roussillon.

Wylie wanted to make a study of a typical French village. Among the reasons why he chose Roussillon was that it was a largely agricultural community, away from the main lines of communication but without being too backward or isolated, and that it was in an area which so far had not been subject to the onslaught of tourism. His observations on his stay here were put down in what was to become a sociological classic, *Village in the Vaucluse* (first edition 1957). It is easy to open this book with a certain amount of scepticism, wondering as you might about how someone who is both a foreign sociologist and a 'middle-class urbanite' (Wylie's own phrase) is able to reach any close understanding of a traditional farming community; and your suspicions seem partly confirmed on reading in the preface that Wylie tried the Rorschach ink-blot test out on the locals and found that they really enjoyed it. The book turns out to be a pleasant surprise, for it uses neither jargon nor meaningless statistics but brings together anecdotes illustrating every possible aspect of village life – from the toilet training of young children to caring for the elderly – to create a very human picture of the place. The Roussillon which emerges (Wylie disguises the village under the name of Peyrane) is a village healthily balanced between progress and tradition. For instance, there are a proportionately high number of car owners in the village, but the cars happen to be battered machines of the 1920s and 30s; farm equipment is modern, but so shabby that it 'might recall an American automobile graveyard rather than a modern farm'. The conclusion of the book is slightly sentimental, but appears justified on the strength of the evidence presented: Roussillon is a 'hard-working, productive community', which for all its feuds and tensions manages also to be sane and caring. Certainly this is a different Roussillon from the claustrophobic, inhospitable village to which a reluctant Samuel Beckett was briefly exiled during the Second World War.

It was also different from the Roussillon which Wylie regularly revisited after the 1950s. By 1960 empty houses had been turned into well-appointed secondary residences and numerous modern villas built; the simple local bistro had become a famous restaurant awarded a star in the Michelin Red Guide; droves of tourists had started coming every weekend to visit Roussillon's celebrated ochre quarries. The place had become more impersonal and less caring. This process of transformation has gathered speed since then, and the Roussillon of today would be barely recognizable to Wylie, whose book on the place is admiringly quoted by many of the Americans who have been attracted here after reading it. In Wylie's time houses remained unsold for years, and could be bought for ridiculously low sums of money: Wylie was offered a windmill and much of the hill on which it stood for $90 – today a sum one hundred times that amount would scarcely buy you a *borie*. Most of the artists and writers who settled here in the early 1950s could not do so today. Their search for the simple life has been taken over by the very rich.

An important chronicler of this recent period in Provençal village life is Jean-Paul Clébert, a novelist and prolific writer on Provence. His autobiographical book, *Vivre en Provence* (1977), chronicles the changes that have taken place in the Lubéron since he moved here from Paris in the early 1950s. At first he lived alone in an isolated, primitive stone hut on the plateau behind Bonnieux. Later a series of articles by J. Held in the Paris magazine *Nouvel observateur* began promoting the region as a 'Saint-Germain-du-Lubéron', and a growing number of intellectuals were drawn here. The wealthy sophisticated and not so sophisticated came next, and began building houses on the Bonnieux plateau that Clébert considers pretentious, absurd, and totally out of keeping with the surrounding countryside. He describes the altered character of the plateau in terms of a change from 'Giono to Tati'. His own position as a left-wing intellectual in the middle of this changing Lubéron is a difficult one, for he finds himself 'in between the *cabanon* and the swimming pool', distrusted by many of the locals and despised by many of the rich. For many years now he has been living in a lovingly restored house in the once totally abandoned village of Oppède, where I went to visit him. Shortly after sitting down I was made to get up and look out of the window at a prominent sign marked EXPOSITION (Exhibition), which had recently been put up on a neighbouring building: for Clébert the very presence of an art gallery in Oppède, let alone of a sign so brazenly advertising it, is an insult to the quiet dignity of the place. His attitude towards most visitors and alien settlers in the Lubéron is one of the utmost contempt, even though he himself, as he likes to admit, was responsible through his highly successful guide-books for bringing many of them here in the first place.

Clébert looks back to the Lubéron of the early 1950s as an idyllic haven. Locals older than him prefer to think further back, and, in recent years, various nostalgic memoirs have appeared with titles such as *Lourmarin à la belle époque*. The author of the latter work, Henri Meynard, wrote that 'it is impossible not to think about this wonderful period at the turn of the century without a certain nostalgia. Life was led then to such a regular rhythm over so many years that it was difficult to imagine that any change was possible ... friendship and unity ruled among families, neighbours always helped each other out ... life was rustic and of a great simplicity ...' The period of which Meynard writes was of course for Mistral already one seriously threatened by change and progress. The problem with rural nostalgia is that it invariably has a life of its own unrelated to any real changes in the environment. Distant memories of village life tend to tell more about the character of the person who wrote them than about the real nature of the places on which these memories are based.

My own experience of Provençal village life is derived mainly from lengthy stays at Lacoste. Lacoste is a place of remarkable beauty, an old hill village dominated by a ruined castle and overlooking the dark flanks of the Petit Lubéron to the south, the more distant range of the Ventoux to the north, and, directly across from the village, the perfect triangle of Bonnieux, over which hovers the light-blue mass of the Grand Lubéron. Scanning the landscape, it is difficult to find any obvious signs of modern civilization apart from some far-away apartment blocks on the outskirts of Apt. The village itself has picturesque cobbled streets and gives a superficial impression that little has changed here over the years. I came here with a preconception of Provençal village life influenced largely by the films of Pagnol, but soon had to revise this. The atmosphere was on the whole unwelcoming and slightly sinister, more suited in fact to the pen of Giono than to the lens of Pagnol. It was not reassuring to be told about the psychopathic butcher of neighbouring Ménerbes, and it was even less reassuring to find out that he held a particular grudge against Lacoste and had written a message in blood on my employer's door telling him that he had only a few more weeks to live. After further exposure to the village's stories I began fancifully to think – and in this I was not alone – that the Marquis de Sade had left an indelible mark on the place.

Broadly speaking, the history of Lacoste since the Marquis's time has not been very different from that of Roussillon or many other villages in upper Provence. A period of agricultural prosperity in the first half of the nineteenth century was followed in the second half by one of decline. Towards the end of the century, when Roussillon began mining for ochre, Lacoste reopened its Roman limestone quarries. However, the new life which this brought to the village was only short-lived and was not sufficient to curb the gradual de-population of the place at the beginning of this century. By the Second World War the upper part of Lacoste was as empty and ruinous as the castle which stood over it. The remaining villagers had little inter-est in the Marquis, whom they considered simply as a lecherous man. They were far more proud of their turn-of-the-century miller with the unfortunate name of Malachier ('Bad Shit'), an eccentric recluse who lived behind the castle and devoted all his spare time to carving primi-tive but powerful figure sculptures. One of the few times that he went far from his mill was to walk to Paris, excited by reports of the newly built Eiffel Tower. His sculptures lay scattered behind the castle after his death, and one of these – of a couple making love – was a great source of interest to the unmarried girls of the village. A few of the sculptures remain, as does his mill. The present occupier is the mason responsible for supervising Bouer's restoration of the castle. He is a loquacious and highly intelligent person, whose life has been the sub-ject of much local speculation.

The mason with the mysterious past is typical of the countless strange people who have been moving to Lacoste since the early 1950s. As with Roussillon, the price of property then was extremely cheap. An American artist bought one of the abandoned houses in the top half of the village for as little as $50, and later cheaply acquired various other properties with the intention of setting up an art school in the village. A number of other artists came to the village around the same time as he did, including a Hungarian-born member of the surrealist movement and a Swedish sculptor who had begun his career in the then moribund artist colony at Pont Aven in Brittany. The process of rebuilding and prettifying the village gathered momentum in the 1960s and 70s, and led finally to its once bare, rocky streets being lined with cobblestones and given quaint, old-looking signs; the former Rue de la Juiverie (Jew Street) became known, ominously, as the Rue de la Four (Oven Street). One of the more colourful of the later arrivals was a retired Breton translator who had spent much of his life associated with radical causes; at Lacoste he supported himself partly by producing grotesque papier-mâché reliefs, a group of which were entitled 'Homage to the Divine Marquis'. Up to the present day there has also been a large number of transitory residents in Lacoste, many of whom have turned out to be foreigners escaping prosecution in their native countries; usually they find employment as stonemasons, and sometimes they suddenly disappear from Lacoste, leaving behind only large debts.

Wylie noted in his study of Roussillon that every village invariably has its feuds, and that these feuds – which sometimes result in neighbours not speaking to each other for years – have often been provoked by the smallest of incidents. Returning to Roussillon after many foreign 'city-dwellers' had moved into the village, Wylie found that the atmosphere was far 'tenser than before, for these outsiders seem to get along even less well than the people born and raised in the commune'.

Over the last two decades Lacoste has been torn apart by feuds, and surely at no previous stage in its history could so many people have been threatening or actively pursuing law-suits against each other. For the outsider these quarrels have often an absurd, comic aspect. Thus the Breton translator had dog turds thrown against his window by the eight-year-old daughter of his neighbouring artist enemies, who in turn were later to bring another quarrel to a head by attempting to knock down the walls of a house which was impeding their view of the valley. Then there is the man who calls himself the 'Count' and who has quarrelled with so many of his neighbours that he has earned himself the untranslatable name of 'le merdeux du village'. His most long-standing feud has been with the baker, whom he tried to expel from the village on the grounds that the noise of the man's oven would disturb the clients of a hotel he was building alongside the bakery; the hotel is now built, and it is claimed that the water from its small swimming-pool has been dripping into the baker's oven. At present Lacoste is without any governing body to intervene in such quarrels, a state of affairs which has resulted from yet another quarrel, this one involving the village Mayor and a couple who wish to set up an antique shop. The Mayor consistently refused planning permission to the couple, who did not help matters by referring to the Mayor as a 'sale Corse' or 'dirty Corsican'. Eventually, though, the couple

successfully appealed and then the Mayor and his assistants all re-
signed. No one wishes to take over their jobs.

Quarrelling and masonry seem sometimes to be the principal activities of present-day Lacoste, certainly the ones in which its foreign
residents are largely engaged. You might well wonder how the village
spends the rest of its time, and if much remains of its traditional life.
In search of this life you should perhaps begin with Lacoste's lower
street, which has much less of the toy-town character of the upper
village, and around which are situated such essential elements of a
village community as the bakery, post office, *tabac* and two cafés. Yet
the people who run these establishments nearly all turn out to be from
outside Lacoste. Even before artists and other such 'foreigners' began
settling in Provence, it was rare to find Provençal villages which had
kept the same families over the centuries. Wylie himself said that the
traditional image of a stable rural community was an 'inaccurate one,
developed principally by middle-class city people nostalgic for a stability they lack but which they wrongly ascribe to rural communities'.
Lacoste is typical of much of upper Provence in having a strong
Spanish element. Many Spanish workers took refuge in the district
before the Civil War, and though they were often badly treated to
begin with, they now occupy leading positions within the villages.

The few local families of long standing in Lacoste are mainly active
in farming, an activity which has become increasingly unpopular in
recent years: more and more young people are giving it up in favour
of emigrating to Paris or Marseille, and those few who have persevered
in their forefathers' footsteps now experience great difficulties in finding anyone to marry them. Furthermore, the farming community has
to a certain extent been affected by too much exposure to artists and
other foreigners with romantic notions of rural life. Students from the
village's recently formed art school join in the grape-picking and other
such agricultural pursuits, and, at the beginning of each term, are
taken to watch a shepherd herding his flock. This 'shepherd', I later
found out, had a large library and was very conversant with Sartre
and structuralism. A good friend of his, also a farmer, was living with
one of the many young American women who have been taken in by
the romance of the region and fallen in love with a local. Most of
these relationships soon fall apart, usually after the American has
been seriously beaten up by her often deceptively civilized lover.

Against all odds this particular relationship had lasted: the woman had found a position teaching a course at the art school entitled 'The Self in the Environment', while her friend gave periodic lectures at the school on 'The Aesthetics of Farming'.

The unchanging side of Provençal rural life is perhaps best observed in the weekend and leisure activities of the Lacoste villagers. Every Saturday morning, unfailingly, a high proportion of the inhabitants of Lacoste and numerous other villages in the area end up at Apt. They come here on business errands, to stock up with supplies for the week, and to take part in the market, which extends over the main streets of the old centre. Apt on a Saturday morning is one of the most animated spectacles in Provence. It is a spectacle which has remained fundamentally unchanged since the last century, with the main difference that ageing hippies now sell herbal recipes alongside the traditional stalls specializing in sausages and goat's cheese, and that the café where everyone meets up afterwards – the Café Grégoire – has become so popular with intellectuals that Clébert has described it as the Apt equivalent of the Coupole in Paris.

The rest of a Lacoste weekend is spent in a manner very much in accordance with traditional images of Provence. Much time is spent in the cafés, sipping *pastis* or playing the much-loved card game of *bolote*. The outdoor game of *boules* – in which competitors try and roll large leaden balls as close as possible to a small wooden one – is as popular here as films on Provence like to make out: one of the most important civic improvements carried out in Lacoste in recent years was the creation of a floodlit *boules* court behind the local church. Hunting is another traditional Provençal pastime, and on Sunday mornings in the autumn is indulged in by the men of Lacoste with the fervour described by Pagnol in his *Gloire de mon père*. Country walks during the hunting season are fraught with danger for those not taking part in the sport themselves. The hunters appear to shoot haphazardly and with little respect either for public footpaths or for those walking on them. I was surprised once to find hunters stationed at regular intervals along a large path I was walking down in the Grand Lubéron. It was only then that I realized that I had inadvertently stumbled on a 'boar drive', and that at any minute wild boars and bullets could be rushing past me.

Though hardly a traditional entertainment, the regular showing of films on an improvised screen in a back room of one of the cafés in Lacoste has been going on since the 1940s and has become an important mid-week activity. Many of the films shown are French films of the 1930s, including many by Pagnol himself: Wylie found that the film most liked in Roussillon in the 1950s was Korda's film of Pagnol's *Marius*, an escapist tale with which the villagers could none the less closely identify ('*C'est comme ça la vie*', 'That's what life is like', they kept on explaining to him after repeated showings of the film). Today the films shown at Lacoste are mainly organized by the local cinema society, but in Wylie's time they would be brought to the village by an itinerant projectionist. Living today near the village of Saignon beyond Apt is François Morénas, a passionate cinéaste who spent much of the 40s and 50s wandering around Provence projecting films from his own extensive collection. His first trip was done on foot to the remote Alpine valley of Tinée, where he found that there was sometimes not even enough electricity to work the projector. After over ten years of this itinerant existence he gave it up to devote himself to his youth hostel at Saignon, the endearingly eccentric character of which is summed up in a notice on one of its outside walls: 'Please do not piss on the parsley, you might be eating it tomorrow.'

Films shown outside in the village square open the most important event in the Lacoste social calendar – the annual fête held at the end of July. Provence has always been famous for its fêtes, and Papon noted in the eighteenth century how the villagers of the region would organize one on the slightest pretext. The aloof Marquis de Sade, who generally shunned contact with the villagers of Lacoste, enthusiastically joined in the dancing which accompanied these occasions. A fête in Provence has different connotations from those which it has in England, and is not a genteel affair but a raucous, animated celebration. Preparations for the summer one in Lacoste begin weeks beforehand and culminate with the putting up of lights all around the lower street and village square. The fête itself lasts for three days. During the daytime there are such activities as *boules* competitions, and a donkey race between the two cafés. The first evening is taken up by the film show, which always includes a short film featuring shots of local sights and people. Dancing in the village square, accompanied by a local band of often dubious quality, animates the next two evenings, the first of which is given over to traditional music, the second to bizarre imitations of American and English rock ('Teechere, teechere, leeve those keeds alone' is a perennial favourite). People from miles around come to these dances, and there are indeed some people who spend most of their evenings in the summer months going to whatever village has a fête. This is Provençal life at its most open and attractive, and one of the few times when the Provençal people show their proverbial gaiety.

Any serious study of village life in Provence should ideally be centred in the cafés. Wylie himself virtually turned the Roussillon café into his own office, and found the place by far the best location for carrying out his Rorschach tests. Cafés have occupied a leading position in Provençal life since the late nineteenth century. Around that time cafés sprang up all over the region to meet a greatly increased consumption of alcohol; prompted by the economic crisis of those years they also often functioned as informal banks. From that time too they have been important centres of political activity. The café-owners tended to subscribe to newspapers reflecting their own political views, and this in turn affected the type of customers they attracted. Political opinion in a village was often divided between the place's cafés: in 1873, for example, the Var village of Salernes had cafés of Bonapartist, republican and monarchist persuasions. The political nature of cafés was often seen as a threat to the authority of the Church, and in fact in some of these places the public reading of political tracts became an alternative to the Sunday sermon.

Lacoste's two cafés could hardly be more different from each other. The more traditional of the two has, paradoxically, the more sensational name, the Café de Sade. Its owner is Lilianne Ségura, a beautiful woman of partly Spanish origin who is generally regarded as the mother of the village. She listens sympathetically to everyone's problems, lends money, and takes it upon herself to look after some of the village's more unfortunate types, such as the bearded gypsy who speaks to no one and spends his day drinking, chuckling to himself, and staring madly at other people (Lilianne gives him food, board and a small allowance in return for odd menial duties such as carrying out the rubbish). Maurice Grau, the owner of the village's rival café, the Café de France, is an ageing Bohemian with long white hair and a love of drink and good food. He is illiterate and can be aggressive, but has a sharp intelligence and a rich if slightly cruel sense of humour. Whereas the Café de Sade appeals to the relatively sedate day-time drinkers, the Café de France, with its juke-box, dancing facilities, and large contingent of American girls from the local art school, gets going mainly in the evenings and draws in a slightly disreputable crowd from sometimes as far afield as Avignon. The steeply rising crime rate in Lacoste is attributed by the villagers to the presence of these outsiders.

The hatred which exists between Lilianne and Maurice is not simply the result of professional rivalry: it goes so deep that even their respective dogs have been trained to savage each other. Lilianne feels that Maurice's establishment is a centre of drugs and corruption; Maurice believes that the outwardly friendly and open Lilianne is little more than a police informer. Lacoste society is divided between the two places, and there are many who frequent the one who would never be seen in the other. The division is not a political one, because in principle everyone in Lacoste is a socialist. The division is somehow connected with the complex tangle of personal feuds which splits apart the village. People can count on their chosen café to support them in their feuds: thus when someone was accused of being a collaborator during the Second World War, it was Lilianne who rushed to his defence by exhibiting in her café documents attesting beyond doubt to his innocence.

Lacoste might be overrun by foreign settlers, but as yet it has not become a tourist resort. The few tourists who come here are struck by the unspoilt beauty of the place, and think that they have come across a survival of the old Provence. How different Lacoste is from other Provençal villages is difficult to say. Subsequent experience has taught me that Lacoste is perhaps not so unusual, that all these villages are not immediately open to outsiders, and that they too have their stories worthy of the pen of the Marquis de Sade. However, any generalization about the character of Provençal villages is suspect, for they are all worlds in their own right, existing in remarkable isolation from each other. Living in Lacoste is like living on an island. The village seems cut off from the real world, and this sense of alienation has undoubtedly contributed to the strangeness with which many here are affected. Apart from the Saturday trip to Apt, the villagers and many of the foreign settlers rarely stray much beyond Lacoste. An excursion to Mont Ventoux or even to the Grand Lubéron is talked about for years afterwards. A visit to the sea is a virtual impossibility.

6

Provence and the Sea

Glamour and corruption have been the two words most commonly used to describe the Provençal coast, the history of which is also to a large extent the history of modern Provence. Marseille and Toulon have played the key role in the industrial development of the region; the rest of the coast, the so-called Côte d'Azur, has been known since the early nineteenth century as Europe's leading playground, and as such has acted as a barometer of the tastes and fashions of the modern world. Neither aspect of the coast has been welcomed by the region's traditionalists. Mistral, in his *Calendau* of 1867, eulogized the then unspoilt fishing village of Cassis but otherwise took little interest in the coast. Giono contemptuously dismissed the entire Côte d'Azur, believing it to have a sophisticated, international character which was alien to the region as a whole. With the exception of Pagnol, not a single major writer native to Provence has found inspiration either in Marseille or Toulon.

The history of Marseille and Toulon has evolved separately from that of the inland towns of Provence. Whereas the latter either declined or remained little changed after the Middle Ages, these two cities shot to new heights of prosperity. After 1669 the importance of Marseille was enormously increased when the port was granted the monopoly of commerce with the Levant. Pierre Puget, the artist sometimes referred to as Provence's Leonardo da Vinci, produced ambitious plans for the redevelopment of the city, and, though these were never executed, Marseille under Louis XIV was greatly expanded and embellished. At the same time Puget's native city of Toulon rose to fame: Cardinal Richelieu made it a base for the French navy, and Louis XIV's minister, Colbert, consolidated its importance by instituting a programme for naval reform. Among the changes which this programme brought about was the abandonment of the quaint practice of adding elaborate painted decoration to warships, a practice which had hitherto provided the young Puget with his most regular source of income.

The sordid underside to Marseille's and Toulon's rapid commercial and naval expansion was the creation of dangerously overcrowded slums. The dark, narrow and dirty side streets behind the two ports became breeding grounds for disease. When, in the summer of 1720, a ship from Syria landed at Marseille with two sailors suffering from the bubonic plague, it was not long before the plague spread from the slums into the rest of the city, and from there to Toulon and many parts of Provence's interior. During the four months for which it lasted, almost half the population of Marseille and Toulon died. One of the survivors was the heroic Jean Belzunce, Bishop of Marseille, who continued to administer the Last Sacrament at a time when families were abandoning their dying members only to die lonely deaths themselves. The bishop is prominently portrayed in two large and intricately detailed canvases of the Marseille plague by Michel Serre, a pupil of Puget.

These two canvases, now in the Musée des Beaux Arts in the Palais Longchamp, are among the greatest works of art originating from Marseille and were always praised and described by early travellers. In fact they were among the few tourist attractions in a city which for its size preserved very little of artistic or architectural distinction. Marseille, like Toulon, appealed to travellers for the magnificence of its position and, to a lesser extent, its animation. Toulon, an even duller city architecturally, had as its greatest draw a visit to the royal galleys. All tourists went on board the galleys for the morbid pleasure of seeing the manacled, unkempt convicts, a sight which inspired a mixture of fascination, horror, and occasionally indignation. It is tempting to see a reference to the plight of these convicts in the struggling captive figures which Puget sculpted for the exterior of Toulon's town hall.

Despite the setback of the plague, Marseille continued to prosper in the eighteenth century and received a further boost through distributing the textiles and other goods brought into France by the East India Company. The Revolution was warmly welcomed here, and during the hostilities between France and Austria and Prussia in 1792 the enthusiastic singing by a group of 500 Marseille volunteers of a national anthem composed in Strasbourg gave to this anthem the name of 'The Marseillaise'. Toulon meanwhile became a royalist stronghold, which, on siding with the English fleet in 1793, was subdued on the intervention of an obscure Corsican captain by the name of Napoleon Bonaparte; Napoleon later established the port as a base for his Egyptian campaign.

After the Revolution Marseille took over from Aix as the capital of Provence. As a cultural and intellectual centre Marseille was never to achieve the eminence which Aix had reached, for the Marseillais were a notoriously philistine people, to whom, according to Stendhal, 'the most absurd act possible was the opening of a book'. But Marseille was always an infinitely more lively town than Aix. Count Moszynski, writing from Marseille in 1784, wrote that 'at Aix everything is sad and deserted; there is hardly any noise. Here, everything is gay, glittering and alive.' This view was to become ever more pertinent in the course of the nineteenth century.

The French conquest of Algeria in 1830 brought renewed activity to Marseille's port and led to the creation of new industries such as the extraction of sesame and palm oil, and the making of tiles and bricks. With the opening of the Suez Canal in 1869 and the colonial expansion of France to include New Caledonia and Indo-China, Marseille became known as the 'Gateway to the East': it was a town filled with turbanned North African immigrants, and exotically dressed merchants from all over the eastern hemisphere. From the early nineteenth century onwards Marseille, together with Toulon, began also receiving more and more Italian workers, who, though at first contemptuously treated, made a vital contribution to the culture of the two cities. At the centre of Marseille's bustling life was the café-lined street of La Canebière, one of Europe's most famous boulevards. Marseille was not just a port and major industrial town: after being linked to Paris by railway in 1848 (the line was extended to Toulon seven years later), it became a stopping-off place for travellers from every part of Europe.

The decline of Marseille set in after the First World War, when its once unrivalled port was superseded by Rotterdam, Hamburg and Antwerp, and the valley of the Rhine became a more important commercial thoroughfare than that of the Rhône. In 1927 King Alex-

ander I of Yugoslavia was assassinated as he drove down La Canebière, a notorious incident which did little to enhance the reputation
of a street which subsequently went increasingly to seed, its sumptuous
cafés being transformed eventually into tacky shops and gambling
halls lined with pin-ball machines. During the Second World War the
Germans, under the pretext of hygiene, destroyed the old streets
around the ports of both Marseille and Toulon, and in so doing
deprived the two towns of much of their remaining picturesque character. Recent travellers have chosen not to linger long in either place,
most of them finding the towns both ugly and threatening. B. Collier,
in his book of Provence reminiscences, *I Wore my Linen Trousers*
(1940), wrote that his real objection to Marseille was 'its air of being
steeped in vice ... Unimaginative as one is determined to be, it is
impossible not to feel that an aura of immemorial and abiding evil
emanates from its grey house fronts and lurks in its narrow squalid
alleys.'

Vice has been endemic to Marseille from at least the time of Count
Moszynski, who reported that windows would be broken purely to
steal the curtains. In the late nineteenth century Marseille, followed
closely by Toulon, boasted the highest incidence of prostitution and
venereal disease after Paris. Today, anyone with a curiosity about the
darker side to Marseille life should brave a visit to the Rue Vincent
Scotto, just to the north of La Canebière: swarming with prostitutes,
pimps and petty criminals, this street is sordid and frightening enough
by day, and at night is positively dangerous. The sense of unease
experienced by the white visitor is heightened by the fact that the
street is in the middle of an entirely North African ghetto. There are a
number of such ghettos in both Marseille and Toulon. Racial tensions
are another of the major problems that the two towns have recently
had to face, and it was perhaps inevitable that the leader of the French
National Front, Jean-Marie le Pen, should have scored here his greatest
successes with voters.

Marseille's main claim to fame as a criminal centre was its domination of the world heroin trade in the 1960s, a reputation popularized by the two highly successful Hollywood films, *The French
Connection*, Parts One and Two. The star, if that is the right word, of
the heroin traffic was Auguste Ricord, a man who began his career in
crime as a procurer in the shady back streets of Marseille between the

wars; later he became a collaborator and a restaurateur before fleeing France in the 1950s and emigrating to Argentina. A Buenos Aires restaurant owned by him called El Sol (later renamed L'Auberge Provençal), with a décor suggesting apparently a cross between Provence and the Pampas, was made the headquarters of his illicit trade. Among the Marseille men caught up in this trade were Joseph Cesari, a hard-working chemist who manufactured the drug in Marseille; Edmond Taillet, a cabaret and night-club singer known as 'the Frank Sinatra of the Côte d'Azur', and Edouard Rimbaud, a highly imaginative man who alternated his real life in crime with writing crime novels for the Parisian publishers, Gallimard. In the early 1960s the French police paid relatively little attention to Ricord's drug-trafficking, but by the end of the decade, when heroin addiction became widespread in America and the United States government accused Marseille of producing 80 per cent of the country's supply of the drug, they closed in on Ricord and finally exposed his ring.

Crime along the coast has not just been concentrated on Marseille and Toulon but has also spread to towns whose superficial image has generally been one of glamour. Nice, France's fifth largest town, is today a more crime-ridden place than Marseille. In July 1976 there took place there one of the biggest robberies of this century. The main person behind this crime was Albert Spaggiari, a picturesque character with a professed love of blondes, Nietzsche, right-wing political organizations, and himself. Making ingenious use of the Nice sewers, he broke into the supposedly impregnable Société Générale bank and got away with a load of jewellery, gold, diamonds and money worth millions of pounds. For a long while Spaggiari avoided capture, and he was even rumoured to have mysteriously accompanied the long-standing Mayor of Nice, Jacques Médecin, on a visit to Tokyo to promote the culture of Nice. Finally Spaggiari was caught, but he escaped in a dramatic manner worthy of his robbery: he jumped out of the court-room window, breaking his fall on the roof of a parked Renault; an accomplice with a motorcycle was waiting for him there, and the two of them were soon lost in the midday Nice traffic. Since then nothing has been heard of Spaggiari, except for a cheque and a letter of apology addressed to the man whose Renault he dented, and an immodest autobiographical manuscript recording his extraordinary adventures.

Spaggiari represents Nice crime at its most seductive, but it has also a far more sinister side which the novelist Graham Greene recently did his best to expose in his powerful booklet, *J'Accuse: The Dark Side of Nice* (1982). Greene, a resident for many years in Antibes, was first made aware of the extent of corruption in Nice while trying to help out Martine Cloetta, the daughter of old friends of his. This unfortunate woman had married one Daniel Guy, who, unknown to her, had had a criminal past. Life with Guy became a misery to her and eventually she left him, for which act of 'disobedience' she was to be punished in psychologically the most cruel ways possible. Guy, an insignificant and not very intelligent man, would have been unable to have done much on his own, but he had the constant support of Nice's criminal 'milieu', which always remained faithful to its associates. Cloetta's experiences revealed a series of cover-ups in high places that extended to Jacques Médecin himself. The right-wing Médecin family has ruled Nice since 1928; Jean Médecin, Jacques's father, was Mayor of Nice for thirty-seven years and was succeeded by Jacques on his death in 1965. The romantic novelist Madeleine Henrey wrote an autobiographical book, set in Nice, called *Milou's Daughter* (1955), which she dedicated to Jean Médecin, whom she had known since she was a child. 'This Médecin family,' she said, 'reminds me of the stories I read as a little girl about the Bonaparte family.' Returning to Nice later in life, she was guided around the city by Jacques Médecin, who emerges from her book as charming, highly cultivated and with an enormous passion for the history and culture of his native city. It is hard to believe that this is the same Médecin to whom Greene points in *J'Accuse*; it is similarly difficult to accept that the corrupt Médecin was also the author of an engaging book on Nice cookery, published in England by Penguin at the same time as Greene's booklet.

J'Accuse opens in a way which might shock those who see Nice and its surroundings primarily as a haven for the pleasure-seeker:

Let me issue a warning to anyone who is tempted to settle for a peaceful life on what is called the Côte d'Azur. Avoid the region of Nice, which is the preserve of some of the most criminal organizations in the South of France; they deal in drugs; they have attempted with the connivance of high authorities to take over the Casino in the famous 'war' which left one victim, Agnès Le Roux, the daughter of the main owner of the Palais de la Méditerranée, 'missing believed murdered'; they are involved in the building industry which helps to launder their illicit gains; they have close connections with the Italian Mafia.

This corrupt city which Greene describes was, only two centuries before, a sleepy, out-of-the-way town just beginning to be discovered by hardy Englishmen in search of health and winter sun. In those days considerable determination was needed to get there. The mountainous coastal route from Menton was described by the seventeenth-century English traveller Mocroft as 'absolutely the worst way in Europe'. If, on the other hand, you approached Nice from Toulon, you had to brave first the bandits of the Esterel and then the crossing of the river Var, which was not served by a bridge until after the Revolution: for much of the eighteenth century travellers had to trust themselves and their luggage to the shoulders of villagers from Saint-Laurent. The whole journey from Calais to Nice took at least fifteen days. The first English people to spend a season at Nice were reputedly Lord and Lady Cavendish, who came here in 1731. But the man who did most to open up the appreciation of Nice and the surrounding coast was the writer and doctor Tobias Smollett, who decided to seek a cure for his consumption here rather than in Montpellier, as was then far more usual. He spent a long period in Nice in the 1760s, and afterwards included a lengthy account of his experiences here in his *Travels through France and Italy* (1766). In refreshing contrast to so many later descriptions of the Côte d'Azur, the tone of the book is far from being uncritical, and in fact was so grumbling that Laurence Sterne gave Smollett the nickname of 'Smelfungus'. His constant moaning about Nice (in particular about its shopkeepers, whom he described as 'poor, greedy and over-reaching') made those passages in which he actually praised the town stand out the more. The situation and climate of the town he thought incomparable, as well as very beneficial to the health: 'The air in Nice being very pure, dry, heavy and elastic must be agreeable to the constitution of those who labour under disorders arising from weak nerves, obstructed perspiration, relaxed fibres, a viscidity of lymph, and a languid circulation.' To the surprise of the local doctors he took up sea-bathing, and even seemed to improve after the experience. He strongly recommended the exercise to fellow consumptives, though he added that women would have difficulty in imitating him 'unless they laid aside all regards to decorum'. A growing number of Englishmen were inspired by his book to come to Nice, including one Joseph Price, an Anglican clergyman whose consumption had become so bad that he spat blood at the slightest exertion: in 1792 he had begged the Archbishop of Canterbury to give him an undemanding parish so that he could travel to Nice in the hope of a cure. In the following century the inhabitants of Nice, though still upset by Smollett's criticisms of them, felt obliged to honour his memory in recognition of all that he had done to promote their town. They named one of the local streets the 'Rue Smolet', which, as one H. Macmillan noted in 1885, was 'incorrectly spelt, as we should have expected from a people given to orthographical mistakes'.

The flow of English travellers to Nice was briefly interrupted by the Napoleonic wars but then revived with added vigour after 1815, by which date the inhabitants of Nice had come to realize how important a role tourism now played in the town's economy. The tourist season lasted strictly from late November to early March and was to continue to do so until the 1920s, the summers being thought of as too hot and unhealthy. By 1850 most of the prominent aristocratic families of England had started 'wintering' in Nice, and they had left their imprint on the town through the prolific construction of villas and other amenities. In 1830 the Reverend Louis Way had been briefly diverted from his life-long crusade against anti-Semitism to take up a cause which was to have immeasurable consequences for the future appearance of Nice. He encouraged members of the colony to donate funds for the enlargement of the path along the sea-front to a width of two yards: this scheme had the dual advantage of providing work for the unemployed and reducing the risk of young English girls being waylaid by uncouth, half-starving beggars. The enlarged path, later made passable for horse carriages and lined with pillars, mimosa and pepper trees, became known as the Promenade des Anglais, one of the main thoroughfares of fashionable Europe.

What Smollett did for Nice, Lord Brougham did for Cannes. In the autumn of 1834 this well-known parliamentary orator and co-founder of the *Edinburgh Review* was travelling to Italy, but was prevented from getting further than the Var by a *cordon sanitaire* which had been established because of an outbreak of cholera. To pass this barrier he needed permission from Paris, and, while waiting for this, he searched for accommodation in the area. Eventually he ended up at the Hôtel de Poste in Cannes, then no more than a tiny fishing village. So taken was he by the mild climate of the place that he decided to end his journey here, thus endorsing a view which was to be held by numerous later travellers to the Riviera: 'Why cross the sea to Algiers, why go to semi-barbarous Spain, when we have but to come to the South of France to change dark November into smiling June.' He purchased some land on the western side of Cannes on which to build a villa, and shortly afterwards suggested to the King of France that a grant of money should be given to make a harbour in the village. Brougham's presence at Cannes soon encouraged a number of other English arrivals, while the construction of the harbour brought immediate economic benefit to the area. Brougham's villa no longer survives, but his memory is preserved by a statue on Cannes's main square.

The most important of the new arrivals was Lord Woolfield, who later wrote an account of how he came to the village. 'After seven years' travelling in Spain, Egypt, Palestine, Syria, Asia Minor, Turkey and Greece, hoping to find some spot where I might pass my remaining days, I found nothing to tempt me in comparison with Cannes.' A very religious man, one of his first tasks on coming to Cannes was to build – despite much Catholic opposition – the Anglican church of Christ Church. He was also a keen horticulturalist and could count among his many achievements the introduction to the Riviera of the gooseberry, the Jamaican sweet potato, the acacia, and the eucalyptus tree (the seed for which was sent direct from the Royal Botanic Gardens in Sydney).

Undoubtedly Woolfield's example in growing exotic plants in Cannes in the middle of winter gave an extra incentive to the garden-obsessed English to come here. Conveniently, Woolfield also indulged in property speculation and was able to provide houses or land for some of those who followed him to Cannes. He himself lived at first in a building now incorporated into the Hôtel Majestic, but at the same time he began constructing the massive Château de Riou, 'which occupied four years, as much of the work was what Cannes workmen were not then accustomed to do; indeed, without my English foreman, Obadiah Pulham, it could never have been finished'. Soon after completing the Château de Riou he sold it to the Duke of Londesborough, who in turn later sold it to the Duke of Vallombrosa, the man who built Cannes's main social venue, the Cercle Nautique; the magnificent neo-gothic 'Château Vallombrosa' still dominates the western end of Cannes, though, like so many of the Riviera villas, it has now been divided into apartments. Woolfield later settled in the Villa Victoria, a building which he had constructed almost as a symbolic gesture on a burial ground containing the remains of Napoleonic conscripts. At this stage of his life he passed on most inquiries about property to his gardener, John Taylor, who also found himself having to deal with visitors' inquiries about banking and wine. Taylor was no fool. He gave up his job to set up in turn an estate agency, a bank and a wine business; his estate agency is still running and up to recently was looked after by his great-grand-daughter Jacqueline.

Cannes prospered, but retained a more exclusive atmosphere than Nice. Edward Lear, looking for a home in the south of France in the early 1860s, took a great dislike to Nice ('a queer place, Brighton and Belgravia and Baden by the Mediterranean: odious to me in all respects but its magnificent winter climate') but found all that he wanted in the as yet much quieter Cannes, where he stayed for seven years. One of his neighbours here was Prosper Mérimée, who became a good friend of his and encouraged him to make his productive visit to Corsica in 1868.

Mérimée had first been to Cannes in the 1840s, in the course of his inspection of historic monuments. He returned over twenty years later and found the climate agreeable to his asthma and hypochondria. In a letter written to the French architect Viollet-le-Duc in 1866, he commented on how little the French knew their own country and how they underestimated the value of a place like Cannes. Certainly the French lagged way behind the English in the colonization of the Riviera; the one resort in the nineteenth century which remained almost exclusively French was Saint-Raphael, which had been popularized in the 1850s by the French journalist and florist Alphonse Karr.

The English on the other hand were ubiquitous, and, as Alexandre Dumas had noted in 1851, every new arrival on the coast was thought immediately to be from England. Mérimée was not alone in generally disliking the English, who kept their distance from the locals and often behaved with exceptional arrogance, as if, in Mérimée's words, they represented some 'invading army'. Tensions between the English and the French were inevitable, and already by 1780 one Frenchman, the Abbé Expilly, had felt obliged to move on from Nice to Genoa after hearing that the English contingent in Nice that year would be even larger than it had been the year before: 'I do not wish to give the English a pretext of any kind that will allow them to try and humiliate me.'

Though the English were undeniably the most numerous of the coast's winter visitors, other foreign colonies were rapidly forming at Nice and Cannes. Empress Alexandra of Russia, advised by her Saint Petersburg doctors to visit Nice on account of her neurasthenia, acted as the vanguard to countless other members of the Russian aristocracy who wintered first at Nice and then at Cannes; splendid traces of their former presence on the coast are the onion-domed Orthodox churches at Nice and Cannes, the former based heavily on the church of Saint Basil in Moscow. Royalty and aristocracy from Germany, Austria-Hungary, and Scandinavia formed their own communities on the coast, as did a growing number of wealthy American visitors.

The foreign invasion of the Côte d'Azur intensified after 1860, when the County of Nice was relinquished once and for all to France. In 1865 Nice was finally linked by rail to Toulon and Marseille: to the detriment of many local business concerns, the station at Nice was built outside the town so as to disturb as little as possible the prestigious foreign residents. Five years later, through an ingenious piece of engineering, the railway line was extended to Menton, the popularity of which as a resort increased enormously. From the 1880s onwards Queen Victoria repeatedly visited the coast, patronizing Menton and later Cimiez, where she stayed at the Hôtel Excelsior Regina Palace (now an old people's home). Through Queen Victoria, the fame of the Côte d'Azur spread to the remotest corners of the British Empire.

The belief in the healthy properties of the Riviera climate remained constant right up to the end of the nineteenth century. The English doctor J. Henry Bennet reported that in Menton in 1861 every foreign family had an invalid, most of them suffering from pulmonary consumption. Bennet himself, in his popular *Mentone and the Riviera as a Winter Climate* (1861), outlined the virtues of this climate to the consumptive. Many other doctors did the same, while feeling it fair to draw the patient's attention to some of the less healthy aspects of the Riviera, for instance the greasiness of the food, the excitability of the atmosphere, and the wearing nature of sightseeing, especially if this entailed plunging out of burning sunshine into an ice-cold cathedral. C. Home Douglas, the author of an 1874 health manual 'dedicated to British and American Invalids', believed that 'there is probably no human occupation more incompatible with health-seeking than sightseeing'. Another, not immediately obvious danger of the Riviera, and one liable to turn a hitherto perfectly healthy person into an invalid, was the abundance of marble floors used in the houses and hotels of the area. W. Miller, in *Wintering in the Riviera* (1879), gave a cautionary tale to his readers by relating how he once slipped on his back coming down a marble staircase, and might easily have caused himself permanent injury had his fall been a more direct one. How real this danger in fact was, was illustrated by the tragic case of Queen Victoria's consumptive son, Prince Leopold, who was killed after a fall in the Cercle Nautique in Cannes.

Throughout the eighteenth and nineteenth centuries attempts were made to give climatotherapy the respectability of a science, and patients were given such advice as how many minutes they should expose their chests to the sun, or how many deep breaths they should take in at 8.00 a.m. However, as the French writer Emmanuel Foderé noted as early as 1821, the failure of experiments in climatotherapy was revealed when the English community had to carry out as their first duty in Nice the building of a cemetery. The Côte d'Azur was more than just a large hospital, it became also a massive burial ground, one of the tombs in Nice being appropriately that of the Rev. H. F. Lyte, the author of 'Abide with Me'.

The foreign cemeteries at Nice, Cannes, Menton and Hyères are filled with the bodies of wealthy young men and women whose hopes for a cure were in vain. One of the most publicized young deaths on the Riviera was that of the consumptive Tsarevitch Nicholas in 1865; the sumptuous villa in Nice where he had been nursed was demolished after his death, and on its site was erected in his honour the present Orthodox church. The young R. L. Stevenson came to the Riviera in search of health in 1875, staying first at Nice and then at Hyères, where his lungs began haemorrhaging and he hovered for several months between life and death. Stevenson recovered (at least for the time being) but Aubrey Beardsley was not so lucky, dying at Hyères in 1898 aged only twenty-five. An especially poignant reminder of the futility of most sea cures is the story of one Henry Dundas Shore. Travelling back from Nice to England, the twenty-five-year-old Shore fell ill in the Lubéron village of Lourmarin, which fortunately had a large Protestant cemetery. His tombstone here, pointing towards England, as he himself had requested, records that he died 'on his return from Nice, whither he had gone for the restoration of his health'.

The pursuit of health was ultimately less rewarding than the pursuit of pleasure. The life of most of the winter visitors to the Riviera was an endless struggle to keep amused. Much pleasure could be had simply from being seen and recognizing distinguished people. Marie Bashkirtseff, a Russian aristocrat who later became a painter and the mistress of the artist Bastien-Lepage, spent much of her consumptive teens riding up and down the Promenade des Anglais in a pony carriage, her spirits sustained by the prospect of having a meeting with the Duke of Hamilton. Flirtation and affairs took up an inordinate amount of time, adding a necessary zest to the constant round of Riviera balls and dinner parties. The Prince of Wales – the future Edward VII – repeatedly visited the Riviera after 1872 and was by no means unusual in the number of mistresses whom he lavishly entertained here.

Concerts and opera had their part to play in the Riviera social life (Paganini, Offenbach and Berlioz were among the many famous musicians to perform in Nice in the nineteenth century), but not to the same degree as games or sports. The short-lived Prince Leopold, Duke of Albany, introduced croquet to Cannes in the 1850s, where it remained exceptionally popular until 1874, when the fashion for lawn tennis superseded it, to be followed in turn by a brief craze for cricket. Pigeon-shooting was a perennial favourite on the Riviera, though the banning of this sport in the 1930s was to be warmly welcomed by a number of people: no more would sensitive souls be distressed by the sight and sounds of dying pigeons on their hotel window-sills.

The most celebrated entertainment on the Riviera was gambling, the story of which is closely linked to that of the Principality of Monaco. By the mid 1850s the Regent of Monaco, Charles III, was nearing bankruptcy after his subjects had refused to pay taxes on oil and fruit. The only solution was to try to turn the place into a fashionable resort on the lines of Nice, Cannes and Hyères. The construction of a sanatorium, a pump-room, and a number of luxury villas was envisaged; in addition a large part of the rocky plateau directly in front of Monaco was cheaply bought, with a view to building a casino there at some future date. The backers of Charles III soon forgot about everything except the casino, which was opened in 1857 not on the rocky plateau which was later to be called Monte-Carlo, but in the one private property in Monaco itself, the Villa Bellevue. Gambling was at that time forbidden everywhere in Europe apart from in some of the minor German principalities such as Homburg and Baden; by using Monaco's independence to allow gambling within the principality, it was naturally thought that Charles III could not fail to make money. At first, however, he did not. The relative inaccessibility of Monaco at this date, combined with the slightly sordid nature of the Villa Bellevue, succeeded in putting off people from coming here: there is a famous illustration showing Monaco croupiers scanning the horizon with a telescope in a desperate search for prospective clients making their way along the stony coast road.

The whole situation changed with the arrival of the railway in 1868, and the taking over of the casino management by the brilliant entrepreneur François Blanc. Winter residents from the main coastal resorts now made it their habit to come to Monaco at least three times a week, and the number of visitors was further increased with the opening of the magnificent new casino in 1878, on the plateau of Monte-Carlo. The new casino, by the leading Paris architect Charles Garnier, shared a building with an equally splendid opera house, for it was always the intention of the Monaco authorities to balance the worldly game of gambling with more elevated activities. The opera house soon outshone that of Nice to become one of the leading opera houses of the day, commissioning works from composers of the calibre of Massenet and Saint-Saëns (later it was to achieve further fame through hosting Diaghilev and his Ballets Russes).

In the meantime the passion for gambling intensified. Up to now the gamblers had mainly been very wealthy people, playing for the fun of it and prepared to lose large sums of money. Now more and more people were gambling in the hope of paying off debts or making their fortune, in other words taking the game very seriously indeed and endlessly devising 'unbeatable' systems for winning at the roulette table. The great inspiration to such people was a shady confidence-trickster called Charles Deville Wells, who turned $400 into $40,000 in the course of three days and was immortalized in the popular song, 'The Man who Broke the Bank at Monte-Carlo'. Most gamblers were not so lucky. The number of suicides at Monte-Carlo reputedly got larger every year, though as the casino took pains to cover up these deaths, the exact statistics are not known. One of the suicides, which was so spectacular that it was reported in the press, was that of an Englishman who, after losing at roulette, fired at the casino's grand chandelier, jumped out of the window, broke both his legs, and with what remaining strength he had left finished himself off with a bullet through the head. The bodies of victims such as these were thought variously to be hidden in the holes and cracks of the limestone cliffs at Monte-Carlo or else put in weighted cases and dropped at sea.

Monaco's legendary reputation for its suicides was seized upon by those who regarded the place as the home of the devil. The Rev. S. Baring-Gould, the author of a book on the Riviera (1886), was not alone in regretting that 'one of the fairest spots of Europe, this earthly paradise, should be given over to harlots and thieves, and Jew moneylenders, to rogues and fools of every description'. In 1887 Queen Victoria famously snubbed the principality by both sending back a bouquet of flowers sent to her by the Casino and later failing to pay her respects to Charles III when passing by Monaco on her way to Menton. Shortly after the Queen had left the Riviera, an earthquake shook the coast, disturbing a large group returning from a Monaco fancy dress ball. God, it was thought, was punishing the principality, accusing it of being some latter day Sodom and Gomorrah. No one thought it worth remarking that the main casualties of the earthquake were 300 church-goers attending mass in San Remo.

Around the beginning of this century, medical opinion was coming round to the view that the bracing air of the mountains was more beneficial to the consumptive than the temperate climate of the Riviera. But by then the Riviera had become so established as the pleasure resort of Europe that its popularity remained scarcely affected by this change of opinion. New coastal resorts such as Beaulieu and Villefranche were springing up all the time, and hitherto under-developed areas such as Cap Martin or Cap Ferrat were now turning into exclusive residential areas: only the coast to the east of Saint-

Raphael, where the *mistral* blew with particular ferocity during the winter, remained as yet little built up, frequented almost solely by small groups of artists or local visitors from Toulon or Marseille. Monaco remained the gambling capital of Europe, even though France and then Italy had cautiously begun to legitimize the game. The ownership of the casino had by now passed into the hands of François Blanc's illegitimate son, Camille Blanc, a man who had inherited all his father's enterprising spirit. Camille devised other entertainments to maintain Monaco's popularity. For instance, he arranged the first of the Monte-Carlo rallies – the famous car race to the principality from different parts of Europe. Thanks to him too the principality saw such diverse novelties as the taking off of the first plane across the Mediterranean, and the first tarmac road in Europe – the invention of tarmac came about as a result of Camille's concern that the distinguished onlookers of a car show he had organized should not be covered in dust. The growing reputation of Monaco and the Riviera seemed unstoppable. Then came the First World War.

The era which the First World War brought to an end, the so-called *belle époque*, has left as perhaps its greatest legacy to the Riviera a series of extraordinary and fantastic buildings. Serious lovers of architecture did not take so kindly to them at the time. Already by the 1850s Prosper Mérimée, one of the most perceptive nineteenth-century writers on architecture, was expressing his disapproval of the type of buildings which the new residents at Cannes were putting up: 'The English,' he wrote to a friend in 1856, 'deserve to be impaled for the architecture which they have introduced to this beautiful land. You wouldn't believe how distressed I am at seeing these cardboard castles placed on these beautiful mountains. It's like having paper flowers in the middle of a *parterre*. Couldn't you get your friends to show a bit more taste?' In 1897 Augustus Hare, describing Cannes in his guidebook to the Riviera, echoed Mérimée's views that 'the hills are covered with hideous villas, chiefly built by rich Englishmen . . . Most of the modern villas are pretentious white palaces, utterly without beauty.' The tastes of Mérimée and Hare were firmly grounded in the Middle Ages, and Hare for one was certainly led by Ruskin into thinking that wealth, sophistication and eclecticism were synonymous with architectural decadence. Today there is no excuse for holding such prejudices and yet the architecture of the nineteenth-century

Riviera is still treated with suspicion and lack of seriousness. Not a single book on Provence has dared to suggest that the 'pretentious' hotels, villas and other such buildings of the Riviera's *belle époque* represent unquestionably the most exciting series of architectural monuments in the region after the romanesque period.

Such was the variety of buildings erected on the Riviera that it is difficult clearly to define a 'Riviera style'. None the less, the most influential architect to have worked here was probably Charles Garnier, whose reputation had been made in the early 1860s with the building of the Paris Opéra. Like the Paris Opéra, his casino and opera house at Monte-Carlo – his most important work on the Riviera – can loosely be described as neo-baroque: it displays a love of massive scale, sweeping staircases, undulant ornate forms, coloured marble, gilt stucco, chandeliers and illusionistic fresco decoration. These same elements are to be found in many of the Riviera's turn-of-the century hotels, which are well worth a visit even if you cannot afford their suitably exorbitant prices. In Monte-Carlo, right opposite the casino and clearly imitating its style, is the magnificent Hôtel de Paris, a cream-coloured confection on the outside, and, inside, a sombrely lit palace with a chandeliered dining-room dominated by Rubens-inspired frescoes. At Cannes there is the Hôtel Carlton, the main façade of which is flanked by two pointed domes rumoured at the time to have been inspired by the breasts of the notorious Spanish dancer and courtesan, La Belle Otero. Cimiez boasts what was perhaps the largest of the Riviera's hotels, the Hôtel Excelsior Regina Palace, described by Hare as a 'frightful building'; its architect was a local man, Sébastien Marcel Biasini, the most prolific architect working in the Nice area in the late nineteenth century.

The last and in many ways the most famous of the *belle époque* hotels is the Hôtel Negresco in Nice. It was the brain-child of Henri Negresco, a Romanian émigré who had been a gypsy violinist before entering the hotel business. The architect whom he chose was Edouard Niermans, who described himself as a 'Parisian born in Holland by an error of nature'. Niermans had worked before on countless grand hotels, casinos, restaurants, and theatres (including the Folies Bergères and the Moulin Rouge in Paris), but the Hôtel Negresco was his masterpiece. The exterior emulates the architecture of the French seventeenth century and is articulated by gigantic columns and pilasters supporting a vigorously projecting entablature; the entrances at each of the rounded corners are crowned by Art Nouveau canopies in glass and iron. The highpoint of the heavily altered interior is the oval Salon Royal, which is spanned by an etherially light dome cut into by a large glass opening. The hotel was inaugurated in 1912, and so had only two years in which to enjoy its prodigious success.

The owners of the grand hotels and casinos were interested primarily in effects of the greatest possible ostentation, and so tended to favour the 'neo-baroque' style popularized by Garnier. The owners of private villas were more catholic in their tastes, and freer to express their personal fantasies. So international, wealthy and eccentric was the Riviera that you could realize your wildest architectural dreams without inspiring too much curiosity or bewilderment. The classical archaeologist, Théodore Reinach, longed to live in an ancient Greek villa, and so built at Beaulieu the Villa Kérylos (now open to the public), a building in which every detail, down to the beds and dining-room chairs, is as close as possible to a Greek original. The exiled novelist Blasco Ibañez, homesick for his native Valencia, covered the walls of his Villa Fontana Rosa at Menton with Valencian colours and tiles, and created an extraordinary garden with tiled benches recalling those on which he sat as a child. The Duke of Albany lived at Cannes in a half-timbered house straight out of the English countryside; Michael Henry Scott, the Scottish industrialist who marketed cod-liver oil, built in the same town the now ruined Château Scott, a Scottish medieval fantasy based on Glasgow University.

One of the most impressive of the coast's architectural extravagances is the building known variously as the Château de l'Anglais or the Folly Smith, a turreted fantasy in pink dominating the fashionable hill of Mont Boron on the eastern side of Nice. Its owner and architect was Colonel Robert Smith, who in 1803 had gone to India where he had worked as a military engineer for the Bengal Army and had carried out extensive studies of Indian architecture. On his return to England in 1830, inspired by his memories of India, he built at Paignton in Devon a prototype of his Nice folly. The latter building (now turned into apartments) dates from after 1856 and is a bizarre amalgam of English and Mogul elements. Smith was also a painter, and inside this magnificent castle is a suitably ambitious canvas over twenty metres long portraying the Fall of the House of the Grand Mogul.

Every architectural style possible is represented somewhere along the Riviera, ranging from neo-Florentine and neo-Palladian to the so-called 'troubadour style', a style imitating French medieval castles. A particularly popular style was the 'Moorish style', which was thought highly appropriate to the Riviera, this land once occupied by the Moors and Saracens, and, with its palms and citrus trees, still retaining an exotic, North African appearance. Napoleon's campaigns in Egypt, followed by the conquest of Algeria in 1830, had helped foster a taste in France for what was then called 'the Orient', a taste popularized by romantic writers such as Lamartine and Gérard de Nerval, and painters such as Delacroix and Fromentin; even the pastry chef Carême had started, after 1828, producing cakes modelled on Moorish and Arabian pavilions.

Two of the early promoters of 'Moorish-style' architecture in France had begun their careers working in North Africa and the Middle East: the Marseille-born architect Pascal Coste had been employed for ten years by the Sultan of Egypt; Marius Michel, who came from Sanary near Toulon, had been made 'Michel-Pacha' for his work supervising the construction of lighthouses for the Ottoman Empire. Michel-Pacha, on his return to the south of France in 1860, commissioned as one of a number of buildings at Tamaris, on the outskirts of Toulon, a Moorish-style Institute of Marine Biology: at the time there were criticisms that the style was unsuited to a building of such serious purpose. The architect whom Michel-Pacha employed at Tamaris, Paul Page, made a far more fanciful use of Moorish elements when he created a delightful house for himself (now known as the Cabanon Mauresque) at Pierrefeu, outside Hyères. In Hyères itself are two further outstanding examples of Moorish-style architecture, both by the little-known Pierre Chapoulart. One, dating from the 1870s and on the Avenue de Beauregard, was originally called the 'Villa Algérienne' and then renamed the 'Villa Tunisienne'. The other is the 'Villa Mauresque' on the Avenue Jean Natte.

It was of course very common to mix styles, and in fact Chapoulart's Moorish pavilion in the Villa Mauresque adjoins a building of vaguely Anglo-Norman inspiration. Sometimes the owner of a building would decide to have a change of style: Somerset Maugham attempted to make Italianate his own 'Villa Mauresque' at Cap Ferrat, while the owner of the Villa La Bocca at Nice turned an Italianate structure into a Moorish one.

A masterpiece of Riviera eclecticism, and one of the few great villas which are open to the public, is the Villa Ephrussi de Rothschild at Saint-Jean-Cap-Ferrat, which was built in the late nineteenth century to house the Baroness Rothschild's superb collections of art. Each of the rooms is in a style appropriate to the works displayed, Italian Renaissance for the tapestries and furniture taken largely from Italian palaces; Venetian rococo for the ceiling paintings by the great Venetian eighteenth-century decorator, Gian Domenico Tiepolo; and French rococo for the Sèvres pottery and canvases by Boucher. The eclecticism is continued into the enchanting gardens, which conjure up in turn images of Florence, Japan and Spain.

The Villa Ephrussi de Rothschild remains exactly as it was in the nineteenth century, but this is not always the case with the Riviera villas. Though the Riviera today is hardly poor, there is no longer enough wealth to maintain all the monuments of the *belle époque* in their original state. A great many of the palaces and villas have been broken up into apartments; others, such as the Château Scott, have been abandoned completely; others still have been kept on by the original families but, through lack of funds, have been left slowly to decay. A visit to the Villa les Colombières at Menton is an especially moving experience. The villa, in a Hellenic-cum-Roman style, was designed and owned by Ferdinand Bac, a humorist writer and, allegedly, the illegitimate son of Napoleon III. The place looks now deserted, though a faded notice announces that it is open to the public and recommends prospective visitors to ring the doorbell. After a while you might be welcomed in by the elderly woman who lives here on her own. You can take a cup of lemon tea in her sombre house and then wander afterwards around the vast hillside gardens, full of cypresses, urns, statues and ornamental pools, all hopelessly overgrown and sadly evoking a past glory.

The First World War radically changed the character of the Riviera. The Hôtel Negresco in Nice, badly damaged during the war after being turned into a military hospital, lost much of its wealthy clientèle, and Henri Negresco died bankrupt in Paris in 1920. Royalty and aristocracy continued to come to the coast, but there were notable absences – the German princelings, the Baltic barons, the Austrian archdukes and, above all, the Russians, whose presence had marked the Riviera more than any other race after the English. Scott Fitzgerald referred to bygone days in a passage in *Tender is the Night*, describing a drive along the coast taken by a young Hollywood actress called Rosemary Hoyt:

> The chauffeur, a Russian Czar of the period of Ivan the Terrible, was a self-appointed guide, and the resplendent names – Cannes, Nice, Monte-Carlo – began to glow through their torpid camouflage, whispering of old kings come here to dine or die, of rajahs tossing Buddha's eyes to English ballerinas, of Russian princes turning the weeks into Baltic twilights in the lost caviare days. Most of all, there was the scent of the Russians along the coast – their closed bookshops and grocery stores. Ten years ago, when the season ended in April, the doors of the Orthodox Church were locked, and the sweet champagnes they favoured were put away until their return. 'We'll be back next season,' they said, but this was premature, for they were never coming back any more.

The Riviera of the 1920s was a more Bohemian and socially more varied place than before, a world in which jazz musicians and Hollywood film stars enjoyed the prestige of royalty, and where artists and writers swarmed, and not just the wealthy and successful ones. To Americans, escaping from Prohibition, the Riviera held a particularly strong appeal, and it was the Americans who brought about the most significant change in the Riviera's life-style.

The group of Americans described in *Tender is the Night* are shown relishing the coast out-of-season, staying on into the summer months. Scott Fitzgerald based his two protagonists, Dick and Nicole Diver, partly on Gerald and Sara Murphy, a wealthy and sophisticated American couple who spent the summer of 1922 at Cole Porter's villa at Cap d'Antibes, and discovered near there the small and deserted beach of La Garoupe. 'At that time,' Gerald Murphy recalled, 'no one ever went near the Riviera in summer . . . We dug out a corner of the beach (the seaweed was four feet thick) and bathed there and sat in the sun, and we decided this was where we wanted to be.'

A few years later another American, Benjamin Finney, met a young Frenchman named André Sella who ran the small Hôtel du Cap at Cap d'Antibes. In the spring of 1926, Sella was preparing as usual to shut down the hotel for the summer when Finney told him that he

would like to give a Fourth of July party at the hotel and wondered if
Sella would be prepared to stay open for this. Sella agreed, and Finney
went ahead and invited sixty guests down to the deserted Riviera for
the occasion, including Noël Coward, Ernest Hemingway, and Zelda
and Scott Fitzgerald. The Fitzgeralds later moved into the Hôtel du
Cap, Scott describing it as 'just a real place to rough it and escape
from the world'. The craze for spending the summers at the Riviera
soon began in earnest, and the Hôtel du Cap, together with the
adjoining rocky promontory, the Eden Roc, was at the forefront of
the new fashion. Finney eventually took over the management of the
hotel, while at nearby Juan-les-Pins a compatriot of his, Frank Jay
Gould, opened the Hôtel Provençal, an establishment which shortly
rivalled Finney's as the fashionable centre of the Riviera. Among the
guests at the Provençal were Harpo Marx, Somerset Maugham, Mary
Pickford, Douglas Fairbanks, and Gerald Murphy. There was also an
attractive American divorcée, as yet unknown to the world at large,
Wallis Simpson.

The French, as before, were slow to join in the new craze, finding
the summer sun too hot for them. However, the invention of air
conditioning and insecticides, combined with a series of poor summers
in the mid 1920s in the hitherto fashionable coastal resorts of northern
France, managed to win people over generally to the idea of a summer
on the Riviera. In 1930, following an exceptionally rainy summer in
the north, even the Carlton Hotel announced that it would be re-
opening on 1 August; after 1936, and the introduction of the paid
holiday in France, more people than ever started coming to the south
of France. An obsession with tanning, so alien to the mentality of the
true Provençal, accompanied the new fashion for the summer season.
The Riviera became crowded with sun-worshippers, and it was certainly appropriate that in the early 1930s an idealistic French doctor
opened on the wild Île du Levant a pioneering nudist colony, named
after a famous city in lower Egypt which had a temple sacred to the
sun, Heliopolis. Heliopolis amused and intrigued many of the Riviera
visitors, and it is still running today, though in the light of recent
hedonistic developments on the coast it seems merely quaint and old-
fashioned.

A great many of those who have written up the history of the
Riviera have done so in the most glowing terms, largely because they

themselves took an active part in the glamorous social life which they are describing. The journalist Charles Graves, one of the finest and most prolific historians of the Riviera, is no exception. To Graves the 1920s and 1930s on the Riviera were halcyon days, and, like many of his ilk, he enjoyed describing how, when the rest of Europe was preparing to go to war again, he and his fellow socialites on the Riviera were carrying on obliviously with their champagne parties:

The week before the outbreak of the war, Eden Roc was stiff with stars. Marlene Dietrich was leaving within twenty minutes for Paris and Hollywood to make *Destry Rides Again*; George Raft walked down from the hotel to the bathing pool with Norma Shearer; tousle-haired Simone Simon in a flower-patterned bathing-dress hurried past for a swim with hairy-legged Charles Boyer; while Edward G. Robinson was looking more like himself than ever.

Graves himself did not return to the Riviera until after the war. Others stayed on here, and many more from other parts of France joined them, for to begin with the Riviera was a relatively safe place to be. While the north of France was occupied by the Germans, the south was administered by Marshal Pétain and the Vichy government and was technically an unoccupied zone. Monaco was a particularly favoured place of refuge, for though governed by France since the nineteenth century and tied to it economically, geographically and militarily, it still had a nominal independence and preferred to maintain a neutral stance during the war. As it turned out, the Germans and Italians scarcely respected Monaco's neutrality, and, moreover, the situation was confused by the difficulty of knowing exactly where Monaco ended and France began. The stones supposed to show the boundary were hard to locate and often incorrect: a number of wealthy Jews who had escaped to Monaco at the start of the war were to find out that by being kicked by German soldiers from one pavement to the other, they were being forced into France and were thus liable to be sent off into the concentration camps. The situation for the whole of the south of France deteriorated rapidly after the British and American invasion of North Africa in the autumn of 1942. Having got off relatively lightly up to now, the Riviera was subjected to the worst battering of any part of France apart from the battlefields of Normandy.

No sooner was the war over than Charles Graves returned to his beloved Riviera. The moment he and his companion entered the luxury Blue Train from Paris and indulged in a 'six-course dinner of clear soup, red mullet, pâté with truffles, choufleur au gratin, cheese, fruit and coffee', he felt 'that the war was really over', and that everything on the Riviera would be as before. He found instead a truly devastated place, with a number of towns such as Saint-Raphael and Saint-Tropez reduced to rubble. Malcolm Muggeridge, visiting the Riviera at around this time, wrote in the *New Statesman* that 'the Riviera's day was done never to return'. 'THE RIVIERA TODAY: EUROPE'S DESERTED PLAYGROUND', ran the headline of a *Daily Telegraph* article for 1946.

None the less, as Graves predicted, the Riviera soon picked up and its former gaiety returned, together with its reputation for glamour and fashion. A new attraction was the Cannes International Film Festival, which had been inaugurated in 1939 and was taken up again in 1946. The festival, held in late May, became immediately one of the highpoints of the social calendar of the Riviera, and a magnet for international celebrities; a sign of the times was the pulling down of Cannes's celebrated Cercle Nautique to make way for the festival building. It was in the festival of 1955 that the hitherto little-known Prince Rainier of Monaco met his actress wife-to-be, Grace Kelly. Their well-publicized marriage the following year enhanced the fairy-tale-like attraction of Monaco, a place which received further world-wide attention a few years later when the Greek shipping magnate, Aristotle Onassis, made it the headquarters of his company.

The image of the Riviera as a liberated sensual paradise was furthered after the war by the promotion on its beaches of a swimming costume which scandalized much of Europe. The costume was named after a tiny Pacific island called Bikini Atoll, where the world press had gathered in June 1946 to watch the first post-war atom bomb explosion. Just why the new two-piece swimming costume should have been named after this island is not immediately obvious, though at the time many suggested that it was because of the costume's 'explosive impact'. A few weeks after the Bikini Atoll tests, Mario Brun, a popular Riviera reporter, forecast that the Aphrodite of 1946 will bathe in an 'atomic swimsuit'. In the Cannes Film Festival of that year the 'sex goddess' of the time, Martine Carole, had already shocked many by wearing such a costume. But accusations of bad taste and indecency did little to check the 'bikini's' increasing popularity, and as one wag later commented, the costume just got smaller as the atom bombs got bigger.

The 'bikini' came to symbolize the young, informal generation of the post-war period, a generation which to begin with had no Riviera resort which it could call truly its own. Places such as Nice, Menton and even Cannes were too heavily steeped in their nineteenth-century associations, while the newly fashionable Cap d'Antibes was becoming ever more exclusive. Only after 1957, with the so-called 'rediscovery' of the small Var fishing town of Saint-Tropez, was an answer found to the young person's dreams.

Stéphen Liégeard, the inventor of the term 'Côte d'Azur', had visited Saint-Tropez in 1887 and had been both enchanted and depressed by the deserted beauty of the beaches on its peninsula. 'But what sadness is imprisoned in this emerald crescent! Who can bring life to these melancholy pines? There is talk of a railway: you would need first of all a road, and on this road, a colonizing Brougham, inspiring France and England to follow in his footsteps.'

At a time when only a 'winter season' existed on the Riviera, the prospects of the north-facing Saint-Tropez developing as a resort must have seemed slight. Yet, contrary to what is often said, the town did not have to wait until the late 1950s before attracting its first admirers. The avant-garde painter Paul Signac came here in 1892, and, charmed by its position and quaint old houses, stayed here for much of his remaining life, encouraging many other important artists to paint here as well. The novelist Colette helped increase the town's reputation by buying a house here just after the First World War; by the mid 1920s she was already complaining that so many tourists were coming to Saint-Tropez to try and catch a glimpse of her that the town was in danger of becoming spoilt. In the following decade the Prince of Wales, shortly before the furore caused by his friendship with Wallis Simpson, took a shine to Saint-Tropez and in so doing gave further substance to Colette's fears.

The heavy destruction of Saint-Tropez during the Second World War put a temporary stop to its development as a resort. The town was reconstructed but was slow to recapture its former appeal. The middle-aged parents of an aspiring film actress bought a house here in the early 1950s because they could not afford to do so at Cannes. The actress was Brigitte Bardot, and the house was one of the reasons why her husband of the time, Roger Vadim, decided to make at Saint-Tropez *And God Created Woman*, the film which would launch Bardot into stardom and give the town a popularity far greater than it had ever had.

Much of Vadim's life had been spent on the Riviera. A poor Polish refugee, he had been brought up by his mother at La Napoule near Cannes, where, aged twelve, he had had his first sexual experience – on the beach with a bold eleven-year-old girl whose parents had been murdered by a gang of Nice thugs. In his early twenties he struggled in Saint-Germain in Paris to write novels and screenplays, and, according to his immodest autobiography, *Memoirs of the Devil* (1975), came to know Cocteau, Gide and Genet and had a girlfriend who was Hemingway's mistress; in the summers he would go to the Hôtel du Cap, where he once found himself swimming with the young John F. Kennedy. He met and married Bardot in Paris, and soon afterwards made *And God Created Woman*, the woman in question being an orphan whose budding sexuality is too much for the orphans' home. The heroine is clearly based on a combination of Bardot and Marilyn Monroe. Containing as it did scenes of Bardot making love and swimming naked at Saint-Tropez, the film caused certain problems for the censor, who reputedly remarked of its director, 'He's the devil!' The controversy contributed greatly to the success of the film, which had a particularly wide following in America. 'For the first time,' Vadim explained, 'the Americans had been shown the female nude on the screen as a work of art, and they had been told that love for the pleasure of loving is not synonymous with sin.'

The message of sexual liberation which the film seemed to be advocating was borne out by the highly publicized lives of those associated with it. Bardot, before the making of the film, had apparently pulled a face after her first meeting with her co-star, Jean-Louis Trintignant. 'How do you expect me to play a love scene with him?' she had shouted at Vadim and the producer. 'He's too small. He's ugly. And in any case he's not my type.' Trintignant for his part had not been particularly taken with her either, finding her too conceited and too devoted to the idea of stardom. Five weeks into the shooting, however, Bardot walked out of the Hôtel Negresco in Nice where she was then staying with Vadim, and moved in with Trintignant.

Vadim remained on good terms with the two of them, and in the following year he married the actress Annette Stroyberg, who soon left him for his closest friend, Sacha Distel, while Bardot married Jacques Charrier. Happily they would all get together at Saint-Tropez, where they spent an increasing amount of their time after 1957. One of their circle was the writer Françoise Sagan, who had achieved instant notoriety and a cult following at the age of eighteen with the publication of her novel *Bonjour Tristesse* (1954), the story of a young woman discovering her sexuality in an unspoilt Riviera setting. What with the antics of Vadim and his circle, and the presence there of the precocious Sagan, Saint-Tropez became fully established in the public imagination as a centre of youth and free love.

Vadim, together with Annette Stroyberg, had first returned to Saint-Tropez in the summer following the shooting of *And God Created Woman*:

When summer came we migrated to Saint-Tropez. 'Chez Palmyre', where everyone danced the *galop* and the *java* to the strains of a barrel-organ and accordion, was still unspoilt. We had the great white beach at Pampelonne almost to ourselves. The dreadful crime Brigitte Bardot, Françoise Sagan and I had committed in making this little fishing port famous the world over had not yet taken its appalling toll. The day of retribution wasn't far off, but as yet we were blissfully ignorant. The papers were full of our extravagant spending sprees, scandals and debauchery. Our cha-cha-cha sessions on the Esquinade and our pitched soda and syphon battles took on epic proportions when described by the press. And yet it was only the carefree uproarious expression of children who refused to grow up despite being successful and almost thirty.

Saint-Tropez was rapidly overwhelmed by its success. 'Phoney Saint-Tropez will die of asphyxiation under the offensive of the bogus, the bluff and the counterfeit,' warned an article in *Paris Match* in 1961, dramatically entitled 'THE AGONY OF SAINT TROPEZ'. Only a year or two later the town became so crowded that teenagers unable to produce a legally witnessed letter from their parents permitting them to be on their own here were promptly expelled by the police.

Vadim, Bardot and their friends remained at the centre of Saint-Tropez's life, and led all the fashions. One journalist referred to Saint-Tropez in the early 1960s as 'a tight dictatorship which is run by a bunch of precocious, untidy-looking, unwashed, inextricably intermarried and dazzlingly talented kids'. Bardot, who at times came to regret having bought a house here in 1958, was mobbed wherever she went; and everything she wore was immediately imitated. 'The year Brigitte appeared early on in the season wearing three butterflies of pink-and-white checked gingham,' wrote David Dodge in *The Rich Man's Guide to the Riviera* (1962), 'it is said that by August you could not tell where the tablecloths of the Saint-Tropez waterfront cafés ended and the beach began, except that the beach had navels.'

The habitués of Saint-Tropez developed a reputation for their beauty, but this beauty, like their life-style, was governed by a strict set of rules. A look of studied informality was the norm, with both men and women tying their shirts above the navel, the women often wearing little else apart from a tiny pair of shorts or the bottom half of a bikini. At night, when not going to boat parties, they often gathered at the Café des Arts, a bar described by Graves in 1948 as 'full of old codgers', but now the place in town to see and be seen. The fashionable beaches changed from year to year, one year being the Tahiti beach, the next the Pampelonne, the next the Épi Plage, and so on. All these beaches were, as the writer John Ardagh put it, 'a study of exotic hedonism'. From the late 1960s the fashionable women of Saint-Tropez began removing their bikini tops, and the fashion soon spread to the rest of the Riviera, even reaching the elegant beaches alongside the Promenade des Anglais in Nice.

Bardot still lives in Saint-Tropez, but the fashionable people have by and large moved on: they have left the coast altogether and 'discovered' the Lubéron. The advent of mass tourism succeeded finally in destroying the Riviera, at least according to those snobbish authors who have written up the coast's history. Already by 1963 Geoffrey Bocca, in *Bikini Beach, The Wicked Riviera as It Was and Is*, was noting with undisguised contempt how 'the new tourist has taken to pitching his tent in a field outside Cannes rather than check in at the Carlton in the centre of the city'. 'The Scots and the Germans,' Bocca went on, 'are the worst. They stand in long lines thumbing lifts with propitiatory leers, long expanses of hairy leg between short shorts or kilts and dirty tennis shoes. Both nationalities carry bulging rucksacks, the Scots usually decorating theirs with the Red Lion of Scotland or the Union Jack.'

The passing of the *belle époque* left the Riviera with a magnificent architectural heritage. The modern Riviera will not be remembered in this way, and certainly not for its villas: wealthy settlers on the coast in recent years have preferred to restore old buildings than to create new ones. The lasting legacy of the modern Riviera will probably be its art galleries, a reflection of the massive influx of artists to Provence this century. The coast has a greater concentration of galleries devoted to modern art than any other comparably sized area in the world.

7

The Artist in Provence

'The future of modern art,' wrote a young Dutch painter in 1888, 'lies in the south of France.' The statement seemed a preposterous one, and the man who made it was known to be unbalanced. His name was Vincent Van Gogh.

When Van Gogh made the eccentric decision early that year to move from Paris to Arles, Provence had not as yet established any reputation as a haven for artists, neither had it had since the Middle Ages a strong artistic tradition of its own. The region had given birth to few important artists and most of these had been based mainly in Paris, for instance the eighteenth-century portraitist Duplessis and his immensely successful contemporary, the marine painter Claude-Joseph Vernet.

The painter of rococo fantasies, Jean-Honoré Fragonard, was by far the greatest Provençal painter before the nineteenth century and the only one whose work has been thought to have a distinctively Provençal character. In fact he spent even less time in his native region than either Duplessis or Vernet, and, unlike Vernet (who did a number of scenes of the Provençal coast), he never once referred to the place in his work. He was born in Grasse in 1732, but when he was only six, his father, a glove-maker, became involved in a disastrous financial enterprise and had to move with his family to Paris; Fragonard returned briefly to Grasse in 1790 to escape the Terror, but that was all. Writers on his art have insisted, however, that the first six years of Fragonard's life were critical for his artistic development, the earliest to do so being the Goncourt brothers in the late nineteenth century. 'And we may recognize throughout his work,' they wrote, 'an artist whose earliest youth had been blessed by a southern sky, and received the accolade of Provençal sunlight. He reflects the gaiety and the happiness of light like a man whose childhood has been saturated in its glow.' Fragonard was an artist of great vivacity, colour and sensuality, and these same qualities have been found in the paintings of most later artists who have worked in Provence.

Marseille in the early nineteenth century saw a renewal of artistic activity in the region. The painter Émile Loubon was instrumental in forming the École des Beaux Arts in this city, and through him a number of renowned artists from Paris – most notably Delacroix, Corot, Couture, and Rousseau – were invited to exhibit in Marseille alongside local artists. Nearly all the successful Provençal painters of this time studied under Loubon, including the prolific landscapists Brest, Cordouan, Guigou and Papety. The best known of Loubon's pupils were Félix Ziem and Adolphe Monticelli. Ziem evolved a romantic, luminous style of landscape painting similar to that of the English artist Turner, and, like Turner, did a number of views of Venice, a city which he visited almost every year from 1842 to 1895; a favourite site of his in Provence itself was a town often compared to Venice, Martigues, which lies across the Étang de Berre and is divided by water and canals. Van Gogh had a great respect for Ziem, whom he once referred to as the 'worthy Ziem'; on another occasion, describing the beautiful leafage of trees in autumn, he wrote that 'Ziem has many a time given us that splendour already'.

But Van Gogh's main passion was for Monticelli, someone with whom he identified both as a painter and as a personality. Monticelli was the archetypal Bohemian outsider. Born illegitimately in Marseille in 1824, he was sent shortly after his birth to be looked after by a nurse in the Basses-Alpes hamlet of Ganagobie, next to the famous priory. After a solitary childhood there, he came to Marseille to work in a drug store, the money he earned there being used to finance his formal training as a painter. His first teacher was Ziem, who became a close friend. A romantic figure and a bit of a dandy, Monticelli was extremely popular with women but preferred always to remain a bachelor. He divided his life between Paris and Marseille, and also spent much time wandering around the Provençal countryside, sleeping rough. Though he had a small, enlightened group of admirers in Paris, for example the Impressionist patron, Dr Paul Gachet, he made most of his money in Marseille, where, like the other painters of this city, he sold his works by hawking them around the luxurious cafés along the Canebière. César Boyer, the owner of the Café Univers, held Monticelli's paintings in particular esteem and encouraged many of his clients to buy them. For a while the artist prospered, even though he had yet to make a name in the art world at large.

Monticelli's canvases are characterized by their heavy impasto and their use of pure colour straight from the tube; the exuberance of many of his fantastic landscapes and figure scenes owes a clear debt to Fragonard. Unfortunately his methods were so slap-dash that his paintings have deteriorated considerably, and are now difficult fully to appreciate. His style became even freer after 1880, and though by then he had begun to build up a certain critical reputation (the first article on him appeared in 1881), he now started to lose even his most fervent admirers. The problem was thought to lie with his excessive drinking, which had perhaps developed as a result of his having to spend so much time in cafés. Only Van Gogh consistently defended Monticelli against this charge. For him Monticelli was not a careless inebriate, but an inspired if slightly mad genius. Monticelli died in poverty in 1886.

Van Gogh, who had taken up painting in 1880 after a chequered career as an art dealer and lay preacher, had moved to Paris in 1886 to continue his art studies. The fashion then among young artists studying in Paris was to spend the summer and autumn months painting out of doors in the country. The villages or small towns where the artists based themselves were chosen for their picturesque, old-fashioned qualities and the presence there, preferably in large numbers, of other artists. By the 1880s 'artist colonies' of this type had been formed all over northern France, the main ones being in the Forest of Fontainebleau and in Brittany. Several of Van Gogh's artist friends from Paris, including Gauguin and Émile Bernard, went off to the Breton colony of Pont-Aven. They shared with the many artists there a fascination with the traditional costumes and life-styles of the local peasantry; but they differed from them in their preference for bright colours and simplified forms. The vast majority of the artists associated with the nineteenth-century colonies were concerned primarily with conveying with as much detail as possible the grey reality of rural life. Their mentor was Bastien-Lepage, who painted life-sized, grey-toned scenes of rural poverty. Sunshine was an anathema to Bastien and his followers, and would often interrupt a day's painting.

An otherwise very conventional artist called Howard Russell Butler was thought eccentric by his fellow artists because of his love for painting in sunny conditions. Sunny weather came to be known disparagingly as 'Butler weather'.

This, then, is the background against which Van Gogh's solitary move to the sunny south of France must be seen. At times Van Gogh seems to have regretted not being with his friends in Pont-Aven, for there was one side to his character which needed the constant advice, criticism and companionship of his colleagues. Yet he also had another, socially maladjusted side, which compelled him to stay away from others, in particular other artists. In choosing to go to Arles, he could not have found a better place to do so.

Van Gogh's love of Monticelli's art was probably a strong reason for his having gone to Provence, and it has been suggested that he was on his way to Marseille before being side-tracked to Arles. The writings of Alphonse Daudet and the Aix-born Émile Zola, his favourite modern authors, were other possible factors. The escapades of Daudet's Tartarin de Tarascon never failed to amuse Van Gogh, one of whose Arles paintings was of the Tarascon coach so lovingly described in the novel.

But why Van Gogh settled in Arles itself is more difficult to understand. It is true that the town's outstanding classical and medieval sights, and the famed beauty of its women, had led many tourists and topographical artists to pass through it; moreover, the Félibres had further publicized the place as a centre of Provençal traditions and folklore. None the less there was a world of difference between the Arles of the tourist books and the Félibres, and the town as it actually was in the 1880s. Arles was beginning to be heavily industrialized, and only shortly before Van Gogh's arrival one of the largest railway works in the south of France had been built there, an enterprise which had brought a large foreign element into the town. 'Arles,' wrote Augustus John, visiting the place some twenty years later, 'once the capital of Provence, in earlier times a Greek colony and then a Gallo-Roman town, has been celebrated for the beauty of its women; but latterly the influx of Belgian workmen employed in the building of the railway, has modified to some extent the famous classic features.'

Van Gogh came to Arles with some of the hopes and preconceptions of the ordinary tourist. He had read all about the beautiful women of

Arles, and was not at first disappointed by their looks. He even harboured romantic notions about the troubadours and on one occasion, contemplating the ruins of Montmajour by moonlight, imagined himself briefly back in the Middle Ages: 'It was romantic, you can't get away from it. Like Monticelli . . . you would not have been a bit surprised to see knights and ladies suddenly appear, coming back from hunting or hawking, or to have heard the voice of some old Provençal troubadour.' He visited all the famous classical and medieval monuments of the town and was undeniably impressed by them. Yet here his resemblance to the conventional tourist ends: he was momentarily distracted by the town's celebrated monuments, but was far more absorbed in its more modern and less obviously beautiful aspects. His attitude towards Arles's past was best summed up in his description of the sculpted portal of Saint-Trophime: 'There is a gothic (sic) portico here, which I am beginning to think admirable, the porch of Saint-Trophime. But it is so cruel, so monstrous, like a Chinese nightmare, that even this beautiful example of so good a style seems to me to belong to another world and I am glad not to belong to it as to that other world, magnificent as it was, of the Roman Nero.' During the year which he was to spend in Arles, Van Gogh virtually never drew or painted any of the town's historic monuments, with the major exception of the neglected, out-of-the-way Alyscamps, next to which the railway works had been built.

From the very start there had been a perverse and highly personal side to Van Gogh's appreciation of Provence. The artist's vision of paradise was based on the landscapes in Japanese prints, and on his journey down to Arles from Paris Van Gogh had fancifully thought that he was approaching this paradise, that Provence was going to resemble the Japan of his imagination. He first saw Arles and its surroundings in the most unusual conditions possible, covered under a thick blanket of snow. The snow lent a delicacy and purity to the scene which indeed transformed Provence into Van Gogh's Japanese heaven; but even long after the snow had melted, Van Gogh kept on comparing the region to Japan, just as others in their excitement had compared it to Spain, Greece, Africa and Italy.

As with so many later artists who painted in Provence, Van Gogh was overwhelmed by the brilliance of the region's colours. He believed that there was something in the air here which preserved colours –

even those of a painting – far better than was possible in a northern climate. 'I have read that the Rubens in Spain have remained infinitely richer in colour than those in the north. Ruins exposed to the open air remain white here, while in the north they become grey, dirty, black etc. You may be sure that if the Monticellis had dried in Paris they would now be much duller . . .' Such a statement reveals how opposed Van Gogh's artistic ideals were to those of Bastien-Lepage and his followers. Yet his attitude towards colour was also very different from that of later 'colourists' working in the region. Colour for him did not just bathe everything in a joyful sensuality; it also highlighted the sordid, ugly elements of the everyday world.

'I think that the town of Arles has been infinitely more glorious once as regards the beauty of its women and the beauty of its costume. Now everything has a worn and sickly look about it.' Van Gogh's feelings towards Provence were complex and ambiguous. Even before his initial elation had subsided, he had ceaselessly recorded in his works the ugliness of modern Arles. This was the Arles which he knew best, for throughout his stay in the town he was based in the outlying district of the Cavalerie, a poor, shoddily constructed area next to the railway station. After a few weeks at the Hôtel Camel at 30 Rue de la Cavalerie he moved to the nearby Place Lamartine, where he hired for use as a studio a decrepit room in a house painted a lurid yellow on the outside, and slept and ate at the Café de l'Alcazar on the eastern side of the square. He painted the bleak back room of the Café de l'Alcazar in his famous *Café Interior by Night*; he also painted the 'Yellow House', as well as the new iron footbridge behind this. In his letters to his brother Theo he constantly referred to the 'ugly' subjects he was portraying, and indeed, even when he walked outside the seedy district where he lived, he could not help taking an interest in buildings or constructions that other visitors would at best have politely ignored. Van Gogh's *Bridge at Arles* is today such a well-known work of art that it is easy to forget that the drawbridge which inspired it formed part of a brand new irrigation scheme which would have been considered an affront to the landscape by many tourists of the time, and certainly by the Félibres.

Van Gogh greatly admired the Félibres' writings, and in one letter to Theo he actually enclosed one of their articles on Provence. He explained to Theo who the group were, and even expressed a naïve hope that they might enjoy seeing his paintings: 'If the Félibres some day cease to ignore my existence, they will all come to the little house. I would rather this did not happen before I have finished my decorations. But since I love Provence as frankly as they do, I have perhaps a right to their attention.' The contrast between the Provence of the Félibres and that of Van Gogh is a striking one. Neither one makes up a particularly balanced portrait of the region, but it is tempting to think that Van Gogh's, in the freshness of its vision and avoidance of the conventionally picturesque, is probably the more truthful of the two.

As his year in Arles dragged on, Van Gogh felt more and more the need to share his perceptions of Provence with other artists. He repeatedly asked Gauguin to come and join him, and dreamed of turning Arles into an artist colony similar to those in Brittany and the Fontainebleau Forest. His dream of establishing what he called 'an Academy of the South' was at that time as unrealistic as his expecting recognition from the Félibres: the heavy presence of industry immediately ruled out the possibility. Gauguin did eventually come, but his stay was a disastrous one, for Gauguin had a much more conventional attitude towards his surroundings than Van Gogh. He thought Arles 'the most filthy place possible', and found that the only subject worth painting was the traditional costume worn occasionally by some of the town's women. There was of course the added problem of Van Gogh's difficult personality.

The story of the circumstances leading to Gauguin's sudden departure from Arles is well known. Tensions between the two men reached such a point that one evening Van Gogh threatened Gauguin in the street with an open razor. Gauguin spent the night in a hotel, and Van Gogh went home to cut off his own ear; the ear was delivered by Van Gogh to a prostitute, and Gauguin took the first train back to Paris. Van Gogh was so distressed by his own actions that he even apologized a few days later to the prostitute, who reassured him by saying that such actions were quite normal and that the brothel was quite used to receiving other people's ears. However, the townspeople as a whole had by now had enough of the mad Dutchman and wrote a petition to the Mayor requesting that something be done about him, both for his good and theirs.

The Musée des Alpilles Pierre de Brun at Saint-Rémy has as one of its exhibits a nineteenth-century newspaper advertisement promoting Dr Rey's sanatorium outside the town, an institution described as in 'beautiful, peaceful surroundings' and with 'all the latest medical equipment'. Into this charming, well-appointed place Van Gogh voluntarily admitted himself in November 1888, staying there until March of the following year; discharged by Dr Rey with the words 'completely cured', he went to stay with a doctor friend at Auvers outside Paris, and shortly afterwards shot himself, muttering as he lay dying, 'I would like to go home now.'

In emulation of the main psychiatric hospital at Budapest (named after Hungary's mad poet, Joszef Atila), the sanatorium at Saint-Rémy now calls itself the 'Hôpital Psychiatrique Vincent Van Gogh'. The hospital is the most important memorial to the artist in Provence, and a hideous bust of him by the sculptor Zadkine has been placed outside it. There are always tourists demanding to see the room where Van Gogh stayed (a room later occupied by Albert Schweitzer as an internee after the First World War), though they are always turned away unless they pretend to be prospective patients. In Arles itself Van Gogh is commemorated by a street named after him, a small, dingy display of photographs and reproductions in the Museon Arlaten, and a notice in the Alyscamps recording the spot where he once set up his easel. None of these attempts to preserve his memory compensate for the total lack of original works by him in the town. The Cavalerie district was largely destroyed during the Second World War, and the bridge of the *Bridge at Arles* was pulled down in 1926 (a copy called the Pont Van Gogh has since been built at Port-de-Bouc near Martigues). Though there are few specific monuments connected with Van Gogh in Arles, the town's associations with the artist have become as important an attraction for tourists as the relics of its classical and medieval past.

The other outstanding painter to have popularized Provence was Paul Cézanne. Cézanne too was a loner who worked for most of his life with only the recognition of a small group of artists and critics. By the time Van Gogh came to Arles, Cézanne had been painting in the region for over twenty years. But Cézanne had a more understandable reason for being there than his Dutch contemporary, for he had been born in Aix-en-Provence (in 1839) and had developed as a child an obsession with the surrounding landscape. The house of his birth is at

28 Rue de l'Opéra and is marked by a plaque. His father had made his fortune in the hat trade and as a money-lender, and was one of the town's wealthiest citizens. The main family home was an elegant early nineteenth-century mansion (which still survives but cannot be visited) in the middle of a wooded estate called the Jas de Bouffan. One of Cézanne's closest friends as a child was Émile Zola, who greatly encouraged Cézanne's ambitions to become a painter. The young Cézanne had all the dedication and energy of a great artist, as Zola recognized, but lacked at first the technical sophistication. Highly conscious of this limitation, he was upset while at art school in Paris by the way his fellow students made fun of his powerful but somewhat crude figure studies. The reaction to his works of the townspeople of Aix was even more mocking, and was to remain so for many years afterwards. He soon found a way of getting his own back on his deeply reactionary town: whenever a local asked to see his paintings (and they generally did so only to criticize and make fun of him afterwards), he simply said, 'I shit on you.'

Cézanne's relations with the people of Aix, including his own family, deteriorated, but the inspiration he found in the local landscape intensified. In his youth he painted many works in and around the Jas de Bouffan, including one (*The Railway Cutting*, c. 1870) which portrays the Marseille railway line at the point where it crosses the estate; in the background is represented for the first time what is to be the most famous motif in his art, the Montagne Sainte-Victoire. Another favourite painting-ground of Cézanne in the 1870s was the coastal village of L'Estaque near Marseille. Already this village was turning into the industrialized suburb which it is today. Cézanne, like Van Gogh, did not shy away from the ugly, modern elements of a landscape. The difference between the two artists was that Cézanne simplified and idealized these elements, so that the factory chimneys in his L'Estaque paintings lose their industrial connotations and are perceived merely as cylinders poised against the deep blue of the sea.

An advantage of working at L'Estaque was that Cézanne could stay there with his Parisian mistress Hortense Fiquet and their small son Paul, the existence of whom he was trying to hide from his father. The father died in 1886, leaving Cézanne an inheritance which rid him of all his previous financial worries, and encouraging him to live almost uninterruptedly at Aix. He stayed at the Jas de Bouffan until 1899, then moved into an apartment at 23 Rue Boulegon (today marked by a plaque); between 1901 and 1902 he constructed a studio on the northern outskirts of the town and worked here until his death in 1906. In contrast to Hortense, to whom he was now married, he hated having to leave the town, and even made little attempt to have his work exhibited in Paris. In Parisian circles he came to be thought of as a boorish provincial, a recluse with few social graces, a stereotypical Provençal lout. The American painter Mary Cassat met him in 1894 and wrote that 'Monsieur Cézanne is from Provence and like the man from the Midi whom Daudet describes'; later she had to concede that her first impression had been misjudged and that 'far from being fierce or a cut-throat, he has the gentlest nature possible, "comme un enfant", as he would say'. In Aix itself he continued to be regarded with suspicion, though in 1898 he at least received here some recognition as an artist after a chauvinistic local journalist, Joachim Gasquet, had written that Cézanne's landscapes expressed the 'soul of Provence'.

That Gasquet's judgement was not taken seriously by others in Aix is shown by the town's failure to purchase important works by Cézanne. Even the museum to him, opened in 1954 in his last studio, is a desultory, little-cared-for place, the atmosphere of which is epitomized in its sad reconstructions of the artist's still-lifes, featuring apples in a now advanced stage of decay.

Happily, the disappointment at not finding any proper memorial to Cézanne in Aix is balanced by the excitement of seeing the landscape motifs which he continually painted. It is impossible to come to Aix without being reminded of his work everywhere, for he has completely altered the way in which we look at this part of Provence. Many of the motifs of Cézanne's maturity are to be found along the D17 leading from Aix to Le Tholonet, a road now renamed the Route Paul Cézanne. Half-way along this, in the middle of a forest of parasol pines, is the misleadingly named Château Noir, which is in fact a farmhouse built of yellow stone, with gothic windows. Cézanne loved this place and painted it repeatedly, and though he failed in his attempts to purchase it, he was allowed to rent one of the rooms in its west wing as a studio. Around the building can be identified numerous motifs of Cézanne's art, including the millstones and other remnants of an old mill. To the north are the quarries of Bibémus, in whose pools Cézanne used to go swimming with Zola as a child; these too he painted frequently, though they are difficult to recognize now owing to the brief reworking of the site in recent times. The landscape between Aix and Le Tholonet is one of emerald green trees set against a vivid red earth (the 'blood of Provence', as Gasquet termed it); jutting above all this is the limestone wedge of Montagne Sainte-Victoire, which becomes larger and larger the further east you drive.

Cézanne, in the hundreds of oil-paintings, watercolours and drawings that he did of this mountain, preferred to represent it from a distance. In his middle years he often painted it from a spot to the south-west of Aix, Bellevue, where the view of the mountain is interrupted by a railway viaduct; in Cézanne's hands this viaduct was made to seem like a Roman construction, thus enhancing the classical quality which he was trying to achieve in his works. In old age Cézanne chose a more majestic viewpoint, the ridge of Les Louves, just behind his last studio. From his *Railway Cutting* of 1870 to the works painted from Les Louves, Cézanne had perfected his representation of the mountain to the point where nothing detracted from the bold classical splendour of its triangular form. Cézanne's landscapes, and in particular his views of Montagne Sainte-Victoire, gave new life to the myth of Provence as a noble, harmonious land steeped in antiquity.

A growing number of avant-garde artists, many inspired by the example of Van Gogh and Cézanne, began coming to Provence from the 1890s onwards. They favoured the coast rather than the interior, which was not to be colonized by artists until a much later date. The main coastal resorts had already an attraction for wealthy and successful artists, who came here for the same reasons that the other visitors did – to enjoy high society and the mild winter climate. One of these artists was Rosa Bonheur, who had made a fortune with her paintings of animals; she owned a villa in Nice and was a familiar sight on the Promenade des Anglais, with her velvet pantaloons, animal trainer's blouse, and prominently displayed ribbon of the Légion d'Honneur. The artist whose work best evokes the spirit of the *belle époque* is Jules Chéret, who wintered regularly at Nice and died at a villa in the fashionable Nice suburb of Mont Boron. His fame today rests largely on his lively, boldly coloured Art Nouveau posters of the 1880s and 90s, works that greatly influenced Toulouse-Lautrec. He worked in the style of a latterday Fragonard, throwing together with considerable panache the worlds of mythology and the contemporary fashion plate. The Nice Préfecture has walls and ceilings covered with delightful decorations by him; and the town's municipal art gallery – housed in a magnificent *fin-de-siècle* palace built for a Russian prince – has the largest collection of his works to be seen anywhere.

As one of Europe's famed beauty spots, the Riviera naturally attracted its fair share of topographical artists. These were mainly conventional watercolourists, working with the tourist trade in mind and with little feeling for such special features of the Mediterranean environment as its intense light and colours, and even its olive trees. B. Becker, in *Holiday Haunts by Cliffside and Riverside* (1884), noted how the Riviera's most prolific watercolourist, Pownall Williamson, never once painted an olive grove. 'Considered as a tree,' Becker explained, 'the olive is distinctly a failure. It is small, it is dusty, and grey, and generally old. It is of little use to painters . . . I have watched the olive in all weathers, and have never found it, pictorially, good for anything.'

Becker's attitude illustrates the enormous gulf which separated the topographical artists of the coast from the Impressionists and other avant-garde painters who worked here towards the end of the nineteenth century. One of the first Impressionists to capture the sensual colouring of the coast was Claude Monet, who visited Antibes in 1884 and again in 1888. In 1895 Monet's fellow Impressionist Auguste Renoir moved from Paris to the village of Cagnes, where he was to live until his death in 1919. After staying for a short while in a house in the centre of the village, Renoir bought a property called Les Collettes on the road between Cagnes and the sea. The main attraction of this place (now a museum to the artist) was its magnificent olive trees, later described by Renoir's son, Jean, as 'among the most beautiful in the world'.

The earliest artist colonies in Provence had been formed by the first decade of this century. One was the hill village of Èze, a place spectacularly situated above the coast between Nice and Monaco; Nietzsche had fallen in love with the village in the 1890s, and in the following decade numerous artists, mainly of the conventional topographical kind, had begun dotting its streets with their easels. Martigues was another, more important colony, which had first been popularized by Corot and Ziem and came later to be frequented by such diverse artists as Augustus John and the future Dadaist, Picabia. The place which was central to Provence's emergence as a pioneering artistic centre was Saint-Tropez, where Signac had bought a house (La Hune) in 1892. Signac was a follower of Georges Seurat, the so-called 'pointillist' painter who had tried to rationalize the working methods of the Impressionists by the evolution of a style based on the juxtaposition of tiny dots of pure colour. During his year at Saint-Tropez, Signac developed a bolder and more sophisticated version of this style. In 1904 Matisse was invited to stay at La Hune and fell heavily under the influence of both Signac and the Mediterranean.

For Matisse, who had been brought up in a grey, industrial area of northern France, the discovery of the Mediterranean seems to have had a remarkable liberating effect. In his early years as an artist, based mainly in Paris, he had worked in a relatively dark and conventional style, and, like most artists of the time, had been unaware of the work of the Impressionists until as late as the mid 1890s. A stay in Corsica in 1898 had helped to lighten his palette somewhat, but it was not until his visit to Saint-Tropez in 1904 that his art underwent the dramatic change which was eventually to turn him into one of the great colourists of this century. His main work inspired by the visit was *Luxe, Calme et Volupté* (1904), which shows female nudes bathed in brilliant sunshine besides the Saint-Tropez seashore. Cézanne's paintings had already promoted an image of Provence as a modern Arcadia; but Matisse's canvas of 1904 lent to this image a quality of overpowering sensuality.

In *Luxe, Calme et Volupté* Matisse employed a loose 'pointillist' style, inspired by that of Signac. He soon abandoned this style and adopted a much broader one. After 1905 he became associated with a group of artists whose boldly applied use of vivid colour earned for them the nickname of 'Les Fauves', or the wild beasts. These artists included Derain, Van Dongen, Vlaminck, Marquet and Dufy, all of whom worked in Saint-Tropez in the early years of this century and found inspiration in the sight of the port's white, pink and yellow houses, reflected against the clear blue of the sea. Many of the group painted also on the coast near Marseille, more specifically at Cassis, La Ciotat, and L'Estaque. The choice of the latter was a conscious homage to Cézanne, an artist whose simplification of form was a powerful influence on the development of twentieth-century art and paved the way for complete abstraction. Working with Raoul Dufy in L'Estaque in 1908 was Georges Braque, an artist then experimenting with Picasso in a style aimed at reducing the natural world to simple, geometrical shapes. The term 'cubist' to describe this style was coined by the critic Vauxcelles after seeing Braque's Cézanne-inspired Estaque landscapes.

The reputation of Provence as a Mecca for those interested in the arts was fully established in the years between the wars. Somerset Maugham and Scott Fitzgerald were just two of a galaxy of successful British and American authors who now frequented the coast, among whom were Ernest Hemingway, Frank Harris. D. H. Lawrence, Cyril Connolly, H. G. Wells, Virginia Woolf, Katherine Mansfield and Aldous Huxley. The revolutionary dancer Isadora Duncan was a famous figure here during the 1920s, and it was on the Promenade des Anglais that there occurred in 1927 her fatal accident with the scarf. The presence at the Monte-Carlo opera house of Diaghilev and the Ballets Russes brought many other pioneering dancers, musicians, and painters to Provence. The composers Georges Auric and Darius Milhaud (both of them members of 'Les Six'), Pablo Picasso, Picabia, and the artist, writer and film-maker Jean Cocteau all worked for Diaghilev, as did the former 'Fauves' Dufy and Derain. Matisse kept his distance from Diaghilev but remained one of the most prominent artists of the Riviera. In 1916 he had taken to spending the winters in one of the grand sea-front hotels in Nice, and in 1921 had purchased an apartment belonging to Frank Harris on the Place Charles Félix, in the heart of Nice's old town. It was in this apartment that Matisse painted most of his celebrated *Odalisques*, half-naked women in oriental guise placed against a sensual, exotic background.

Numerous lesser painters took to working in Provence during this period, many of whom were pale imitators of Van Gogh, the Fauves, and, above all, of Cézanne, whose art suddenly began to enjoy a popularity far greater than ever before. The widespread obsession with Cézanne among French artists after the First World War had a strong nationalist basis to it. While the art of the Fauves had uncomfortable associations with German expressionism, that of Cézanne represented the great classical tradition in French culture and had come to symbolize, like the harmonious south in general, the hope for a renewal of national identity. A passion for Cézanne also infected those great British Francophiles, the Bloomsbury group. Duncan Grant, Vanessa Bell and Roger Fry all spent much time in Provence in the 1920s and 30s, and Fry – England's most passionate spokesman for Cézanne – bought a house near Saint-Rémy in 1931 and thought he had found paradise.

The popularity of Cézanne during this period led to the production of an enormous amount of bad art. Jacques-Émile Blanche, a highly perceptive art critic and patron, described in his memoirs, *Propos de peintre* (1928), a beautiful drive from Hyères to Saint-Tropez and asked rhetorically: 'Why should there not be a Renaissance of painting on the Mediterranean Coast?' His answer to this was characteristically caustic:

From Marseille to Vintimille, on the coast and inland, there is scarcely a village but someone, dreaming of Cézanne, has come and set up an easel there. I see nothing but hackneyed motifs, colours and lines which the artist has vulgarized. They have made your Provençal countryside more un-interesting for us than the forest of Fontainebleau. Every little shack in these paintings done by 'Independent' artists looks to me as if it were about to tumble down . . . Am I suffering from dizziness? Trees, mountains, clouds, the horizon, the sea, they are all dancing! – and would Cézanne have beaten time for this sort of farandole? I breathe comfortably only when the rain obliterates the blue sky.

Artist colonies proliferated in Provence after the First World War, as they had done in the Fontainebleau Forest and in Brittany in the nineteenth century. The main difference between these new places and their northern French prototypes was that the most interesting artists associated with the former tended to be those who rarely if ever painted their surroundings and who worked there purely because they found the atmosphere sympathetic. Martigues continued to be a favourite haunt, though growing industrialization drove away many of its older habitués by the late 1920s. Saint-Tropez was still popular with artists, but the new craze was to frequent the many picturesque hill villages which lay behind the coast, places such as Le Cannet, Seillans, Tourette, Vence, Mougins, Cagnes and Saint-Paul. Bonnard lived in Le Cannet from 1925 until his death in 1940; D. H. Lawrence's last months were spent in Vence; Picabia bought a house, Le Château de Mai, in Mougins in 1924; and Picasso, Fernand Léger, Paul Éluard, Jean Cocteau and Isadora Duncan all stayed in Mougins's Hôtel Vaste Horizon.

Cagnes, at the time of Renoir's arrival there in 1895, had had few visitors apart from the odd English couple searching for a quiet holiday away from the main coastal resorts. Now it emerged as one of the liveliest of the Provençal colonies, and was used as the model for Trou-sur-Mer (nicknamed 'Montparnasse-sur-Mer') in Cyril Connolly's first and only novel, *The Rock Pool* (1936). This book, rejected at first by Connolly's English publishers for being too obscene, tells the story of a mediocre young Oxford graduate contemplating writing a novel on the antics of the village's incestuous community of artists and writers, who tease and take advantage of him, eventually to drag him down to their own pagan, degenerate level.

The leading artist colony in Provence by the mid 1920s was indisputably that at Saint-Paul, near Vence. As with most of the great nineteenth-century colonies such as those at Barbizon and Pont-Aven, Saint-Paul became popular with artists largely through the activities of an enterprising local hotelier, in this case Paul Roux. Roux, an uneducated hill farmer, decided after the First World War to give up his hard life as a farmer and open up a small restaurant and hotel at Saint-Paul. This establishment, after several changes of name, became known as the Colombe d'Or. One of the first to 'discover' it was an obscure American sculptor called Jo Davidson; in his wake soon came artists such as Picasso, Léger, Rouault, Braque, Chagall and so on. Faced with all these artist guests, Roux soon acquired a passion for contemporary art. Following a tradition dating back to the famous artist inns of nineteenth-century France such as Père Ganne's at Barbizon, Roux began accepting works of art in lieu of payment for his hospitality; moreover, he now spent much of the money he was able to earn buying further works. The artists loved him, and Picasso called him 'Roux the Magnificent'.

The hotel had the appeal of an old and unostentatious family home. This was a look which Roux had carefully cultivated: the whitewashed walls of this relatively modern building had been waxed to give an impression of age; there was no concierge, reception desk or porter. The informality of the Colombe d'Or was to be imitated by other fashionable Provençal hotels of more recent date and came to be preferred by many to the intimidating elegance of the grand coastal hotels. After the Second World War, film stars and other celebrities chose to stay here rather than at the Hôtel Carlton in Cannes. In the early 1950s the singer Yves Montand became a regular sight at the poker table, while the film actress Simone Signoret could often be seen helping in the kitchen or serving drinks behind the bar. Roux died in 1954, leaving behind just £200 and an art collection worth then close to a million. The hotel is still running, and is filled with paintings and sculptures by some of the greatest artists of this century. At one time tourists were freely able to see this collection but they are now obliged to have at least a meal here, a costly experience. The Colombe d'Or, despite its deceptively unpretentious appearance, is one of Provence's most luxurious establishments.

The Second World War if anything increased the flow of artists and writers coming to Provence. Before the war itself broke out, Thomas and Heinrich Mann, Alma Mahler, Bruno Frank, and a number of other distinguished German intellectuals escaped to France from Nazi Germany, and headed to Provence because it was both hotter and cheaper than Paris. Partly on the recommendation of Cocteau, and partly because of the presence there of the renowned German art critic Meier-Graefe, they settled around the port of Sanary near Toulon, where they were soon visited by friends and compatriots such as Bertolt Brecht and Stefan Zweig. Sanary thus became quite a centre of German culture, much to the annoyance of Aldous Huxley, who had recently purchased a villa here (named, on account of a local builder's error, the 'Villa Huley'). Huxley and his circle were treated condescendingly by the Germans, and came to refer to them as 'Haute Culture' because of their pompousness and intellectual snobbery.

The occupation of Paris in July 1940 led to many other intellectuals taking refuge in the south of France. André Breton, Jacques Hérold, Yves Tanguy, Max Ernst, and other members of the surrealist movement moved to Marseille, turning the town briefly into a major surrealist centre. This was the subject of a fascinating if rather chauvinist exhibition inaugurating Marseille's dynamic new cultural centre, housed in the refurbished Charité: it was the contention of the exhibition's organizers that Marseille, filled at that time with an international crowd of exiles from Paris, acted as an important centre for the diffusion of surrealist ideas across the world. By 1942 Breton, Ernst and Tanguy had emigrated to America, where their ideas possibly influenced the development of abstract expressionism. Jacques Hérold and many other exiles moved to the Lubéron, an area considered then as secluded and relatively free from German interference.

Samuel Beckett came to the Lubéron village of Roussillon in 1942 and found himself in the company of a number of exiles staying at the local hotel there, run at the time by the widow of the chef Escoffier. Beckett finally returned to Paris in 1945, glad to have left Roussillon, where he had suffered a nervous breakdown (later described in his novel, *Watt*) brought on by the boredom of village life. While in the village he had worked briefly for a wine-grower called Bonnelly, to whom he was later to refer in a passage in his play *Waiting for Godot*: 'But we were in the Vaucluse together, I'd swear it. We worked in the harvest together at Bonnelly's farm in Roussillon . . . Everything is red down there.'

Consuelo de Saint-Exupéry, the artist wife of the novelist and Resistance martyr Antoine de Saint-Exupéry, was another exile from Paris who had ended up in Marseille shortly after the Occupation. While there she heard of a group of young artists and architects who had moved into the Lubéron village of Oppède, and she decided to join them there. The old village of Oppède, perched on a rock directly underneath the Lubéron range, was at that time almost completely in ruins, the remaining 700 villagers having moved down to the plain and formed the community now known as Oppède-les-Poulivets. The artists and architects camped in the ruins of the village and its castle, and began making some of the buildings habitable and suitable for use as studios. The group aimed to be self-sufficient, and to teach their skills to others so that, in the words of one of them, the survivors of the war would 'be able to rebuild once the age of destruction was over'. They were great idealists and romantics. Consuelo de Saint-Exupéry, in the middle of her first sleepless night spent alone in the overgrown castle, was approached by one Bernard, the leader of the group. They talked to each other by the light of the moon, and Consuelo asked him to tell the story of the village and its castle.

Bernard spoke to her about Raymond VI of Toulouse, the original owner of the castle, and about his support of the Cathars and the troubadours, who took refuge in Oppède to escape the forces of the French and the papacy. 'Bernard,' Consuelo replied after hearing this rather simplistic and questionable historical account, 'we are the new troubadours. We are slightly mad, as they surely were. We are young. We have nothing but our hearts. We have been chased away too, we have been persecuted. Our houses have been destroyed, then our towns. Oppède must once again be a refuge.'

Bernard's answer to all this was to appoint Consuelo the troubadours' Princess. Consuelo's book, *Oppède* (1945), reads more like a fantasy than a realistic description of the colony, but there must have been times when Consuelo and her colleagues found it genuinely difficult to distinguish fantasy from reality, as when, one day, an old man calling himself a marquis rode on a white horse all the way from the Camargue to visit them. The man was none other than the Marquis Baroncelli-Javon. Numerous stories had circulated about the Oppède colony: some said that they were a religious sect, others that they believed in free love. The Marquis wanted to find out for himself. He rode back to his home towards sunset, deeply impressed by what he had seen. Their art had meant nothing to him, but their youthful ideals had warmed the heart of this eternal romantic.

After the war the members of the Oppède colony dispersed, and the buildings that they had restored soon fell into ruins again; but it was not long before artists and writers were to move back into Oppède, and into the Lubéron generally. In the meantime the coast and its nearby hill villages remained as popular with artists as ever.

Matisse was still alive, and staying mainly in the exclusive Nice suburb of Cimiez, where he had an apartment in that huge masterpiece of *belle époque* architecture, the Hôtel Excelsior Regina Palace: contrary to prevailing 'modernist' tastes, Matisse had a love of the fanciful elaborate forms of the *belle époque* style and often wrote about the beauties of the arabesque. Between 1949 and 1951 he was engaged on his greatest contribution to the art and architecture of the Riviera, the Chapel of the Rosary at Vence. The building was intended as a gift to the nuns of a Dominican convent who had looked after him during the war while he had convalesced from a serious illness. He designed every detail of the chapel down to the candlesticks of the altar table and the vestments worn by the officiating priests. The interior has dazzlingly white walls decorated with black line drawings representing the Stations of the Cross and Dominican monks; the main colour was provided by some beautiful stained-glass windows. Few religious buildings are quite as moving as this, or emanate such an atmosphere of serenity.

Matisse died in 1954, after which Picasso had no serious rival as the greatest and most celebrated artist working in Provence. Unlike Matisse, Picasso was far more affected by encounters with people – in particular with women – than with places. As he was neither an outstanding colourist nor someone who frequently represented his surroundings, it cannot be said that the impact of Provence was as great on his art as it had been on that of Matisse. Picasso lived in Provence because of his love of the Mediterranean environment and because the region reminded him of his native Spain, to which his opposition to Franco made him unable to return: a nostalgia for Spain led him to be a regular attender of the bull-fights held in the amphitheatre at Arles.

Picasso had been a frequent visitor to Provence before the war, but it was not until 1945 that he settled here permanently. He stayed at first at Antibes, where he was offered the use of the Château Grimaldi as a studio. Two years later he moved into the nearby village of Vallauris, which he had first visited in 1936. On that occasion he had been excited to find out about the existence of a pottery industry dating back to classical times; now he took up pottery himself, and helped to revive this industry. He left Vallauris in 1954 and bought a nineteenth-century villa, La Californie, on the northern outskirts of Cannes. Soon he found himself troubled by too many tourists and visitors, and in 1958 he sold this place and acquired a magnificent part-fourteenth-century castle in the remote village of Vauvenargues, underneath Montagne Sainte-Victoire. As an artist whose development of 'cubism' had been strongly influenced by the works of Cézanne, he was only too conscious of being under the shadow of Cézanne's favourite motif: to his friends he even boasted of having 'bought' the mountain. Picasso kept on his Vauvenargues home after he later purchased a house at Mougins, where he died in 1973 at the age of ninety.

Other celebrated masters of twentieth-century art settled in Provence during the latter half of their lives – Chagall lived at Vence from 1949 to his death in 1985; Max Ernst spent most of his last years at

Seillans, where he had bought a house in 1963. There was also much new talent coming into and even originating from the region. Nice experienced a brief artistic renaissance in the 1960s with the creation of the so-called 'School of Nice', a group comprising Arnan, Yves Klein, Tinguely and the Marseille-born sculptor César. They devised highly entertaining works, often made up of discarded pieces of machinery; Arnan's villa outside Vence is largely covered with the drums of spin-dryers, and is one of the few modern villas to be a worthy successor to the fantastic creations of the *belle époque*. The main focus of cultural life in Provence since the war has been the district of the Lubéron, which has boasted such diverse talents as the writers Camus and Julio Cortazar, the photographer Henri Cartier-Bresson, the abstract artists André Lhote and Nicholas de Staël, the 'op-artist' Vasarély, and the now highly fashionable English creator of life-sized terracotta reliefs, Raymond Mason.

Despite the continuing presence of good artists in Provence, the region no longer plays a central role in today's art world. The good artists have been vastly outnumbered by the bad ones, and the place has been overrun by galleries and 'craft shops' selling usually the most mediocre works. Yet, whatever happens next, however much Provence might decline artistically, the region will always be remembered for the quantity and quality of its permanent collections of twentieth-century art. The Musée des Beaux-Arts Jules Chéret in Nice has in addition to its work by Chéret the finest groups of paintings by Dufy and Van Dongen to be seen anywhere. All the Fauves are represented in Saint-Tropez's Musée de l'Annonciade, a museum housed in a beautiful seventeenth-century chapel overlooking the very port which these artists so frequently represented. The importance of Saint-Paul as an artist colony is recalled in the Maeght Foundation, a cultural complex seductively spread over a landscape of pools and exotic shrubs and interspersed with important works by most of the greatest French-based artists this century. Then there are the museums devoted to single artists: Matisse and Chagall at Cimiez, Picasso at Antibes, Léger at Biot, Cocteau at Menton, Vasarély at both Gordes and Aix. The sheer quantity of modern art in Provence is overwhelming, and, after visiting the Vasarély museums, you might well begin to feel the need for something different. Perhaps the time has come for some good food.

8

The Food and Drink of Provence

'Somewhere between Vienne and Valence,' Ford Madox Ford continues, 'below Lyon on the Rhône, the sun is shining and south of Valence Provincia Romana, the Roman Province, lies beneath the sun. There there is no more any evil, for there the apple will not flourish and the brussels sprout will not grow at all.'

The mysterious boundary which separates Provence from the rest of France is not just a geographical and historical one, it is also a culinary one. The appearance of the first olive trees below Valence marks the change between a gastronomy based on dairy produce and one based on olive oil. The cuisine of Provence is as much a reflection of the colourful, exuberant world of the Mediterranean as was the soggy brussels sprout a symbol of the drab north for Ford Madox Ford. To many writers, Provençal food has epitomized all that is special to Provence. In 1840 a journal of Provençal poetry was inaugurated with the name of the famous Provençal fish dish, *Bouillabaisse*. Over fifty years later Mistral brought out a literary and political journal named after the region's garlic-flavoured mayonnaise, *Aïoli*. Explaining why he chose such a name, he said that aïoli is like 'a distillation of all the heat, strength and joy of the Provençal sun'.

The olive, that prerequisite of Provençal food, has always been worshipped by the region's writers. To them the olive has an ancient sacred character, no doubt because the first olive trees in Provence are reputed to have been planted by the Greeks. Among Mistral's last published works was a collection of poems entitled *L'Oulivado* (The Olive); the rituals surrounding the growing and the picking of the olives are the subject of Giono's book, *Le Chant de l'olive* (The Song of the Olive); a poem of praise to the olive opens *La Cuisine provençale de tradition populaire* (1962), a manual of traditional Provençal cookery written by a chronicler of the Félibres, René Jouveau. The central role which the olive once played in Provençal life is illustrated in an anecdote concerning Cézanne, whose wife's dowry had been squandered by her thoughtless and generally disliked brother. At table once, when everyone was listing this man's faults, Cézanne was able to find in him a single virtue, 'He knows how to buy olives.'

In a footnote to his epic poem mainly in praise of Provence, *Le Grandeur de Dieu dans les merveilles de la Nature* (1744), the Marseillais poet P.-A. Dulard wrote that 'the oil which the olive produces, above all in the district of Aix, is preferred even to that of Italy and Portugal'. Opinions today vary considerably as to which is the finest olive oil of Provence; the *bon viveur* Mayor of Nice, Jacques Médecin, believes that the oil pressed by the Nice firm of Nicolas Alziari is unquestionably the best; another school of thought maintains that the oil improves the further north you go up the Rhône valley. Whatever brand you decide to buy, you should look out for the designation *extra vierge* (extra virgin), which means that the oil is the result of a first pressing of the olives; the olive grower adds cold water to the residue of this pressing to produce a second pressing, labelled *fine* or sometimes *extra fine*; a third pressing, made with the addition of warm water, is never commercially sold. The one problem of the *extra vierge* is that the flavour of the olive is sometimes so strong that if you use the oil unadulterated to make mayonnaise, the result can be somewhat bitter; in this respect the *extra vierge* Nicolas Alziari is the perfect oil, retaining all the flavour of the olive while being smooth and subtle. One of the few small olive mills I know of which still functions is at the Lubéron village of Oppède-les-Poulivets (marked by the sign 'Moulin à huile'). Should you buy your oil here, you should try afterwards to visit the nearby Moulin des Bouillons, three kilometres to the south of Gordes. This small museum, devoted to the history of the olive and its products, is built around a fascinating old olive press of a type devised by the Greeks over 1,500 years ago.

After olive oil, the next essential element of Provençal cuisine is garlic. Garlic has not quite the same solemn connotations as the olive and indeed is regarded by many foreigners with a combination of suspicion and amusement. The unshaved peasant reeking of garlic is a widely held image of the Provençal man, while the phrase 'French laced with garlic' was used by Anne Dempster in 1886 to describe what were to her the quaint, amusing nasal sounds of the Provençal language. Almost every dish is flavoured with garlic in Provence, a region which after all even has a place on the coast named Cap d'Ail, Garlic Cape. Those who have defended its extensive use in the region's food have often argued that the garlic from here has not such a strong or bitter taste as that of northern districts. This line of defence seems unnecessary. All prejudices against garlic must be dropped if you are to appreciate Provençal food.

'A whiff of thyme from a marinade,' wrote the author of the preface to Jouveau's *La Cuisine provençale*, 'transports you across the Alpilles at sunrise.' The aromatic herbs which grow in such abundance in Provence have made another major contribution to the local cuisine. Even before being added to a dish, they often subtly flavour the meat of the animals who graze on them, Sisteron lamb or *agneau de Sisteron* being a particularly tasty example of this. At one time herbs were even thrown into the baker's oven, thus giving a delicate aromatic flavour to the local bread; this practice was referred to approvingly by the Arles author Quiqueran de Beaujeu in a lengthy passage extolling the quantity and variety of the region's herbs in his *La Provence louée* (In Praise of Provence) of 1551. In the course of any walk in the Provençal countryside you will soon be able to amass a considerable quantity of herbs, most notably rosemary, fennel, sweet bay, sage, thyme, and, above all, savory, of which there exist over twenty different types in Provence. Should you prefer instead to buy herbs, you will find everywhere in the region sachets of often precious appearance containing a mixture of 'Herbes de Provence'.

By far the best of the many shops devoted to herbs and herbal products in the south of France is the Paradis des Plantes in the Languedoc town of Sommières. This is run by Ludo Chardenon, one of France's few remaining *ramasseurs des plantes* (plant gatherers), and a person sometimes referred to as 'the magic plant man'. For many years he ran a herb stall in the Arles market, where he was discovered one day by Lawrence Durrell, then searching for a cure for chronic eczema. Durrell found relief in one of Ludo's medicinal herbs and encouraged him to write down the herbal cures that he had picked up from his grandmother, together with a few tips about the use of herbs in cooking. The resulting book, *Memoirs and Recipes of Ludo Chardenon* (1982), is on sale at the Paradis des Plantes along-side a wide selection of medicinal and culinary herbs and such won-derful home-made products as a jam made with apples, figs, almonds and tomatoes, and a hot, herb-flavoured olive oil for garnishing pizzas.

'Prince Curnonsky' (the *nom de plume* of Maurice Sailland), one of the great gastronomes of this century, believed that no other part of France was so rich in natural products as Provence. The wealth of its herbs is matched by that of its fruit and vegetables, which makes the region the foremost market garden in France. Meat might be limited mainly to mutton and pork, but the region's fish and sea-food are exceptionally varied, as Quiqueran de Beaujeu and later. Tobias Smollett both emphasized. The ways of dealing with all this produce are befitting to a region of such geographical and cultural diversity: the cuisine changes not just between coast and hinterland, but between one town and the other. Foreign influences have greatly contributed to this gastronomic variety: the Italians in particular have made an impact on local cuisine, and not just on that of the former County of Nice, but, through the large presence of Italian workers in Marseille, Toulon and elsewhere, on Provençal food generally. The North Africans have added another exotic element, and J.-F. Reboul, the author of the first major book on Provençal food, *La Cuisinière provençale* (first edition, 1895), included *couscous* among his Pro-vençal recipes because this had become so common in the region. Similarly, among the Nice specialities which Jacques Médecin writes about in his *Cuisine niçoise* (English edition, 1983), is a dish of mutton, raisins and pine-nuts which was introduced into the city in 1913 by a large colony of Armenian expatriates, and was soon adopted by even the most traditional milieux.

Like so many other aspects of Provence, the subject of Provençal food is surrounded by myth. The earliest attempts to define a dis-tinctively Provençal cuisine date only from the late nineteenth century, and can be seen as part of that romantic nationalist movement led by Mistral. To Mistral, food played as important a part as literature and folklore in the promotion of a national identity. He devoted much of his *Le Trésor de la Félibrige* to the description of Provençal dishes; he persuaded Reboul to translate into Provençal the names of the dishes given in *La Cuisinière provençale*; he was a close friend of the greatest cook Provence, and perhaps even France, has produced, Auguste Escoffier. Mistral's belief in a traditional Provençal cuisine going back to the time of the Greeks and Romans, and surviving throughout the centuries of French domination, is as misleading as his sentimental view of medieval, independent Provence.

Extensive research on Provençal food of the fourteenth and fifteenth centuries has shown that the food of the peasantry was the same as that of the rest of Europe, and that even the special dishes eaten by the aristocracy and the clergy had an international and not specifically Provençal character. Olive oil was used only for the cooking of fish and eggs, and was supplemented by walnut oil (Provence still ranks with the Dordogne as the greatest producer of walnut oil in France). The tomato, which today is a vital component of any dish *à la Provençale*, was not of course brought to Europe until the sixteenth century; to Provence it in fact came later still, and, thanks to the *mistral*, it was not widely cultivated here until after 1850. Whenever you read of a 'traditional' Provençal dish, you can generally be sure that the tradition in question goes back no further than the nineteenth century.

Moreover, most of these dishes – the sort that you find in restaurants and cookery books – bear little relation to the everyday food of the Provençal people. Until comparatively recently meat and even fish was never eaten more than once a week, and often only on feast days or special occasions: at the beginning of this century the two butcher's shops in the Vaucluse town of L'Isle-sur-la-Sorgue were open only around Christmas and Easter. The main sustenance of both the countryfolk and the urban dweller was provided by soup and vegetables: vegetables were nearly always boiled and served with vinaigrette, and the water in which they had been cooked served as the basis of the soup. The Toulon and Marseillais worker of the nineteenth century could rarely afford olive oil, and used corn or sunflower oil instead. Local fruit, though so abundant, was too expensive for the poor city-dweller, who tended to buy the cheaper and inferior fruit from Algeria; the one cheap Provençal fruit, the melon, was often avoided because it was a notorious source of dysentery. To the immigrant Italian worker even the diet of his fellow workers, with its occasional extravagances such as meat, fish, or slices of cheese, seemed a luxury. Like many of the poorer inhabitants of the interior, he survived almost exclusively on pasta, flavoured with herbs or meagre portions of vegetables; the water used to cook this was poured afterwards into the empty plates, swirled around to mop up what remained of the frugal sauce, and then drunk.

The famous Lyonnais restaurateur Paul Bocuse wrote that 'Provençal food is amusing, but it will never be *haute cuisine*.' Bocuse is right in suggesting that even the most special Provençal dishes, the ones that actually benefit from the region's wealth of natural produce, have a fundamental simplicity. However, we no longer share the snobbish view that the greatest food is necessarily the richest and most complex. The cookery writer Elizabeth David, who has done more to influence present-day attitudes towards food than anyone else of her generation, made her name with *Mediterranean Food* (1950), much of which deals with Provence. In this she made a case for 'honest cooking' which had nothing to do with 'the sham Grande Cuisine of the International Palace Hotel'. She has always believed that simple food is by no means primitive food, and that food can be civilized without being over-civilized. Provençal food, with its simplicity, reliance on fresh vegetables, and absence of butter and cream sauces, meets many of today's criteria for healthy eating and is in accordance with the principles of '*nouvelle cuisine*'. I feel I should add that anyone who tries cooking the dishes listed below should not do so in too respectful a manner. I do not believe, like some purists, that making a small alteration to a 'classic' dish such as a *bouillabaisse* is like changing a masterpiece by Cézanne. From the time of Mistral, nationalists and gastronomes alike have talked about the 'correct' way of doing certain Provençal dishes, and in so doing have often invested them with a bogus mystique. Authenticity is a highly questionable concept is an essentially humble cuisine such as that of Provence, especially since almost all the region's famous dishes exist in numerous versions. And surely, as Elizabeth David suggested, is not one of the charms of simple food the scope which it allows for 'brilliant improvisation'?

Any introduction to the gastronomic specialities of Provence should perhaps begin with *aïoli*, which is often called the 'butter of Provence'. A mayonnaise made with at least two cloves of garlic per person (a litre of olive oil will need up to fifteen cloves), *aïoli* was for Mistral both a symbol of Provence and a test to sort out the true lover of the region from the half-hearted and the wimp; according to him it even kept away the flies. 'Around a good solid *aïoli*,' he once said, 'fragrant, gilded like a thread of gold, tell me where are those men of Provence who do not recognize each other as brothers . . . ?' Charles Maurras, a well-known writer from Martigues who supported the Germans during the Second World War, was clearly a true male and a true Provençal, for he did not consider any meal complete until he had had at least two or three soupspoons of the stuff. Traditionally *aïoli* is served on a special occasion as an accompaniment to boiled food, such as vegetables, mutton, eggs and salt cod. An *aïoli garni*, as this is called, is a meal in itself, although a dish of *aïoli* and snails often forms a separate course during a Christmas feast.

A normal Provençal meal begins with salad or soup, though sometimes this might be preceded by simple *hors d'oeuvre* such as *saucisson* (dried sausage). The most famous *saucisson* of the region is that of Arles; it is very popular with tourists, who perhaps do not realize that it is made of donkey. Many Provençals consider that a finer *saucisson* is that of the Basses-Alpes town of Sault, which is famous generally for its charcuterie.

An *hors d'oeuvre* more special to Provence is *tapenade*, a paste made of oil and crushed olives. *Tapéno* means capers in Provençal, and a good home-made *tapenade* will also have in it capers, tunny fish, anchovies and lemon juice. *Anchoïade* is anchovies pounded with oil and vinegar; as an *hors d'oeuvre* it is generally eaten with raw celery, and when spread over a stick of French bread it used to be a popular lunchtime snack with Marseille workers. *Pissala* is a more refined, Niçois version of this, and involves marinading the fish with thyme, cloves, peppercorns and bayleaves, and putting the whole mixture through a fine sieve; if made properly, writes Médecin, the fish used must be *palaïa* (small fry) of sardines and anchovies, and this should be steeped for at least one month in the other ingredients, renewing the oil and stirring the paste each day. *Pissala* serves often as the base for the *pissaladière*, a pizza of olives, anchovies and a generous helping of cooked onions; the dough version of this is sold in slices at street corners, while the pastry version tends only to be served at home, where it makes an excellent *hors d'oeuvre*.

Another Provençal fish paste is *brandade*, a creamy mixture of cooked salt cod, olive oil and milk, the whole slowly amalgamated as in a mayonnaise, but over a gentle flame. Garlic, parsley, lemon juice, or even truffles can be added to this mixture, which is often served on fried *croûtons* of bread; a rather bland *brandade* sold in jars is marketed at Nîmes. *Poutargue*, a speciality of Martigues, is the caviar of Provence, and consists of the eggs of the thin-lipped grey mullet, which have been washed, salted and dried in a shady place. Eulogized by Mistral in his *Calendau*, *poutargue*, according to Charles Maurras, was offered to someone as a sign of respect and friendship.

For a humbler *hors d'oeuvre* you should try *socca*, which is a porridge-like mixture made with water and chick-pea flour and then baked or cut into slices; in *panisses* the mixture is deep-fried in oil. The shouts of street vendors selling piping-hot *socca* at lunchtime were once regularly heard in the main towns of Provence.

One of the most basic and, at one time, common Provençal soups, is the *aigo-boulido*, which literally means boiled water. The water is boiled with crushed garlic and sage, and then is tipped over bread soaked in oil. Mistral got away with the addition of nutmeg, but other refinements, such as grated gruyère cheese and the breaking in of an egg at the last minute, have been frowned upon by purists and considered too 'bourgeois'. The staple of the poor, *aigo-boulido* inspired the Provençal proverb, 'L'aigo boulido sauvo la vido' ('boiled water saves life'), to which was later added the ironic refrain, 'Au bout d'un Tèms, tuio li gènt' ('after a while it kills off people'). While very insubstantial as a daily dish, *aigo-boulido* has been considered the perfect food both for the invalid and for those suffering the after-effects of a Provençal fête.

Soupe au pistou is as hearty and filling as *aigo-boulido* is thin and unsatisfying. Italian in origin, and derived from the vegetable soup known as *minestrone*, *soupe au pistou* is now one of the great dishes of the region. A meal in itself, it is best made in the summer, when fresh and white beans replace the dried ones used in winter. The soup's other vegetables usually include courgettes, string beans, tomatoes, potatoes and onions; but whatever vegetables are put in, the important thing is that they are plentiful and that the final result is very thick. Vermicelli pasta is usually added, and occasionally grated cheese; the one essential is the *pistou* itself, a Provençal variant of the Italian basil, garlic, pine-nut and olive-oil sauce known as *pesto*.

Unlike *pesto*, *pistou* is used only for this soup, and never for pasta alone.

To many Provençals, the one true salad is made from wild ingredients from the garden such as dandelions; another, strong-flavoured, salad common here is the *salade frisée*, comprising curly endives and capers. The one salad for which Provence is generally remembered is the *salade niçoise*, which has become a standard international dish often bearing little resemblance to its prototype. The genuine *salade niçoise* has hard-boiled eggs, tomatoes (cut in quarters), anchovies, cucumber, spring onion, and perhaps broad beans or small globe artichokes, depending on the time of the year. For Médecin the replacement of tunny fish with anchovies is just about acceptable, even though in the past tunny would rarely have been added because it was too expensive. But 'Never, never,' he begs, 'include boiled potato or any other boiled vegetable.' A *salade niçoise* served in a large bun is called a *pan-bagnat*, one of the most popular and ubiquitous of all Provençal snacks. The words *pan-bagnat* mean 'soaked bread', and delicious though this snack is, it is one liable to leave you with a trail of vinaigrette down your front.

Boiled vegetables dressed with oil and vinegar tend to accompany the main dish. Giono thought that chick peas were the vegetable which best brought out the flavour of the olive oil. Another very popular vegetable in Provence is asparagus, which is traditionally the speciality of the village of Lauris near Lourmarin; the asparagus from Lauris was originally eaten when white, until Escoffier persuaded the local growers not to pick the vegetable until the stalks had gone green, a state which he found his sophisticated clientèle generally preferred. The most common Provençal vegetable is the *blette* or Swiss chard, and indeed the people of Nice eat so much of this that they are sometimes called the *caga-bléia*, or 'chard-shitters'.

At the other, refined end of the gastronomic scale is the truffle, an underground black mushroom associated mainly with the region of Périgord but known also as the 'diamond of Provence'. It grows here in the Vaucluse, in particular on the southern slopes of Mont Ventoux. The legend goes that there once lived on these slopes an old woman called La Rabasse, who survived purely through collecting dead wood. Huntsmen would take pity on her and give her some of the birds that they had caught, but she only accepted the live ones, which she looked

1a. The 'Miroir aux oiseaux', a much painted corner of Martigues, the 'Venice of Provence'.

1b. The west portal of the twelfth-century priory church of Ganagobie. Christ in Majesty is shown above the twelve Apostles.

2a. The fourteenth-century Saunerie
Gate at Manosque.

2b. General view of Bargemon.

3a. The duct of the Roman aqueduct at Barbegal.

3b. The highest point of the Fort de Buoux. The duct and basin were possibly used by the Ligurians for sacrificial purposes.

4. The main entrance to the fortified town of Entrevaux.

5. The coast near Cassis, in between the Calanques de Port-Pin and d'En-Vau.

6. Street scene, Saorge.

7a. The author's moped taking a rest on top of the pass of La Bonette. Nice seems very distant from this bleak scene.

7b. View of Saorge from the N 204.

8a. Sculpted group of the Crucifixion at La Sainte-Baume.

8b. On the Île de Port-Cros.

9a. The twelfth-century priory of Notre-Dame-de-Salagon.

9b. The eighteenth-century Château de Sauvan.

10. The cliffs at Cap Canaille, with a distant view of Cassis.

11a. The seventeenth-century Château de Barbentane.

11b. Fourth of July celebrations in Lacoste.

12a. Apse of the twelfth-century
priory church of Carluc.

12b. 'Sur le pont d'Avignon . . .'
view of Avignon from the twelfth-
century Pont Saint-Bénézet, with the
Petit Palais in the background.

13. View of the Grand Canyon of the Verdon in between the Chalet de la Maline and the Point Sublime.

14. The four remaining columns of the Roman temple at Riez.

15a. View of the fourteenth-century ramparts at Avignon from the Boulevard Limbert.

15b. A corner of the folk-museum at Sainte-Étienne-de-Tinée.

16. The twelfth-century chapel of Saint-Gabriel.

after until they were better and then released. One bird, in gratitude for having been saved, told her a secret. She was to take some charcoal and plant it as if it were a seed next to an oak tree. In December she was to return to this tree, where she would see a patch of bare soil with a black mouth; digging underneath this she would find the charcoal grown bigger and edible. To this day a truffle in Provence is called a *rabasse*, and those who hunt for it *rabasseurs*. Moreover, the presence near an oak tree of black earth around which no grass or other plants have grown is a sure sign that there is a truffle underneath.

The tomato is the one vegetable, after garlic, which people always associate with Provence. *Tomates à la provençale* are tomatoes cut in half, covered in oil and diced garlic and parsley, and cooked under the grill. Alternatively they can be hollowed out and their pulp added to a cooked mixture (later bound together with an egg) of onion, garlic, parsley, and spinach or chard; the hollowed tomatoes are then stuffed with this mixture, sprinkled with breadcrumbs and put into the oven. Another common way of preparing the tomato in Provence is to stew it with peppers, onions, courgettes and aubergines to make a *ratatouille*, a dish of Nice origin, the fame of which has spread well beyond the confines of the region. Less well known is the *tian*, which Mistral called the national dish of Provence. This is named after the deep terracotta gratin dish into which are put a mixture of eggs and assorted vegetables. The exact make-up of this varies considerably, but, unlike the *ratatouille*, it is a main dish in itself and not an accompaniment to meat.

The Italian workers who came over to Provence in the early nineteenth century were at first teased for their constant eating of pasta. However, after 1840, pasta began to be widely adopted by the Provençals themselves and its popularity soon rivalled that of the *tian*; Provençal doctors started worrying that children were being given too much of it. Pasta dishes as prepared in Provence, though differing slightly from district to district, never achieved the sophistication of those of Italy, and were treated mainly as an extremely cheap way of feeding oneself.

The small folk museum of the Alpine village of Saint-Étienne-de-Tinée has a group of photographs and utensils which give a fascinating insight into the pasta-eating habits of this remote valley bordering on

Italy. The photographs are of some of the older villagers who continue to this day to make fresh pasta, using the rollers, long wooden boards, cutters and other objects on display in the museum. The simplest forms of pasta are known in the local dialect as *lous andeirouls*, in which the pasta dough is kneaded with a small amount of water and then roughly cut into small pieces which are often cooked with slices of potato. A slightly more sophisticated dish is *lous crous*, or 'little ears'. The pasta dough, made in this case with flour, eggs and walnut oil, is rolled into long sticks which are divided into half-inch pieces, each of which is then flattened out into 'little ears' with the finger; sometimes potato is incorporated into the dough, creating a pasta similar in type to *gnocchi*, another speciality of this district and known here as *lous gnocs*. These pasta dishes are served either with a tomato or garlic sauce, or sometimes just with salt and pepper or even a few leaves of mint; elsewhere in Provence you might find anchovies used, or chard, or a mixture of sage and rosemary; you will never find the complex meat sauces favoured in such places as Bologna. For a special occasion in the Tinée valley, notably Christmas Eve, *las raviolos* (ravioli) will be made. The pasta is cut into rounds, filled with a vegetable (usually chard), shaped into what are called 'gendarme hats', and served with a sauce made with walnuts and bread dipped into the cooking water.

In Italy pasta is always a dish on its own, but in Provence it is often an accompaniment to a beef stew. *Estouffade de boeuf* is a dish of the Camargue and involves beef simmered for many hours with tomatoes, olives and red wine; in *daube à la provençale* the beef is combined with wine, garlic, onions, herbs, orange peel, carrots and anything else readily available, such as smoky bacon or even pigs' trotters. A now forgotten stew is *la chouio*, a favourite dish of the Rhône boatsmen and referred to by Mistral in his *Chant du Rhône*: it includes beef, capers and anchovies. Many Provençal families keep an old earthenware pot specially for cooking beef stews in. This pot is never washed, but simply dried over a flame: the brownish crust of sauce which is formed impregnates the cracked surface and enhances the flavour of later stews. Colette had one such pot in her Saint-Tropez home, and regarded it 'almost as a sacred vessel'. Jean-Paul Clébert has a sorry tale to tell of an old '*daubière*' lent to a Parisian couple and returned immaculately clean and shining. For this reason Parisians and other foreigners are often dissuaded from entering a Provençal kitchen.

Pork and mutton are far more common meats in Provence than beef, which is perhaps why they are not treated with quite the same respect. At best they are just grilled and flavoured with herbs. Sheep's tripe stuffed with salt pork cooked in tomatoes and red wine forms the 'packages' of a well-known Marseillais dish, *pieds et paquets*; the *pieds* are supposedly calves' trotters, but these are never found in the dish today. Thanks to the Provençal love of hunting, game can often be had in the region. During the boar-hunting season in the autumn, whole wild boars or *sangliers* hang in the butcher's shops as if in some still-life painting by Rubens or Jordaens; at other times of the year grotesque chunks of the animal fill up the freezers of super-markets. The boar, a very rich meat, is always served in stews made with a heavy wine-based sauce. In complete contrast to the boar in terms of size, delicacy of taste and digestibility, is the *grive* or thrush (a species protected in England); it is wrapped here in bacon and sautéed with tomatoes and crushed olives. Also good is the *perdrix aux lentilles*, partridge cooked with lentils.

The Catholic tradition of eating fish on Fridays created problems for those living in remote parts of the Provençal hinterland. In the days before refrigerators, wagons carrying fresh fish would leave the coast and travel around the interior for periods of up to several weeks; though protected by blocks of ice, the fish would usually be rotting by the time it was sold and would have to be disguised by strongly flavoured sauces. Salted or wind-dried cod (stockfish) did not create the same problems as fresh fish, but none the less needed similarly strong sauces to make it interesting. Cod is not a Mediterranean fish, but it has been exported in a preserved state from Sweden since the Middle Ages and from America since the eighteenth century. It was the ideal convenience food, and has always been (both in the interior and along the coast) the most popular fish in Provence. Among the better ways of cooking salted cod (*morue*) are frying it in garlic and tomatoes, or covering it with spinach and anchovies. *Morue en raito* is a traditional Provençal Christmas dish in which the cod is cooked in a rather overpowering sauce of capers, tomatoes and red wine. Even less to foreigners' tastes is the Niçois treatment of stockfish or *es-tocaficada*: the fish, together with its guts, is stewed in eau-de-vie, onion, garlic, olives, potatoes, peppers and herbs. The Niçois are so proud of this potent concoction that they have named a local gastronomic organization after it.

So vast is the range of fresh fish available in Provence that the names of many of them will mean little if translated into English. The same is true of the region's shellfish, and a visit to the shellfish market in Marseille is an extraordinary experience. Just how you eat many of the bizarrely shaped molluscs on sale here is a mystery to me, and should you wish to find out, I can only recommend that you turn to the opening section of Reboul's *La Cuisinière provençale*. As an example of one of the shellfish, I quote Reboul's description of something called a sea-squirt (*violet*):

> This gastronomic eccentricity is only eaten live, and its sticky substance is not to everyone's taste. None the less it has its enthusiasts. The shape of the animal is like that of a closed purse, with a corrugated surface and an earthy, generally reddish colour. The edible part is inside and can only be obtained by splitting open the animal to its full length; this has to be done with the aid of a good knife, the horny substance which surrounds it being very hard and rough.

For Colette the finest way of preparing Mediterranean fish was to grill it over red-hot charcoal and cover it with good oil, vinegar, and herbs. One of the simplest and tastiest of the fish specialities served in the fancier Provençal establishments is sea perch grilled over a bed of fennel stalks (*loup au fenouil*). But most people who come to Provence will not be happy until they have tasted one of the region's more elaborate fish dishes such as *soupe de poissons* or a *bouillabaisse*. The assorted fish contained in the *soupe de poissons* generally include spider crabs, sea eel, and the *rascasse* or scorpion fish; these and other fish are cooked in water together with saffron, tomatoes, leeks and garlic, then sieved and put back into the broth; vermicelli is usually added later, and the soup is served with grated gruyère or parmesan and a *rouille*, an excellent sauce comprising sweet peppers, garlic, soaked bread, and some of the liquid from the soup.

A certain amount of mystique is attached to the *soupe de poissons*. The inhabitants of Saint-Tropez, for instance, claim that the soup can be properly made only in their town, because it requires certain fish exclusive to the gulf of Saint-Tropez; the gastronome Waverley Root had to wait around the town for days before these obscure fish were found and the soup could be made. The passions that this soup arouses, however, are as nothing in comparison to those provoked by the *bouillabaisse*. One of the issues at stake is which town makes the finest *bouillabaisse*. Excellent versions of the dish are prepared by almost every coastal town from Marseille to Menton, though the true Provençal will always insist that the only real versions are those found between Marseille and Toulon. Even narrowing down the contest to these last two towns, it is impossible to decide upon a winner. The Marseillais version is the one best known to tourists, and the town's claim to have invented the dish can perhaps be seen as a compensation for its having failed to father the 'Marseillaise'. Others swear by the Toulon version, which contains, horror of horrors, potatoes.

Ford Madox Ford summed up rather too succinctly the dispute as to which ingredients should be used in the *bouillabaisse*: 'It should be premised that there exist three schools of *bouillabaisse* – those who sanction langouste (lobster), those who sanction potatoes and those who sanction neither – though very occasionally you will find both together in the *bouillabaisse* of quite famous practitioners.' I shall not bore the reader with a description of the many other schools of *bouillabaisse* that in fact exist. The only consensus of opinion is that the seasoning of the water in which the fish is cooked must include saffron, that the many types of fish or sea-food used should all be spanking fresh from the Mediterranean (it is useless to try to prepare this dish in London), and that of these fish the one essential is the *rascasse*.

The *rascasse* is a revoltingly ugly fish but it is one with a legendary reputation. The Marseillais poet Paul Méry wrote a poem about *bouillabaisse* in which he suggested that the *rascasse* absorbed through its skin all the aromatic herbs of the cliffs by which it feeds. The *rascasse* is actually a fish with relatively little flavour, and it is never a dish on its own; the vital role which it plays in a *bouillabaisse* is dependent on the belief that – like a kiwi fruit in a fruit salad – it has the capacity of bringing out the flavours in other fish. Because its cheeks are meant to be its tastiest part, it is always cooked with its head on, so that those eating it can fully appreciate its ugliness. All the fish in a *bouillabaisse*, by the way, are served separate from the stock, which is poured into soup bowls over slices of toast, accompanied by *rouille*.

The *bouillabaisse*, it is sometimes said, was invented by Venus ostensibly as a treat for her husband Vulcan, but really so as to put him into a deep sleep so that she could slip off with one of her lovers (a saffron-flavoured fish soup was considered a soporific in antiquity). Méry believed instead that the dish was first thought up by an eighteenth-century abbess from Marseille, looking for something new to give the nuns of her convent on a Friday. The origins of the dish are probably rather more prosaic. Like the *soupe de poissons*, the *bouillabaisse* was almost certainly a dish devised by fishermen to find a use for all the small, unsaleable fish which they picked up. By the early nineteenth century this humble fare had become *haute cuisine*, and the poor people who used to eat it could no longer afford to do so. Today the dish, however well done, does not seem worth its exorbitant expense. Tourists will always be seen entering the restaurants around the Marseille harbour that specialize almost solely in *bouillabaisse*; but many of those who go in with high expectations come away disappointed. One such person was the travel writer Percy Allen, who, as soon as he reached Marseille, rushed into a restaurant to try the dish. 'I may as well tell you,' he wrote in *Impressions of Provence* (1910), 'that the famous Provençal dish did not appeal to me as a "manger exquis". A lobster and something else upon a dish; and, accompanying it, a vessel that was a compromise between a sauce-boat and a soup tureen, many islands of bread floating in a lake of yellow gravy. I have not ordered *bouillabaisse* again. It is best to have one's ideals unrealized.'

Charles Maurras, a passionate enthusiast of *bouillabaisse*, was shocked that this 'royal and imperial' dish was thought by some to be inferior to what he described as the admirable but humble *bourride*. The *bourride* consists of any firm-fleshed white fish cooked in a fish stock and served with a sauce containing a mixture of the stock and *aïoli*. An eighteenth-century Provençal poet, Jean-Baptiste Germain, devoted a poem to it, *Bourrido dei Diéu*, and in this described how the gods, tired of Olympus, would every so often descend on Marseille to savour the *bourride*. For Elizabeth David, the *bourride* is far better than the *bouillabaisse* and 'perhaps the finest fish dish of Provence'.

The best way to end a meal in Provence is with the excellent fruit of the region. The little town of Le Thor near Carpentras is famous for its table grapes; oranges and lemons come from around Nice; cherries are a speciality of Lauris and Lourmarin; the finest figs are traditionally from Marseille, and the best prunes from Brignoles. The great melon centre is Cavaillon, and in the height of summer delicious honeydew melons can still be bought for practically nothing (though without the dysentery). Alexandre Dumas had a passion for these melons, and when he read once that the library at Cavaillon could not afford to buy his books, he immediately offered to give them some, on condition that they would send to him in Paris twelve melons a year; this the library accepted.

The cheeses of Provence are made almost exclusively from goat's milk; an authentic Provençal cheese platter brought to you in a restaurant is likely to consist entirely of small rounds of goat cheese flavoured with garlic, thyme, bay and so on. Sweets are not a great Provençal speciality, and the few ones distinctive to the region are rarely to be found in a restaurant. Pies would be made for special occasions, and often given to the local baker to put in his oven. The *tarte de citron*, a lemon pie, is the best known and most sophisticated of these; but equally good, if of a more rustic appeal, are those made either of sweetened squash, spinach or chard. Honey, often flavoured with lavender, is sold throughout the hinterland, and is used as the binding element of an excellent walnut pie made in the Tinée valley. The oil-based bread known as *fougasse* is usually salted and speckled with pieces of bacon, but it can also be coated in sugar. A sweet version exists of 'little ears' (see page 194), the pasta dough being sprinkled with sugar after having been deep-fried in oil. Almond biscuits called *calissons* are a celebrated product of Aix, while Apt has been famous since the sixteenth century for its jams and candied fruits. Among the great admirers of these fruit products were Catherine de Medici and the Marquis de Sade.

Despite Ford Madox Ford's passion for Provence, he could never raise much enthusiasm for the local food. 'The traveller in Provence,' he wrote, 'will never, I feel sure, be able to enter an unknown town and go into any restaurant with any certainty of good food.' This is no longer true today; the general standard of restaurants in the region has improved enormously in recent years, and you are now as likely to eat well in Provence as you are in any other area of France. Yet if you come here expecting always to find restaurants specializing in good, simple Provençal fare, you might well be disappointed. Most restaurants here – including the very finest, such as the Oasis at La Napoule, the Beaumanière at Les Baux and the Chantecler at Nice – serve only a few dishes that can be called typically Provençal. The places calling themselves 'oustalou' and producing food mainly labelled 'à la Provençale' tend in fact to be the worst, the food being not only inauthentic but also poor and fussy. Other than being lucky enough to eat in someone's home, the nearest you are likely to get to a true Provençal cuisine is by going to one of those cafés or modest country restaurants catering for large parties of hunters. The Basses-Alpes district of Sault is famous for these, and if you go to one of them during the hunting and mushroom season, you will almost certainly be outstandingly fed.

Ever since the nineteenth century, when tourists started coming to Provence in large numbers, restaurateurs have had to adapt their cuisine to meet the demands of foreigners, in particular the English. The region was constantly criticized for its food, the main sources of complaint being the lack of good dairy produce, the oiliness of everything, and the over-generous use of garlic. Countess Blessington's stay at Aix-en-Provence in 1780 was partially ruined by her inability to procure good cream or milk 'or at least any that is palatable'. For her, goat's milk utterly destroyed the flavour of tea and coffee, while the butter she was once brought (it had come from a long distance) had to be sent back because 'its odour was really offensive'. Characteristically, the only cow in Aix-en-Provence was owned by an English family who had settled here; when, over one and a half centuries later, a Hollywood actress moved to the Riviera, she had to have a cow specially imported from England.

Augustus Hare, after considerable searching, finally discovered in the centre of Menton 'a restaurant from where we get a dinner which is very tolerable, after it has been stripped of its oils and garlic and has had some extra cooking bestowed upon it by our own servants'. Hare's numerous compatriots, who had come to the Riviera for the sake of their health, believed that Provençal food, if left in its native state, was not just unpleasant but positively dangerous. C. Williams, in *The Climate of the South as Suited to Invalids* (1870), wrote that 'the cooking, except in the best hotels, is not of that plain wholesome character which best agrees with the delicate appetite of an invalid, and often contains a large amount of grease and oil, which in a warm climate tends to produce biliousness and liver disturbance'. Fortunately there was a remedy to this. 'By strict injunction to the cooks, this objectionable quality in the food may be corrected . . .'

Garlic was perhaps the main source of discontent, and one which united all the visitors to Provence, including the French themselves. The prejudice against it was based largely on ignorance. Sarah Bernhardt, for instance, had a great dislike of garlic and had no idea that her favourite chef, Escoffier, always speared a clove of garlic on the knife with which he beat up eggs; to the end she remained ignorant of his secret, and found that no one else made scrambled eggs better than he did. Two other great enthusiasts of Escoffier, a Russian prince and his mistress, regularly ordered from Escoffier a dish of saddle of lamb served with a Provençal sauce. One day they asked Escoffier for the exact ingredients of the sauce, and were horrified to find that it contained garlic. 'But I hate garlic,' the woman said, 'and I cannot imagine how it can be used in a first class restaurant.' 'But Madam,' Escoffier replied, 'since you enjoyed the sauce so much . . .' As late as 1961, Elizabeth Fearon in *The Marquis, the Mayonnaise and Me* could write that 'there is more prejudice attached to garlic than to any other item in Continental Cookery'. Fearon herself ran a boarding house in Cannes in the 1950s, and in her cooking had to put up with complaints about most things Provençal, ranging from garlic to olive oil and even to herbs (one woman told her on arrival that she could only accept parsley as a flavouring). Most of her clients, including the parsley woman, eventually began to come round to local tastes. 'However,' she said, 'I put a firm limit on culinary adventures and refuse to shock them with too Provençal a table.'

The presence on the coast of wealthy and aristocratic foreigners led to the setting up here of some of the most exclusive restaurants in Europe. By one of those great paradoxes of which Provence is full, Provence, the home of simple cooking, became host to a culinary tradition which was diametrically opposed to its own, *haute cuisine.*

Someone who helped greatly to enhance the gastronomic reputation of the Riviera was Henry Gordon Bennett, the eccentric proprietor of the *Paris Herald Tribune* and the man who sent Stanley to search for

Livingstone. Bennett, who had a villa at Beaulieu, founded two of the earliest great restaurants of the Riviera, La Réserve at Beaulieu and Ciro's at Monte-Carlo. Moreover, if any other of the Riviera restaurants won his approval it was assured a great success, for he would write about it at great length in his paper. One such restaurant was that of the Hôtel de Paris in Monaco, which had at one time a chef called Henri Charpentier, later to achieve fame as a restaurateur in America. As a fourteen-year-old chef at the Hôtel de Paris, Charpentier accidentally invented one of France's most famous desserts. Edward VII, then Prince of Wales, had come to dinner, and Charpentier had prepared for him a pancake to be covered at the last moment with curaçao, kirsch and maraschino. By mistake the liqueurs caught alight. Charpentier thought the dish was ruined, but on tasting it he realized that the burning had improved the flavour. The prince was impressed by the dish; asking if it had a name, he was told that it was called a 'crêpe princesse'. He then wondered if this could be changed to 'crêpe Suzette' in honour of the woman companion whom he was with.

Edward VII played an important part in launching the international career of the greatest chef to have worked on the Riviera, Auguste Escoffier. Escoffier, 'the king of cooks, and the cook of kings', was born in 1846 at Villeneuve-Loubet, a small town between Nice and Cagnes. The house of his birth is now a museum devoted both to him and to the 'art of cookery'. His father was a blacksmith, and on an outside wall of the house can be seen an iron ring where the father used to tie up the horses to be shod. Aged thirteen, Escoffier went to work in his uncle's restaurant at Nice, and in 1865 he was appointed *commis rôtisseur* to Le Petit Moulin Rouge in Paris. During the Franco-Prussian War he served as *chef-de-cuisine* to the Rhine army at Metz, after which he began dividing his life between Paris and the Riviera. In Paris he now worked as main chef to Le Petit Moulin Rouge, which had become one of Paris's most fashionable restaurants. It was here, during the 1870s, that he first met the future Edward VII, who was to be a life-long enthusiast of his cooking.

In the early 1890s Escoffier formed the most important partnership of his career, with César Ritz, a brilliant young hotelier and another protégé of the Prince of Wales. Ritz called in Escoffier to work as head cook at the Grand Hotel in Monte-Carlo and, in the summer months, at the National Hotel in Lucerne. The Grand Hotel was a great rival of the Hôtel de Paris, and its reputation was much enhanced in 1881 when the Prince of Wales chose to stay there. The prince told Ritz that there was not a single hotel in London where one could eat well, let alone 'dine as Gods as one does here'. Ritz, with Escoffier as his chef, was encouraged to take over the management of the Savoy Hotel in London, and in 1890 to open his own London establishment, the Carlton. Escoffier remained based in London for nearly twenty years, leaving shortly after the Carlton was badly damaged by fire. While the fire had lasted, a large group of spectators had anxiously waited outside, fearful that Europe's most famous chef had been killed. But Escoffier eventually emerged from the blazing building, calmly announcing to the assembled crowd, 'The thousands of chickens I have roasted here did not succeed in taking their revenge.' He retired to his villa in Monte-Carlo in 1919 and died there in 1935, having enjoyed the longest career in the history of cookery.

The Escoffier Museum at Villeneuve-Loubet is a charming place. The room in which he was born has been turned into a typical Provençal dining room of the nineteenth century, while the kitchen has been furnished with all the traditional utensils used in Provençal and Niçois cooking. Elsewhere is a 'culinary pantheon', with photographs and other documents relating to the great cooks of France, including Eugène Herbodeau and Paul Thalamas, two pupils of Escoffier and the authors of his biography. Throughout the house are exhibits testifying to the wide range of Escoffier's achievements. As a child he loved to draw and paint, and in later life he developed a passion for sugar and wax-flower decorations, the subject of his first book, *Les Fleurs de cire* (1885); in the cellar of the museum is a permanent collection of works made of sugar-drops and boiled sugar. Escoffier was also a very practical person and gave much thought to the subject of kitchen utensils; he invented, among many other things, a device for stoning fruit and olives (this is exhibited in the museum), and introduced the sauté pan into England. His practicality made him one of the first to appreciate the value of tinned food, and it was through his efforts that the manufacturing of tinned tomatoes developed on an industrial scale. The library of the museum contains his complete writings, which include, in addition to his culinary bible, *Guide culinaire* (1903), a number of philanthropic tracts featuring proposals for social insurance and for financing rest homes. In another room is displayed a collection of his menus and other records of his famous culinary creations. One of the panels has a photograph of the singer Nellie Melba, signed by her and inscribed 'to the inventor of the "Pêche Melba"'. Escoffier had devised the dish as a surprise for her following her first night as Elsa in *Lohengrin*. He had served peaches and vanilla ice cream in between the wings of a swan carved in ice and coated with *sucre filé*. The dish had first been known as *les pêches du cygne* (swan peaches), but was later given its more familiar name of peach melba after Escoffier had added a raspberry purée.

Right to the end of his career Escoffier never forgot the cuisine of his childhood, and in his cookery books and menus are a number of dishes clearly inspired by those of his native region. But his debt to Provence goes much deeper than this, and is reflected in his fundamental attitude towards cooking. Memories of simple Provençal cuisine, combined with his experiences of having to produce good food with limited means for the French army at Metz, made him highly critical of the extravagances and fussiness of other cooks. The menus of his exhibited at Villeneuve-Loubet might now seem to us long and elaborate, but at the time they were short and engagingly simple. *Haute cuisine* was for him not a question of showing off but had to take into account the enjoyment and stomach capacities of those who ate the food. While his artistic side made him enjoy sugar-flowers, silver wings, and other such decorative touches, he did not believe, like Carême and all the other great chefs up to his day, that the presentation of food was of the utmost importance, and that the work of a cook was identical to that of a display artist. More important to him was the role of nutrition, and the importance of having easily digestible ingredients. He abandoned the then common practice of preparing all meat in flour, and favoured a light veal stock over flour-based sauces.

Outstanding chefs have continued to work on the Riviera since Escoffier's day, and the place remains one of the most sophisticated gastronomic districts of Europe. One of its best-known chefs today is Roger Vergé, who in 1969 bought a sixteenth-century olive-oil mill outside Mougins and turned this into one of the famous restaurants of

France, Le Moulin de Mougins; Vergé is also the author of a highly successful cookery book, *The Cuisine of the Sun* (1979).

A cook considered by some to be superior even to Vergé is Jacques Maximin, who first came to Provence to work as an assistant in Vergé's restaurant in 1977, when he was twenty-nine. Maximin was persuaded to take charge of the Chantecler Restaurant in the Hôtel Negresco in Nice, where he remains still. The dynamic hotelier who brought him here, Michel Palmer, had been made manager of the hotel in 1964 and had revived its reputation as one of Europe's most luxurious hotels. The new decoration might not be to everyone's taste, but no one disputes his foresight in appointing Maximin as head cook.

Two years after coming here, Maximin entered the notoriously difficult competitive examinations for 'le Meilleur Ouvrier de France', and won. His cooking, unlike that of Vergé, has not yet been awarded the Michelin three-star rating, but through no fault of Maximin's: Michelin refuses on principle to give more than two stars to a restaurant attached to a grand hotel. However, Maximin has received the highest possible accolade in a culinary guide which many now find more reliable than Michelin's, Gault and Millau's; in this he is described as the 'Bonaparte of the kitchen'. The travel writer Eric Newby ate recently at the Chantecler and concluded that the meal was 'the best, the most imaginative and the most beautifully presented I have ever eaten in my entire life, and am ever likely to eat'. Maximin, an extremely inventive cook and one of the apostles of the *nouvelle cuisine*, sometimes transforms and lightens traditional Provençal dishes, as in his version of *aïoli* in which the garlic to be used is simmered beforehand in water, and hard-boiled eggs are incorporated with the fresh yolks. The food and wine editor of the *Observer*, Paul Levy, wrote that Maximin 'can take dishes of *haute cuisine*, and of *nouvelle cuisine*, and of local origin, and abstract the essential features so that their ingredients appear simple and fresh and their flavours clear and strong'. 'There is,' he added, 'a lesson in this for every cook.'

A similar contrast to that which exists between everyday Provençal food and the *haute cuisine* of the region can be found in the region's wines. Most Provençal wines are what are often described as 'homely', and have been treated with the same snobbery which in the past was reserved for the local food. Yet Provence incorporates within its boundaries much of the lower half of the Rhône valley, and as such also boasts some of the oldest and most distinguished wines of France.

The first vines of the Rhône valley were planted by the Greeks of Phocis, and there is a theory that the best of the Rhône red grapes, the so-called Syrah grape, was brought by the Greeks from the Phocian town of Shiraz, at that time the wine-growing centre of Asia Minor. The Romans continued to cultivate the Rhône vines, which remained concentrated on the northern end of the valley; their most famed vines were those of the Côte Rôtie near Vienne and L'Hermitage near Valence. Viticulture declined markedly after the departure of the Romans but revived in the ninth century, with the Church emerging as the most prolific owner of vineyards. The vital impulse for the development of viticulture in the lower Rhône valley was given by the arrival of the popes in Avignon in 1309. Clement V, Archbishop of Bordeaux and the first of the Avignon popes, was a great lover of wine and someone whose name was given to one of the best of the Bordeaux wines, the Château Pape-Clément. He planted many vines around Avignon, as did his successor, John XXII. The most notable of the new vineyards was at a place now called Châteauneuf-du-Pape, a small hill village between Avignon and Orange where John built for himself a summer residence. By the end of the fourteenth century the reputation of the vines surrounding the papal palace at Châteauneuf-du-Pape was such that Petrarch cynically gave it as one of the reasons why certain members of the papal entourage were reluctant to return to Rome.

The palace was burnt down in the sixteenth century and survives now only as an imposing ruin; but the fame of the vines has continued to grow. In the middle of the nineteenth century a local wine owner, the Marquis de Nestle, did much to broaden the wine's appeal: he had the name of the village changed from Châteauneuf-Calcernier to Châteauneuf-du-Pape, and ascribed to the wine his virility in old age. In the early 1920s another proprietor, Baron Le Roy, persuaded his fellow wine-growers to adopt a scheme whereby they alone were able to market their wine as Châteauneuf-du-Pape; this resulted a decade later in the present system of the Appellation Contrôlée, a guarantee of the origin of good wines and a way of maintaining their quality. The vigilance of the Châteauneuf-du-Pape proprietors over their wines was so strict that in 1954, when reports of sightings of flying saucers were constantly in the news, a decree was passed in the village stating that 'the flying overhead, landing or taking off of aeronautical machines called "flying saucers" or "flying cigars", of whatever nationality they be, is strictly forbidden in the territory of the commune of Châteauneuf-du-Pape'.

The finest of the village wines are the red ones, which are dark and strong and take between two and six years to mature. Almost as good as these are the red wines of the nearby village of Gigondas, which received its Appellation Contrôlée in 1971. The third Appellation Contrôlée of the neighbourhood is Beaumes-de-Venise, which specializes in a sweet muscat wine, now much drunk in the region as an apéritif. This wine has also been well known since the Middle Ages, and it received the praise of Mistral, who referred to it as 'the good Muscat of Beaume' in his *Miréio*.

Up to the nineteenth century the Châteauneuf-du-Pape district was by no means the only important wine-growing area of Provence. Viticulture thrived generally in the region, which was second only to Bordeaux as a wine exporting centre. Provençal wines enjoyed a good reputation, and Keats could even sigh for a 'draught of vintage ... Tasting of Flora and the country green/Dance, and Provençal song, and sunburnt mirth'. Then in the 1870s and 1880s came the scourge of phylloxera, which affected Provence more severely than most areas of France, and from which, some say, the region has never fully recovered. The respected wine authority, Hugh Johnson, gave this rather cruel verdict on Provençal wines in 1977:

An optimistic description of Provençal wines always mentions the sun-baked pines, thyme, and lavender, and claims that the wine takes its character from them. This is true of some of the best of these ... Others get by on a pretty colour and a good deal of alcohol. 'Tarpaulin eyed with lace' is a realistic summing-up of one of the better ones.

Among the Provençal wines most highly regarded are those of La Palette near Aix-en-Provence, notably the rosés and the reds, the latter praised even by Johnson for their 'aromatic' quality. The coastal districts of Bandol and Cassis produce, respectively, excellent reds and whites, the whites of Cassis (not to be confused with the black-currant liqueur made in Dijon) being thought by many to be the ideal accompaniment to a *bouillabaisse*. The other Appellation Contrôlée of Provence is Bellet, a small wine-producing centre near Nice, which is renowned equally for its reds, whites and rosés, all highly fashionable but extremely expensive.

Johnson characterized Provence as the land of the 'V.D.Q.S.', 'Vin de Qualité Supérieure', the second category of French wines. Of these and the ones labelled 'Vin de Pays' (the third category), the best in Provence are usually the rosés, and at least a chilled glass of rosé makes a refreshing drink on a hot day. Yet Provençal wines have improved enormously in recent years, thanks largely to state aid and increased tourism. The wines of the Lubéron are a case in point. During the 1950s Elizabeth David had a stay in the Lubéron partly spoilt by a combination of the *mistral* and 'the truly awful wine of that particular district'. Today she would no longer have to limit her drinking to the rough wines produced by the district's cooperative societies, and would find such good Lubéron wines as those of the Château-la-Canorgue, a tiny wine producer near Bonnieux which only started up in 1983 and has already won widespread recognition in France (the 1985 vintage has almost all sold out). How snobbish one should be towards Provençal wines is of course another matter, for it is difficult to imagine any other wines which so perfectly complement the simplicity of the local cuisine.

If a symbol of Provence, as potent as the *aïoli* or the *bouillabaisse*, has to be found among the region's drinks, this would not be a wine at all but rather an apéritif, the *pastis*. The *pastis*, this legendary drink of the Provençal worker, has its origins in a legend. At an unspecified time in history, a mysterious man with an unknown past settled in the Lubéron. He lived frugally in a crude forest hut hung with branches of herbs, which occasionally he would be seen putting in a cauldron. One year a plague descended on this part of Provence, one of its symptoms being a terrible thirst. When the plague was in its final stages, the man descended from the mountain to the village of Cucuron, where he surprised the weakened surviving inhabitants by his cheerful, healthy appearance. The secret of his good health, he said, was the brew which he had concocted from his herbs. The villagers drank this and immediately their thirst passed away. Later the man moved to Marseille and opened by the port a bar selling his concoction. He called his place 'Au Bonhomme Passe-Soif', 'The Good-Natured Thirst-Quencher'.

Later this was Latinized to 'passe-sitis', which in turn became *pastis*.

Pastis is a liquorice-flavoured drink, similar to *anis* or the Greek *ouzo*. The one brand which most people drink in Provence is Ricard, devised and promoted by a man many people would consider (himself included) the greatest living Provençal.

In June 1909 the Provençal village of Verrègues was struck by the worst earthquake in French history, and in its wake was born a man destined to create an even greater impact on his native region. So begins the immodest autobiography of Paul Ricard, *La Passion de créer* (The Passion for Creation, 1983). Ricard, born and brought up in the Marseille suburb of Sainte-Marthe, was the son of a wine-merchant. His enormous range of interests as a boy could have started him on many a glorious career. He had a natural aptitude for painting and drawing; he loved the theatre; he was a passionate scholar who would stay up reading until three o'clock in the morning; he dreamt of becoming a fisherman and in charge of a fleet in the Mediterranean, the Atlantic and the Pacific. But in the end he decided to follow in his father's footsteps. Naturally such a genius could not so easily be contained by the job of selling wine, and it was not long before he thought up a variation on the traditional *pastis*, made from 'liquorice, fennel, mint and all the aromatic herbs'. The difference between Ricard's *pastis* and the other brands was actually not so great, but Ricard had the advantage of exceptional energy and a brilliant gift for self-promotion.

Walking from bar to bar in Marseille selling 'Ricard, the true *pastis* of Marseille' soon reaped its rewards, and within months his product had 'conquered the city' (his own phrase). The question now was if something labelled 'the true *pastis* of Marseille' would have an equal success in those parts of France – such as Lyon – which had a traditional antipathy towards Marseille. The older *pastis*-manufacturers were doubtful of Ricard's chances, but sure enough Ricard went on to conquer first Lyon, then Paris. Ricard's empire expanded in inverse proportion to his remaining modesty. Ricard bought up a large area of the Camargue for his factory, and made even the Marquis Baroncelli-Javon accept the necessity of the enterprise. Ricard encouraged agriculture in the Camargue and taught the French people how to cook rice properly. After Pagnol had closed his film studios in Marseille, Ricard opened his own in Sainte-Marthe and made there the first colour film in France. The subject of the film was the Tour de France, which had recently been sponsored by Ricard and festooned with flags bearing the yellow and blue colours of his trademark. The film was made, developed, and shown at selected seaside resorts all on the same day, another first for Ricard. Ricard's name began appearing everywhere, at song recitals, bull-fights, and so on. Ricard turned even the 1957 Suez crisis to his advantage. His supplies from overseas had been held up, and the reserves of Ricard were becoming dangerously low in the French cafés. Ricard came to the rescue with a caravan of camels all bearing the Ricard label. The election to the papacy in 1958 of Monsignor Roncalli, who had visited Ricard in Provence, gave Ricard another, more ambitious idea. He hired a whole train and sent in its wagons marked R I C A R D a procession of costumed 'Arlésiennes', and thirty horses and white lambs, to greet the new pope in Rome. He planned similar expeditions to America and Russia, but for once considerations of expense and practicality prevailed.

In 1950 Ricard had bought the barren, deserted island of Bendor off the coast near Bandol. He had envisaged a simple retreat for his family, but nothing could remain simple with Ricard for very long. At first he limited himself to the construction of a number of Provençale-style villas intended for people who, like him, needed a quiet place to escape to. But by the mid 1960s this little community had grown to include restaurants, two hotels, a gift shop, a bar, a theatre, a sea museum, a nautical club, a naval quarter, an underwater centre, a glass factory, an art gallery, and a zoo. 'To give the history of Bendor would take up a whole book. The island is known the world over.' By now he had also acquired the nearby islands of Embiez, which he was in the process of turning into the 'leisure centre of the future'. It was his hope, he has said, that should one day these islands become deserted again, those who looked on the ruins of his centre would see them as 'the Delos of twentieth-century France'. Ricard retired as director of his company in 1968, but that was not the last that was to be heard of him. In his home at Tête de l'Évêque he has conducted numerous experiments with solar energy; he has fulfilled his life-long ambition of building up a library containing every book ever published on Provence and Marseille; and he has created 'probably the largest art gallery in Provence, if not in France'. 'I have inexhaustible supplies of enthusiasm', he concludes.

Were it not for his phenomenal energy and success, Ricard, with all his absurd boasting and flights of fantasy, would be a stereotypical Provençal, a latterday Tartarin, a comic, larger-than-life figure. The very basis of Ricard's existence, the exploitation of drink and entertainment, seems to confirm that image of Provence as the land of the pleasure-seeker. But Ricard, though he has appropriated *pastis*, is not Provence; he represents only one small aspect of a land of fascinating and endless contradictions.

9

A Gazetteer of Provence

The scale of modern-day Provence is intimidating, and almost every place within this vast area has something of historical or artistic interest. No general gazetteer can hope to be exhaustive, and the aim of the following pages is simply to direct the reader to and around the most important towns, villages and natural curiosities within the region as well as to give a personal selection of some of the lesser-known sights. The information given is intended largely to supplement that of the main body of the text, which is why I have often enthused over some eccentric little sight and given only a cursory mention to some of the more important monuments discussed at greater length elsewhere.

Places are arranged alphabetically, ignoring 'La', 'Le' or 'Les'. A place in small capitals within an entry indicates that it has a separate entry of its own. Small villages and isolated monuments are sometimes combined with larger places nearby; in these cases cross-references are always given. The references at the end of each entry are to the map printed on pages 10–11; the reader is also strongly advised to use the gazetteer in conjunction with the excellent Michelin map no. 245, which covers the whole of the region.

Good train and bus facilities link the towns and villages of the coast, but a car is essential for anyone who wishes to travel widely in the hinterland. Those planning a seaside holiday should bear in mind that the finest beaches are all to the west of Antibes, the ones to the east being nearly all of gravel. Every town in Provence, and many of the villages as well, has a public swimming-pool, though these are generally open only during the summer months.

In my entries I have occasionally given details of walks, sports, traditional shops, and places and activities of family interest; lists of market-days and fêtes and festivals appear at the end of the gazetteer, on pages 346–54. By and large I have avoided mention of restaurants and hotels, unless these have either an outstanding reputation for food, a beautiful situation, or are of architectural or historical interest. For fuller information on restaurants and hotels you should consult the annual guides produced by Gault and Millau and Michelin (Guide Rouge), and John Ardagh's excellent *American Express Guide to the South of France* (London, 1983).

Many of the smaller churches listed in the gazetteer are locked for most of the year, but keys can generally be had from the local town hall (*mairie*). As a rule museums, castles and archaeological sites are closed on Tuesdays and public holidays, and between 12.00 a.m. and 2.00 p.m. But it is always best to check beforehand with the local tourist office or Syndicat d'Initiative, to which you should also refer for up-to-date details concerning all practical aspects of travel in Provence. Below are the addresses and telephone numbers of the main tourist offices in the region:

AIX-EN-PROVENCE: Place du Général de Gaulle. Tel: [42] 26-02-93

ARLES: Palais de l'Archevêché, 35 Place de la République. Tel: [90] 96-29-35

AVIGNON: 41 Cours Jean Jaurès. Tel: [90] 82-65-11

CANNES: Palais des Festivals, Boulevard de la Croisette. Tel: [93] 39-41-20

GRASSE: Place de la Foux. Tel: [93] 36-03-56

MARSEILLE: 4 La Canebière. Tel: [91] 54-91-11

MONACO: 2a Boulevard des Moulins. Tel: [93] 30-87-01

NICE: 32 Rue de l'Hôtel des Postes. Tel: [93] 85-25-25

SAINT-TROPEZ: Quai Jean Jaurès. Tel: [94] 97-03-64

LES-SAINTES-MARIES-DE-LA-MER: Avenue Van-Gogh. Tel: [90] 97-82-55

TOULON: 8 Avenue Colbert. Tel: [94] 22-08-22

VAISON-LA-ROMAINE: Place du Chanoine-Sautel. Tel: [90] 36-02-11

For detailed information on fishing, mountain-climbing, and sailing schools, contact, respectively, the Fédération Départementale des Sociétés de Pêche (20 Boulevard Victor Hugo, 06000 Nice. Tel: [93] 88-19-92); the Club Alpin Français (15 Avenue Jean Médecin, 06000 Nice. Tel: [93] 87-95-41); and the Centre d'Information Jeunesse Côte d'Azur (Esplanade des Victoires, 06000, Nice. Tel: [93] 90-93-93).

AIX-EN-PROVENCE: On a small butt of land skirted by the dual carriageway of the N296 stand the ruins of the citadel of Entremont, which was founded in the third or fourth century B.C. as the capital of the notorious Salyans, a Celto-Ligurian tribe famed for their barbaric practices and cult of decapitation. The ruins share the site with a military radar station, but have recently been opened to the public. There is little to see save for the foundations, and the view of Aix-en-Provence to the south, encircled by motorways but made dignified by the powerful wedge of Montagne Sainte-Victoire rising behind it, like Vesuvius over Naples.

Roman forces led by Caius Sextius Calvinus stormed Entremont in 123 B.C. and founded the present city of Aix-en-Provence three kilometres to the south. Named Aquae Sextiae after its thermal springs, this was the first Roman settlement in Gaul. With the completion of the Aurelian Way during the reign of the Emperor Augustus, the city became a major stop between Fréjus and the Rhône, and its prosperity increased markedly. However, the Roman emperors and later the Holy Roman Emperors continued always to favour ARLES over Aix, and though it was made a bishopric in the fourth century A.D., Aix went into a long decline, hastened by devastating attacks from the Visigoths, the Lombards, and later the Saracens. Its fortunes did not revive until the twelfth century, when the Counts of Provence made the city their capital. In the fifteenth century a university was established here and the city enjoyed a brief period of intense cultural activity under René of Anjou, whose court attracted many of the international artists and musicians in the orbit of the so-called Avignon School.

Sentimental writers on Provençal history from the eighteenth century onwards have looked back on the days of 'Good King René' as the greatest in Aix's history. Yet in many ways the most interesting period in this history were the three centuries between the annexation of Provence to France in 1487 and the Revolution. Aix was kept on as the capital of Provence, and also became, after 1501, the seat of its supreme court of justice, the Parlement. The presence of wealthy and ennobled magistrates in the city led to the building of countless splendid palaces, particularly in the seventeenth and eighteenth centuries. During this period the centre of Aix acquired more or less the appearance it has today. In the process it lost the few remaining

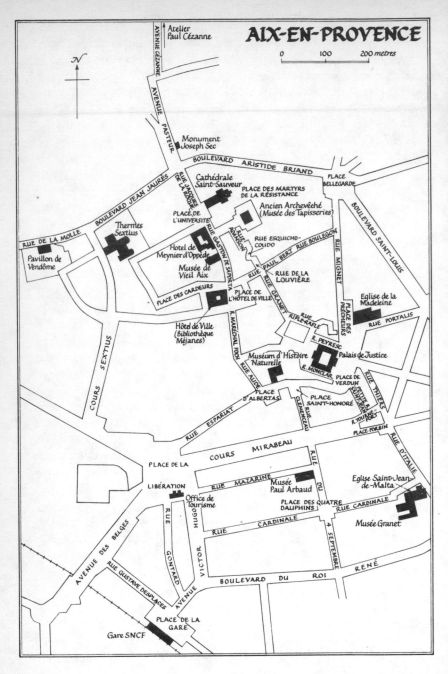

AIX-EN-PROVENCE

0   100   200 metres

Atelier
Paul Cézanne

AVENUE CÉZANNE

N

AVENUE PASTEUR

Monument
Joseph Sec

BOULEVARD ARISTIDE BRIAND

PLACE
BELLEGARDE

BOULEVARD JEAN JAURÈS

RUE JACQUES DE LA ROQUE

Cathédrale
Saint-Sauveur

PLACE DES MARTYRS
DE LA RÉSISTANCE

Ancien Archevêché
(Musée des Tapisseries)

BOULEVARD SAINT-LOUIS

RUE DE LA MOLLE

Thermes
Sextius

PLACE DE
L'UNIVERSITÉ

RUE GASTON DE SAPORTA

RUE ADANSON

RUE ESQUICHO-
COUDO

RUE PAUL BERT RUE BOULEGON

RUE MIGNET

Pavillon de
Vendôme

Hôtel de
Meynier d'Oppède

RUE DE LA
LOUVIÈRE

Église de la
Madeleine

Musée de
Vieil Aix

RUE DES PRÊCHEURS

PLACE DES CARDEURS

PLACE DE
L'HÔTEL DE VILLE

RUE CRAME

RUE PORTALIS

RUE MARÉCHAL FOCH

RIFLE-RAFLE

RUE

COURS SEXTIUS

Hôtel de Ville
(Bibliothèque
Méjanes)

R. PEYRESC

Muséum d'Histoire
Naturelle

R. MONCLAR

Palais de Justice

RUE AUDE

PLACE DE
VERDUN

RUE THIERS

PLACE
D'ALBERTAS

PLACE
SAINT-HONORÉ

RUE CLÉMENCEAU

R. TOURNE-
FORT

RUE ESPARIAT

PLACE FORBIN

COURS MIRABEAU

RUE D'ITALIE

PLACE DE LA
LIBÉRATION

RUE MAZARINE

Musée
Paul Arbaud

RUE DU

Église Saint-Jean
-de-Malta

Office de
Tourisme

PLACE DES QUATRE
DAUPHINS

RUE CARDINALE

RUE HUGOU

RUE
CARDINALE

4 SEPTEMBRE

Musée Granet

RUE GONTARD

AVENUE VICTOR

RENÉ

AVENUE DES BELGES

RUE GUSTAVE DESPLACES

BOULEVARD DU ROI

PLACE DE LA
GARE

Gare SNCF

216

monuments of the Roman city, and many of its important medieval ones, but it gained in compensation one of the finest complexes of seventeenth- and eighteenth-century buildings in France. Even the terrible plague of 1721, which spread to here from MARSEILLE, had favourable consequences for the look of the city: the city's water supply had to be renewed, and as a result many of the delightful and numerous fountains that so greatly enhance the elegance of Aix were built.

Though an aristocratic and important city, Aix was never a very animated one, even before the Revolution. When the far livelier and socially more varied city of Marseille was made capital of Provence in 1790, Aix easily slipped into somnolence and dignified retirement, a position reflected in its simultaneous renewal as a thermal resort. This century its importance as a thermal resort has increased further, its university has expanded, it has become the seat of a number of American colleges, and it hosts in July and August an internationally renowned music festival. Yet it remains a deeply reactionary town, wonderful to visit, but dull to live in.

The main car park in central Aix lies behind the Place de la Libération, at the eastern end of the town's main thoroughfare, the Cours Mirabeau. This elegant street, punctuated by fountains and bordered by four rows of trees which curve inward to form an arbour, was constructed between 1649 and 1651 on a site previously occupied by the town's southern fortifications. It was intended as a promenade where the aristocratic families of the town could parade up and down in their carriages. The palaces that were built overlooking it were among the most fashionable addresses in town, and there was much protest when in 1748 a '*limonadier*' proposed to set up a café here. Today the street is lined both with cafés and some of the smartest shops in town. The Café des Deux Garçons at no. 53 *bis* was an important literary meeting-place in the eighteenth and nineteenth centuries, and its dining-room (in many ways the finest restaurant in town) retains its magnificent Empire decoration. Paul Cézanne preferred to meet his friends at the more modest Caf Clem opposite (at no. 44), and, with his boorish nature and hatred of pretentiousness and elegant manners, might well have favoured today Le Quick Burger at no. 39; his father's hat shop was at no. 55, which still keeps its original sign, 'Chapellerie du Cours Mirabeau, gros et détail'. At nos. 12 and 36 are L. Bechard and Brémond Fils, two good pâtisseries where you can buy Aix's most famous gastronomic speciality, the almond biscuits known as *calissons*. These biscuits have been made in Aix since at least the sixteenth century and were at one time distributed in churches on certain feast days; today no church could afford to do so. Far more distinguished, to my taste, are the hand-made chocolates sold at Puyricard (no. 7 of the nearby Rue Rifle-Rafle). Though there is nothing specifically Provençal about these chocolates (and the firm is now even Belgian-run), they are among the best you will find in France.

From the Cours Mirabeau you should turn north on the Rue Clemenceau into what was once the medieval town of Aix. The walk from here to the cathedral of Saint-Sauveur at the northern end of the old town is a delightful one, especially as much of the area is now traffic-free. At the Place Saint-Honoré turn left into the Rue Espariat, where at no. 6 you will find the seventeenth-century Hôtel Boyer d'Éguilles. The pleasant interior, with seventeenth-century ceiling paintings and elaborately carved doors, contains a natural history museum: busts of famous Aix scholars of the sixteenth and seventeenth centuries such as de Gassendi, de Tournefort, d'Adanson and de Peiresc (a close friend of Rubens) are reminders of what an important centre of botanical and biological studies Aix once was.

Further along, the Rue Espariat opens up into the Place d'Albertas, a tiny cobbled square with a fountain in the middle, created in the eighteenth century by Jean-Baptiste d'Albertas to make a theatrical approach to his palace behind it; the palace had been built for Jean-Baptiste's father, the first president of the Audit Court. To the north of this square is the Place de l'Hôtel de Ville, on the western side of which is the seventeenth-century town hall. A part of this building is taken over by the Bibliothèque Méjanes, the basis of which was a remarkable collection of books and manuscripts presented to the town in 1786 by Jean-Baptiste Piquet, Marquis of Méjanes and first consul of Aix; among the manuscripts which are on regular exhibition here is the Book of Hours of King René. In 1975 Saint-John Perse, who was both an outstanding diplomat and a poet who won the Nobel Prize for Literature, left all his papers and collections of art and books to the town of Aix, and a selection of these are now on permanent display in the museum to him set up in two of the most beautiful rooms of the town hall.

At no. 17 Rue Gaston de Saporta – the road which leads from the town hall to the cathedral of Saint-Sauveur – is the Musée du Vieil Aix. The museum has a charming folklore collection, particularly interesting in its exhibits relating to the Fête Dieu celebrations instigated by 'Good King René' (see page 87); but its chief glory is its setting, a seventeenth-century palace boasting a superb grand staircase with intricately-fashioned wrought-iron railing. Further north, at no. 19 Rue Gaston de Saporta, is the seventeenth-century Hôtel de Châteaurenard, the place where Louis XIV stayed on a visit to Aix in 1660 and now a citizen's advice bureau; you should go inside to see the staircase well, which has an impressive *trompe-l'oeil* decoration by a leading Flemish painter of the seventeenth century, Jean Daret. The palace at no. 23 Rue Gaston de Saporta is now divided between the University and the Departmental Archives, but was from 1490 to 1730 the family home of the Mayniers d'Oppède, one of Aix's most important families; four of its members were presidents of the Parlement, including the infamous Jean de Maynier, the man responsible for the Vaudois massacre in the Lubéron (see page 83). The palace was heavily remodelled in the mid eighteenth century.

Opposite the palace, at the far end of the Place des Martyrs de la Résistance, is the former Archbishop's Palace, a large seventeenth-century structure built around a courtyard and today housing the Musée des Tapisseries. The museum mainly comprises three series of Beauvais tapestries that were purchased by the archbishops in the seventeenth and eighteenth centuries and put into hiding during the Revolution; they were discovered in the building's roof in 1847. The most endearing of these series is that devoted to the life of Don Quixote, which was woven between 1735 and 1744 using designs supplied by the French rococo artist Natoire.

The cathedral of Saint-Sauveur adjoins the museum. It has a long and complex history, with a baptistery (immediately to your right after entering the church through the west door) dating back, at least in its foundations, to the fifth century. The baptistery columns are Roman, and were certainly taken from the Roman forum on which the cathedral stands. The right aisle was once the nave of the romanesque church of Notre-Dame, which was later incorporated into the present building. The greater part of the cathedral was built between 1285 and 1350, and is one of the better examples of gothic architecture in Provence; the west façade, a flamboyant gothic structure with intricately carved Renaissance doors by a Toulon artist, was not completed until the early sixteenth century. The main attraction of the interior is the *Triptych of the Burning Bush* in the nave (ask the sacristan to open the panels for you), which was painted *c.* 1476 for King René by his court artist Nicolas Froment. The King is represented on the left-hand panel together with Saint Mary Magdalene, Saint Anthony and Saint Maurice; his wife Jeanne de Laval is on the opposite panel in the company of Saint John the Baptist, Saint Catherine and Saint Nicholas. The central panel shows the Burning Bush with the Virgin and Child in its flames appearing to Moses: in the Middle Ages the Bush (which burned but was not consumed) came to symbolize the virginity of the Virgin Mary. This masterpiece of the Avignon School is notable for its Flemish-inspired realism, such as the minutely observed landscape background.

Making your way back to the Cours Mirabeau, bear left before the Rue Clemenceau and you will reach the huge Palais de Justice, on the Place de Verdun. It was for this that the medieval palace of the Counts of Provence was pulled down in the late eighteenth century. This act of vandalism was heavily criticized at the time, but at least the building which replaced the palace is a striking neo-classical structure with a vaulted and arcaded courtyard of monumental proportions. The seventeenth-century church on the north side of the square, Sainte-Marie-Madeleine, is worth a visit for its fifteenth-century *Annunciation*, a major painting of the Avignon School (see page 77).

The area to the south of the Cours Mirabeau, the Quartier Mazarin, is one of the quietest and least visited districts of Aix. Built in the seventeenth century for Michel Mazarin, Archbishop of Aix, it is an aristocratic quarter arranged as a grid of narrow streets lined with severe but distinguished palaces. Take the Rue du 4 Septembre, where you will find at no. 2a an early eighteenth-century palace housing the Musée Paul Arbaud. This building, opposite the birthplace of the Marquis Folco de Baroncelli-Javon (see page 33), was the home of Paul Arbaud, a nineteenth-century scholar and collector. The place has been left as it was in Arbaud's day and has a fascinating array of objects, ranging from sixteenth-century manuscripts to eighteenth-century pottery, and no less than 350 portraits of the Marquis de Mirabeau (see page 294). Though no single object stands out, the whole is a great treasure trove of curiosities.

At the lovely Place des Quatre Dauphins, with its seventeenth-century fountain of dolphins, turn left on to the Rue Cardinale, at the end of which is the former priory church of Saint John of Malta, an early example of Provençal gothic. Next to this, housed in the seventeenth-century priory building, is the Musée Granet, which has one of the finest collections of old master paintings in Provence. The museum, named after the Aix neo-classical painter François Granet, was used as an art school in the nineteenth century and Paul Cézanne was one of its pupils (he is represented in the museum only by a small group of drawings and watercolours). The paintings are on the first and second floors, but before going upstairs you should take a look at the powerful Salyan heads, which were found at Entremont.

The finest of the foreign school paintings are nearly all of the seventeenth and eighteenth centuries and include good works by Guercino, Rubens, and Rembrandt. The real strength of the collection, however, is its extensive holdings of nineteenth-century French paintings. These are displayed mainly in a dark and seedy room, with a skylight so thick with dirt that even on the sunniest day the visitor is led to believe that a storm is brewing outside. Matters are made worse by the room having no electric light, which is why it always closes an hour before the rest of the museum (try to get here early in the morning). Unlabelled works are hung nineteenth-century-fashion on top of each other, and a large notice tries to justify the whole shoddy display with the excuse that the paintings are shown as they appeared in Cézanne's time. The outstanding paintings are by artists of the neo-classical school, David, Gérard, Gros, and, above all, Ingres. Ingres's portrait of Granet (1807) in front of the Villa Medici in Rome is a painting of extreme subtlety in terms of both colouring and psychological perception; at the other end of his range is the enormous *Jupiter and Thetis*, a strangely memorable work despite absurd details such as the toe of Thetis brushing against that of Jupiter.

Aix has many attractions on its perimeter. On the north side of the town, off the Rue de la Molle, is the Pavillon Vendôme: this attractive seventeenth-century building, once the summer home of the Cardinal de Vendôme and now a setting for temporary exhibitions organized by the Musée Granet, sits in the middle of well-kept formal gardens. Nearby, off the Boulevard Jean Jaurès, is an eighteenth- and nine-teenth-century spa complex, built on the site of the town's Roman baths and containing in the garden a tower from the town's medieval walls. The Avenue Pasteur, which leads north from this part of the town in the direction of the Cézanne Studio Museum, is notable for its late eighteenth-century mausoleum to Joseph Sec, an extremely bizarre work whose astonishing sculptures and inscriptions trace the ascent of man's soul.

Cézanne's studio – where the artist worked for the last four years of his life – comes as a disappointment after the Sec Mausoleum, being a poorly maintained place lacking in real character; there are a few personal mementoes, but only reproductions of his works. This modest museum is a telling comment on a town which never cared much for the artist when he was alive. It is certainly ironic that – as with Van Gogh at Arles – Aix's associations with Cézanne are today one of the town's major draws for tourists.

Throughout his life Cézanne repeatedly painted the same motifs, and a great many of these motifs have changed little since his day. In the latter half of his career much of his work was done near the D17 leading east from Aix to Le Tholonet (the road has now been renamed the Route Paul Cézanne). Beyond Le Tholonet is a path which leads steeply up the most famous of the artist's motifs, Montagne Sainte-Victoire; the view from the cross at the top is outstanding, but you should bear in mind that Cézanne himself never did the climb: he remained happy to look at the mountain from below.

In his youth Cézanne painted much around his family home, Le Jas de Bouffan, on the western outskirts of the town. This elegant nine-teenth-century house in its large wooded garden still survives, but is not open to the public. Visitors to this part of town will have to content themselves with a tour of the nearby Vasarély museum, which sits, appropriately, at the ugly junction of the Avignon and Marseille motorways. The building was designed by Vasarély himself, an 'op-artist' who specializes in cold, abstract works that are often literally painful to the eyes. The museum – inaugurated in 1976 and already beginning to show its age – is intended apparently to serve some didactic purpose. 'Man,' Vasarély grandly explains, 'needs to nourish his sense of harmony, just as he needs oxygen.' Fresh air is certainly needed after this museum. As a more pleasant farewell to the Aix area you should follow the D67 west from the museum to the quiet village of Ventabren; on the way you will pass under the Roquefavour aqueduct, a striking example of nineteenth-century engineering in a most romantic wooded setting.   [4B]

ANSOUIS, a toy-like village built around a hill on the southern side of the Lubéron, is dominated by its castle, one of the most enchanting in Provence. This building has been in the possession of the Sabran family since the twelfth century. Visitors are shown around by elderly family retainers, and the Duchess herself occasionally puts in an appearance. You enter through an elegant late Renaissance wing of around 1600, behind which is the original twelfth- to fourteenth-century fortress. The interior was extensively redecorated in the eighteenth century with delicate *rocaille* ornamentation, but a number of earlier rooms have preserved their medieval character; one of these contains mementoes of those famous medieval virgins, Saints Elzéar and Delphine (see page 98). The old kitchen is especially delightful, and, unlike many kitchens of this sort, is still in use: the guide takes pride in pointing out the recently installed Aga. The castle is surrounded on all sides by beautiful hanging gardens of the eighteenth century.

As you descend to the village, make sure to look into the romanesque church which is attached to the castle walls and was originally the castle's Court of Justice. Further down you might be intrigued by signs pointing to the 'Musée Extraordinaire'. A group of hideous ceramic sculptures of fish at the bottom of the village signifies your arrival at this place, which really is extraordinary, though not perhaps for the same reasons which its owner, Georges Mazoyer, would have you believe. Mazoyer is a charming and energetic Marseillais man who has devoted much of his life to sea-diving, collecting Provençal furniture, and trying to reproduce in paint, ceramics, and many other media the underwater world. His many interests come together in the Musée Extraordinaire, which has rare shellfish and some interesting pieces of furniture but which is really fascinating as a monument to extraordinarily bad taste. The part of the museum of which Mazoyer is most proud, and which I urge all children and lovers of the curious to see, is his underwater grotto, which resembles less a grotto than the entrance to a tacky night-club, and makes use of dangling pieces of felt, stained glass, coloured lighting, and sub-aqueous sounds. [3B]

ANTIBES: Originally a small Greek trading port, Antibes became from the fourteenth century onwards a fortress town on the border between Provence and Savoy. A small lively medieval quarter survives, as well as a large section of the seafront fortifications. The Musée Archéologique, housed in a bastion designed by the seventeenth-century military engineer Vauban, possesses a large collection of amphorae, jewels, coins and other objects illustrating Antibes's rich archaeological history. A few minutes' walk to the north of here is the Château Grimaldi, built between the twelfth and sixteenth centuries and now containing the Musée Picasso. In 1946 Picasso was given the use of the castle as a studio by the Mayor of Antibes; he worked here between July and December of that year. Three years later, in memory of his happy and very productive stay in Antibes, he donated to the castle many paintings and drawings executed during that period, to-gether with a large collection of tapestries, lithographs, sculptures and ceramics. This bright and cheerfully laid out museum also displays works by various other contemporary artists, including many canvases by the abstract painter Nicholas de Staël. After years of poverty and lack of recognition, de Staël finally achieved critical and financial success in the early 1950s. He bought a house in MÉNERBES, installed his wife there, then came to Antibes to be with his mistress. He killed himself here in 1955, at the age of forty-one.

Immediately to the north of Antibes is the resort of La Brague, which has a lively Marineland featuring Icelandic whales and per-forming dolphins. Further fun can be had at the nearby La Siesta, which functions both as a luxurious beach establishment with special facilities for children and dogs (the latter even have their own res-taurant!) and as an extravagantly decadent night-club with flaming torches and flood-lit waterfalls. But the traditional playground of Antibes is the Cap d'Antibes to the south, now a spacious, verdant suburb covered with luxury villas and apartment blocks. The Ameri-cans discovered this little peninsula in the 1920s and soon turned it into the first summer resort of the Riviera. Cole Porter had a villa here, and an international jazz festival is held every July in the Palais des Congrès at Juan-les-Pins, at the northern end of the peninsula. In the centre of Cap d'Antibes is the sanctuary of La Garoupe, an eighteenth-century church with a magnificent medieval Russian altar (next to the main altar), and an extensive collection of sailors' ex-votos. Just to the west of the sanctuary is the delightful Jardin Thuret, a park created in 1856 and containing a wide selection of exotic plants, among which are some of the earliest eucalyptus trees planted in Europe. The famous Eden Roc, haunt of film stars and other celebrities in the 1920s and 30s, is at the southern tip of the peninsula. Nearby is an old coastal fortification with a naval and Napoleonic museum; Napoleon was based in Antibes in 1794, while in charge of the defence of the coast. [4E]

APT: 'Colonia Apta Julia' was an important Roman town named after Julius Caesar, probably on his return from his Spanish campaign. Later the place became an important centre of pilgrimage because of its associations with Saint Anne, who is reputedly buried in the cathedral church named after her. Apt is today an important market town, famous for its truffles and candied fruits. It comes alive on Saturday mornings, when its market is held, and the squares and narrow streets of its small medieval quarter are jam-packed with stalls and people. Because of this area's reputation as a resort for artists and intellectuals, Apt bears on these occasions a certain resemblance to Saint-Germain-des-Prés. The great meeting-place for locals and Bohemians alike is the Café Grégoire on the Place de la Bouquerie.

Apt's principal monument is the former cathedral of Sainte-Anne, a gloomy building discreetly tucked away in the medieval quarter. The building is of many periods, and perhaps the most interesting part is the pre-romanesque lower crypt, a rare survival of early Christian architecture in Provence. The rest of the church is mainly of the eleventh and twelfth centuries, with a fourteenth-century north aisle, and, off this, a large seventeenth-century chapel (Saint Anne's or the Royal Chapel) commemorating the pilgrimage made here in 1660 by Anne of Austria, wife of Louis XIII: inside the chapel is a reliquary containing the 'shroud of Saint Anne', in fact an eleventh-century Arabian standard brought back from the First Crusade.

The recently modernized Archaeological Museum is housed in an austere eighteenth-century building on the Rue de l'Amphithéâtre. There are a few Roman finds here but the main objects of interest are the ceramics, all dating from the late eighteenth century onwards, when a small but thriving pottery industry was established in the town.

By far the finest Roman monument in the vicinity is the Pont Julien, a magnificently preserved bridge eight kilometres to the west of Apt, off the main road (N100) to Cavaillon. On the other side of the N100 to the bridge is the junction of the D108 to Roussillon; it was supposedly while waiting at this spot that Samuel Beckett had the idea for his play, *Waiting for Godot*.

Four kilometres to the south-west of Apt, off the D3 to Bonnieux, is the Château de Mille, a medieval castle perched on a rock and heavily rebuilt between the sixteenth and eighteenth centuries. The place produces what is generally regarded as the best wine of the Lubéron (the reds are particularly good).   [3B]

LES ARCS: In the now ruined castle of Villeneuve, which dominates this small village, Saint Rosseline was born in 1267. As a girl she gave considerable help to the poor, much to her wealthy father's annoyance; one day her father prevented her from distributing her provisions, and these turned into flowers. The miracle is represented in a sixteenth-century fresco in the village church, which boasts a splendidly elaborate mechanical crib.

In 1300 Saint Rosseline became prioress of the Benedictine convent of La Celle, four kilometres north-east of Les Arcs, and in the middle of flat countryside extensively covered in vineyards. The only remaining part of the convent is the romanesque chapel of Saint Rosseline, which contains the remarkably well preserved body of the saint, some fine baroque furnishings and a number of modern works, including a mosaic by Chagall and a bronze relief of the life of Saint Rosseline by Giacometti's brother, Diego.   [4D]

ARLES: The Roman word for Arles is 'Arelate', which means the town on the marshes. Situated on the Rhône, and in the middle of a vast area of marshland, Arles was little more than an island from ancient times right up to the Middle Ages. The town developed initially as a port and trading centre, possibly used by Phocians from as early as the sixth century B.C. In 104 B.C. its importance as a port increased greatly when the Roman general Marius cut a canal into the swamps and created a more direct link with the coast. In 46 B.C. Arles profited

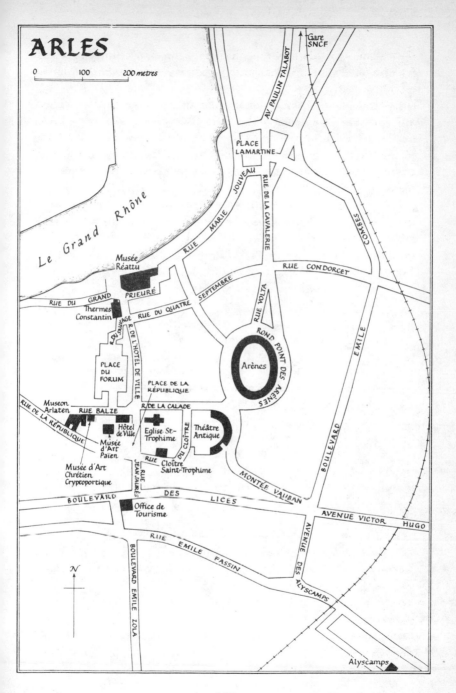

ARLES

0   100   200 metres

Gare
SNCF

AV PAULIN TALABOT

Le Grand Rhône

PLACE
LAMARTINE

RUE MARIE JOUVEAU

RUE DE LA CAVALERIE

RUE COMBES

Musée
Réattu

PRIEURÉ

RUE CONDORCET

RUE DU GRAND

SEPTEMBRE

RUE DU QUATRE

RUE VOLTA

Thermes
Constantin

R. DE L'HÔTEL DE VILLE

ROND POINT DES ARÈNES

PLACE
DU
FORUM

PLACE DE LA
RÉPUBLIQUE

Arènes

Museon
Arlaten

RUE BALZE

R. DE LA CALADE

BOULEVARD EMILE

RUE DE LA RÉPUBLIQUE

Hôtel
de Ville

Eglise St-
Trophime

Théâtre
Antique

Musée
d'Art
Païen

DU CLOÎTRE

RUE

Musée d'Art
Chrétien
Crypteoportique

RUE JEAN JAURÈS

Cloître
Saint-Trophime

MONTÉE VAUBAN

BOULEVARD

DES

LICES

BOULEVARD EMILE ZOLA

Office de
Tourisme

AVENUE VICTOR HUGO

RUE EMILE FASSIN

AVENUE DES

N

ALYSCAMPS

Alyscamps

further after taking the side of Julius Caesar in his struggle against Pompey; veterans of the Sixth Legion were settled here, and the town was endowed with riches seized from the disgraced MARSEILLE, which had opposed Caesar. Arles, Caesar's favourite town in Gaul, prospered enormously under the Romans as a result of its being at the intersection of their major trade routes. In the early fourth century the Emperor Constantine made Arles the capital of the Roman Empire, and though it soon lost this status, it was made instead the capital of the 'Four Gauls' (North and South Gaul, England and Spain). A contemporary of Constantine, the poet Ausonius, described Arles as 'the Rome of Gaul', and indeed the town is rivalled only by the nearby Nîmes in the extent of its Roman monuments.

Arles was a vital focus of early Christianity, and under Constantine became a host to the first council of Christian bishops and an archiepiscopal see. The former cathedral of Saint-Trophime was one of the most revered buildings in Europe, and saw in the sixth century the consecration of Saint Augustus as first Bishop of Canterbury, and in the twelfth century the coronation of Barbarossa as Holy Roman Emperor. However, in the course of the Middle Ages Arles's economic and political importance declined, and the town has since played a minor role in Provence in comparison with AVIGNON, AIX-EN-PROVENCE, and MARSEILLE. Its reputation in the eighteenth and nineteenth centuries was due largely to its strong folklore tradition. Much of the traditional Provençal furniture that you find in homes and museums throughout the region is by or based on the work of eighteenth-century Arles craftsmen. Moreover, the district of Arles is the only one in Provence to have kept a distinctive folk costume. This costume, particularly as worn by the town's women – who have always had a reputation for their beauty – helped further a very romantic image of Arles during the nineteenth century. Daudet's play L'Arlésienne, for which Bizet wrote the music, was a typical product of this romanticism. So too was the Museon Arlaten, the delightful folklore museum which Mistral founded at Arles.

Van Gogh came to Arles in 1888, his imagination filled with visions of costumed beauties, but came away later with a series of canvases that gave a much more realistic picture of Arles. The Arles which he painted was a town which was beginning to be heavily industrialized, and where one of the largest railway works in France had been recently established.

Much of the ugly, makeshift area of Arles where Van Gogh lived and painted has now either gone or been tidied up (the Tourist Office on the Boulevard des Lices will give you an excellent map marking all the sites in and around the town associated with him). The town none the less still has a rough quality to it. It is not a show-piece like so many other places in Provence, nor has it the genteel elegance of Aix. Tourism has brought much animation to the place in recent years, and has been responsible for the establishment of an annual photography festival, the most important of its kind in Europe and an attraction which turns the old streets every July into a lively thoroughfare of all nationalities. But you feel that Arles has a strong life of its own quite independent of tourism. Thanks to the reclamation of much of the Camargue (see LES-SAINTES-MARIES-DE-LA-MER), Arles is now at the centre of a thriving agricultural district, and the market held here on Saturdays is one of the rowdiest in Provence. The market stalls cover much of the Boulevard des Lices, and you can buy there, among countless other local products, the town's most famous speciality, the dried sausage known as *saucisson d'Arles*. The food stalls jostle with the extraordinary flea-market, where you will be able to pick up outstanding antique and old book bargains.

The best places for leaving your car in Arles are off the Boulevard des Lices (but not on Saturdays!) or on the Place Lamartine in the opposite, northern end of town. The latter square, situated by the Rhône, was where Van Gogh had his 'Yellow House' and adjoins one of the two remaining sections of the town's old walls. In the relatively small area between the Place Lamartine and the Boulevard des Lices are crammed the town's main attractions. A sensible idea is to purchase a combined ticket which will allow you access to all the town's museums and monuments.

The most prominent of these monuments is the Roman amphitheatre, which is especially exciting to visit when a bull-fight is on (the fights are held on Sunday afternoons from Easter to late September; tickets can generally be had for them on the day itself). The Roman theatre just to the south of this is not in such a good condition, but is situated in a quiet and pleasant garden which makes a lovely setting for plays, dances and concerts in the summer months. A few minutes' walk to the west takes you to the main square of the old town, the Place de la République. The magnificent romanesque west portal of

Saint-Trophime, with its powerful *Last Judgement*, overlooks the square. The building stands on the site of a church commissioned in the fifth century by Bishop Hilarius; it dates back to the eleventh century, but was heavily altered in the twelfth century (when the west façade was added). Even the celebrated cloister (entered from the square) is not all of one period, the south and west walks being fourteenth-century additions. The joy of the cloister is the carvings on the east and north walks, which rank with the sculptures of the west portal as the greatest examples of romanesque sculpture in Provence. Hilaire Belloc wrote in 1906 that 'silence inhabits the place', though this is no longer true, especially as the rooms above the cloister have been turned into popular exhibition halls for contemporary art and photography.

On the opposite side of the Place de la République is a collection of Roman statues and sarcophagi (the Musée de l'Art Païen) installed in an attractive early seventeenth-century church. Arles's best-known Roman sculpture, the *Venus of Arles*, is now in the Louvre in Paris, but a copy of this work can be seen on the grand staircase of the town hall, on the northern side of the square. This building is in itself of great interest, being partly designed by France's renowned baroque architect, Jules Hardouin-Mansart. It is one of the major seventeenth-century buildings of Provence, and has a most ingenious flat vault in the ground floor hall. Walk through here and turn left on to the pedestrian street of Rue Balze and you will reach the Museon Arlaten (see page 116). Nearby is the Musée d'Art Chrétien, housed in a seventeenth-century Jesuit chapel and containing a major collection of paleo-Christian sarcophagi taken mainly from the cemetery of the Alyscamps; within the building are steps leading down to the vast and gloomy Roman granary, the Cryptoporticus.

On the way north from here to the Musée Réattu, you will pass through the delightful Place du Forum, which marks the site of the Roman forum and incorporates within the walls of one of its buildings an eloquent fragment from a Roman temple. This small and lively square is dominated by a statue of Mistral, who regularly frequented the open-air cafés here together with many other of the town's intellectuals. Van Gogh painted his *Café by Night* on the east side of the square, but this particular café is now a furniture shop below the Vaccarès restaurant.

Sad and rather ugly ruins of Roman baths – all that remains of the palace which the Emperor Constantine built for himself at Arles – stand next to the Musée Réattu. The museum, overlooking the Rhône, occupies the sixteenth-century former priory of the Knights of Malta. After the Revolution it belonged to a local painter, Jacques Réattu, whose dull neo-classical paintings are on show here. In addition the museum has large holdings of contemporary art and photography, most notably fifty-seven drawings by Picasso, executed between 31 December 1970 and 4 February 1971 and presented to the town by the artist in gratitude for the many bull-fights he had enjoyed here.

One of the outlying attractions of Arles is the cemetery of the Alyscamps, to the south of the Boulevard des Lices and once one of Europe's most celebrated burial grounds (see page 62). Today it has been reduced to a single shaded avenue leading to the romanesque church of Saint-Honorat. The place has a quiet and neglected character, and there is a sign saying that Van Gogh was 'moved by the beauty of the site'.

Next to the Alyscamps are the important nineteenth-century railway workings. One of the warehouses has recently been converted into the main exhibiting hall of the International Photography Exhibition. The photographs shown here might not be to everyone's taste, but the setting is remarkable, with abandoned train engines, dramatically lit steel girders and an evocative overall gloom, the whole reminiscent of a painting by the surrealist artist Delvaux.

Seven kilometres north of Arles on the D17 is the abbey of Montmajour, which, like the nearby Mont de Cordes, was once an island in the middle of marshes. This major abbey was founded by Benedictines in the tenth century, supposedly on the site where Saint Trophimus hid from the Romans. The tiny tenth-century chapel of Saint-Pierre is next to the rock seat where Saint Trophimus is meant to have prayed; special permission is now needed to visit this chapel. The main abbey church, together with its crypt and cloister (exhibitions of contemporary art are put on in the rooms adjoining this) are all of the twelfth century and have a powerfully austere character. You should also climb up to the top of the tower, which has an extensive view towards the flat, mysterious expanse of the Crau: the large mound immediately to the south is the Mont de Cordes, an important prehistoric site but now in private possession (see page 40).

The abbey declined in the seventeenth century, and was left in ruins after the Revolution. Outside the grounds, to the north, is the eleventh-century chapel of the Sainte-Croix, an interesting cruciform structure with paleo-Christian tombs carved into the rock in front of it.   [4A]

AUPS, a large village in the middle of a wooded, fertile plateau, has become the lively tourist centre of an area of Provence which has only recently been 'discovered'. At the bottom of the village is the attractive late gothic church of Saint-Pancrace; further up the main street is a former Ursuline convent now housing a modern art gallery (the Musée Simon Segal) of questionable value. The charming sixteenth-century clock tower at the top of the village was probably originally a watch-out tower and is today the most picturesque element on the Aups skyline.   [4D]

AURON, see SAINT-ÉTIENNE-DE-TINÉE

AVIGNON has not always had the tourist appeal which it has today. 'There is little of interest in this town,' wrote the Abbé Jean-Pierre Papon in 1780. He admired its position by the Rhône and the fertile countryside around it, but found that the place itself had 'nothing which matches the beauty of its situation'. He regretted that there were no traces of its Roman past, and that the Avignon popes had so little interest in antiquity and had not built a series of glorious classical monuments as the Italian popes had done. By the middle of the nine-teenth century, medievalism had come into fashion and Avignon had begun to fascinate travellers. But even then the town did not always inspire immediate enthusiasm. Henry James, for instance, had to come here three times before beginning to fall for its charms. The *mistral* is thought to be harsher here than in any other place in Provence, and James had to put up with it on all three of his visits. Then there was the dirt and decay of Avignon's back-streets, romantic for some, but also depressing when seen in conjunction with a grey, bleak day and the lugubrious dark green of the Rhône. 'Avignon!' exclaims the nar-rator of Lawrence Durrell's *Monsieur* (1974). 'Its shabby lights and sneaking cats were the same as ever; overturned dustbins, the glitter of fish scales, olive oil, broken glass, a dead scorpion.'

Avignon was built around a rock, the rock which is today called the Rocher des Doms. Neolithic man lived here, and later the Romans

AVIGNON

came, establishing a small colony and possibly building a temple to Diana on the top of the rock. The town flourished for a time as a trading post, yet never achieved anything like the importance of places such as ARLES or AIX-EN-PROVENCE. The most dramatic moment in its history prior to the arrival of the popes was its siding in the thirteenth century with the Albigensians, and the consequent razing of the town and pulling down of its defensive walls.

As a consequence of the Albigensian wars, the papacy acquired in 1274 the territory known as the Comtat-Venaissin. In 1309, threatened by the political ambitions of the powerful Italian families, Clement V abandoned Rome for Avignon, which had the advantage of being a relatively peaceful town, conveniently situated by the Rhône and almost on the border with the Comtat. He took with him the College of Cardinals, the Bishops Legate and the huge administrative body known as the *Curia*. Artists, diplomats, courtiers, ecclesiastics and pilgrims poured into Avignon from all over Europe. The prostitute population of Avignon grew enormously to cater for all these new customers, as did the number of local criminals and swindlers. After 1348, when the town was finally purchased by the papacy, many more people moved in, finding it a safe haven from French justice or, in the case of Jews, persecution. To Petrarch, one of the most distinguished of the Italian residents, Avignon was a living hell, 'the sewers of the earth'.

The papacy returned to Rome in 1377 but the so-called 'anti-popes' ruled until 1403 (see page 76). Moreover, the town remained a papal possession until 1790, and for a while leading artists continued to come here, so strong was its reputation as a centre for artistic patronage. Up to the Revolution, numerous religious orders remained based here, important palaces were still built, the Jewish community expanded, and Avignon thrived as a publishing centre, thanks to its freedom from French censorship. Even after the Revolution, when the religious orders were expelled and the Jewish community dispersed, the town's publishing houses stayed on and played a major role in fostering the literary group known as the Félibrige. Avignon became the favourite meeting-place of this group, and later on was to be known as 'the cradle of the Félibres'. While Arles and Aix slumbered, Avignon thrived intellectually, and it has remained to this day one of the liveliest cultural centres in France. An enormous boost in recent

years was the instigation in 1956 of Europe's most important international theatre festival, an event which spills all over the streets,
has inspired an ever growing number of 'fringe' attractions, and draws
crowds from all over the world. But even outside the festival weeks (in
July and August) much of the animation remains, the cafés are packed,
major rock concerts are put on here, and the local cinema club, the
Utopia (15 Rue Galante), has one of the best programmes in Provence.

Avignon is still entirely surrounded by its fourteenth-century walls,
even though these now contain only a fifth of the town's total population. These walls, like those at Carcassonne, were in fact heavily
'restored' (rebuilt would be a better word) by Viollet-le-Duc in the
nineteenth century; none the less they greatly contribute to the town's
romantic appeal. Near their north-western perimeter are to be found
Avignon's most famous monuments. Attached to the walls, and projecting half-way across the Rhône, is the Pont Saint-Bénézet, the bridge
which inspired the celebrated nursery rhyme, 'Sur le Pont d'Avignon/
On y danse tous en rond' (On the Bridge at Avignon everyone
dances in a circle). One of the oldest surviving monuments in Avignon,
this was built in the late twelfth century, and there is a small romanesque chapel in the middle. Dancing never took place on the bridge
in the past (if it happened at all, it was done on the island in mid-
stream), but you will always find tourists trying to do it today.

The impressive Rocher des Doms, which rises in a sheer cliff above
the river, stands just to the east of the bridge and has been incorporated
into the fortifications. Entering the town by the gate at its foot (the
Porte du Rocher), you will soon reach the large traffic-free Place du
Palais, the tourist heart of the town. A multi-storeyed car-park has
recently been built underneath this square, and for those who leave
their car here there is the curious experience of taking a lift and
finding yourself emerging directly in front of the Papal Palace. This
palace is by no means the only attraction of the square. Directly
facing it is the Old Mint, a seventeenth-century structure with a
baroque façade comprising powerfully sculpted swags of fruit and
other such ornamentation. Adjoining the palace to the north, on top
of a flight of steps, is the cathedral of Notre-Dame-des-Doms, a large
building dating mainly from the romanesque period; two frescoes by
the Sienese artist Simone Martini remain in the entrance porch (the
others have been taken to the palace), while inside is the flamboyant

gothic tomb of John XXII, and a beautiful central dome supported by an elegant, pillared lantern.

At the northern end of the square is the Petit Palais ('Little Palace'), an archbishop's residence built in 1317 but enlarged and heavily remodelled in the fifteenth century and extensively restored in recent times. In the 1970s the place was converted into a museum of medieval paintings and sculptures. A great many of the paintings are Italian thirteenth- to early sixteenth-century works acquired in Rome in the early nineteenth century by the Marquis G. B. Campana (this collection was confiscated in 1861 when the Marquis was accused of misappropriating papal funds, and was later sold to Napoleon III). These paintings are charming but largely unmemorable, with the major exception of a *Virgin and Child* by Botticelli. The so-called Avignon school (see pages 76–7) is represented principally by Enguerrand Quarton's very sculptural *Virgin and Child between Two Saints and Two Bishops*, an interesting work which nevertheless pales in comparison with the same artist's *Coronation of the Virgin* at Villeneuve-lès-Avignon (see page 242).

In between the Petit Palais and the cathedral of Notre-Dame-des-Doms is the entrance to what is perhaps the most enjoyable attraction lying off the square, the public park built in the 1830s around the summit of the Rocher des Doms. Stendhal, Dickens, Prosper Mérimée, and Henry James are among the many who have enthused over this place, with its lawns and shaded paths leading up to a pool with ducks, an erotic statue, and a grotto. Steps take you to the top of the grotto, from where you can enjoy a magnificent view over the Rhône valley. There could be no better place to recover from the ordeal of a tour around the Papal Palace.

The Papal Palace is in fact not one but two palaces, the first being built by Benedict XII between 1334 and 1342, and the second by Benedict's successor, Clement VI, between 1342 and 1352. The guided tour of this massive complex takes an hour and has unfortunately become obligatory to any visit to Avignon (few people bothered to come here before the mid nineteenth century, and at any rate the place was then largely taken over by a barracks and prison). The frescoes by Simone Martini, Matteo Giovannetti and others are lovely, but the interior is otherwise bare, having been stripped after the Revolution. To Henry James the palace always remained 'the dreariest of all historical buildings'. 'The place,' he continued, 'is as intricate as it is vast and as desolate as it is dirty. The imagination has, for some reason or other, to make more than the effort usual in such cases to restore and repeople it.'

South of the Place du Palais is the Place de l'Horloge, the most animated square in the town and a place crowded with open-air cafés and buskers; on its western side are the nineteenth-century town hall and theatre. The Rue de la République leads south from here, almost all the way to the railway station beyond the southern gate, and is the main artery of the town. To those disappointed by the Papal Palace, Avignon offers a remarkable range of other possibilities to the west and east of this street. There is little point in listing all the town's medieval and baroque churches, nearly all of which have fine baroque altarpieces by the local artists Mignard and the Parrocels; these paintings were the only objects Papon thought worth commenting on in his description of the town. There are also numerous museums, quiet squares, and an endless number of palaces, particularly from the sixteenth century onwards. Many of these sights are little known and hidden away, and you feel a great sense of discovery in coming across them. Durrell referred to the 'putrescence' of Avignon's squares, and though the town has been much tidied up recently (and even a group of characterless modern apartments has been constructed in a small quarter to the west of the Place du Palais), the place still has a great many corners with a romantically decrepit character; central Avignon, in other words, has still the feel of a real town.

The western half of the town is in many ways the most elegant part of Avignon. At the junction of the Place de l'Horloge turn west into the Rue Saint-Agricol. Immediately to your left is a tiny alley leading after a few yards to the flamboyant gothic portal of the Palais du Roure (no. 3 Rue du Collège-du-Roure). You should step inside to see the enchanting fifteenth-century courtyard. The palace was built for a Florentine mercantile family, the Baroncellis, who kept the building until the end of the nineteenth century. The last member of the family to own it was the Marquis Baroncelli-Javon, the poet rancher of the Camargue and a protégé of Frédéric Mistral; inside the palace Mistral edited his Provençal literary journal, Aïoli, and the place has now become a library and archive devoted to Provençal history, folklore and literature. Further down the Rue Saint-Agricol, at no. 19, is another important place associated with the Félibres, the Librairie Roumanille. This is today an excellent bookshop specializing entirely in books on Provence; at the back of the shop is a delightful nineteenth-century room where the Félibres used to meet, and where Joseph Roumanille directed his small publishing company, which is still running today.

Beyond the fifteenth-century church of Saint-Agricol, the Rue Saint-Agricol joins the Rue Joseph Vernet, a beautiful street with many eighteenth-century palaces and various antique shops and quiet cafés. The Rue Baroncelli at its northern end leads into the Place Crillon, a pleasant small square adjoining one of the western gates of the town and boasting a good flea-market on Saturdays. On its northern side stands Avignon's oldest and most famous hotel, the Hôtel de l'Europe. Originally a sixteenth-century nobleman's house, this had already become a hostelry by the time Napoleon first stayed in 1799. In the nineteenth century the hotel put up a remarkable succession of distinguished guests, many of whom were English, for it was the English who were among the earliest enthusiasts of Avignon. Robert Browning, eloping with Elizabeth Barrett, stopped here; Dickens came, and so did George Eliot, the future Edward VII and Cardinals Manning and Newman.

Another guest was the philosopher John Stuart Mill, who was to win a special place in the heart of the Avignon people. In 1858 he was staying at the hotel with his adored wife Harriet. They had not been long here before she fell ill and died; she was buried in the large cemetery of Saint-Véran outside the western walls of the town. The distraught Mill, reluctant to leave her tomb, bought a house overlooking the cemetery and moved into this all the furniture from their room in the Hôtel de l'Europe; he spent much of his later life in Avignon, and died here in 1873. The main entrance to the Saint-Véran cemetery is on the street now named the Avenue Stuart Mill; nearby is the Stuart Mill swimming-pool. Many eminent Victorians came to pay their respects to Harriet's tomb, including George Eliot, who noted that the effusive essay which Mill penned to her on top of the slab was so long that there was room for little else; when Mill himself died and was laid beside her, his name had to be discreetly squeezed into the side.

Back on the Rue Joseph Vernet head south, and turn right after the

Rue Saint-Agricol on to the Rue Victor Hugo. At the end of this road is a large nineteenth-century house which belonged this century to a wealthy industrialist and collector, Louis Vouland. Vouland left the house and its collections to the town on his death in 1973, and the place has now been turned into the most recent and least visited of Avignon's museums. The interior is disappointingly bland, but there is much fine eighteenth-century furniture and porcelain. Return to the Rue Joseph Vernet, continue south, and you will reach, on the left-hand side, the Musée Calvet, a museum as full of character as the Musée Louis Vouland is lacking in it.

The eighteenth-century palace which houses this art gallery and archaeological museum is one of the most evocative in Avignon, and has a parched green courtyard where peacocks strut. Stendhal once visited this courtyard, and an almost illegible inscription on one of its walls quotes a passage from his *Mémoires d'un touriste* in which he relates how he came here feeling very depressed, and was soon overcome by a deep serenity which he had only felt before in Italian churches. Most of the building is almost as dilapidated as the inscription, but restoration work has slowly begun; one can only hope that in the process of being tidied up the place is not stripped of its faded elegance, which is so integral to its charm. In complete contrast to the always crowded Petit Palais, this is a quiet museum where the visitor can happily spend hours gradually absorbing the varied collections. There are prehistoric pots, Roman and even Egyptian finds, and a dusty display of wrought-ironwork which puts together, in a single case, instruments of torture and dentistry equipment. Above all there are the paintings, which take over chronologically from where the Petit Palais left off but are particularly extensive in nineteenth- and twentieth-century works. These include an outstanding series of canvases by the expressionist painter Soutine, and good works by Corot, Manet and Renoir. The most famous piece is David's portrayal of the drummer boy *Barra* (1784), who was killed during the Revolution for having refused to shout 'Vive le Roi' instead of 'Vive la République'. This monochromatic, unfinished work is beautifully executed, but is slightly absurd in the treatment of its subject-matter: the naked, androgynous boy seems more in the throes of orgasm than in his death agony. Most of the other paintings range from the indifferent to the downright awful, but there are numerous curiosities. The eighteenth-century Avignon painter Claude-Joseph Vernet (a specialist usually in idyllic marine scenes) is represented by an ingenious *trompe-l'oeil* panel portraying, and actually in the shape of, a canvas on an easel with a palette and reproductions of famous paintings stuck on to it. His grandson Horace was responsible for the museum's silliest painting, *Mazeppa*, which shows a naked man tied to the back of a rearing horse and being chased by ravenous wolves. As for Chassériau's *Sleeping Nymph* of 1880, this has the distinction of being perhaps the first serious portrait of a female nude which shows hair under the armpits.

In another wing of the same building is the Musée Requien, an old-fashioned natural history museum with an interesting history. Esprit Requien, a close friend of Prosper Mérimée and a leading force in Avignon cultural circles in the first half of the nineteenth century, was a naturalist who achieved renown for his work in paleontology, malacology (the study of molluscs) and above all botany. Provence, with its wealth of flora, has always attracted the botanist, and it was through the help and hospitality of Requien that such eminent botanists as A.-P. de Candolle and the Englishman George Bentham came to pursue their studies in the region. The museum, of which Requien was one of the first curators, covers all aspects of Provence's natural life, but its greatest treasure is its herbarium. This collection of pressed plants, one of the largest in France, was initially built up by Requien himself and was enhanced later in the century by a generous donation from John Stuart Mill. Mill had once paid a visit to the museum and met Requien's successor as curator, the famous naturalist, J.-H. Fabre (see SÉRIGNAN). The two men became the best of friends, and Fabre greatly stimulated Mill's interest in botany. Together they explored the Vaucluse, and even planned to write together a treatise on the flora and fauna of this region.

South of the Musée Requien the Rue Joseph Vernet curves to the east and joins the lower end of the Rue de la République. Turn left in the direction of the Place de l'Horloge. At the junction of the first street to your right, the Rue Frédéric Mistral, is a seventeenth-century church inside which is a small lapidary museum containing the Salyan carving found in Noves and known as the 'Tarasque' (see page 43). Leave the Rue de la République at the next street up, the Rue Théodore Aubanel, and turn right into the Place Saint-Didier. The attractive fourteenth-century church of Saint-Didier is famous for its fifteenth-century relief of the *Carrying of the Cross* by Francesco Laurana, the greatest Italian sculptor to have worked in Provence (see pages 76–7). Now you have a choice, either to head north through a shop-filled pedestrian quarter towards the district of Saint-Pierre, or else make a detour to the eastern walls of the town, a rather long but rewarding walk. If you choose the latter you start off by taking the Rue du Roi René, a winding street with numerous sculpted seventeenth- and eighteenth-century palaces (at no. 22 is a plaque recording the site of the convent of Sainte-Claire, where Petrarch first set eyes on Laura, see page 99). This brings you to the Rue des Teinturiers, a most picturesque street which hugs a small exposed section of the narrow river Sorgue. Plane trees and lively bistros line one side of the street, while on the other tiny bridges lead off to buildings across the stream. You could almost be in Bruges, an impression strengthened by the gothic bell-tower of the former convent church of the Franciscans. This tower is all that remains of the convent where Petrarch's Laura was supposedly buried (see page 100). Further down the street, also on the other side of the stream, is the sixteenth-to seventeenth-century church belonging to the Grey Penitents, the first of the many Penitent Brotherhoods which were founded in Avignon during the papal residence, and also the last one to survive. At the end of the street is a quaint nineteenth-century water wheel, the one remaining wheel out of several which once animated this stretch of the Sorgue and provided the power for the textile industry which gave the street its name, 'the Street of the Dyers'.

The Rue des Teinturiers ends up by the western walls, from where you could walk to the cemetery of Saint-Véran and see the Stuart Mill tomb. Alternatively you could head north and visit another of Avignon's pleasant hidden corners, the long shaded square of the Place des Carmes. The church of the Carmelites has kept its beautiful fifteenth-century gothic façade, and next to this is an old-fashioned café, a relaxing stop on a hot afternoon. The road at the southern end of the square, a continuation of the Rue Carnot, will lead you to the Place Carnot, just to the east of the Place de l'Horloge. On the square stands the gothic church of Saint-Pierre, and there are several interesting monuments in the vicinity, including a mid-nineteenth-century synagogue (still functioning), which marks the site of the Jewish ghetto (see page 80). A fine eighteenth-century palace on the Rue de Mons houses an institute named after the actor and director Jean Vilar, the founder of the Avignon Theatre Festival; the institute has much documentation about the festival and puts on small exhibitions devoted to the history of world theatre. Down a small alley behind the church of Saint-Pierre is the Musée Théodore Aubanel, Avignon's most enjoyable small museum and a place with an intimate charm. The Aubanels established a publishing and printing firm in Avignon in the mid eighteenth century and brought out, until the Revolution, the *Courrier d'Avignon*, at that time one of France's most important newspapers. The family firm is still running and the museum is installed in the family home, near the offices and printing works of the firm. Part of the museum is devoted to the history of printing in Avignon, and you are reminded that in 1756 there were as many as twenty printers in the town, as compared to thirty-two in Paris. The rest of the museum has souvenirs of the family's most famous member, the poet and Félibre Théodore Aubanel; there are letters to him by friends such as Dumas and Mistral, manuscripts of his, his writing desk and a portrait of the greatest love of his life, 'Zani', the woman who broke his heart by retiring to a convent (see pages 106–7). A rarity is a small painting by the art critic Théophile Gautier, a friend of Aubanel's.

You cannot come to Avignon without crossing over the Rhône to Villeneuve-lès-Avignon. Though in Languedoc, and thus in French territory in the Middle Ages, the French kings allowed the cardinals in the papal entourage to build for themselves large palaces here, palaces to which they could come to escape the dirt and confusion of Avignon; even today many of the wealthy citizens of Avignon prefer to live here, and the place has numerous luxurious villas. At the southern end of the town is the tall and remarkably well preserved fourteenth-century tower of Philippe le Bel, which once stood guard at the western end of the Pont Saint-Bénézet. Climbing the Rue Montée de la Tour towards the centre of the town you reach a former seventeenth-century palace. First a hospice and then a municipal museum was installed in this building. The museum is a dark and musty place filled with grim and decaying ecclesiastical bric-à-brac, most of which came from the town's two monasteries (see below). The visit is made worthwhile by the outstanding *Coronation of the Virgin* (1454), one of the masterpieces of the Avignon School. The artist, Enguerrand Quarton, was specifically contracted to portray in the background the church of Saint Peter's in Rome and the Castel Sant' Angelo; but Quarton also decided to include elements of local scenery, such as Mont Ventoux and the cliffs of L'Estaque. Next to this painting is a good copy of another work attributed to Quarton, the celebrated *Avignon Pietà*, also originating from Villeneuve but now in the Louvre in Paris.

Just north of the museum is the former collegiate church of Notre-Dame, a fourteenth-century structure with an attractive cloister and an excellent polychrome ivory statuette of the *Virgin and Child*. Further north, off the Rue de la République, is the largest and most important Charterhouse in France, founded in 1356 by Innocent VI, who is buried in the church here. The monastic buildings have been taken over by an organization calling itself CIRCA (Centre International de Recherche de Création et d'Animation), the lofty aims of which are not immediately easy to understand but have led to a number of its countless cells being taken over by historical and artistic exhibitions. The most impressive feature of the place is its sheer size, especially the 80-metre wide graveyard cloister, which also has a chapel off its west walk frescoed by fourteenth-century Italian artists.

A visit to Villeneuve is completed by walking up the barren hill behind the Charterhouse to the even larger Saint-André Fort, which was erected in the fourteenth century and has kept its massive, original walls. Within these walls was once an abbey where pilgrims stopped on their way to Santiago de Compostela. The abbey has now gone, but in its place are delightful terraced gardens with superb views towards Avignon. [3A]

BANDOL is a quiet and sophisticated resort, with a pleasantly laid out zoo in which exotic plants and trees compete with the animals in attracting the visitor's attention. La Ker-Mocotte Hôtel, perched on a cliff above its privately owned beach, was built originally as the home of the famous Provençal actor Raimu (see page 122).

The tiny and once barren island of Bendor, two kilometres from Bandol, is the property of the *pastis*-merchant Paul Ricard (see pages 209–11), who transformed it into a verdant holiday centre complete with such attractions as an imitation Provençal fishing village, an artisans' quarter, a nautical club, and a very enjoyable museum of wines and spirits. [5C]

BARBEGAL: For this Roman aqueduct see FONTVIEILLE.

LA BARBEN: Three kilometres to the east of the hamlet of La Barben is a castle with the most romantic position. Perched high above a densely wooded landscape, the castle of La Barben is a crenellated structure dating back to the twelfth century. Between 1453 and 1474 it was owned by the daughter of 'Good King René', Yolande, Duchess of Lorraine. Since 1474 it has belonged to a family of reputed Scottish ancestry, the Forbins, who extensively remodelled and redecorated the place between the sixteenth and early nineteenth centuries. As you walk up the steep path to the castle, you will notice below you a small formal garden designed by Le Nôtre. The interior of the castle is pleasantly homely and has fine medieval and Renaissance furnishings, as well as some magnificent small rooms in Empire style. One of these is named after Pauline Bonaparte, later Borghese, who stayed here in 1807 when taking a thermal cure at GRÉOUX. The owner of the castle at that time was Auguste de Forbin, who was chancellor to the princess and also a close friend of the leading neo-classical painter, Granet, a pupil of David. Granet was a frequent guest at La Barben and left here a number of small works, including a painting of the castle's attractive old kitchen. [4B]

BARBENTANE: Built on the wooded slopes of the gentle range of the Montagnette, Barbentane is an attractive medieval town with two impressive nineteenth-century gates, a romanesque church and some fine medieval and Renaissance houses. Its market is renowned for its aubergines.

The castle of the Marquis de Barbentane sits in the middle of an elegant formal park at the bottom of the village, overlooking the densely fertile plains of the Rhône valley. Designed in 1674 for Paul-François de Barbentane, the building has remained in the family's possession since then and was undamaged during the Revolution. The ornate and homogeneous interior owes its appearance principally to Pierre Balthazar de Barbentane, an ambassador to Tuscany in the late eighteenth century and a great lover of the Italian baroque. [3A]

BARCELONNETTE: Dwarfed on three sides by high mountains,

Barcelonnette is Provence's northernmost town and a place with a strong Alpine character. Its name is a diminutive of Barcelona, the ancestral home of Count Raymond Bérenger V, who established a fortified settlement here in 1231. From 1388 to 1713 it belonged to the Counts of Savoy. The neatly laid out town centre dates mainly from the late eighteenth and early nineteenth centuries, the old town having been destroyed by serious fires in the mid eighteenth century.

Visitors to Barcelonnette today might well be surprised by the strong Mexican influences on the town. There are Mexican folk objects on display in the town hall museum, shops selling Mexican food and Mexican crafts, an 'Avenue Porfirio Diaz', a 'Camping Tampico', and a Mexican cultural centre (the Casa de Mexico) putting on exhibitions of Mexican folklore, organizing courses in Mexican cookery, and arranging flights to Mexico.

The reason for all this goes back to 1821, when three brothers, the Arnauds (commemorated today by a plaque opposite the church of Saint-Pierre-ès-Liens) left their impoverished native town and made the brave move of emigrating to Mexico. Mexico was then in the throes of Revolution, and the brothers hoped to take over the trade relinquished by the departing Spaniards and other foreigners. In the heart of Mexico City they opened up Las Siete Puertas, a textile shop which survives today as a large department store. In 1830 the Arnaud brothers were joined by two other men from Barcelonnette, both of whom returned home fifteen years later, having made what seemed to the other inhabitants of the town a considerable fortune. From that time onwards began a large-scale emigration movement to Mexico. Some of the Barcelonnettes prospered, and one family became leading Mexican bankers; most of them died in poverty. Several of the successful ones returned home and constructed in the valley between Barcelonnette and Jausiers a number of pompous Mexican-style villas with names such as the Villa Guanajuato. The Casa de Mexico today gives assistance to Mexican families coming to Barcelonnette in search of their Provençal roots. [1E]

BARGEMON, a shaded medieval town set in rolling, wooded countryside, has an extensive surviving section of ramparts. Attached to these is the fourteenth-century church of Saint-Étienne, notable mainly for its flamboyant gothic west doorway. The baroque chapel of Notre-Dame-de-Montaigu has been a centre of pilgrimage since the seventeenth century, when it acquired a miraculous statuette of the Virgin originating from Flanders. [4D]

BARJOLS: With its tree-lined streets and squares, and abundance of fountains and nearby springs, Barjols has come to be known as the 'Tivoli of Provence'. The most striking of these fountains is the one near the town hall. It takes the form of a basin surmounted by a mushroom covered in moss; adjoining it is a plane tree, fifteen metres wide, said to be the largest in France.

Every fourth year, around 17 January, Barjols is the scene of some impressive and unusual celebrations in honour of the town's patron saint, Saint Marcel. The occasion, referred to as 'La Grande Saint-Marcel', begins in the morning with a procession of musicians playing three-holed flutes and narrow drums (these traditional Provençal instruments, known respectively as *galoubets* and *tambourins*, are today made only in Barjols). In the afternoon a cow, decorated with ribbons, is led through the streets of the town, eventually to be blessed by a priest, sacrificed, and placed on a floral float. The day ends with dancing and music in the church where Saint Marcel is buried, the former collegiate chapel of Notre-Dame-de-l'Assomption.

The college of Notre-Dame-de-l'Assomption, a foundation dating back to the eleventh century, was where the Counts of Provence sent their children to be educated in the early Middle Ages. Today only the chapel remains. This was rebuilt in a gothic style in the early sixteenth century, but a relief from the original tympanum has been transferred to an altar in the left aisle.

The finest secular monument in Barjols is the so-called House of the Marquis de Pontèves, with a beautiful Renaissance façade. [4C]

LE BARROUX: The castle of Le Barroux is a massive building over-looking on one side Mont Ventoux and on the other the Dentelles de Montmirail. Originally a twelfth-century structure belonging to the Lords of LES BAUX, it was largely rebuilt during the Revolution. The village below is famous for its so-called 'pink apricots' (*abricots rosés*) and there is an apricot market held here every day throughout July. To the west of the castle is a small road leading to Suzette, a tiny, isolated place set in a landscape of steep hills and vineyards reminiscent of Tuscany. [2B]

BARRY, see BOLLÈNE

LES BAUX: The citadel and ruined village of Les Baux rise from the limestone crags of the Alpilles like some bleached apparition from a fairy-tale. Its position, and its romantic history involving love, poetry and much blood (see pages 96–7), make Les Baux one of the the major tourist sights of Provence.

The citadel of the Lords of Les Baux was built upon a long narrow spur and has now largely been reduced to rock and rubble. The place was razed during the seventeenth century and only parts of the castle survive; the best-preserved fragment is that of the keep, attached to a sheer cliff overlooking the plain of Arles. The village which you have to cross to reach the citadel was a Protestant stronghold during the sixteenth and early seventeenth centuries and features a number of splendid Renaissance buildings, such as the Hôtel de Porcelet (now a small archaeological museum). Tourism has unfortunately destroyed much of the character of the village, which is now filled with souvenir and craft shops. The picturesque Place Vincent has a romanesque church where every Christmas Eve since the sixteenth century there has been celebrated a midnight mass in the form of a Provençal pageant of the Nativity; this is the best known of all the many such pageants in Provence, and you should arrive early to secure reasonable seats. Also on the square is a seventeenth-century chapel which would be wonderful were it not for the painted decorations inside, by the contemporary artist Yves Brayer. The Museum of Modern Art in front of this has more of the truly awful art which this village has inspired in recent years, and is worth a visit solely for the old building (the Hôtel de Mandeville) in which it is housed, and for the works on the ground floor by the wood-engraver Louis Jou, one of the earliest and best of the artists to have settled here. The workshop and Foundation of Louis Jou in the centre of Les Baux are perhaps the most exciting of the village's attractions.

In the valley underneath the village, the so-called 'Val d'Enfer', is the jewel-like garden pavilion of Jeanne de Quiqueran, and the Oustau de Baumanière, one of the famed restaurants of the south of France. [3A]

BEAULIEU, one of the most fashionable Riviera resorts of the late nineteenth century, has today a quiet elegance which makes it a favourite place for the elderly rich. Together with nearby MENTON it enjoys the warmest and most sheltered climate in France, and is full of exotic gardens (mainly private) where even bananas can be found. Splendid examples of *belle époque* architecture abound, including the Hôtel Bristol and the Villas Namouna and Léonine, the homes respectively of Gordon Bennett and the British prime minister, the Marquess of Salisbury. The celebrated restaurant which the former founded here over 100 years ago, La Réserve (see page 202), is still running, and has a magnificent chandeliered dining-room with superb sea-views.

The Villa Kérylos, overlooking the Baie des Fourmis, is one of the few great villas of the Riviera open to the public and is fascinating both as an example of *belle époque* fantasy and as the finest recreation of an ancient Greek villa to be found anywhere. Its creator was the classical archaeologist Théodore Reinach, who had it built at the turn of the century and left it to the state in 1928. Reinach constructed this building with an obsessive concern for detail, and made sure that all concessions to the modern world such as electricity were ingeniously hidden. The materials used were extremely sumptuous (Carrara marble, alabaster, exotic wood), and many authentic Greek pieces (statuettes, vases, mosaics, amphorae) were incorporated into the overall design. This is not Walt Disney make-believe but a highly sophisticated creation, which is further favoured by being set on a little headland of its own, with magical views of the mountainous coast towards Monaco.   [3F]

BEAUMES-DE-VENISE: The wonderful name of this small town on the southern slopes of the Dentelles de Montmirail has nothing to do with Venice but is instead a reference to the Comtat-Venaissin. Since the Middle Ages the town has been famous for its sweet muscat wine. Anne of Austria came here on her visit to Provence in 1660 (see APT), and, in recognition of the excellence of the local wine, presented the parish church with some magnificent liturgical vestments. The Châteauneuf-du-Pape wine grower, the Baron Le Roy, described the Beaumes muscat as 'the nectar of the gods'.

The main monument of artistic interest in the area is the chapel of Notre-Dame-d'Aubune, a kilometre outside the town, off the main road to Carpentras. This is an isolated twelfth-century structure with a most elegant bell-tower and a beautiful position under the Dentelles de Montmirail (the key can be had from the farmhouse below). [2B]

BIOT, north of Antibes, is an attractive village with an arcaded square and a reputation for its ceramic and glass industries. Fifteen days before his death in August 1955, the artist Fernand Léger bought a large property here with the intention of constructing large-scale ceramics in its grounds. After his death his widow Nadia decided to build a museum at Biot to display the 347 works he left to her in his will.

The Musée National Fernand Léger is situated just to the south of the village, off the D4; on your way there you will pass near the Verrerie de Biot (founded in 1957), a famous glass factory which can be visited. The Léger Museum is dominated on the outside by a massive polychrome ceramic by Léger, originally intended for the Olympic Studios at Hannover; further ceramic works by him are scattered around the pleasant gardens of the museum. Léger's greatest achievement was as a painter, and inside the building you will see a wide selection of his works, ranging from his early figurative canvases of around 1905 to his experiments with cubism in the subsequent decade, and, finally, to his rejection of complete abstraction in favour of colourful, simplified portrayals of the everyday life of the worker.

BOLLÈNE, an important market town since the days of the Avignon popes, lies in the middle of one of the most industrialized sections of the Rhône valley. The town has a small but very attractive medieval centre, a municipal gallery with drawings by Chagall and Picasso, and a museum commemorating Pasteur, who discovered an inoculation against swine fever when staying at Bollène in 1892.

A tiny uphill road north from Bollène leads after four kilometres to the abandoned village and castle of Barry, on the border of present-day Provence. Barry, referred to in signposts as '*le village troglodytique*', is an extraordinary place, partially built into the rock and completely overgrown. Prehistoric in origin, Barry was demolished in 1228 after the Albigensian Crusade. [2A]

BONNIEUX, the liveliest of the villages on the northern side of the Lubéron, is shaped like a perfect triangle at the apex of which is the twelfth-century parish church, surrounded by ancient cedars. In the steeply sloping upper half of the village is an old bakery, recently transformed into the Musée de la Boulangerie. This spaciously arranged museum is devoted to the history of bread-making, and you can browse through books and articles on the subject in the comfortable library, or even take these out on to the roof terrace, which enjoys a beautiful view of the Petit Lubéron; in the summer months exhibitions of local artists are put on in the museum.

At the bottom of the village is an ugly nineteenth-century church, which none the less is worth a visit for a group of fifteenth-century German paintings which it possesses. If from here you follow the D149 in the direction of the Pont Julien (see APT) you will come after a kilometre to the Château-la-Canorgue, an atmospheric nineteenth-century mansion which produces one of the finest red wines in the Lubéron.

On the other side of Bonnieux, off the D36 to Lourmarin, is a road marked 'Route des Cèdres', which will take you past a tall nineteenth-century folly in the form of a Tuscan campanile and deposit you at the top of the Petit Lubéron. From here you can walk along the mountain's wooded ridge. After half a kilometre a forest path to the left leads to the edge of the forest, from where there is a beautiful view embracing the Alpilles, Montagne Sainte-Victoire, and, on clear days, the Mediterranean.   [3B]

BONPAS: For this Charterhouse see NOVES.

BORMES-LES-MIMOSAS: Shrouded in mimosa and eucalyptus and enjoying lovely views out towards the Iles d'Hyères (see HYÈRES), Bormes-les-Mimosas is one of the most celebrated of the Provençal hill villages. Its proximity to the sea made it very vulnerable in the past to overseas invaders: the Saracens sacked it in 730, the Corsairs in 1393, the Moors in 1529, and finally the Genoese, under Andrea Doria, in 1539. The village, so brutally damaged in the past, has been over-prettified in recent years, with even the name of the village changed in 1968 from Bormes to the rather precious Bormes-les-Mimosas.

A local nineteenth-century landscape painter, Jean-Charles Cazin, is commemorated in the local art gallery, housed in a pretty eighteenth-century palace, the Maison Taibé, and containing also two terracottas by Rodin and works by the 'pointillist' painters Maximilien Luce, Henry Cross, and Van Rysselberghe.

There are good sandy beaches at Le Lavandou, a modern, characterless resort three miles to the south. [5D]

BOULBON: The small farming village of Boulbon is dominated by its monumental castle, attached impressively to a steep outcrop of rock under the barren cliffs on the eastern slopes of the Montagnette. The castle, standing guard over the Rhône valley between Avignon and Tarascon, was built by the Counts of Provence around 1400 and intended to protect the western frontier of their land.

On the northern outskirts of the town, adjoining the village cemetery, is the solidly built church of Saint-Marcellin. Every year, on the 1 June, an exclusively male procession makes its way to this church for the blessing of bottles of local wine. [3A]

BREIL-SUR-ROYA: Though badly damaged during the last war, this Alpine town near the Italian border retains an impressive and sumptuously ornate baroque church (Sancta Maria in Albis), and, behind this, a number of tall eighteenth- and nineteenth-century houses covered on the outside with *trompe-l'oeil* ornamentation. Enthusiasts of Italian architecture of the period of Mussolini will appreciate the railway station, which, like that of Saint-Dalmas-de-Tende (see TENDE), further up the Roya valley, seems ludicrously large and grand for the small community which it serves. [3F]

BRIGNOLES, an important market town, has been known since the Middle Ages for its prunes, which were exported all over France; the Duke of Guise was reputedly eating some when assassinated at Blois.

There is a small but remarkably unspoilt old town, dominated by the summer residence of the Counts of Provence. The Counts started coming to Brignoles in the twelfth century, and there was a tradition that their wives always gave birth here. Their palace, though dating in part from the twelfth century, was extensively rebuilt in the fifteenth and sixteenth centuries. The interior was further altered in the late nineteenth century in the course of installing here the Musée du Pays Brignolais; the one room to keep its medieval character is the fourteenth-century chapel of Saint-Catherine.

The museum is one of those chaotic, eccentric places which repay the visit for the atmosphere alone. The prize object is the sixth-century sarcophagus of La Gayole, a fascinating example of the intermingling of pagan and Christian elements (see page 65). It says much of the layout of this museum that directly in front of this masterpiece of early Christian art is the sorry shell of a concrete rowing boat, created by a misunderstood local genius, J. Lambot, the inventor of reinforced concrete. Jumbled together elsewhere in the museum are some dinosaur eggs; exhibits relating to the local bauxite industry (the most important in France); works by a well-known family of seventeenth-century painters, the Parrocels (they all spent much time in Brignoles); and an intriguing mechanical crib, activated by a press of a button and guaranteed to absorb the attention of the most blasé museum visitor.   [4D]

LA BRIGUE: Situated in a tiny Alpine area of Provence which remained in Savoy possession until as late as 1947 (see TENDE), La Brigue is a remote unspoilt village with cobbled, arcaded streets and a number of fine monuments. The parish church of Saint-Martin is in a Lombard romanesque style and has an interior rich in sixteenth-century furnishings. On the small main square are two delightful baroque chapels, both with stucco and *trompe-l'oeil* decorations.

The town hall, or any of the main hotels in the village, will provide you with the key to the isolated chapel of Notre-Dame-des-Fontaines, which is four kilometres to the west of the village at the end of the tiny D143. Inside is one of the most extensive and remarkable medieval fresco cycles in Provence. The paintings in the choir and on the arch in front of this are of scenes from the life of the Virgin, and are attributed to an obscure Piedmontese artist of the early fifteenth century, Giovanni Baleison. Baleison's Piedmontese contemporary, Giovanni Canavesio, was responsible for the rest of the decoration, which comprises a *Last Judgement* and scenes from Christ's Passion. The works by Canavesio, with their angular figurative style and grotesquely realistic details, reveal a pronounced Germanic influence. This is crude, provincial art, but none the less art with a very considerable power.   [2F]

CABRIS, a fashionable hill village near Grasse with an extensive view of the coast from Cap Ferrat to the Massif of the Maures, has been especially popular with writers, including Gide, Sartre, Camus, Antoine de Saint-Exupéry, and Herbert Marcuse. A number of these writers stayed at the magnificently situated Hôtel l'Horizon, the exotic patio-garden of which was also an inspiration to the popular composer Leonard Bernstein.

CAGNES-SUR-MER comprises three distinct communities – the brash coastal resort of Cros-de-Cagnes, the modern commercial town of Cagnes-Ville, and, rising aristocratically above all this, the medieval hill village of Haut-de-Cagnes. The latter became popular with artists after Auguste Renoir moved here in 1895 and was later an inspiration to Cyril Connolly in his fictional study of an artist colony, *The Rock Pool.*

Haut-de-Cagnes is crowned by its castle, originally built in 1309 when the Lord of Monaco, Raynier Grimaldi, became also Lord of Cagnes. The Grimaldis thoroughly renovated the place in the early seventeenth century, and brought over the Genoese artists J. B. Carlone and Giulio Benso to paint in the central hall a dramatic illusionistic ceiling fresco of the *Fall of Phaeton.* The castle today is taken over by a museum devoted to olive culture; a largely mediocre collection of works by contemporary Mediterranean artists from Dufy to Vasarély; and – in a boudoir which once belonged to a Grimaldi marchioness – a group of forty portraits donated to Cagnes by a famous artist's model, Suzy Solidor. The portraits are all of Solidor and are by such well-known painters as Van Dongen, Foujita, Dufy, Marie Laurencin, Otto Friesz, and Picabia.

In 1903, after living at first in the centre of Haut-de-Cagnes, Renoir bought a property outside the village, off a road (the D18) leading down to the sea. This property, Les Collettes, is today a tranquil haven on the edge of the noisy, ugly sprawl of Cagnes-Ville. Renoir's house and studio have now been turned into a museum to him and have been reconstructed as they were when the artist was alive; in the studio you will see the artist's easel, coat and cravat, and the wheelchair to which rheumatism confined him during the last years of his life. Perhaps the greatest attraction of the museum is the magnificent olive grove which surrounds it, and it was in fact this feature which inspired Renoir to buy the property in the first place. [4F]

LES CALANQUES, see CASSIS.

CAMARGUE: For National Park of, see LES-SAINTES-MARIES-DE-LA-MER.

CANNES, at one time a seigniory of the abbey of Lérins, was a fishing village when Lord Brougham was forced to stop here in 1834, on his way to Italy (see pages 141–2). He fell in love with the place, built a villa here, and within a year the place began developing as one of the favourite resorts of the European aristocracy, attracting first the British and then the Russians.

The village which Brougham saw in 1834 is marked by the quarter of Le Souquet, built up around a hill on the western side of the town, next to a small port. Most of the old houses have gone, but on top of the hill is the medieval citadel with a gothic church dating from the late sixteenth century. Inside the twelfth-century keep (rebuilt in the fourteenth century) is the Musée de la Castre, containing mainly oriental, African and South American items collected by an eccentric Dutchman, Baron Lycklama, who died in Cannes in 1900 after a lifetime of exotic travelling. The museum has a portrait of the baron dressed in oriental costume.

Lord Brougham's villa has been pulled down, but the main property of the most influential Englishman to have followed him to Cannes, Lord Woolfield (see page 142), still survives, off the Boulevard Vallombrosa, behind Le Souquet. This, the enormous Château Vallombrosa (remodelled in the late nineteenth century and now divided into flats), is a splendid neo-gothic pile in the middle of a large garden. It was built for Lord Woolfield in 1853 and was sold to another key figure in the history of Cannes, The Duke of Vallombrosa.

One of the more attractive streets linking Le Souquet with the modern town of Cannes to the east is the narrow, traffic-free Rue Meynardier. This animated street has a number of excellent traditional shops, including, at no. 31, Aux Bons Raviolis which has a wide range of home-made pastas; Ceneri, at no. 22, is reputedly one of France's best-stocked cheese shops and boasts over 300 types of cheese. The modern town stretches alongside the nine-kilometre-long coastal boulevard of La Croisette, a thoroughfare glamorously described by Scott Fitzgerald in *Tender is the Night* and now an exceptionally noisy thoroughfare lined with characterless modern apartment blocks and chic private beaches. At the opening of this street, on a site overlooking the old port, is the ugly post-war festival and conference building, which today is famous as the main venue of the town's International Film Festival; this festival, inaugurated in 1939 and held always in May, has helped maintain Cannes's reputation for glamour but is now little more than a glorified trade fair. The building replaced the Cercle Nautique, which was founded in the mid nineteenth century by the Duke of Vallombrosa and was one of the great aristocratic meeting-places of Europe.

Many other great monuments of Cannes's *belle époque* have also disappeared in recent years. One of the fortunate survivors is the Carlton Hotel at 58 Boulevard de la Croisette, a dazzlingly white wedding cake of palatial proportions, built in 1902 in a neo-baroque style. A more poignant, less ostentious reminder of bygone Cannes is the Russian Orthodox church, off the Boulevard Alexandre III on the peninsula of La Croisette. This colourful structure topped by a blue onion dome was built shortly after the arrival at Cannes in 1879 of the Tsarina Maria Alexandrovina.

Just to the north of this church is the fashionable suburban district of La Californie, where Picasso lived in the mid 1950s. Cannes's suburbia spreads in all directions and virtually engulfs the much-prettified medieval hill villages of Le Cannet and Mougins, places that were once very popular with artists (Bonnard lived at Le Cannet from 1925 to his death in 1947, and Picasso died at the Mas de Notre-Dame-de-Vie in Mougins in 1973). In a converted sixteenth-century olive-oil mill south-east of Mougins on the D3 is Roger Vergé's Le Moulin de Mougins, one of the famed restaurants of the south of France and still a great venue for celebrities.

The loveliest excursion you can do from Cannes is to take a boat trip from the old harbour to the Îles de Lérins, two wooded islands with a fascinating history. The Île Saint-Honorat, the further of the two, was where Saint Honoratus stayed in the fourteenth century and formed what was to be one of the most important early Christian monasteries in Europe (see page 63). The island is a tiny one and can be walked round in less than half an hour. At its eastern end is the small chapel of the Trinity, a fifth-century structure which has been heavily restored in recent years. The original monastery was almost entirely destroyed in the course of Saracen and other raids during the Dark Ages. In the eleventh century a fortified monastery was built on the island's southern shore. This tall, crenellated structure has a most romantic position, lapped by water on three sides. Inside is a cloister and a chapel (both revaulted in the fourteenth and seventeenth centuries), and a terrace from where you can see, on clear days, the snow-capped Alps rising above the mainland. The island was bought after the Revolution by a well-known Parisian actress, Marie-Blanche Sanival, a beautiful woman reputed to have put on orgies here. Cistercian monks from Sénanque later took over the island and remain here to this day. The buildings which they occupy, in the centre of the island, incorporate a twelfth-century cloister.

The Île Sainte-Marguerite, a finer place for swimming, is dominated on its northern shore by a large citadel, built by Richelieu, and reinforced by Vauban in 1712. Protestant prisoners were incarcerated here in 1689, and there is now a small museum, installed in one of the cells, devoted to the persecution of the Protestants in Provence; an adjoining cell is supposed to have been the cell after 1687 of the mysterious 'Man in the Iron Mask', the identity of whom was never revealed. A '*son-et-lumière*' show is put on regularly at the citadel throughout July and August.   [4E]

LE CANNET, see CANNES.

CAP CANAILLE, see CASSIS.

CAP D'ANTIBES, see ANTIBES.

CARLUC: For priory of, see CÉRESTE.

CARPENTRAS: A Ligurian and then a Roman settlement, Carpentras became in 1320 the capital of the Comtat-Venaissin, an area of Provence which had been ceded to the papacy in 1274; when the Comtat was re-attached to Provence after the Revolution, Carpentras was made capital of the *département* of the Vaucluse. It is a lively commercial town, famous for its truffles and its mint-flavoured sweets known as *berlingots*, and hosts an important international arts festival in late July and early August.

A ring of tree-lined boulevards marks the site of the medieval fortifications, of which only an impressive fourteenth-century gate – the Porte d'Orange – survives. The one vestige of Roman Carpentras is a badly preserved triumphal arch attached to the north side of the cathedral. The cathedral itself, situated in the middle of a large pedestrian district in the centre of the old town, has a small romanesque section but was built largely between the fifteenth and sixteenth centuries. Its most attractive feature is its southern portal, in a flamboyant gothic style and known as 'the Jew's Gate' because it was through here that Jews on the point of being baptized had to pass.

The Jewish community in Carpentras was one of the largest in Provence. Persecuted and impoverished at first, by the eighteenth century the community had begun to play a vital role in the commercial life of the town. A sign of their new-found prosperity at this time was their pulling down of their old synagogue to make way for the large and sumptuously decorated one which exists today (opposite the town hall), one of the most charming examples of eighteenth-century architecture in the region. The building, with its dazzling rococo interior, is still in use, though the Jewish community is reduced to only a handful of families.

The eighteenth century was a period of intense building activity generally in Carpentras, and most of the finest buildings in the town date from this time. A leading force in the cultural life of eighteenth-century Carpentras was Monsignor Malachie d'Inguimbert, who was appointed Bishop of Carpentras, his native town, in 1735. Inguimbert had spent much time in Italy as a young man, and had built up there a large collection of books and manuscripts. In 1745 he opened his library to the public, and on his death in 1757 he bequeathed this to the town. The Inguimbert Library is now housed in a wing of an elegant eighteenth-century mansion off the Boulevard Albin-Durand. This mansion also contains two old-fashioned museums, the Musée Comtadin (dedicated to the history and folklore of the Comtat-Venaissin) and the Musée Duplessis, an art gallery named after a famous eighteenth-century portraitist born in Carpentras. A ticket to the two museums allows you entry into two further ones in the vicinity. On the narrow Rue du Collège is the Musée Sobirats, a decrepit but highly atmospheric eighteenth-century house filled with furniture, porcelain and other applied arts objects from this period. In between here and the Porte d'Orange is the town's Lapidary Museum (ask one of the staff of the Musée Duplessis to accompany you here), interesting principally for the impressive late baroque church in which it is installed.

The other major monument in Carpentras associated with Inguimbert is on the other side of the town's ring of boulevards. The grandiose Hôtel-Dieu was founded by Inguimbert and built between 1751 and 1762 by the leading Carpentras architect, Antoine d'Allemand. The place still functions as a hospital, but visitors are taken to see the magnificent chapel and the well-preserved pharmacy. The former is in an Italian baroque style and contains the tomb of Inguimbert; the latter is a delicate rococo construction, with beautiful pharmaceutical pots and wooded panels decorated by Duplessis.   [2B]

CASSIS, one of the loveliest of the Provençal coastal resorts, sits squeezed between pine-covered limestone hills and the monumental reddish cliffs of Cap Canaille. The medieval citadel (converted now into a luxury residential area) is built on a narrow, wooded escarpment jutting out to sea. The rest of Cassis developed as an important port and fishing village from the seventeenth century onwards. By the time Mistral popularized the place with the publication of his poem *Calendau* in 1867, the town had already begun to be favoured as a weekend retreat for the people of Marseille, and to be frequented by a number of local artists and intellectuals. This century Cassis has been a haunt of the Fauve painters Matisse, Dufy, Vlaminck and Derain, and the surrealist artist Salvador Dali.

The centre of present-day Cassis is a lively, colourful place, thronging with tourists but, happily, closed to cars. The picturesque port is lined with cafés and restaurants, and many people come here to eat *bouillabaisse*, a dish for which the excellent local white wine provides a perfect accompaniment.

For swimming, it is best to make your way to the eastern end of the town (follow the signs marked Calanques) and from here take the beautiful footpath (about a twenty-minute walk) to the Calanque de Port-Pin, a narrow, shaded inlet which manages to remain peaceful even in the busiest days in July and August. If you are still feeling energetic you can walk on for a further half an hour to a more spectacular inlet, the Calanque d'En-Vau, surrounded by tall cliffs and limestone needles. The path is marked but not always easy to find, and the steep descent down to the inlet (arrows indicate where you should place your feet) is more like rock-climbing than walking. An easier but longer approach is to drive for fifteen kilometres along the Cassis to Marseille road, then turn off and follow a dead-end road until you reach the car-park marked La Gardiole; from here it is an hour's walk to the inlet. Alternatively you can take a boat trip from Cassis to the Calanques, but these trips give you only a cursory glance of the inlets and do not stop off there.

A wonderful car excursion from Cassis is to follow the winding D41A the whole length of the dramatic Cap Canaille to La Ciotat. This is not a trip for the faint-hearted, especially if you decide to get out of your car and peer over the sheer, unprotected 350-metre drop down to the sea.   [5C]

CASTELLANE: A thriving tourist centre, popular with those wanting to visit the Grand Canyon of Verdon (see MOUSTIERS-SAINTE-MARIE), Castellane has a number of fine medieval monuments including a fifteenth-century bridge, a large section of the old ramparts, two gateways, and the former parish church of Saint-Victor, built in the twelfth century by monks from the abbey of Saint-Victor in MARSEILLE. The skyline is dominated by a tall outcrop of rock crowned by the chapel of Notre-Dame-du-Roc, which has been a place of pilgrimage since the ninth century. The present chapel (an eighteenth-century structure) can be reached by a tortuous path starting from behind the town's modern parish church (ask for the key at the presbytery). On 31 January each year a festival (the Fête des Pétardiers) is held at Castellane to commemorate the successful resisting of a siege led in 1586 by Huguenots under the Baron d'Allemagne.

Seven kilometres to the south of Castellane, near the hamlet of Robion, is the striking romanesque chapel of Saint-Thyrse, impressively isolated in the middle of a gaunt, stony plateau.   [3D]

CAVAILLON has been a prosperous market town since Roman times, when its coins had on their reverse a Horn of Plenty; today the town has the reputation of being the wealthiest town *per capita* in the whole of France. Its honeydew melons (much loved by Dumas, see page 199) are its most famous speciality, and can be bought for very low prices on market-days (Mondays) in August.

Most tourists rush past Cavaillon on their way to the Lubéron, unaware of the very interesting town which lies off the unprepossessing main through roads. You should leave your car in the Place du Clos, a pretty square lined with some splendid nineteenth-century cafés (take a look at the palatial interior of the Café de la Belle Époque). At its eastern end the square widens into the Place François Tourel, where a beautifully ornamented Roman arch (called a triumphal arch, but probably a gate on the Roman wall) has been reconstructed. The town's other monuments lie in a small area to the north of these two squares. Walking along the Cours Sadi Carnot you will soon reach the former cathedral of Saint-Véran, a building of twelfth-century origin and with a delightful small cloister. Further north, along the Grande Rue, is an archaeological museum installed in the chapel of a former eighteenth-century hospital and containing a number of important Gallo-Roman finds. Tracing your way back to the Place du Clos along the Rue Raspail, turn off at the Rue Chabran to see the famous Jewish Museum and synagogue, a place which many writers – including Judith Krantz in *Mistral's Daughter* (1983) – have found more like an eighteenth-century *salon* than a place of worship.

If you have the time and energy, you should take the stepped path leading from behind the triumphal arch up the tall rock face which dominates the town to the east. At the top is an inscription by Mistral, a viewing table and a tiny twelfth-century chapel (heavily restored) once guarded by hermits. [3B]

LA CELLE: For this abbey see LES ARCS.

CÉRESTE: At the eastern end of this village is a Roman bridge, the main surviving monument of 'Cataiuca', a small Roman settlement on the Domitian Way. A small lane (the GR4) leads north from here to the ruins of the priory of Carluc, romantically set in a wood next to a running stream.

Founded in the eleventh century, Carluc came under the dependency of the priory of Montmajour (see ARLES) around 1116. The one standing section of the priory is the apse of the main church, notable for its capitals carved with animals and vegetable motifs; a hive of bees has unfortunately been established in the roof, discouraging the curious from coming too close. Nearby are the scanty remains of two further churches and a strange gallery partly hewn out of a rock and with tombs embedded in its floor; one of the tombs discovered here was ornamented with scallop shells, indicating that the buried person was a pilgrim on his way to Santiago de Compostela. [3C]

CHÂTEAU DE MILLE: For this castle see APT.

CHÂTEAU DES FINES ROCHES: For this castle see CHÂTEAUNEUF-DU-PAPE.

CHÂTEAU D'IF, see MARSEILLE.

CHÂTEAUNEUF-DU-PAPE: The importance of Châteauneuf-du-Pape dates from after 1317, when the Avignon Pope John XXII began building a summer residence here and planted the surrounding countryside with vines. This residence, crowning the hill beyond the village, has been heavily damaged and is worth a visit largely for the view to be had from the top of its sole remaining tower.

Most of those who come to the village do so to taste and buy the local red wine, the best known of the Rhône valley wines and the first Appellation Contrôlée in France (see page 206). The cellars most visited are those of Père Anselme, largely because these are joined to an interesting museum of wine. For better wines and a more personal reception you should visit the smaller cellars, such as those of Louis Arnaud and Gilbert Establet. Try to avoid coming here during the wine harvest (late September), when most of the wine-owners will be too preoccupied to spare you much of their time. You should also remember that the local red wines take between three and five years to reach their peak.

Three kilometres to the south of the village on the Avignon road is the Château des Fines Roches, a mock medieval castle which once belonged to the Marquis Folco Baroncelli-Javon (see page 33). The 'castle' was a favourite meeting-place of the leading Provençal writers of the late nineteenth century, including Mistral, Joseph Roumanille, and Alphonse Daudet; today the place is an excellent restaurant and small hotel. [2A]

CHÂTEAURENARD: The small old town of Châteaurenard is, along with CAVAILLON, the largest centre in Provence for the export of fruit and vegetables. On the hill behind it are the ruins of a fourteenth-century castle belonging to the Counts of Provence. Only one of its towers – the Tour de Griffon – survives intact, and this is now a tiny local museum. The rest of the ruins have been incorporated into a municipal park, which is enjoyable to visit on account of its extensive view over the Rhône valley towards AVIGNON. [3A]

COLLOBRIÈRES, the only community of any importance in the

middle of the vast forest of the Maures, is a pleasant village with a number of old houses and a rapidly flowing stream running through its middle. This is the best place in France to buy candied chestnuts or *marrons glacés.*

A forest road to the east, unasphalted in its last stages, leads after six kilometres to the Charterhouse of La Verne, a romanesque construction (heavily remodelled in the eighteenth century) in a grandiose forest setting which seems straight out of a canvas by the German romantic painter Caspar David Friedrich (see page 72). [5D]

COLMARS, a small town which once guarded the Provençal frontier, has an impressive setting of forests and mountains. It is flanked by two medieval castles (including the massive and well-preserved Fort de Savoie), and is completely encircled by fortifications designed in the late seventeenth century by Vauban. Inside the old town are a number of quiet small squares with fountains. [2E]

COMPS-SUR-ARTUBY is a small village perched on a hill near the entrance to the Grand Canyon of the Verdon (see MOUSTIERS-SAINTE-MARIE). Standing in isolation above the village is the thirteenth-century chapel of Sainte-Philomène (dedicated to Saint Andrew), a granite structure in a severe gothic style which perfectly accords with the wilderness of the surrounding landscape. [3D]

CRESTET, one of the prettiest of the villages built around the Dentelles de Montmirail, has the appeal of a medieval miniature. The twelfth-century church stands on a minute square lined with an arcade and decorated in the middle with a fountain; from here a narrow cobbled lane leads up to the ruins of the eleventh-century castle, now in the process of being turned into a private residence. [2B]

CUCURON: The name of this village on the southern side of the Lubéron is thought, wittily but wrongly, to be derived from the Latin 'Cur currunt?' (Why are they running?) – a line supposedly spoken by Caesar on seeing the inhabitants of the place flee at his approach. The amused response which this village generally provokes among French people is due also to Alphonse Daudet, who included a story called 'The Curé of Cucuron' in his *Letters from My*

Windmill. This funny story concerns a delightful priest who feels so protective towards his 'Cucuronnais' that he goes to God to see if there are any in Heaven, but finds eventually, after trying Purgatory, that they are all in Hell.

Cucuron is a long attractive village stretched between a romanesque keep crowning a small hill and a square containing the parish church of Notre-Dame-de-Beaulieu. This church has a romanesque nave and a gothic apse, and includes among its fine furnishings a fifteenth-century wooden *pietà* and a large eighteenth-century marble high altarpiece originally intended for a convent chapel at AIX-EN-PROVENCE. In front of the church, in the seventeenth-century Maison des Bouliers, is a recently restored museum of local archaeology and folklore. [3B]

DÉFILÉ DE PIERRE-ÉCRITE: For the Roman inscription of, see SISTERON.

DIGNE has been a thermal resort since Roman times, and the capital of the *département* of Alpes-de-Haute-Provence since the Revolution. In recent times it has become known as the 'lavender capital' of Provence, and from late August to early September a lavender fair is held here.

The life of this quiet town is centred along the shaded Boulevard Gassendi, a street named after Digne's most famous son, Pierre Gassendi, a seventeenth-century philosopher and scientist, and friend of Molière and Cyrano de Bergerac. At the eastern end of the street is the Musée Municipal, housed in a former eighteenth-century hospital which was drearily renovated in 1970: inside are two slight works by the Marseillais painter Ziem, and numerous butterflies and local landscape paintings. Continuing further east along the street, into the outskirts of the town, you will reach the former cathedral of Notre-Dame-du-Bourg, a stunning and very unusual building. The nave is romanesque but the main interest of the church is the elegant gothic façade, made up of alternating white and bluish bands of stone, and far more Lombard than Provençal in style. [2D]

DRAGUIGNAN, originally the site of a Roman military post, was named after a dragon who terrorized the town in the fifth century A.D. The first Bishop of Antibes, Hermentaire, finally killed the monster, and in so doing succeeded in converting the town to Christianity. Medieval Draguignan developed around the hill crowned today by a seventeenth-century clock tower, one of the most elegant in Provence. In the early Middle Ages Draguignan had a sizeable Jewish community, and there survives to this day, on the Rue de la Juiverie, the large façade of the thirteenth-century synagogue.

Draguignan gradually grew in importance, and by the sixteenth century was the fifth largest town in Provence. Made *Préfecture* of the Var after the Revolution, it was criss-crossed in the mid nineteenth century with shaded streets and boulevards, put up on the instigation of the celebrated Baron Haussmann, then serving as the district prefect. In 1975 Draguignan lost its status as *Préfecture* to Toulon, but it still remains an important commercial town, at the centre of a large wine-growing district.

Draguignan, in particular its small animated medieval quarter, is a pleasant enough place to walk around, but without any outstanding attraction. The Municipal Museum has, amid its haphazardly arranged collections of local history and fine and applied arts, a large group of nineteenth-century Sèvres porcelain, some good seventeenth- and eighteenth-century paintings and sculptures, and a few watercolours by Rodin.

Four kilometres south of Draguignan, off the N555, is the village of Trans-en-Provence, which has a cheerful late eighteenth-century town hall with painted ornamentation on its main façade. If, instead of turning into the village proper from the main road, you turn in the opposite direction, up the steep hill of the Clos de l'Hermitage, you will come almost immediately to an enormous honeycombed structure. This is none other than an 'aerial well', invented in 1930 by an eccentric Belgian engineer, Achille Knapen. It works, or rather does not work, on the principle that warm air entering the 'well' by day is stored there until night, when it condenses on contact with cold air. Knapen did not live long enough to perfect his invention, the sole function of which today is as a splendid folly.   [4D]

ENTRECASTEAUX: The main street of Entrecasteaux, a charming village in wooded surroundings, looks over a formal garden by Le Nôtre. Towering over this garden, now a public park, is an austere seventeenth-century castle built over medieval foundations. The man responsible for the reconstruction was the Count of Grignan, the son-in-law of the Marquise de Sévigné, and the Lieutenant-General of the King in Provence. At the death of the Count in 1714 the building passed into the possession of the Brunys, a family of entrepreneurs and adventurers, who soon acquired for themselves the rights to the Marquisate of Entrecasteaux. The Marquis Jean-Baptiste Bruny spent the latter half of his life in a Portuguese gaol after having murdered his young wife; a contemporary of his, Joseph de Bruny, Knight of Entrecasteaux, was a vice-admiral who was killed on an expedition in search of the explorer La Pérouse.

After the Second World War the castle became the property of the village but, through lack of funds, soon fell into a ruinous state. This situation was saved in 1974 by the intervention of a man whose colourful life made him a worthy successor to the Brunys, Ian McGarvie-Munn. McGarvie-Munn, a Scotsman born in India in 1919, combined the life of an avant-garde painter with such glamorous appointments as commander-in-chief of the Guatemala navy. 'I have always felt,' he once said, 'that my vocation was that of a painter, but the exigencies of life have also led me on many different paths: that of a soldier, a sailor, a diplomat, an investor of the stockmarket and latterly an architect.'

After buying the castle, McGarvie-Munn set about obsessively restoring it, a task taken over after his death in 1981 by his architect son, Lachlan. The castle is open to the public and has the most generous opening hours of any building in Provence (daily 10–8, April to September; 10–6 the rest of the year). The atmosphere is in fact so friendly and informal that you are made to feel that you would be welcome at any time you cared to drop in. You enter through the kitchen, sometimes interrupting a family lunch, then proceed to trip over children's toys as you begin wandering around the rest of the house. No attempt has been made to reconstruct a typical seventeenth-century interior, but instead the walls have been whitewashed and the feel of the place made quite modern, and tastefully so. The result is a bright, spacious interior, cheerfully setting off the family's magnificently eclectic collections, which include, in addition to Ian McGarvie-Munn's own interesting paintings, such diverse objects as Provençal kitchenware, Scottish bagpipes, pre-Columbian ceramics, and exhibits relating to the famous admiral of Entrecasteaux. In the summer months a music festival is held here, with classical concerts given on the terrace. [4D]

ENTREVAUX, for centuries a border town on the frontier between Provence and Savoy, has changed little since the time when Louis XIV decided to turn it into a key defensive position and entrusted the rebuilding of its ramparts to the great military engineer Vauban. Vauban's ramparts, constructed from 1693 onwards, survive intact, and, with their moat and drawbridges, give a magical appearance to the place today.

The town lies on the opposite side of the torrential river Var to the main Nice road, and is reached by crossing a single-arched bridge and entering one of the town's three gates. Inside this compact little town are numerous old buildings, some dating back to the early Middle Ages; the former cathedral church of Notre-Dame has a gothic nave and a fine sculpted seventeenth-century façade. Behind the town a series of nine zig-zag ramps – which took nearly fifty years to build – lead up to the citadel, which has magnificent views over the Alps.

In the butcher's shop on the town's main square you can buy an excellent local speciality – a dried salt beef called *socca*, similar to the Italian *bressala* and best eaten sprinkled with olive oil, lemon juice and pepper. An English resident of the town, Roger Greaves, organizes an international two-week festival of baroque music every August. [3E]

EYGALIÈRES, a small village wonderfully situated under the Alpilles, has become popular with artists and writers since the early 1950s. The artist and writer Mario Prassinos lived here from 1950 until his death in 1985 (see SAINT-RÉMY); his book *La Colline tatouée* is a strange mystical autobiography filled with descriptions of the place (the mountain of the title is a reference to the Alpilles). André Brink, the South African novelist, regularly spends his summers at the Auberge Provençale, which provided him with the main setting for *The Wall of the Plague* (1985). At the top of the village, near the ruins of the citadel, is the seventeenth-century Penitents Chapel, which puts on exhibitions by local artists.

Two kilometres to the east of the town, off the main road to Saint-Rémy, is the Mas de la Brune, a beautifully preserved sixteenth-century mansion, now a small hotel with rooms furnished in an appropriate style. On the other side of Eygalières, off the D24B, is the chapel of

Saint-Sixte, a simple twelfth-century structure restored in the seventeenth century. The charm of this much photographed place lies in its tranquil, isolated setting, directly facing the Alpilles and shaded by a small group of cypresses. [3B]

ÈZE: The medieval village of Èze, once a Ligurian stronghold, clings to a spectacular outcrop of rock above the sea near Monaco. Inevitably, given its quite sensational beauty and its proximity to the main coastal resorts, it has been overrun by tourists. The walk through the narrow, over-picturesque streets up to the citadel is a tiring one, not just because of its steepness but because of the jostling crowds and the interminable line of souvenir shops. The climb is none the less worth it, for surrounding the ruins of the citadel is a fascinating garden of cacti with a literally breath-taking view over the coast.

The verdant path which leads down from the old town to the lower corniche is named after Nietzsche, who loved walking here and thought up while doing so the third part of *And Thus Spoke Zarathustra*. On the outskirts of the town, in the Monaco direction, is a branch of the Fragonard perfume factory (see GRASSE), a favourite stop for coach parties. [3F]

FONTAINE-DE-VAUCLUSE has been one of the major tourist attractions of Provence since at least the sixteenth century. Early travellers came here, in homage to Petrarch, who spent much time in the village between 1337 and 1353 and composed during these reclusive stays many of his sonnets to his beloved Laura (see pages 101–2). Today's tourists are interested mainly in the extraordinary resurgent spring, reached from the village by a shaded footpath along the river Sorgue. The river issues from a large cave at the bottom of a sheer cliff-face: during the winter and spring months the water gushes out with a mysterious force, covering the mouth of the cave completely; at other times of the year the sight has a quality of lurking menace.

The ruined castle on top of the hill overlooking the fountain belonged to Philippe de Cabassole, Bishop of Cavaillon and a friend of Petrarch's. In the centre of the village is the parish church of Notre-Dame-de-Saint-Véran, a unified romanesque structure with fluted Roman columns flanking the apse and – in the eight-century crypt – the tomb of Saint Véran, the bishop saint of Cavaillon who rid the village of the Coulobre, a monster who lived in the famous spring. [3B]

FONTSÉGUGNE: For this castle, see LE THOR.

FONTVIEILLE is a small, attractive town which became prosperous through the quarrying industry established here in the Middle Ages. Its great attraction is Daudet's Windmill, which lies just to the south of the village, off the D33, and was one of a large series of windmills that once dotted the countryside. Daudet never owned the windmill, but simply imagined it as the home of the narrator of his *Letters from My Windmill* (1886), the book which made Daudet's name. The windmill has been heavily restored and the working mechanism is now in good order. Inside you can see also a small Daudet museum, containing, amid numerous personal mementoes, engravings by José Roy, the original illustrator of *Letters from My Windmill*.

Continuing three kilometres further south along the D33, and then turning left in the direction of Paradou, you will come to the evocative ruins of a Roman aqueduct. Parking your car here and following a path between the aqueduct and an olive grove, you will reach the ruins of a group of Roman mills (Le Grand Barbegal), once activated by water.   [3A]

FORCALQUIER: A small independent state throughout the twelfth century, Forcalquier was tied to Provence in 1209 after Gersende de Sabran, Countess of Forcalquier, married Alphonse II of Provence. Thereafter Forcalquier became a favourite residence of the Counts of Provence, who turned it into the capital of upper Provence and an internationally renowned cultural, political and economic centre. The town suffered badly in the late fourteenth century from assaults of the notorious Raymond de Turenne of Les Baux, and was further devastated in the sixteenth century by a combination of plague and the wars of religion. In 1601 the castle which crowned it was pulled down by Henry IV, thus consolidating the town's decline. Today Forcalquier is a quiet market town basking in the middle of rolling, luxuriant scenery.

The main square, the Place du Bourget, lies underneath the picturesque old town and is flanked on one side by the town hall (with a small local museum open only in July and August), and on the other by the former cathedral church of Notre-Dame, an austere building dating back to the twelfth century but with thirteenth-century apsidal chapels (a gothic feature rarely found in Provence) and many seventeenth-century additions. Nearby is the twelfth- to fourteenth-century Couvent des Cordeliers, which was originally the residence of the Counts of Forcalquier. In 1236 Count Raymond Bérenger V gave this building to the Franciscans (known in France as the Cordeliers, because of their *cordes liés* or pieces of rope that they used instead of belts). The building, one of the earliest Franciscan monasteries in France, contains in its well-restored rooms an interesting museum of medieval religious art.

On the Rue d'Orléans, one of the dark narrow streets running up the slopes of the old town, is the Centre d'Art Moderne, a privately owned gallery which puts on some of the most exciting contemporary art exhibitions in Provence. The gallery is spread out over the evocative if rather lugubrious rooms of a fifthteenth-century hospital; its eccentric owner will be pleased to show you his private art collection, which features many portraits of himself by famous artist friends such as Bernard Buffet. At the top of the hill a nineteenth-century church set in a wooded cemetery marks the site of the former citadel. An orientation table here helps you identify the many distant mountains that surround the town on all sides. [3C]

FORT DE BUOUX: The D943 from Apt to Lourmarin takes you suddenly into a wild landscape of forests and limestone crags dominated by the monumental mass of the Grand Lubéron. Leaving the road shortly after the Col de Pointu, and following the D113 towards Buoux, you will soon see a tall, extremely elegant, romanesque bell-tower, the sole remains of the priory of Saint-Symphorien. Descending further, and ignoring the turning to Buoux itself (a tiny unremarkable hamlet), you will enter the wooded river valley of the Aiguebrun, where there are several sheltered places for swimming. This valley is hemmed in on both sides by sheer cliffs which are popular with rock climbers and are pitted with caves used in prehistoric times. The Fort de Buoux, barely visible from the road, sits on top of a high sloping plateau, surrounded by spectacular drops. It takes a good forty minutes to walk from the road to the top of the fort, but you will be rewarded by one of the most evocative and least spoilt sights in the whole of Provence (see pages 43–4). The fort, with its strategic position overlooking what was once the main pass across the Lubéron, has overgrown remains from the Ligurian times right up to the seventeenth century, when the place was destroyed on the orders of Louis XIV. [3B]

FRÉJUS, known to the Romans as Forum Julii, was founded by Julius Caesar in 49 B.C. as a small market town and military post on the Aurelian Way. Shortly afterwards the future Emperor Augustus, having quickly to form a fleet to fight the forces of Sextus Pompey, turned the town into a naval base and arsenal: among the many ships that were built here were those that conquered Antony and Cleopatra in the Battle of Actium of 31 B.C. Though a bishopric from the fourth century until the Revolution, the town never fully recovered from being ravaged by the Saracens in the tenth century and its decline was hastened a few centuries later when its port silted up.

The varied but very fragmentary ruins of Roman Fréjus surround the old town, and include an amphitheatre, a theatre, an aqueduct, and extensive portions of the ancient port. In the summer months bull-fights, plays and light entertainment are put on in the theatre and amphitheatre.

The complex of episcopal buildings at the centre of the old town is one of the finest in France. The earliest part of it is the fifth-century baptistery, the most unified and best preserved of the four baptisteries of this type in the country. The rebuilding of the cathedral to which it is attached began after the departure of the Saracens but was carried out mainly in the twelfth and thirteenth centuries. The architecture is sturdy and fortress-like, and is also an early example of gothic influence in the region. Also of this later period is the attractive cloister, a visit to which is included in the guided tour which you are obliged to follow if you want to see the baptistery.

Sandy public beaches are to be found at Fréjus-Plage, one mile south-east of the old town. On the latter's northern outskirts meanwhile are a couple of exotic curiosities from the early years of this century. One is a Buddhist pagoda, situated off the N7 in the direction of Mougins; it commemorates 5,000 Annamite soldiers killed in the First World War. Off the D4 to Bagnols-en-Forêt is a rather dilapidated mosque, built by soldiers from the former French Sudan in imitation of a famous mosque at Djenne in North Africa. Nearby, appropriately enough, is a zoo and safari park, with lions, tigers, elephants, monkeys and so on, in a natural environment.   [4E]

GANAGOBIE: The priory of Ganagobie is inaccessible by car from the nearby village of Ganagobie, and is reached from the Manosque to Sisteron road by the steep and winding D30. Founded in the tenth century on a high wooded plateau with a magnificent outlook over the Durance valley, the priory was given as a gift to the Cluniac order. Enriched in the twelfth and thirteenth centuries by generous donations from the Counts of Forcalquier and Provence, it later received from the monks of Lérins the remains of Saint Honoratus. After changing hands repeatedly from the late fifteenth century onwards, it declined rapidly, and was left in a sad, ruinous state after the Revolution. An intensive restoration campaign was started in the early 1960s and is still continuing.

The tympanum of the priory's romanesque church is famous for its vigorously carved *Christ in Majesty*, one of the few large-scale sculptures of this period in Provence. The fantastical zig-zag arches which frame the work are not, as is sometimes said, contemporary with this, but date from the sixteenth century. The greatest treasures inside the church are the twelfth-century mosaics in the apse, executed solely in black, white and red and featuring bizarre figurative and geometrical motifs of strong oriental inspiration. In the transept is a crude painting of the Virgin by the eccentric Marseille painter Monticelli, who spent much of his childhood in Ganagobie.   [2C]

LA GARDE-FREINET, a village high up in the Massif des Maures, was occupied between the eighth and tenth centuries by the Saracens, who used it as a base for their raids on the Provençal interior. The ruined castle which rises on a rocky outcrop above it is said to have been built for them, though in fact it is of a much later date. At the bottom of the village is a small museum commemorating the writer Jean Aicard, a nineteenth-century novelist who lived here and was inspired by the place to write his romantic historical novel, *Mauris des Maures*.   [5D]

GASSIN, see SAINT-TROPEZ.

GIGONDAS, on the eastern slopes of the Dentelles de Montmirail, belonged to the house of Orange in the Middle Ages. It has remains of its medieval walls and castle and a heavily restored eleventh-century church with a terrace offering a fine view of the Rhône valley. But its main attraction for tourists is its famous wines, made an Appellation Contrôlée in 1971. On the village's main square is a 'Caveau de Dégustation', where you can taste the wine of a great variety of local wine-growers. [2B]

GORDES, one of the most visited villages in the Vaucluse, comprises a harmonious series of terraces leading steeply up to an early Renaissance castle, visible for miles around. It is difficult at first glance to imagine that the place has changed greatly since the fifteenth century, but in fact much of what you see is the result of extensive rebuilding after the Second World War. In August 1944 a German soldier was killed by the local Maquis, and in retaliation the Germans set fire to the place, blew up many of the houses, and killed thirteen people; only the intervention of a monk from nearby Sénanque prevented others from the village from being executed.

The village has been popular with artists ever since the academic cubist painter André Lhote started coming here in 1938. It was at the castle of Gordes that the 'op-artist' Victor Vasarély (see AIX-EN-PROVENCE) set up the first museum in Provence dedicated to his dreary abstract works. For the inauguration ceremony in 1970 the Mayor of Gordes covered up an offending sign from the nearby co-op, unaware that this was in fact one of Vasarély's best-known designs. The castle is at least worth a visit for a marvellously elaborate Renaissance fireplace, and the extensive views from its terrace.

There are many attractions in the immediate vicinity of Gordes, the best one being the twelfth-century abbey of Sénanque, dramatically set at the bottom of a wild cliff-lined valley four kilometres to the north of the town. Sénanque, one of the three Cistercian abbeys of Provence (see pages 71–2), has permanent exhibitions devoted to the history of the abbey and to the nomads of the Sahara Desert (the place has a Centre for Sahara Studies); a more exciting bonus are the outstanding concerts of medieval music put on in the abbey church throughout the year.

Nearer Gordes, at the end of a small road off the D2, is the Village des Bories, a group of stone huts dating from the seventeenth century and lived in until the nineteenth century (see page 40); they have now been turned into an informative museum of rural life. Further south, on the road to Beaumettes, is the Moulin des Bouillons, a house which contains a fascinating old olive-mill surrounded by exhibits relating to olive culture since Greek times. The owner of the house, the stained-glass artist Frédéric Durand, has built in the garden a small museum of stained glass. Durand's own works are exhibited alongside panels describing the history and technique of stained glass, and photographs and fragments of medieval and Renaissance glass. The knowledge, enthusiasm, and engaging eccentricity of Durand's wife – who acts as curator and guide – gives this place a very special quality.

The hamlet of Saint-Pantaléon, two kilometres west of the Moulin des Bouillons, is interesting for its small but extraordinary eleventh-century church (the key can be had from the village shop). Both the apse of this church, and some paleo-Christian tombs outside, have been carved into the rock on which the building stands.   [3B]

GOURDON occupies a quite startling position on top of a rock thrust up nearly 1,500 feet above one of Provence's great natural attractions, the Gorges du Loup. The main building of this small, much-visited village is the thirteenth- to fourteenth-century castle. Heavily restored and remodelled after 1610, the castle now houses two museums. The Musée Historique has furniture and works of art from the Middle Ages up to the seventeenth century (most of its paintings are minor studio works). The other museum is devoted to the vastly overrated phenomenon of 'Naïve Painting'. The Douanier Rousseau – represented here by a small portrait – was genuinely charming, but the artists who have followed him and self-consciously promoted their 'naïvety' have generally been little more than poor artists with a shrewd business sense.   [4E]

GRASSE: This large hill town, facing seaward across a landscape of flowers and exotic plants, was in the early Middle Ages a miniature republic with close commercial and political links with Genoa and Pisa. In the thirteenth century the struggles between the Guelphs and Ghibellines eventually forced its citizens to side with Raymond Bérenger IV of Provence.

The traditional industry of the town was tanning, in particular the making of leather gloves; in the sixteenth century the fashion for scented gloves led to the development of its scent industry, an industry hitherto exclusive to Italy and one which Henry IV's wife, Catherine de Medici, had been anxious to introduce to France. By the eighteenth century Grasse had risen to be the perfume capital of the world, a position which it still holds.

After the Revolution Grasse was created capital of the Var, but it was to lose this status in 1860 when it was incorporated into the newly formed *département* of Alpes-Maritimes. The nineteenth century saw its development as a health resort and winter residence, something to which its balmy climate made it ideally suited. Pauline Bonaparte, who stayed here between 1807 and 1808, was one of the first to see its potential as a resort, and to this day the terraced garden where she loved to walk is called the 'Jardin de la Princesse Pauline'. A later visitor was Queen Victoria, who spent several winters at the Grand Hotel.

The old town of Grasse is very well preserved, and there are numerous narrow winding streets lined with tall medieval houses with a strong Italianate character; the daily market on the Place aux Aires is one of the most picturesque in the region. The cathedral dates from the twelfth century and has some remarkable paintings, most notably three canvases by Rubens, painted by the artist in Rome in 1601 and presented to the town in the nineteenth century. Another painting, sadly damaged by a recent fire, is the *Washing of the Feet*, a rare religious work by Grasse's most famous son, Jean-Honoré Fragonard.

Fragonard, the son of a glove-maker, was born at 23 Rue Tracastel (marked by a plaque) on 5 April 1732. His family left the town soon afterwards and settled in Paris, where Fragonard himself was to remain for most of his life. The artist's one return trip to his native town was in 1790, when he flew Paris to escape the Terror. He stayed with his cousin Évariste Maubert, a wealthy glove-maker and perfumer, who had a villa just outside the old town. This elegant villa, set in a beautiful exotic park, is now the Villa-Musée Fragonard. When Fragonard came from Paris he brought with him a famous series of large canvases, *The Pursuit of Love*, which had been turned down as being too frivolous by the woman who had commissioned them. The artist had them set up in the dining-room of his cousin's villa, where copies of them can still be seen (the originals ended up in the Frick Collection in New York). Upstairs there is a youthful self-portrait by Fragonard in Renaissance costume, and many works by his painter son, Alexandre-Évariste, who was responsible for the pleasant *trompe-l'oeil* decoration on the staircase.

A ticket to the Villa-Musée Fragonard allows you entry as well into the nearby Musée d'Art et d'Histoire de Provence, which is housed in the eighteenth-century Hôtel de Cabris; the works of art here are mainly slight (there is a pastel by Berthe Morisot, and an oil painting of Cannes by Maurice Denis), but the old-fashioned interior, furnished with eighteenth- and nineteenth-century furniture, porcelain and other objects, has considerable charm.

Next to this are the Parfumeries Fragonard (another branch of which is at È Z E), the town's most popular attraction. You are led on a free guided tour of the factory, taken through a small museum on the history of the perfume industry, and finally brought to a small shop selling Fragonard products. There is no obligation to buy any of these, and the promotional purpose of the tour should in no way put you off from going on it. What you learn about perfumes is fascinating, if sometimes alarming, as when you are told that one of the 'fixatives' used in the scent's manufacture is whale vomit.

Grasse has two well-known, if not very subtle, gastronomic specialities – *tripes à la mode de Grasse* (tripe) and *sous fassoun* (Provençal for *chou farçi*), an extremely filling dish comprising cabbage stuffed with rice, sausagemeat, bacon, pig's liver, peas, lettuce and leeks, and cooked in a pot together with ham, beef, turnips, carrots and so on. [4E]

G R É O U X - L E S - B A I N S: The thermal baths at Gréoux-les-Bains have been famous since antiquity, and in the grounds of the modern thermal establishment can be seen a *stele* of 126 A.D. dedicated to the nymphs of the site.

A small, much-rebuilt old village survives, but the greater part of Gréoux is now taken up by large modern hotels and luxury residences serving the many who come here suffering from rheumatism, arthritis and chest complaints. [3C]

G R I G N A N: The château of Grignan, one of the grandest Renaissance structures in the south of France, overwhelms the attractive but tiny old village beneath it. Grignan lies just outside the present-day boundaries of Provence (since 1979 it has belonged to the *département* of Drôme), but it has played a central role in Provençal history.

The castle belonged for many centuries to the Adhémar family, one of the oldest in Provence. The medieval building was completely transformed in the early sixteenth century by Louis Adhémar, Francis I's ambassador in Rome and a man with a great interest in contemporary Italian architecture. The place was further embellished in the late seventeenth century by François de Castellane-Adhémar de Monteil, Count of Grignan and the Lieutenant-General of Provence.

The Count of Grignan is best remembered today as the son-in-law of the Marquise de Sévigné. The Marquise was born in Paris in 1626, married there in 1644, and was widowed seven years later after her errant husband had been killed in a duel. Never remarrying, the Marquise spent the rest of her life devoted to her beautiful if cold-hearted daughter Françoise. In 1669 Françoise married the ugly Count of Grignan, and soon afterwards she moved with him to Provence. The pain of being separated from her daughter, to whom she began to write almost daily, turned the Marquise into one of the great letter-writers of the seventeeth century.

The Marquise stayed three times at Grignan. The abundance of local herbs and fruits and the view of Mont Ventoux from the castle's terraces enchanted her. However, the extremes of the Provençal climate, in particular the violence of the *mistral*, greatly wore her down. She was also horrified by the 'pagan' Provençal custom of burying a dead woman in her finery, and with her face exposed. 'I would hate to die in Provence,' she once wrote. When she died at Grignan in December 1691, she did not even have the consolation of being next to her daughter, who at the time lay ill in another part of the huge castle.

The upkeep of the castle was neglected in the eighteenth century, and the place was abandoned for a long while after the Revolution. Restoration work has been continuing since 1912, but the interior still remains rather bleak. Outside the castle grounds is the entrance to the austerely impressive church of Saint-Sauveur, where the Marquise de Sévigné is buried. Her tomb was vandalized by phrenologists in the eighteenth century, and the skull of the Marquise is now claimed to be in the possession of a Belgian convent.   [1B]

GRIMAUD, a hill village in between LA GARDE-FREINET and

the bay of SAINT-TROPEZ, boasts the imposing ruins of an eleventh-
to fifteenth-century castle, pulled down on the orders of Cardinal
Richelieu. Port-Grimaud, a modern residential resort on the sea five
kilometres away from the old Grimaud, was designed by the Alsatian
architect François Spoerry. This town of canals and alleys (there are
no roads) aims to suggest a cross between Venice and a Provençal
fishing port, and has been thought by some to be a masterpiece of post-
war French architecture. It already seems somewhat dated.   [50]

HYÈRES: The town of Hyères, which is set back slightly from the sea,
was founded near the Greek trading port of Olbia, the ruins of which
are still in the process of being excavated (they are to be found in
what is now the suburb of Costebelle, four kilometres to the south of
the town centre). In 1254 Saint Louis of France is supposed to have
stopped here on his return from the Seventh Crusade; at all events the
town became during this period a port for those visiting the Holy
Land, and a base of the Knights Templar. The pulling down of the
town castle during the wars of religion led to a period of decline, from
which it emerged in the late eighteenth century as one of the pioneering
health resorts of Provence: Napoleon, Pauline Bonaparte, Tolstoy,
Queen Victoria and R. L. Stevenson were among its distinguished
visitors in the following century.

The character of much of present-day Hyères is that of an elegant
spa town gone somewhat out of fashion. There is also a small medieval
quarter, surrounded by some of the original gardens and containing
the austerely impressive Commandery of the Knights Templar.

In its heyday as a resort, Hyères's popularity was due to the wooded
hills on its northern side, and only this century was the tourist potential
of its coast exploited. The flat and now heavily built-over landscape
immediately to the south of the town is not in fact attractive, and you
would be advised to drive quickly past this on your way to the wooded
promontory of Giens, reached by a narrow spit of land lined by salt
banks. From here it is a short boat journey to the island of Porquerolles, the largest of what are in many ways the least spoilt attraction
of the Provençal coast, the Îles d'Hyères.

These islands have been known since the sixteenth century as the
Golden Islands, on account of the golden colour of their southern
cliffs. Though scarcely inhabited today, they have been occupied in

the past by Ligurians, Greeks, Romans, monks from the Lérins (see CANNES), Saracens, Turks, pirates and criminals. Their importance was due largely to their strategic position, and scattered throughout them are forts dating from the fifteenth century onwards, of enormous interest to students of military architecture. Francis I, optimistically, granted convicts and criminals asylum on the islands on condition that they would defend them against corsairs and pirates. Naturally they became pirates themselves, and ruled the islands unchallenged until the intervention of Louis XIV. The islands remained under threat from invaders (including the English) until the time of Napoleon. The only invasion since then was that of the Americans in 1944, who landed here prior to their moving to the Provençal mainland.

The village of Porquerolles was built in the last century as a military base, and has more the look of a colonial settlement in North Africa than a Provençal village. The island itself, like that of Port-Cros to the east, is densely covered with pines, eucalyptus and exotic shrubs. A forty-five-minute walk to the south of the village takes you to a lighthouse, from which there are wonderful views of the cliffs which extend the whole length of the island's southern coast. The beaches are all on the north, and those with time should follow the shaded coastal path from the village to the Plage-Notre-Dame on the north-eastern end of the island (about an hour's walk; alternatively you could hire a bicycle). This long, sandy, unspoilt beach, set in a hilly bay, is one of the finest in Provence.

Whereas Porquerolles has a number of hotels and even vineyards, the privately owned island of Port-Cros (best reached from the port of Le Lavandou) is virtually one large nature reserve and enjoys the status of a National Park. The walk around this lovely island takes at least a day and is both arduous, owing to the hilliness of the terrain, and also slightly frustrating, because of the way the trees keep on blocking your view of the sea. One of the most popular walks for those with little time is along the so-called 'Valley of Solitude' to the cliff-lined southern coast (about two hours return); shortly after leaving the port you pass the island's one hotel, Le Manoir, an atmospheric eighteenth-century mansion with the feel more of a private house than a hotel (you have to book several months in advance). A shorter walk is from the port to the tiny bay of La Palud (about half an hour), a walk which takes you along the *sentier botanique*, a footpath lined with a wide range of exotic Mediterranean plants; before you reach the bay you should make a short detour to the fort of L'Estissac (built by Cardinal Richelieu), which has good views both of the island and of the mainland. A curious footnote to the island's history is that D. H. Lawrence stayed here as a guest of a young Englishwoman, who told him of an affair she had had with a local labourer: this account inspired *Lady Chatterley's Lover*, which of course has a rather less exotic setting.

A short crossing from Port-Cros takes you to the Île de Levant (the boat from Le Lavandou usually stops off here on its way to Port-Cros). In contrast to the other two islands, Le Levant is largely barren and precipitous. The eastern half of the island is used by the French navy and is out of bounds to visitors. The western half is a pioneering nudist colony which was set up by a doctor in the 1930s. Non-nudists are allowed, but the sight of nudists being carried around on open trucks like cattle is not a welcoming one.   [5D]

ÎLE DE RÂTONNEAU, see MARSEILLE.

ÎLES D'HYÈRES, see HYÈRES.

ÎLES DE LÉRINS, see CANNES.

L'ISLE-SUR-LA-SORGUE, between Capentras and Cavaillon, is crossed and surrounded by the multiple branches of the river Sorgue and is a charming small town known inevitably as the 'Venice of the Comtat'. The best time to come here is on a Sunday morning, when many of the streets are taken over by a much-visited flea-market; even at other times of the week this is a good place to buy antiques and old furniture.

The gothic parish church in the centre of the town was renovated in the seventeenth century and given one of the most lavishly baroque interiors of any Provençal church. Another attraction of the town is an eighteenth-century house (at 20 Rue du Docteur Tallet) which until recently displayed a collection of works of art belonging to the famous local poet, René Char. Today this well-restored house provides an elegant, spacious setting for major art exhibitions.

JUAN-LES-PINS, see ANTIBES.

LACOSTE, a hill village on the northern side of the Lubéron, has steeply sloping cobbled streets leading up to the ruins of a castle (see pages 126–33). Much of the upper half of the village forms part of an American art school linked to the Cleveland Institute of Art; every August the school hosts the Deller Consort, who give concerts of early music in the village church and other places in the vicinity.

The ruined castle dates back to the eleventh century and was owned in the Middle Ages by the Simiane family. Sacked in the sixteenth century when it became a place of refuge for the Vaudois, it later passed into the hands of the Sades, one of the oldest families in Provence. The notorious Marquis de Sade spent an important part of his life here and gave the place an ill-repute through his debaucheries; the castle is described in many of his writings, including *Justine* and *120 Days of Sodom*. The Marquis spent much of his wife's money (he himself was never very well off) restoring and embellishing the place, and was responsible for the tall façade which you see when approaching the castle from the village. The place is now owned by an eccentric retired teacher, André Bouer, whose self-identification with the Marquis has led to a mad scheme to restore the castle to its original state. Bouer's additions are totally out of character with the rest of the castle, and only detract from what would otherwise be an evocative ruin. The place is open to the public, and Bouer himself gives a vivid if over-long guided tour, gleefully pointing out the places where orgies took place.

Walking along the plateau behind the castle, you will find to your left an abandoned house and garden, inside which are some of the few remaining sculptures by a visionary turn-of-the-century miller called Malachier. Continuing further and taking a turn to the right, you will descend into one of the village's former quarries. Now owned by the art school, this forms a magnificent arena filled with sculptures and covered with curious late nineteenth-century graffiti.

An exciting way of touring the countryside is by horse. Lilianne Ségura, the owner of Lacoste's Café de Sade, organizes excursions by horse for both beginners and experienced riders (ponies are available for children).   [3B]

LOURMARIN, situated in the middle of flat agricultural countryside on the southern side of the Lubéron, boasts a splendid Renaissance castle. Work was begun on this in the late fifteenth century but was mainly carried out in the 1540s. The tastefully restored apartments, with their impressively large ornamented fireplaces, contain old Provençal and Spanish furniture, a few early Italian paintings, and, on one of the walls, some mysterious graffiti. Locals believe that the latter were the work of gypsies, who stayed here in the last century on their way to LES-SAINTES-MARIES-DE-LA-MER and put a curse on the place when they were thrown out. Laurent Vibert, the man who saved the castle from ruin in the early 1920s, was killed in a car crash four years after buying the place. In his memory there was set up here a foundation for artists and writers.

Albert Camus bought a house in the village shortly after winning the Nobel Prize for Literature in 1957. But he too did not stay long here, dying in 1960 in the same way as Vibert. He is buried in the local cemetery, under a simple headstone.   [3B]

LE-LUC-EN-PROVENCE, a thermal resort and busy market town, is squeezed unprepossessingly between the N7 and the Autoroute du Soleil. Its interest, historically, is that it became after the Edict of Nantes one of the three towns in Provence where Protestants could freely practise their cult.

Next to its abandoned parish church is an interesting hexagonal bell-tower of 1517. Historical and philately museums have been installed respectively in the seventeenth-century chapel of Sainte-Anne and in the attractive eighteenth-century castle of the Vintimille. On a hill in the eastern outskirts of the village is Vieux Cannet, a tiny and most charming village built around an eleventh-century church.   [4D]

LUCÉRAM, a village with a strong Italianate character, is a remarkably unspoilt place considering its enormous beauty and proximity to the coast. Situated high up in the Nice hinterland, it overlooks a mountainous, sun-baked landscape once covered entirely in shrubs and pine-trees. Sadly, a disastrous fire almost engulfed the village in August 1986 and charred much of the surrounding forest.

Narrow, stepped alleys wind their way around tall old houses up to the parish church of Sainte-Marguérite, with its beautifully positioned terrace, pastel-green seventeenth-century façade, and onion-domed eighteenth-century clock tower. The colourful interior – late gothic in structure but rococo in decoration – is notable for a Renaissance retable of the school of Ludovico Bréa and a well-endowed Treasury.   [3F]

MAILLANE: This quiet village in the middle of the flat agricultural land of the Rhône valley has been a place of literary pilgrimage for over 100 years, and yet it has remained pleasantly unaffected by tourism. Its fame is due entirely to Frédéric Mistral, who spent most of his life here. He was born on 8 September 1830 at the Mas du Juge, a large farm (now much altered) one kilometre outside the town on the Saint-Rémy road (D5). After studying at SAINT-MICHEL-DE-FRIGOLET and at AIX-EN-PROVENCE, he came back to help his father, now blind, in running the farm, and to devote himself to poetry. In 1855, one year after the foundation of the literary group, the Félibrige, Mistral's father died, and Mistral and his mother moved to the Lézard House in the centre of the village. Shortly after marrying, Mistral built a house opposite his mother's and lived here from 1876 until his death in 1914. Countless admirers of the poet came to see him in this house, including Augustus John, who was disappointed at not being allowed to do a sketch of the master. The house, now a museum to Mistral, has been perfectly preserved, and there is a statue to the poet in the lovely surrounding garden. His tomb is in the local cemetery and is an imitation of the so-called 'Pavilion of Queen Jeanne' at LES BAUX. Copies of his books, and works about him and the Félibres, can be bought in the village tabac. The anniversary of Mistral's birth is commemorated each year by a folk festival and a mass in Provençal. [3A]

MALAUCÈNE, an attractive small town with scattered medieval houses and other monuments, has been from the time of Petrarch a popular setting-off point for excursions to Mont Ventoux. At Groseau, two kilometres from the village on the road climbing up the mountain (D974), Clement V built a summer residence, next to an abundant spring (now a favourite picnic spot). The residence has gone, but there remains a tiny rural chapel with a fourteenth-century fresco executed for the Pope and bearing his arms. During his residency at Groseau (1309–14), Clement V pulled down the romanesque church at Malaucène and replaced it with a massive, heavily built structure, at one time attached to the village's fortifications.

The D974 from Groseau to the summit of Mont Ventoux is a steep, winding and exciting road with breathtaking views of the endless folds of mountains to the north. Those who have at least a day to

spare and wish to make the ascent on foot should do so by heading off
at Groseau on to the Grande Randonnée 4, a spectacular and well-
marked footpath with an exhausting final stretch. The summit itself
can be disappointing unless you choose a particularly clear day: the
mountains to the south are much more distant than those to the north
and are often shrouded with haze during the summer. With its various
converging roads, unattractive gravel surface, and numerous ugly
twentieth-century structures, the summit itself bears an unfortunate
resemblance to a large adventure playground. [2B]

MANDELIEU-LA-NAPOULE: La Napoule is the seaside suburb of the
characterless small town of Mandelieu. There are two major reasons
for coming here. One is the Oasis restaurant, one of the finest restaurants of Provence, with an enchanting flower-filled patio dominated by the tall palm tree which gives the place its name. The second
reason is the Henry Clews Foundation, which was the extraordinary
home of a little-recognized American sculptor and is now both
museum to him and an American-run art school. In 1917 the wealthy
and decidedly eccentric Henry Clews decided to buy up the seaside
ruins of the fourteenth-century castle of La Napoule, destroyed in the
eighteenth century by Savoy troops. With the help of only two masons
he embarked on its reconstruction, on which he spent the remaining
seventeen years of his life. This was no ordinary reconstruction but a
fantasy of romanesque, gothic and oriental motifs, and covered everywhere with grotesque carvings of animals and monsters. Bizarre
inscriptions abound, such as the one in the sombre, enormous dining-
room, 'Save me, Marie, from Gynocrat, scientist, democrat.' Clews is
buried in his folly, and naturally he himself designed the funeral
chamber and had the tomb inscribed with the words:

> If God grant me three score and ten,
> I shall be ready to depart.
> I shall have finished with my art
> And with the ways and wiles of men.

'To judge by his work,' Charles Graves wrote in 1957, 'he was a
cynic, a sadist and Communist.' The Michelin Green Guide describes
Clews's art in terms of its '*réalisme atroce*', but the word '*atroce*' alone
would perhaps have been sufficient. Clews's sculptures are so

monumentally awful and tasteless that they remain strangely memorable. His was the sort of imagination that the British film director Ken Russell would have wholly approved of. Bloated baboons cling to terrified elephants; writhing naked forms struggle with crocodiles; genitals turn into skulls. [4E]

MANE: Standing among cultivated fields just to the south of Mane, off the N100, is the former twelfth-century priory of Salagon. Originally a Benedictine institution, the priory changed hands constantly until the Revolution, when it was abandoned and fell into ruins. The romanesque church, with its fifteenth-century rose window, has recently been restored, and the adjoining fifteenth-century buildings are in the process of being turned into a museum dedicated to the rural life of upper Provence. The stripped interior of the church has some charming romanesque capitals and other carvings. Two kilometres further south on the N100 is the Château de Sauvan, a mansion built in the early eighteenth century for Michel-François de Forbin-Janson, brigadier of the Royal Army. The style of this elegant classical building surrounded by formal gardens is more characteristic of the Île-de-France than of Provence, and for this reason the place has sometimes been dubbed 'Le Petit Trianon Provençal'. Forbin-Janson ran out of funds before completing the interior, and the house, which fell into neglect after the Revolution, was damaged by an earthquake in 1904. Its present owners, who bought the building in 1980, have made it habitable once more and have brought back some of the original furniture. [3C]

MANOSQUE and its surrounding district were made famous this century by Jean Giono, who lived here for most of his life and set all his novels in the surrounding countryside. Giono dubbed the town 'Manosque-de-Plateaux', and questioned the story that had led to the town's more usual nickname of 'Manosque la Pudique' (Manosque the Modest). This rather silly story concerns a visit to the town in 1516 by the young Francis I. The King was greeted at the fourteenth-century Saunerie Gate by a local dignitary, who was accompanied by his beautiful daughter Péronne. Péronne made an immediate impression on the King, who started being flirtatious. Rather than comply with his desires, she decided to disfigure her face with sulphur.

The tall and splendid Saunerie Gate, crowned by projecting crenellated towers, still survives and is the town's greatest architectural attraction. Behind this is a pedestrian street leading through the heart of medieval Manosque to the Soubeyran Gate on the other side. On the way you will pass two churches dating back to the twelfth century (the first with a gothic façade, the second with an elegant Renaissance one), both set in attractive small squares with fountains.   [3C]

MARSEILLE: Crowned by the amazing pinnacle of Notre-Dame-de-la-Garde, set against a broad skyline of savage limestone peaks, Marseille presents a most extraordinary spectacle when viewed from the sea. This is how the town has so often been described in literature: while there are a relatively few novels describing the city itself, there exists a large body of works relating the feelings of those arriving at or departing from its port. The excitement which the distant view of Marseille inspires must have been even greater in the nineteenth century, when the place was the unrivalled port of Europe and 'the gateway to the East'. For many travellers then the sight of Marseille was their first glimpse of Europe after months of exotic travel; for many others it was both a farewell to Europe and a foretaste of the exotic unknown lands to come.

Marseille itself has inspired feelings that could kindly be described as 'mixed'. The capital of Provence, and the second largest town of France, Marseille must be one of the least loved cities of Europe. Much of the architecture is indescribably ugly; the main streets in the city centre are very seedy while the dark and narrow side ones are often dangerous as well; the crime level is frighteningly high, and the racial tensions the worst in France; the name of Le Pen, the leader of the French National Front, is scrawled in graffiti on the bleak walls of grey apartment blocks. Tourists tend not to stay in Marseille longer than it takes to eat a *bouillabaisse* or to pay a visit to the Château d'If.

And yet Marseille has corners of great beauty and interest, and is full of fascinating buildings and museums, many of which are exciting for being little visited. It is also a very lively city, and there is always something worth watching on the streets around the port. One admirer of the city was the English surrealist artist Edward Burra, who had a taste for low life. 'If you feel a little relaxed and down,' he wrote to a friend in 1927 in his usual idiosyncratic style, 'go to Marseille its like Berwick Street gone mad with six lines of trams a sprinkling of nigs in blue boiler suits and a bevy of café bars all over the pavement.'

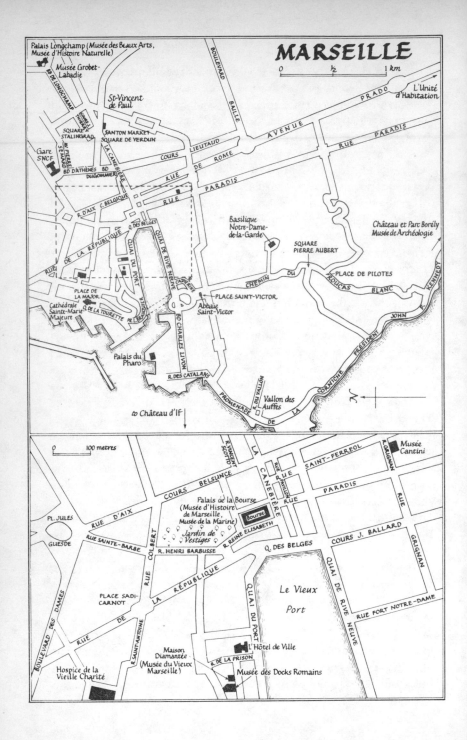

Whatever criticisms are levelled against Marseille, it can always be proud of being the oldest city in France. Founded around 600 by Greeks from Phocis in Asia Minor, it remained a thriving port until the mid first century B.C., when it allied with Pompey in his fight against Caesar and suffered terrible reprisals as a result. Though it lost its political importance, it remained a leading centre of Greek studies, and early editions of Homer were brought out here. Its port revived during the crusades and was greatly expanded under Louis XIV, against whom the city had previously rebelled. A plague in 1720 wiped out half the city's population, but this proved to be only a temporary set-back to a place whose fortunes were otherwise rapidly rising. Superseding AIX-EN-PROVENCE as the capital of Provence in 1792, Marseille experienced added prosperity after the opening of the Suez Canal in 1869. An enormous area of dockland was built to the east of the old port, and heavy industries spread out in all directions. The decline of the port set in only this century, with the development of the Rhine valley as the leading commercial thoroughfare of Europe and the loss of most of France's colonies. Today a number of docks (which can be visited on Sundays) are empty, and there is much unemployment.

The old port is the best place to begin a tour of Marseille. Much of the district around the port was once an aristocratic area, but it had become a slum by the 1930s and was pulled down by the Germans in 1943. The buildings that replaced the old ones after the war were rather dismal, but at least the Quai des Belges, on the eastern side, is enlivened by its daily fish and seafood market. Moreover, the construction of a new shopping district behind this led to the uncovering of remains of the Greek port and town of the third and second century B.C.; these ruins have now been incorporated into the Jardin des Vestiges, off the Rue Barbusse.

Important monuments have remained on the other two sides of the old harbour. Guarding the entrance of its southern side is the impressive Palais du Pharo, a palace built by Napoleon III and now used by the local legislature. Further in, on the same side, is the heavily fortified church of what was once one of Europe's most important abbeys, the abbey of Saint-Victor. The abbey was founded in the fifth century by Saint John Cassien in honour of Saint Victor, patron of sailors and millers. The saint is buried in the crypt, which is all that remains of the fifth-century abbey; the church above was rebuilt in the eleventh century and remodelled in the fourteenth.

On the other side of the harbour is the baroque town hall, an attractively ornamented building in the style of a Genoese palace. Two important museums lie behind this, the Musée des Docks Romains and the Musée du Vieux Marseille. In the basement of the former are the excavated remains of the town's ancient Greek and Roman docks, and helpful information panels tracing the history of Marseille as a trading centre. The adjoining Musée du Vieux Marseille is less interesting in its contents but has a more attractive setting, a sixteenth-century house known as the 'Maison Diamantée' on account of the diamond-shaped stones studding its exterior. This charming, old-fashioned museum contains some fine eighteenth-century Provençal furniture and enjoyable displays of eighteenth-century cribs and nineteenth-century crib figures or *santons*, a speciality of this town (see pages 85–6).

To the north of these museums is a district which has retained its filthy but fascinating old alleys. On its western edge, overlooking the new docks, is the hideous neo-Byzantine cathedral of Sainte-Marie-Majeure. When work was begun on this in 1852, the intention was to pull down the small old cathedral next to it; this latter building, known as the Major, was fortunately saved and is a masterpiece of Provençal romanesque, with an elaborate and beautiful dome above the crossing. One of the most unusual and distinguished monuments in Marseille lies in the heart of the old district to the east of the cathedral. This, the Old Charity Hospice (Hospice de la Vieille Charité), is a seventeenth-century hospital with a large arcaded court-yard dominated by a tall, domed church; the architect was that genius of the French baroque, Pierre Puget (see page 79). After having been left to decay for many years, the place has recently been imaginatively renovated and is now an exciting cultural centre putting on important and ambitious exhibitions.

The wide street of La Canebière, which runs east from the Quai des Belges and is the main artery of Marseille, was once one of the famed streets of Europe and was lined with splendid cafés. The cafés have been either taken down, badly modernized, or turned into sleazy amusement arcades. One of the few remaining buildings of interest is the palatial nineteenth-century former Stock Exchange building facing the inaptly named Rue Paradis, and now housing on its ground floor a rather bleak naval museum. Much of the area north of the Canebière to the railway station of Saint-Charles is today a drab ghetto, and includes the infamous Rue Vincent Scotto, a dark and sinister prostitute street; the station itself is worth a visit for the nineteenth-century steps and statues that lead up to it, a truly monumental approach. At the eastern end of the Canebière, in front of the large neo-gothic church of Saint-Vincent-de-Paul, is the long shaded square where the town's famous *santon* market is held on Sundays from late November to January. (At other times of the year you can buy *santons* at Marcel Carbonel, 84 Rue de Grignan.)

Further east, along the tree-lined Boulevard Longchamp, you reach a more modern and distinguished area of town. At the far end of the Boulevard, opposite the Palais Longchamp, is a late nine-teenth-century building housing the Musée Grobet-Labadie. This was once the residence of the local violinist and painter Louis Grobet, whose widow bequeathed it and its collection of furniture, iron-work, porcelain, musical mementoes, sculpture and painting to the city in 1919. Each of its tiny, charming rooms is crammed with the most varied and surprising assortment of items, ranging from original manuscripts by Beethoven and Paganini to old microscopes. Amid all this are minor paintings by Greuze, Corot, Daubigny and Monticelli.

The Palais Longchamp, a grandiose nineteenth-century structure standing at the top of a tall flight of steps, comprises two wings linked together by a massive curved arcade. One of the wings is taken up by the city's main art gallery, and has large decorations in its staircase well by Puvis de Chavannes. The museum has a genre scene by Annibale Carracci which belonged to Louis XIV, an *Adoration of the Shepherds* by Rubens formerly in the church of Saint-Jean in Malines, and paintings by David, Corot, Courbet, and Dufy. But its fascination lies essentially in its holdings of locally-born artists. Both Pierre Puget and the nineteenth-century caricatur-ist Honoré Daumier have rooms devoted to them. Two of the paint-ings most admired by visitors to Marseille in the eighteenth and nineteenth centuries were the two large canvases of the 1720 plague by Puget's pupil, Michel Serre: these two works have astonishing power, and are also an absorbing if rather grotesque human document, being filled with minutely observed scenes recording individual incidents in the plague.

South of the Canebière, off the Rue Paradis, is another of the town's art galleries, the Musée Cantini, installed in an excellently modernized seventeenth-century palace. The museum, curiously, is divided between collections of porcelain (over 600 Provençal works, most notably from MOUSTIERS-SAINTE-MARIE) and modern art (including works by Léger, Balthus, Bacon, Vasarély, and Soulages). The best-known Marseille artist of recent times is the sculptor César, who was a member of the so-called 'School of Nice' (see page 183) and specializes in witty irreverent work often making use of unorthodox materials. The most striking work by him in the museum is *Homage to Louis Renault*, an enormous pillar made out of compressed car bumpers.

The nineteenth-century church of Notre-Dame-de-la-Garde, also on the south side of the town, is in the same depressing style as the cathedral; but you should climb up here to see its good collection of ex-votos and the magnificent view. At the foot of the steep hill on which it stands begins the long Chemin du Roucas Blanc, which winds its way through a beautiful nineteenth-century residential district, full of tall, elegant villas and stepped alleys dropping down to the coastal road, the Promenade de la Corniche President John F. Kennedy. Tucked away underneath this promenade is the tiny, picturesque port of the Vallon des Auffes, an excellent place to come and visit at night, for it is lined with animated, small restaurants serving some of the best pizzas in town: these restaurants are far cheaper and more authentic than the tourist establishments around the old port.

Driving south along the coastal road for another four kilometres, and turning left at a huge, ungainly reproduction of Michelangelo's *David*, you will reach the Parc Borély. This park, with its ponds and fairground stalls, comes alive on Sunday afternoons, when it is packed with Marseille families. The eighteenth-century palace in the middle of it has an archaeological museum with Greek, Roman and Salyan finds (above all a reconstructed Salyan portal from Roquepertuse, see page 43) and one of the most important groups of Egyptian antiquities in France; also kept here is a large collection of old drawings, mainly of the eighteenth-century French School. East of the park, on the

Boulevard Michelet, is a pioneering example of post-war architecture, Corbusier's Unité d'Habitation (1952). This tall concrete block of flats incorporating a 'shopping street' (half-way up) and community centre (on the roof) was What Le Corbusier imagined future living would be like. It was originally intended to be one of six such blocks, which Corbusier named the 'Cité Radieuse' – the 'Radiant City'. The 'Unité d'Habitation' was to result in the construction of many of the dreadful high-rise blocks of the 1950s and 60s, and, in its present dirty and neglected state, is the very opposite of 'radiant'.

Essential to any visit to Marseille is a boat trip from the old port to the barren island of the Château d'If. This will give you a chance both to view Marseille from the sea and to visit the sinister sixteenth-century prison immortalized by Dumas in *The Count of Monte-Cristo*. You can go inside all the cells, each of which has the names of its illustrious prisoners, including Mirabeau and the mysterious 'Man in the Iron Mask'; a plaque on one of the walls commemorates the 3,500 Protestants incarcerated at the Château d'If before being sent to the galleys. A nearby and much less visited island is the Île de Râtonneau. On this stand the haunting ruins of the Caroline Hospital, a majestic neo-classical structure built in 1821 to isolate sufferers from yellow fever, a new illness which had recently been brought over from America. [5B]

MARTIGUES, a town at the mouth of the Étang de Berre, was formed in 1581 by the amalgamation of three fishing villages – Ferrières to the north, Jonquières to the south, and, in the middle, the island village of Brescon. With its canals lined with boats and coloured houses, Martigues has often been likened to Venice, and for once such a comparison is a fairly accurate one: parts of Brescon could easily be mistaken for quiet districts of Venice such as the Canareggio. Ziem, a nineteenth-century Provençal painter famous for his views of Venice, had a studio at Martigues. Corot, Augustus John, Picabia and Roy Campbell are among the many other artists and writers who found inspiration here in the late nineteenth and early twentieth centuries. The heavy industralization of the Étang de Berre from the 1920s onwards destroyed much of its charm, but it still remains a lively resort, shunned by the rich and smart, and as such far more welcoming to the ordinary tourist than many other more fashionable places. A particularly good time to come here is during the second half of July, when the town has its festival – an animated two-week event with illuminated streets, open-air theatre and concerts, and even free offerings of sardines and seafood.

The best vantage-point in Martigues is the bridge crossing the Canal Sébastien, in the heart of Brescon. On one side is the Quai Brescon, known as the 'Bird's Mirror' and once a favourite spot for painters. On the other side is the seventeenth-century church of Sainte-Madeleine-en-Île, which has a richly ornamented façade and a gilded baroque organ. The town's recently re-installed museum, the Musée Ziem, is in Ferrières, and is far superior to most provincial museums. Its clearly displayed collections include Greek and Roman finds from the area, paintings by Ziem and other nineteenth- and twentieth-century artists who have worked in Provence, and a large and highly entertaining collection of ex-votos. [4B]

MÉNERBES, one of the prettiest villages on the north side of the Lubéron, is stretched out over a long narrow hill covered in trees. Its shape has frequently been compared to that of a boat.

In the middle of the village is a castle, built in the late sixteenth century following a siege carried out in 1577 to rid the village of its recently settled Huguenot community. The castle received a small garrison during the seventeenth century, then fell into ruins; bought in 1962 by the American art historian John Rewald (the pioneering chronicler of the Impressionists) it has been impressively restored (no visits). At the western end of the village, past a small church dating back to the fourteenth century, is a small, atmospheric cemetery, with a terrace commanding an excellent view. Immediately below is the fortified house of Le Castellet (built probably in the fifteenth century on a twelfth-century foundation), which formed part of the village's original defence walls. In the late eighteenth century the Danish Count Rantzau took refuge there after escaping from Denmark, where he had been implicated in the assassination of the queen's lover, Frederick Struensee; he is buried outside the castle. The abstract painter Nicholas de Staël bought the place in the 1950s, and his widow still lives there (see ANTIBES). Another distinguished resident of Ménerbes is Dora Maar, the beautiful Yugoslav photographer with whom Picasso had an affair in the 1930s and for whom he subsequently bought a house in Ménerbes after becoming infatuated with Françoise Gilot. [3B]

MENTON, a possession of the Grimaldi family of MONACO from 1346 until 1848, became a favourite resort of the English after 1850. In its heyday in the late nineteenth century the town had about 5,000 English residents in the winter, many of whom were consumptives attracted by the town's reputation as having the warmest winter climate on the coast. The English had their own church, club, newspaper, lending library and estate agency.

Today the English have all but gone, but the town remains one of the most dignified of the famed coastal resorts of the *belle époque*. Moreover, its old quarter, rising up on a hill between the town's two bays, is remarkably well preserved, a maze of stepped alleys lined by tall seventeenth-century houses. Half-way up, on a square covered with mosaics, is the beautiful baroque church of Saint-Michel, painted on the outside in pale shades of yellow and grey. The citadel above this was turned into a cemetery in the last century and is a wonderful place to visit, both for its views over the coast and for its tombs bearing the names of Europe's greatest aristocratic families.

In the port of the old town is a seventeenth-century bastion which once formed part of the town's seaside fortifications. This now has a museum to the novelist, film-maker and artist Jean Cocteau. The museum, partly designed by Cocteau himself but inaugurated five years after his death in 1963, resembles a down-at-heel bistro and has only indifferent works by the artist. The idea of a museum to himself came to Cocteau after he had been invited in 1957 by the Mayor of Menton to decorate the marriage room of the town hall. This is a nineteenth-century building in the heart of the commercialized district which extends west of the old town and includes the lively traffic-free shopping street of Saint-Michel. Cocteau's decorations here are far more sympathetic than the works in his museum (the same ticket allows you access to both places) and are intended to recreate the interior of a Greek temple; the room would be an ideal setting for a high-class confectioners.

The Jardin Biovès, to the west of here, is a long exotic park with the sea at one end and a splendid *belle époque* Kursaal at the other. Crossing this park you come to a residential district of long tree-lined avenues and sumptuous nineteenth-century parks and villas. The Municipal Museum is housed in the Palais Carnolès (3 Avenue de la Madonne), an eighteenth-century palace built as a summer residence for the Grimaldi Prince Anthony I. Later the building was transformed into a casino before becoming a luxurious furnished villa let out to such illustrious visitors as Elizabeth Louis of Bavaria and the Prince and Princess of Metternich. It was acquired in 1896 by a rich American, Dr. Edward P. Aldiss, who lived here until his death in 1947. Aldiss considerably enlarged the building and lavishly redecorated it. In 1969 it was turned into a museum to house a large number of paintings given to Menton by Wakefield Mori, an English resident. The paintings are mainly of the early French and Italian Schools, but there is also a large group of twentieth-century watercolours on the ground floor, including ones by André Lhote and Paul Delvaux. The collection is not an outstanding one, but the setting and the large garden which surrounds it are superb.

To the east of the old town is the smart residential area of Garavan, descending sharply to the sea down slopes covered with olive trees and exotic shrubs and plants. On either side of the small, neglected station of Garavan (the last stop before Italy) are streets named after the writers Blasco Ibañez and Katherine Mansfield, both of whom had villas here. Ibañez, who achieved international fame in the 1920s with his novel *The Four Horsemen of the Apocalypse* (made into a film starring Rudolph Valentino), came here as a Spanish exile in 1923 and transformed a characterless group of houses into an exotic Spanish villa and garden (Fontana Rosa, see page 151); the place has now been divided up, and its garden (the 'Jardín de los Novelistas') is sadly overgrown. The villa where Katherine Mansfield lived, the Villa Isola Bella on the Rue Katherine Mansfield, has a plaque to her quoting a letter she wrote in 1920 to Middleton Murry: 'You will find Isola Bella engraved on my heart.' You could round off a visit to Garavan by sipping lemon tea in the villa of the nineteenth-century humorist writer, Ferdinand Bac. This, the Villa Les Colombrières, high up on the Boulevard Garavan, has a large wooded garden which, like the villa itself, is in an evocative state of decay (see page 153). [3F]

MEYRARGUES: High above the ugly small town of Meyrargues is a twelfth-century castle, which was reconstructed in the seventeenth century and is now a hotel of baronial splendour. Below the castle, to the east, hidden in a wooded ravine, are the poignant remains of a Roman aqueduct (see page 57). [4C]

MIRABEAU: The imposing seventeenth-century castle of Mirabeau was the family home of the celebrated Revolutionary orator, Gabriel Honoré Riquetti, Count of Mirabeau. Riquetti actually spent little time here after 1774, when he had to run away to escape both from his wife and from numerous debts. His dissolute youth was followed by an active career as a journalist, pamphleteer and orator, in the course of which he alienated himself from the aristocracy without becoming fully accepted by the Jacobins. Despite his repudiation of his aristocratic past, his castle was burnt and pillaged during the Revolution. It was well restored the following century, when it became the property of the romantic novelist Maurice Barrès. [3C]

MONACO: The Principality of Monaco is a tiny sovereign state whose citizens are exempt from income tax and military service. It is ruled by the Grimaldis, the oldest reigning family in Europe. This family, of Genoese origin, were expelled from Genoa during the conflicts in Italy between the Guelphs and the Ghibellines. They purchased the high spur of rock on which the town of Monaco now stands in 1309; within the rocks were caves which had been lived in by some of the earliest inhabitants of the south of France.

The Grimaldis soon expanded their territory to include, among other places, MENTON and ROQUEBRUNE, but after a turbulent history were left in the mid nineteenth century with just Monaco itself. Faced with bankruptcy in the mid 1850s, Prince Charles III of Monaco decided to turn his principality into a health and leisure resort and to allow gambling, which was banned in both France and Italy. A rocky plateau to the east of Monaco was purchased, and a large gambling hall built on this. The town which grew up around the hall was named Monte-Carlo after Charles III, and was soon a magnet for the aristocracy, the rich and the would-be rich.

The present-day principality, one of the famed playgrounds of Europe, comprises four distinct areas: joining the old town of Monaco with Monte-Carlo is the port district of La Condamine, while below the old town to the west is the small industrial area of Fontvieille. As a result of being hemmed in by steep mountains and the sea, the exceptionally overcrowded principality has had to expand vertically and today resembles from a distance a brash American city, packed with tiers of skyscrapers surrounded by flyovers. Contemptuously dismissed by a number of Frenchmen as the 'Las Vegas of France', the principality has none the less retained much of its aristocratic nineteenth-century elegance. Its combination of the old and the new was symbolized for some by the marriage in 1956 between Prince Rainier I and Grace Kelly, the Hollywood actress daughter of a Philadelphia industrialist.

For a place of its size, the principality has a range of attractions almost unrivalled in the world, and almost every month of the year has its festival or other special celebration. In January there is the Monte-Carlo Rally, which has been running since 1912; February has the International Television Festival; April, the International Tennis Championships; May, the Monaco Grand Prix; July and August, the International Fireworks Festival; August and September, the World Amateur Theatre Festival; November, the Monégasque National Fête; and December, the International Circus Festival.

To appreciate Monaco to the full you have to be very rich, but even for the ordinary day-tripper there is an enormous amount to do and see, beginning – in chronological order of the sights – with a visit to the Jardin Éxotique in La Condamine, which has both a beautiful grotto where neolithic man lived, and one of France's most important prehistoric museums.

The prehistoric rock of Monaco's old town has today largely been hollowed out to make a vast shelter for the cars of *Homo sapiens*. A lift – one of several public lifts throughout the principality – takes you from the bottom of the rock into the old town at the top. The old houses here, though often dating back to the Middle Ages, look like the props of a bad film set, while the crenellated Royal Palace seems as if it is made from icing sugar. The over-quaint character of the palace is reinforced by the white-costumed guards in front of it, who regularly perform a changing-of-the-guard ceremony which seems lifted from a Gilbert and Sullivan opera. The building, despite heavy nineteenth-century remodelling and recent restoration, dates back in fact to the thirteenth century and has a courtyard and several rooms decorated with sixteenth- and seventeenth-century Italian frescoes, some of which are attributed to the Genoese painter Luca Cambiaso. Apart from these frescoes the palace is not an especially interesting place, and a tour round its apartments can be recommended only to those taken in by the glamour of monarchy. (Incidentally, the guides who lead these tours do not do any speaking themselves, but simply switch on a tape-recorder in each room.) Separate to this tour, and more intriguing, is the excellent Napoleonic museum attached to the palace.

Elsewhere in the old town is an ungainly neo-romanesque cathedral (nineteenth century), a building much visited today on account of its harbouring the tomb of the recently deceased Princess Grace. The huge Oceanographic Museum, spectacularly perched over the rock's southern cliffs, is one of the finest of its kind in the world. It was built in 1910 to satisfy Prince Albert I's passion for oceanography, and is directed today by the famous underwater explorer, Commander Jacques Cousteau. You can see skeletons of whales and other sea mammals, an elaborate display of marine technology, a large array of sea-shells, and film shows on marine subjects. It also has an important aquarium, an amusing feature of which is the label attached to the tank containing the *rascasse* or scorpion fish: your sympathies grow for this small and ugly creature innocently floating in its tank after reading that it is '*idéal pour la bouillabaisse*'.

Whether you gamble or not, you should pay a visit to Monte-Carlo's Grand Casino, a masterpiece of the neo-baroque by the architect of the Paris Opera House, Charles Garnier. Row upon row of pinball machines now fill up several of the rooms, and the atmosphere is dense with smoke; but Garnier's fantastically gilded, chandeliered and over-ornate interior manages to shine through the decadent gloom. Equally splendid and renowned are the Opera House at the back of this building (productions are put on only in winter and spring), and the Hôtel de Paris which faces it. Another smaller example of Garnier's work in Monte-Carlo is the villa now housing the Musée National, at no. 17 Avenue Princesse Grace. This museum is taken over almost entirely by a remarkable collection of eighteenth- and nineteenth-century dolls and automatons. It is best to go round this museum with a guide, who will open up the cases of the 'automated dolls', and, with a turn of a key, make these figures come charmingly to life.   [3F]

MONTMAJOUR: For this abbey, see ARLES.

MONT VENTOUX: For this mountain, see MALAUCÈNE.

MOULIN DES BOUILLONS: For this olive-oil mill and stained-glass museum, see GORDES.

MOUSTIERS-SAINTE-MARIE, a village picturesquely set against a back-drop of rocks, is overrun with tourists. Its popularity is due both to its position – at the entrance to the spectacular Grand Canyon of the Verdon – and to its local pottery industry. This industry was established in the late seventeenth century by Antoine Clérissy, profiting from the area's rich deposit of clay. The success of his potteries was immediate, and by the end of the eighteenth century there were eleven others in the village. In the nineteenth century, competition from industrial manufacturers in the north of France helped kill off the local pottery industry, which was none the less revived after 1926. Moustiers ware is characterized by its use of ornamentation derived from classical grotesques; recent products, on sale today throughout the village and in souvenir shops all over Provence, are very expensive and often of poor quality.

The main point of interest in the town is the informative museum of pottery housed in the old town hall. The romanesque parish church, with its beautiful bell-tower, is also worth a visit; and, should you wish to escape some of the crowds, you should climb up to the twelfth-century chapel of Notre-Dame-de-Beauvais. Another short climb behind the village will take you up to the Château de Trigance, a ninth- and twelfth-century castle converted in 1965 into an unusual luxury hotel with exuberant mock-medieval furnishings.

Two and a half kilometres south of Moustiers, the road divides and you are offered two ways of approching the spectacular Grand Canyon of the Verdon. The D952 to Castellane follows the north side of the canyon and passes by, after thirty-one kilometres, the famed viewpoint of Le Point Sublime. The D19 leads along the southern ridge, the Corniche Sublime, and reaches after thirty-eight kilometres what is perhaps the best view-point of all, the Balcons de la Mescla, which overlooks the Verdon at the point where it is joined by the small

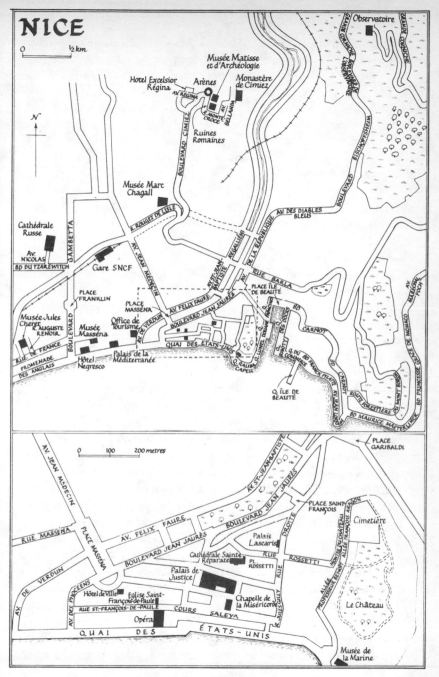

NICE

0   ½ km

N

Observatoire

GRANDE CORNICHE
BOULEVARD DE L'OBSERVATOIRE

Musée Matisse
et d'Archéologie

Hotel Excelsior
Régina

Arènes

Monastère
de Cimiez

AV. REGINA

AV. BELLANDA

R. MONTE
CROCE

Ruines
Romaines

BOULEVARD CIMIEZ

Musée Marc
Chagall

R. ROUGET DE L'ISLE

AV. DES DIABLES
BLEUS

BISCARRA-FESHEIM

BOULEVARD

GRANDE CORNICHE

Cathédrale
Russe

Av.
NICOLAS

BD DU TZAREWITCH

GAMBETTA

Gare SNCF

AV. JEAN MÉDECIN

AV. JEAN-
BAPTISTE

AVIGLIELLO

AV. DE LA RÉPUBLIQUE

RUE BARLA

PLACE ÎLE
DE BEAUTÉ

AV. MARÉCHAL FOCH

PLACE
FRANKLIN

PLACE
MASSÉNA

AV. FELIX FAURE

BD
CARNOT

Musée Jules
Chéret
R. AUGUSTE
RENOIR

Office de
Tourisme

AV. DE VERDUN

BOULEVARD JEAN JAURÈS

Q. LUNEL DRÈME

Q. DES DOCKS

BD PRINCESSE GRACE DE MONACO

RUE DE FRANCE

BOULEVARD

Musée
Masséna

QUAI DES ÉTATS-UNIS

Q. DU
COMMERCE

BD FRANCK-PILATTE

ROUTE FORESTIÈRE

PROMENADE
DES ANGLAIS

Hôtel
Negresco

Palais de la
Méditerranée

Q. RAUBA
CAPEU

BD CARNOT

AV. JEAN LORD

BD DU MONT BORON

Q. ÎLE DE
BEAUTÉ

BD MAURICE MAETERLINCK

0   100   200 metres

PLACE
GARIBALDI

AV. JEAN MÉDECIN

AV. ST-JEAN-BAPTISTE

BOULEVARD JEAN JAURÈS

PLACE SAINT-
FRANÇOIS

RUE MASSÉNA

AV. FELIX FAURE

PLACE MASSÉNA

BOULEVARD JEAN JAURÈS

Palais
Lascaris

RUE DROITE

RUE ROSSETTI

Cimetière

AV. DE VERDUN

AV. DES PHOCÉENS

Cathédrale Sainte-
Réparate

PL.
ROSSETTI

ROUTE DU CHÂTEAU

ALLÉE FRANÇOIS ARAGON

ALLÉE PROFESSEUR BENOIT

Le Château

Hôtel de Ville

Palais de
Justice

Église Saint-
François-de-Paule

Chapelle de
la Miséricorde

RUE ST-FRANÇOIS-DE-PAULE

Opéra

COURS   SALEYA

RUE JULES GILLY

QUAI   DES   ÉTATS - UNIS

Musée de
la Marine

Canyon of the Artuby. Should you intend to walk down into the canyon you should choose the former route and turn right at La Palud-sur-Verdon until you arrive at the Chalet de la Maline, a small refuge and restaurant. A footpath from here sharply descends into the canyon and follows the river to under the Point Sublime, where it ascends in a series of tunnels (bring a torch). The whole walk takes six hours, but is deeply rewarding; at both the Chalet Maline and the Point Sublime you can take taxis to where you left your car. [3D]

NICE: The terrible pun that Nice is 'nice' has frequently been made, most famously in a song in Sandy Wilson's musical *The Boy Friend*, which has the memorably silly refrain, 'But it's nice, much nicer in Nice.'

Helped perhaps by its name, Nice has enjoyed for over 150 years the reputation of being one of the great pleasure capitals of Europe, and today comes after Paris and Florence as the main destination for American travellers on the continent. But Nice is much more than the carefree resort of Wilson's song, it is a place with an impressive history and a character perhaps more varied than that of any other Provençal town.

The Greeks founded the trading port of Nikaia in about 350 B.C., but the Romans abandoned this and created a settlement two miles inland, on the site of the present-day suburb of Cimiez. The Roman town, with its important situation at the entrance to Gaul, grew to a population of around 20,000 but was largely destroyed by barbarian and Saracen invasions. A town was rebuilt on the site of Nikaia, and this was ruled from the tenth to the fourteenth century by the Counts of Provence. In 1388 the people of Nice chose to ally themselves with the Dukes of Savoy, and from that time onwards the town was an Italian possession and the capital of a district known as the 'County of Nice'.

In the fifteenth and early sixteenth centuries the town was the centre of a flourishing school of painting headed by the Bréa family: the works of these artists – which are to be found in churches throughout the district – owe nothing to French art, but are instead a provincial reflection of trends in central and north Italian art of this period. In 1793 Nice and its county voluntarily switched allegiance to France, but were taken back by Savoy after the collapse of the First Empire in 1814. Only with the Unification of Italy in 1860 was Nice finally reunited with France. Interestingly, the man who did so much to bring about this unification, Giuseppe Garibaldi, was born in Nice in 1807.

English visitors, encouraged by the doctor and writer Tobias Smollett, began coming to Nice from the 1780s onwards, and by the middle of the next decade the European aristocracy (especially the English and the Russians) regularly spent the winter months here. The popularity of the town increased further after the arrival of the railway in 1864. One consequence of growing tourism was the creation in 1873 of a carnival in the two weeks before Lent. Ever since the Middle Ages a costumed procession through the streets of Nice had been taking place at this time of year; but the carnival – which remains to this day one of the great attractions of the town – was an altogether more splendid affair, an extraordinary spectacle of flowers, floats, illuminations, and fantastical costumed figures, culminating, on Shrove Tuesday, with a spectacular fireworks display.

The great aristocratic families that had frequented Nice in the nineteenth century were not so much in evidence after the First World War. The appeal of the town broadened considerably, and the place today, while maintaining a very rich clientèle, caters for the mass tourism which has developed since the introduction of the paid holiday for workers in the 1930s. While Nice is not the ideal place for a swimming holiday, as its long beach is covered entirely with shingle, it offers numerous tourist attractions quite apart from its carnival. These include excellent opera and classical concerts, a famous international jazz festival (in July), a lively series of open-air cafés, and some of the best restaurants in Provence (Nice food, with its strong Italian character, is perhaps the most exotic and sophisticated in the region and includes such specialities as *pissaladière*, *estocaficada*, and *tourte de bléa*, a sweet tart made with chard, raisins, pine-nuts and parmesan cheese; see pages 190 and 195.).

Yet Nice, unlike Cannes or most of the other coastal resorts of Provence, does not exist solely for tourists. It is also the fifth largest town in France, with a newly established university, a major international airport, and important light industries; it is also, as Graham Greene emphasized in his booklet, *J'Accuse*, a town notorious for its corrupt, autocratic government and its Mafia-organized crime (see page 138–9). All in all Nice manages to bring together the charms of an animated resort and cultural centre, the staid virtues of a popular place of retirement, and the pace of an exciting if slightly dangerous city.

The complex character of Nice is reflected in the remarkable diversity of its sights, which range from important classical ruins to architectural masterpieces of the *belle époque*. The old town of Nice is one of the most beautiful old quarters of any French town, and quite unlike the rest of Nice: with its many baroque palaces and churches tightly packed into dark narrow streets festooned with washing-lines it could easily be mistaken for an Italian coastal town such as Genoa. It occupies a triangular area of land bordered to the south by the sea, to the east by the basin of the old harbour, and to the north and west by a wide esplanade which leads from the sea to the Place Garibaldi. Its western end is its most orderly and modern section, and comprises a regular grid of streets dating mainly from the late eighteenth century. On the Rue Saint-François-de-Paule are the town's neo-classical Opera House and a large late baroque church. At no. 7 is a shop (Henri Auer) specializing in delicious chocolates, pastries and crystallized fruits, while at no. 14 is one of the finest of all the town's traditional shops, Alziari, famous for its olives, olive oil, and olive-oil based products.

The Rue Saint-François-de-Paule leads on to the colourful heart of seventeenth- and eighteenth-century Nice, the Cours Saleya, a promenade overlooked by the elegant, superimposed *loggie* of the *Préfecture* and animated every day with a large flower, fruit and vegetable market. The oldest part of the town lies to the north and east of here, and is built up against the slopes of a hill dominated by a citadel. On all the tiny streets in this maze-like area you will come across sumptuous baroque portals, small crowded bars and bistros, and fashionable food shops, some selling a remarkable variety of fresh pasta. The Place Saint-François has a fish market selling so many types of fish that you might almost think that the contents of Monaco's aquarium had been emptied out on to its stalls. The most notable of the monuments is the Palais Lascaris on the Rue Droite, a seventeenth-century Genoese-style palace built for the Lascaris-Vintimille family and adorned with vigorous stucco decoration and mythological ceiling frescoes; the place is now a small museum with traditional Niçois furnishings of this period, and, on the ground floor, a charming, reconstructed eighteenth-century pharmacy.

At every corner of the old town there are tantalizing glimpses of the verdant citadel hill. You should certainly climb up to this. Part of the citadel is taken over by the town's old cemetery, which, like that of MENTON, is fascinating for its elaborate tombs containing a distin-guished cross-section of Europe's nineteenth-century aristocracy; attached to this is a large Jewish cemetery, a reminder of the important Jewish community which was once based in Nice. The rest of the citadel has been turned into a lovely municipal park, with delightful views and terraces and even an artificial waterfall, thundering down to the old town below.

To the west of the old town is the vast, arcaded Place Masséna, and beyond this is an extensive area intersected by straight and spacious avenues lined with ornate nineteenth-century hotels and apartment blocks. The Rue Masséna, and a number of small streets leading off it, have now been given over entirely to pedestrians; by day the area is an animated shopping district, and by night a focus of the city's night and café life.

The Promenade des Anglais, the famous coastal thoroughfare built after 1831 on the insistence of the town's English residents (see page 141), runs parallel with the Rue Masséna. One of the many extraordin-ary buildings along this is the Palais de la Mediterranée, a casino built in 1924 and an extremely ambitious example of the Art Deco style. Further down, at the intersection of the Rue de Rivoli, is the Hôtel Negresco, outstanding both for its *belle époque* architecture and for its restaurant, regarded by some as one of the greatest in Europe (see page 205). Next to the hotel, set back from the Promenade by a small formal garden, is a palace built in an Empire style in the late nineteenth century for Prince Victor Masséna, grandson of the famous Marshal of Napoleonic fame. The palace is now the Musée Masséna, and displays furniture and souvenirs from the Empire period and some fifteenth-century Nice school altarpieces from the parish church at LUCÉRAM.

Another splendid nineteenth-century palace which can be visited is the one containing the municipal art gallery, the Musée Jules Chéret, which lies a good ten minutes' walk to the west of the Musée Masséna, off the Rue de France. The building – in the style of a late sixteenth-century Genoese palace – was constructed around 1880 by the Russian Princess Kotschoubey and was later owned by an American millionaire, James Thompson. Though the interior has been given a recent face-lift, it remains magnificently evocative of *fin-de-siècle* Nice. On the ground floor is a superlative *David and Goliath* (*c.* 1615) possibly painted by the Lombard Tanzio da Varallo, an artist known for his tense and disturbing realism. But the nucleus of the collection is of nineteenth- and twentieth-century works, among which is a large group of paintings by the Provençal landscapist Félix Ziem (see page 164). Many of the other works are by artists closely associated with Nice, such as the Russian aristocrat Marie Bashkirtseff (see page 146), Jules Chéret (see pages 173–4), the bizarre symbolist artist Gustave Mossa, and the Fauve painters Raoul Dufy and Kees van Dongen. The latter, who worked as a successful society portraitist on the Riviera from the 1920s onwards, is represented principally by *The Tango of the Archangel* (1927), a triptych which features a girl, naked save for stockings and a garter, dancing with a dinner-jacketed man with wings. This amusing work, so suggestive of high society decadence between the wars, typifies the spirit of this constantly entertaining but little visited museum.

The Boulevard Gambetta leads north from the Promenade des Anglais into the district of Saint-Étienne, which is worth visiting for the Russian Orthodox Cathedral, off the Avenue Nicolas. This poignant testimony to the former Russian presence in Nice was begun in 1903 and completed five years before the Revolution. Crowned by five onion domes dressed in colourful tiles, the building was inspired by churches in Moscow and Jaroslavl and designed by a Russian architectural historian.

Further treasures of the *belle époque* are to be found in Nice's extensive suburbs. On the slopes of Mont Boron, a spacious and luxurious suburb rising up to the east of the old harbour, are countless fantastic villas, including, most notably, the orange-pink pseudo-Mogul castle known variously as the 'Château de l'Anglais' or 'Folly Smith' (see page 151). Mont Gros, the hill to the north of this, is topped by an observatory designed in 1881 by the architect of the Monte-Carlo casino, Charles Garnier, and with an ingenious dome put up by Gustave Eiffel.

The most important of the suburbs is Cimiez, which was popularized as a resort by Queen Victoria in the 1880s and boasts from this period the former Hôtel Excelsior Regina Palace (on the Avenue Regina), once one of the grandest of all the Riviera hotels. Inside and around the nearby public park are a remarkable group of monuments, including a small and rather battered Roman amphitheatre, and extensive and recently excavated ruins of Roman baths. On the eastern side of the park is a Franciscan monastery, with a late gothic church (heavily restored in the seventeenth century) containing three major altarpieces by the leading Nice painter of the fifteenth century, Ludovico Bréa. Both Matisse and Dufy are buried in its cemetery.

Matisse spent much of his later life in Cimiez, staying for some of the time in an apartment in the Regina Palace. Important works from all periods in his career are to be seen in the Musée Matisse, which shares a charming seventeenth-century villa overlooking the Roman baths with a small archaeological museum. Matisse once wrote that art should be 'devoid of any subject-matter . . . [and] as relaxing as a comfortable armchair'. The old-fashioned, unostentatious display of his works in this museum is perfectly in sympathy with these intentions; there is even an armchair which he owned, and a painting which he did of it, *Rococo Armchair*.

Marc Chagall painted little more than pleasing decorations but believed that these had important subject-matter. The museum to him, at the lower end of Cimiez on the Avénue du Docteur Ménard, is called the Musée National Message Biblique Marc Chagall, and, in addition to having a permanent display of seventeen large canvases by him, puts on temporary exhibitions often of a religious or mystical nature, such as displays of Tibetan prayer rolls. There is something deeply pretentious about the whole conception of this museum, but at least the building (opened in 1971) is a light airy structure in the middle of an attractive garden with a pool and cafeteria. [3F]

NOTRE-DAME-D'AUBUNE: For this chapel, see BEAUMES-DE-VENISE.

NOTRE-DAME-DE-LUMIÈRES, an undistinguished small village off the main Cavaillon to Apt road, is redeemed by its pleasant wooded setting and views of the Petit Lubéron.

A wooden *Madonna* in the large seventeenth-century sanctuary is the object each year of popular pilgrimage. The statue was discovered in the late seventeenth century, after an old shepherd kept seeing a mysterious procession of candles pass next to the paleo-Christian tombs hollowed out of the rock behind the village. The sanctuary is not of great architectural interest, but contains one of the most extensive collections of ex-votos in Provence.

NOTRE-DAME-DE-LURE: For this priory, see SAINT-ÉTIENNE-LES-ORGUES.

NOTRE-DAME-DE-L'ORMEAU: For this chapel, see SEILLANS.

NOTRE-DAME-DES-FONTAINES: For this chapel, see LA BRIGUE.

NOVES, the home town of Laura de Noves, the supposed 'Laura' of Petrarch's sonnets, is a quiet market town which has kept a portion of its medieval walls. The spacious romanesque church of Saint-Baudile was once attached to the southern ramparts and has a clock tower which served as an observation post.

Three kilometres to the east of the village, on the other side of the Durance, is the lovely Charterhouse of Bonpas, unfortunately situated next to one of the busiest road junctions in the Rhône valley. The stretch of the Durance here was once known as 'malus passus' because it was notoriously difficult to cross and was guarded by criminals. Towards the end of the twelfth century a bridge was built and its protection was entrusted to a group of monks, thus transforming a 'malus passus' into a 'bonus passus'. The nearby chapel which the monks constructed was incorporated in the early fourteenth century into a Charterhouse, which today is at the centre of a small wine domain. Visitors are welcome. After entering through a medieval gate you find yourself in a large courtyard, with a hanging terraced garden above you to the left and, in front, a seventeenth-century hostelry. Crossing the courtyard you descend on the other side into the twelfth-century chapel. At the end of the tour you have the opportunity to taste some of the good red wines produced here.   [3A]

OPPÈDE: The ruined hill village of Oppède, high up on a limestone crag underneath the northern slopes of the Petit Lubéron, is still a most evocative place despite much recent rebuilding and growing tourism.

The village grew around its castle, which was built in the twelfth century and enlarged in the fifteenth and sixteenth centuries. Belonging first to the Counts of Forcalquier, then to the Counts of Provence, it became after 1274 a papal possession within the Comtat-Venaissin. In 1501 Alexander VI entrusted it to the Maynier family, who were soon afterwards granted a baronetcy. Jean de Maynier, the first Baron of Oppède, achieved notoriety for his massacre of the Vaudois in 1545, and, though acquitted at his trial in AIX-EN-PROVENCE in 1551, died shortly afterwards of an agonizing intestinal seizure attributed by some to poisoning (see page 83).

The handing back of the Comtat-Venaissin to France after the Revolution hastened the decline of the village by depriving it of its once active commercial links with Italy. In 1910 the village was abandoned and its remaining inhabitants moved down to what is now known as Oppède-les-Poulivets. During the Second World War a group of artists and architects settled in the ruins (see pages 180–81), and since then many of the medieval houses in the lower half of the village have been made habitable. The one outstanding building higher up is the twelfth-century church of Notre-Dame-d'Alydon, restored in the sixteenth century and again in the nineteenth century (ask for the key in the town hall off the village square). The castle is completely overgrown but is well worth a visit for the spectacular views on its northern side, down to a wooded ravine, and above to the steep slope and limestone scars of the Lubéron.

The impressive position of Oppède is best appreciated by taking one of the two steep footpaths which lead from the bottom of the village up to the top of the Lubéron ridge (about an hour and a half's walk). Another wonderful walk from Oppède is to follow the wooded footpath along the lower slopes of the mountain almost all the way to BONNIEUX (about five hours).

At Oppède-les-Poulivets is a traditional olive-mill, where good oil and other oil-based and local products can be bought.   [3B]

ORANGE, originally a Celtic market town, was presented in 46 B.C. to veterans of the Roman VIIth Legion. The Romans built here two of the finest classical monuments of Provence, most notably a triumphal arch on the northern outskirts of the town, and – in the town centre – a massive theatre (the best preserved one in existence);

on the hill against which the auditorium is set are important ruins of a temple and a gymnasium. In the last two weeks of July an international music festival – operas and classical concerts – is held in the theatre.

Orange was created a principality in the twelfth century by the Emperor Barbarossa, and in the sixteenth century this passed, through inheritance, to William of Nassau ('William the Silent'), Stadtholder of the Netherlands; it remained a Nassau possession until 1713, when it was annexed to France after the Treaty of Utrecht. During the period of Nassau rule much damage was caused to the Roman monuments by the use of their stones to create a palace and fortifications; these latter were later demolished by the French.

Directly opposite the Roman theatre is the town museum, with well-displayed Roman finds, and objects and historical panels relating to the history of the principality. A curious feature of the place is its extensive holdings of the graphic work of Sir Frank Brangwyn, a highly successful British artist of the Edwardian era.   [2A]

PERNES-LES-FONTAINES is often rushed past by tourists on their way down the dull, busy road from Carpentras to Cavaillon. Hidden from this road is a town of great charm, with a fine group of medieval monuments and an important history.

With the handing over of the Comtat-Venaissin to the papacy in 1274, Pernes became the first capital of the Comtat, a position which it held until 1320 when it was superseded by CARPENTRAS. A large section of its fourteenth-century walls survives, and a number of its medieval and Renaissance gates. The most impressive of these is the eastern Porte Notre-Dame (1548), on the bridge leading up to which is a small seventeenth-century chapel. Outside this gate is the large twelfth-century parish church of Notre-Dame-de-Nazareth.

Entering the old town through the Porte Notre-Dame, you will come immediately to the 'fountain of cormorants', one of the thirty-six fountains (mainly dating from the eighteenth century) which give the town its name of 'Les-Fontaines'. Also within the old town is the Ferrande Tower, the sole remaining part of a palace which once belonged to the Hospitallers of Saint John of Jerusalem. The upper room of the tower contains the most important surviving fresco cycle from thirteenth-century Provence: the subjects depicted are scenes from the struggle of Charles I of Anjou (supported by Clement IV) against the house of Hohenstaufen.   [3B]

PEYROLLES-EN-PROVENCE: On a small hill on the southern side of Peyrolles is the intriguing twelfth-century chapel of the Holy Sepulchre, a rare example in Provence of a church with a quatrefoil plan (another is that of the Holy Cross at Montmajour, see ARLES).

The main building of the town, the castle (now the town hall), has great historical interest but is in a most depressing condition. Dating back to the twelfth century, it belonged in the fifteenth century to King René, and later to the kings of France. The present structure is mainly of the seventeenth century, but the seedy, collapsing interior decoration is of a much later date.   [4C]

PONT FLAVIEN: For this Roman bridge, see SAINT-CHAMAS.

PONT JULIEN: For this Roman bridge, see APT.

PORT-GRIMAUD, see GRIMAUD.

RAMATUELLE, see SAINT-TROPEZ.

RIEZ, a thriving Roman settlement, became a bishopric in the fifth century and was thus one of the earliest dioceses in Gaul. It remained a bishopric until 1790.

The town's two main attractions lie just outside the town to the west. Beautifully set among fields on the northern side of the river Colostre are the four remaining Corinthian columns of a Roman temple probably dedicated to Apollo. On the southern side of the river, off the D 952 to Allemagne-en-Provence, is one of the four early Christian baptisteries of France: dating back at least partially to the fifth century, it is also one of the earliest surviving Christian buildings in the country. Inside is a small lapidary museum, and nearby are the scanty ruins of the fifth-century cathedral. Both the baptistery and the cathedral were put up during the rule of Bishop Maximinus, and may owe their foundation to a Council held at Riez in 439, at which Bishop Hilarius of Arles presided.

The attractive old quarter of Riez is in itself worth a visit, and has one of the best natural history museums in the region.   [3D]

ROBION, see CASTELLANE.

ROQUEBRUNE-CAP-MARTIN: Much of the luxuriant mountainous coast between MONACO and MENTON is taken up by the sprawling commune of Roquebrune-Cap-Martin. The oldest part of this conglomerate is the hill village of Roquebrune, a maze of stairways and steep paved alleys, the whole festooned with souvenir shops and over-prettified houses. The Rue Moncollet, the tourist thoroughfare of the village, leads up to the Donjon, which is supposedly the oldest standing castle in France. In fact only a small part of the building dates from the eleventh century, the rest of the fabric being of the thirteenth and fourteenth centuries. The building has been heavily restored in recent times, and is worth a visit primarily for the views from its roof terrace. The best times to come to Roquebrune are on the night of Good Friday and on the afternoon of 5 August, when, in fulfilment of a vow made by the villagers during the plague in 1467, costumed processions recreating the Passion pass through the village streets.

Cap Martin below has been a resort for the rich and famous ever since the Empress Eugénie of France started coming here in the late nineteenth century. Yeats died here, and Sir Winston Churchill and the renowned forger of Vermeers, Van Meegeren, were both frequent visitors. One of the streets is named after the architect Le Corbusier, who drowned while swimming off the cape. The place is filled with luxurious villas in large exotic gardens. You will skirt some of these if you follow the lovely coastal path from the Avenue Winston Churchill on Cap Martin to Monte-Carlo (see MONACO).   [3F]

LA ROQUE-D'ANTHÉRON has a number of seventeenth- and eighteenth-century houses, and an impressive Renaissance château, but it is known to tourists principally for the abbey of Silvacane, one kilometre to the east of the village, off the D23. The name Silvacane (from the Latin *silva cana*) means forest of reeds, a reminder of the marshy terrain which once characterized much of the Durance valley in which this abbey stands. The valley today is much built up, but its ugly, modern elements are hidden from Silvacane.

The abbey, reached from the road by crossing cultivated fields, is nestled in a wooded hollow and set off by the distant bluish range of the Lubéron. It was founded in 1144 by the Cistercians, but has a more modest appearance than the two other celebrated Cistercian abbeys of Provence, Sénanque (see GORDES), and LE THORONET.

In fact it was once the most important of the three. Heavily endowed by Raymond des Baux, it knew great prosperity in the twelfth and thirteenth centuries. Only towards the end of the thirteenth century, when it entered a long conflict with the Benedictine abbey of Montmajour (see ARLES), did its fortunes start to decline. Pillaged by vandals in 1357, annexed to the cathedral of AIX-EN-PROVENCE in 1443, and transformed in the sixteenth century into the parish church of La Roque-d'Anthéron, it finally became a farm after the Revolution. State restoration of the building is still in progress. The complex dates mainly from 1175 and 1230 (the refectory was rebuilt in the fifteenth century) and, like Sénanque and Le Thoronet, is notable for its simplicity and homogeneity. [3B]

ROQUEFAVOUR: For this aqueduct, see AIX-EN-PROVENCE.

ROUSSILLON, a medieval village with a fourteenth-century church and fragments of its ramparts, is red from the dust of the ochre cliffs on which it stands. The place has been much modernized and altered by tourism since the time when an American sociologist, Laurence Wylie, wrote here a classic study of Provençal village life, *Village in the Vaucluse* (see page 123–4). Its attraction for the passing visitor lies primarily in the surreal ochre landscape which lies to the north and to the east. An exciting path from the village car-park leads into this world of strange shapes and lurid colours. The temptation for children and adults alike to roll around in the ochre is a great one, but you should remember that the dust is extremely difficult to remove and remains on your clothes after persistent washing. In Wylie's day the children of the village were not allowed to play here. [3B]

RUSTREL: Five kilometres to the south of Rustrel (follow either the D30 or the D30A) lies the Dôa valley, on the southern side of which is a landscape of pine trees and abandoned ochre quarries. This area is known as the 'Provençal Colorado'. Though not as exciting as the ochre landscape near ROUSSILLON, a number of fine walks can be done here, including one to a group of clay-capped earth pillars fancifully referred to as the '*cheminées de fées*' ('the chimney stacks of the fairies'); to get there, leave your car by the river Dôa, just below the junction of the D30A and the D22, and follow the yellow arrows for about twenty minutes. [3C]

SAINT-BLAISE: The small steep-sided plateau in between the Étang de Berre and the smaller Étang de Lavalduc is of extreme importance for those interested in the earliest history of Provence. The archaeological site of Saint-Blaise, excavated only in very recent times, marks the ancient city of Mastramella, which dates back to prehistoric times. Even before the Greeks from Phocis came to Provence in the seventh century, it was a flourishing trade centre enjoying strong commercial links with Etruria, and, through Etruria, probably with Greece and Asia Minor as well. Falling soon under Phocian domination, it continued to prosper but the political and economic problems that Marseille suffered in the late sixth century affected it too. Plundered in the early fourth century by Celtic tribes, it revived towards the end of the century with the renewal of Marseille's own economic fortunes. The construction of the Fosses Mariennes (see page 45) and the subsequent foundation of the port at nearby Fos threatened the town's prosperity once again by offering a faster route from Marseille to the Rhône valley. The fate of Saint-Blaise seemed finally sealed after the submission of Marseille to Rome in 49 B.C.

Saint-Blaise lay deserted for centuries, but then in the fourth century A.D. its easily defendable position made it an ideal place of refuge for Christians, gathering together to protect themselves against barbarian attacks. They called the new town which they built Ugium, and this survived until 874, when it was finally burnt down by barbarians. It remained half-abandoned until 1231, when the Archbishop of Arles tried to repopulate it and built a new defence wall. This new settlement stuggled on until after 1390, after which it was abandoned for ever.

Vestiges of all the periods in the town's history are to be found at Saint-Blaise, including impressive fragments of the Greek sixth-century fortifications, a Christian necropolis, the foundations of a paleo-Christian basilica, and – outside the excavated site – a section of the thirteenth-century ramparts and the beautiful romanesque chapel of Saint-Blaise.   [4B]

SAINT-CHAMAS: Two kilometres south of Saint-Chamas on the D10 is the Pont Flavien, a bridge constructed by the patrician Flavian in the first century A.D. It gracefully crosses the river Touloubre in a single span, but its most exciting features are the triumphal arches seven metres high at either end. These arches support sculpted lions, only one of which is original, the other three being by an eighteenth-century sculptor. [4B]

SAINT-DALMAS-DE-TENDE, see TENDE.

SAINT-DONAT: For this abbey, see SAINT-ÉTIENNE-LES-ORGUES.

SAINT-ÉTIENNE-DE-TINÉE, the largest village of this wild Alpine valley bordering on Italy, is an unspoilt place of great character and with a magnificent mountain setting. The village was burnt down in 1594 in an attempt to dislodge some Huguenot troops, and was further damaged by fire this century. None the less it has a number of fine old houses, and a church with a tall and striking romanesque bell-tower. A small ethnographical museum has been installed in the old bakery, and gives an insight into a valley whose traditions are a fascinating mixture of French and Italian elements (see pages 193–4).

There are a number of chapels in the vicinity containing fifteenth-century Italian frescoes. Off the D39 to the small skiing resort of Auron is the chapel of Saint-Sébastien, decorated by Giovanni Canavesio and Giovanni Baleison (see LA BRIGUE). At Auron itself is the chapel of Saint-Érige-d'Auron, a romanesque building with a fifteenth-century apse covered in charming scenes of the Magdalene, and Saints Denis and Erigius. [2E]

SAINT-ÉTIENNE-LES-ORGUES, an attractive village at the foot of the wild and densely wooded mountain range of the Lure, owes its existence to the small but renowned abbey founded by Saint Donatus thirteen kilometres to the north (see page 64). The abbey, high up in the Lure at the end of a small track off the D113, is popular today both as a pilgrimage place and as a picnic spot. The surroundings are lovely, but the surviving abbey buildings are unremarkable. The present church of Notre-Dame-de-Lure dates back to the twelfth century, but was heavily altered in later years and has little more than a quaint rustic appeal; the adjoining hermitage is a tiny structure of the seventeenth century, also much restored. The D113 continues up to the crest of the Lure, and from here you can walk for fifteen minutes to the Signal de Lure, an outstanding view-point.

Of far greater architectural distinction are the majestic ruins of Saint-Donat, the abbey which Saint Donatus later founded between the Lure and the Durance valley. To reach this from Saint-Étienne-les-Orgues take the road to Sisteron, then take the right turn just past Mallefougasse on the D101 marked Les Mées. After a four-kilometre drive (with good views towards the strange limestone pinnacles of Les Mées on the other side of the Durance valley) you will finally come to the abbey. The tall abbey church (now undergoing restoration) is a masterpiece of early romanesque architecture in Provence.   [2C]

SAINT-GABRIEL: The isolated chapel of Saint-Gabriel – five kilometres to the south of Tarascon, at the crossing of the N570 and the D33 – marks the site of Eraginum, a small Roman settlement at the junction of the main lines of communication in Roman Provence. Much of the surroundings were covered in marshland, and in the early Middle Ages a small fishing community lived here. The chapel, the only survival of this medieval community, is a gem of the Provençal romanesque, and a persuasive example of the influence on this style of classical art and architecture (see page 68).

SAINT-JEAN-CAP-FERRAT, a verdant peninsula of palms, pines and exotic flowers, is covered with nineteenth- and early twentieth-century villas, including the Villa les Cèdres (which belonged to Léopold II of Belgium) and Somerset Maugham's Villa Mauresque, a magnet for tourists when Maugham was still alive. The lake belonging to the Villa les Cèdres has been drained and now forms the setting of a spacious private zoo which organizes 'chimps' tea parties' six times a day. The only villa in the area which can be visited inside is the Villa Ephrussi de Rothschild, built in the late nineteenth century by the Baroness Rothschild to house her own art collections and those belonging to her father and exceptionally rich banker husband. The collections (particularly strong in works of the French and Italian rococo) are impressive, but the pleasure of the visit lies mainly in the glamorous setting of the house, and the fantastic surrounding gardens (see page 153).   [4F]

SAINT-MARTIN-VÉSUBIE, the foremost mountain and thermal resort in the Alpes-Maritimes, has also an excellently preserved medieval quarter, which is best seen by walking the full length of the narrow and steep Rue du Docteur Cagnoli. The town is a good base for excursions to the Parc National du Mercantour, a large and magnificent wildlife reserve where no cars, dogs, or guns are allowed, and where you are likely to come across marmots and chamois. Details of walking, mountaineering, horse-riding, canoeing and other such activities to be done in the national park can be had from the information office at Saint-Martin.

The valley of the Vésubie turns twenty-four kilometres to the south into a spectacular gorge. At Saint-Jean-la-Rivière take the road which skirts the gorge to the left and you will climb up to a famous viewpoint with a sheer 1,000-foot drop down to the river. This spot is known as the 'Saut des Français' (Frenchman's leap), a reminder of the Republican soldiers who were thrown into the chasm by Nice rebels in 1793. [2F]

SAINT-MAXIMIN-LA-SAINTE-BAUME, a lively market town dominated by its enormous basilica, has been a major centre of pilgrimage ever since the fifth century when a monastery was constructed to house the relics of the Mary Magdalene and of Saints Maximinus, Marcellus and Sidonius (see pages 59–60). These relics were hidden in the eighth century to avoid capture from the Saracens, and did not resurface until 1279. The man responsible for the discovery, Charles of Anjou, afterwards became Count of Provence and in 1295 ordered the construction of the present basilica to house them (they are kept in the crypt). The architect chosen, Giovanni Baudici, had been responsible for the Count's palace at AIX-EN-PROVENCE. The apse and much of the nave were completed in the early fourteenth century, but work on the rest of the church continued up to 1532; the western façade is still unfinished. The vast sober interior has not the elegance or the decorative sophistication of the great gothic cathedrals of the north of France, but is none the less unrivalled as the main gothic building in Provence.

One of the few ornate features of the interior is the late eighteenth-century organ, and it was this organ which reputedly saved the basilica after the Revolution. Napoleon's brother Lucien Bonaparte, then in charge of the local Jacobin club, had the brilliant idea first of using the church as a warehouse, and then of playing the 'Marseillaise' on the organ at the very moment when the notorious Commissionaire of the people, Barras, entered the building. The organ was in itself worth saving, and today excellent recitals of seventeenth- and eighteenth-century organ music are given during the music festival which is held in the town in August.

The large adjoining monastery, the main venue of this festival, was begun at the same time as the basilica and was built over a period of many years. At its centre is an enormous fifteenth-century cloister, sheltering a luxuriant garden dominated by a large cedar tree. The pilgrims' hostelry projecting from the western end of the cloister was put up in the eighteenth century and is now the town hall; the other monastic buildings are given over to a tourist office and cultural centre.

The old town extending to the east of the basilica has several attractive streets, most notably the fourteenth-century Rue des Arcades, an arcaded street marking the site of a small Jewish ghetto.   [4C]

SAINT-MICHEL-DE-FRIGOLET, a large and active monastic complex, lies in a hollow shaded by cedars, pines and cypresses in the heart of the Montagnette, a low range of rocky hills rising above the Rhône valley. The landscape is fragrant with wild flowers and aromatics, and the name 'Frigolet' might well be a derivative of the Provençal word for thyme, *ferigoulo*.

The monastery was probably founded in the late tenth century by Benedictine monks from Montmajour (see ARLES), escaping the unhealthy marshes surrounding their own abbey. The chapel which they built was dedicated to the 'Virgin of the Goodly Remedy', and this soon became a popular pilgrimage stop on the route to Santiago de Compostela. The surrounding monastery declined after the fifteenth century and was dissolved during the Revolution. In 1839 it became for a while a small school, run by a lazy and incompetent old man. One of its first and last pupils was Frédéric Mistral, who studied here between 1839 and 1841. The property was sold in 1859 to the order of Premonstratensians, who largely rebuilt the place and are still its owners.

Many who come here are disappointed, expecting to find a picturesque medieval abbey and finding instead a large neo-gothic complex, entered by a crenellated mock-medieval gate. As a nineteenth-century structure it is none the less most impressive, and the brilliantly coloured interior of the new abbey church forms a pleasant contrast to the sobriety of Provençal churches in general. There also remains more of the old monastery than is immediately apparent. Tucked away at the back of the new church is the tiny chapel of Notre-Dame-de-Bon-Remède, a romanesque structure (on the site of the tenth-century original) heavily disguised by elaborate baroque panelling presented by Anne of Austria in 1638. The main survivals of the medieval complex are the heavily restored twelfth-century church of Saint-Michel, and a romanesque cloister inspired by that of Montmajour.

A tour of the monastery will also take you to a room containing the distilling apparatus used by the monks up to 1880 to make a famous herb-based liqueur (similar to Bénédictine), which inspired one of the tales in Daudet's *Letters from My Windmill*, 'The Elixir of Père Gaucher'. A liqueur named after this tale is on sale in the monastery shop, though the liqueur itself is now produced elsewhere. [3A]

SAINT-PANTALÉON, see GORDES.

SAINT-PAUL-DE-VENCE, a hill village which once guarded the border between France and Savoy, is still surrounded by the ramparts built at the instigation of Francis I between 1537 and 1557. Much frequented by artists after 1918, the village today is one of the most popular tourist spots in the south of France. The place is exceptionally well preserved, though it has been so prettified that it looks more like a museum than a real village – even the streets have been paved with mosaics.

The thirteenth- to fourteenth-century parish church is rich in six-teenth-and seventeenth-century furnishings and works of art and boasts a magnificent baroque chapel, consecrated to Saint Clement and endowed by Giovanni Bernardi, majordomo to Pope Innocent XI and canon at Saint Peter's in Rome. On the Place de Mérier is the Museum of Mechanical Curiosities, an enjoyable collection of mech-anical musical instruments dating from 1750 to 1930. A fine six-teenth-century house on the Place de la Grande Fontaine contains the Musée Provençal, a museum of Provençal life and folklore. The Colombe d'Or, the celebrated hotel around which the village's art colony grew (see pages 178–9), has a stupendous collection of modern art, though to see this you are now obliged either to stay or to have a meal at the place. If you are unable to do so there is always the Maeght Foundation outside the village, off the road to Vence.

This is one of the greatest museums of contemporary art in Europe, both for its collections and for its architecture and setting. Surrounded by exotic trees and shrubs, it was built in the early 1960s by the gallery owners and art-book publishers, Marguerite and Aimé Maeght. Their intention was to increase the knowledge and appreciation of modern art. In addition to a gallery, the Foundation has a library, a bookshop and ceramic and paint studios, and also hosts concerts, ballets and other such performances.

The architect of the Foundation was the renowned Catalan José Luis Sert, who conceived of the place as an asymmetrical cluster of buildings in perfect harmony with the environment. He favoured simple materials, such as stones from a nearby hill and hand-made bricks fired – as was the tradition in this area – in a wood oven. As in many of his other buildings, Sert worked here in close collaboration with artists. Thus his friend and compatriot Miró (whose museum in Barcelona Sert also designed) executed numerous ceramics, mosaics, fountains and sculptures for the museum's terraces, while Braque decorated a pool and provided stained-glass windows for a chapel. The works on display are constantly being changed, the only ones always remaining being a large group of paintings by Chagall and Kandinsky, and a group of bronzes by Giacometti beautifully placed on the museum's patio. [3E]

SAINT-RAPHAEL, today a quiet and rather unfashionable resort, was settled by the Romans at the same time as the adjacent town of FRÉJUS. Roman villas existed on the site of the present casino, but these were destroyed in the course of Saracen raids in the Dark Ages. After the expulsion of the Saracens in the late tenth century, the Counts of Provence entrusted the abandoned site to monks from the Lérins (see CANNES), who built a church here and created a village around it. Defended by the Templars in the twelfth century, Saint-Raphael later developed as a small fishing port, the reputation of which was enhanced by Napoleon, who both landed here on his return from Egypt in 1799 and set sail from here on his way to exile in Elba in 1814. Towards the middle of the last century Saint-Raphael became established as a winter resort, favoured largely by the French. Alphonse Karr, a journalist and a passionate horticulturist, was one of the earliest and most enthusiastic of the town's winter visitors. The garden of the villa which he had built here offered him endless delight, and he constantly wrote about it to his Parisian friends. 'Leave Paris,' he told one of them, 'and plant your walking stick in my garden; when you get up the next day it will already have sprouted roses.' Encouraged by Karr's reports of Saint-Raphael, many other distinguished Parisians started coming here regularly, including Alexandre Dumas and Maupassant; Gounod stayed in 1866, and composed his opera *Romeo and Juliet* in the town.

The history of Saint-Raphael and of Alphonse Karr's stay here is recorded in photographs and other souvenirs displayed in the town's fascinating archaeological museum on the Rue des Templiers. The greater part of the museum is devoted to underwater archaeology, and there are many important finds ranging from Greek amphorae and Roman anchors to eighteenth-century warship cannons. Next to the museum is the church of Saint-Raphael, a twelfth-century structure with a watch-tower probably built by the Templars. [4E]

SAINT-RÉMY-DE-PROVENCE, the successor to the important ancient settlement of Glanum, was founded one kilometre to the north of this town shortly after the latter's destruction by barbarians in the third century A.D. Surrounded by the fertile plains of the Rhône valley, with its skyline to the south marked by the strange crags of Les Alpilles, this lively market town lies at the heart of the Provence praised by the Félibres. Joseph Roumanille, the oldest member of this group, was born here, and Mistral lived for most of his life seven kilometres to the north, at MAILLANE. Within a short radius are some of the most celebrated monuments of all Provence.

Many who come to Saint-Rémy rush off immediately to Glanum, but the town itself is a very pleasant place in which to linger, having many fine old buildings and a lovely series of shaded open-air cafés. Park your car on the large Place de la République (except on Wednesdays when the square is taken over by a market). On the eastern end of the square, at the entrance of the old town of Saint-Rémy, is the parish church of Saint-Martin, a neo-classical structure which has kept its fourteenth-century bell-tower. Turning left behind the church on to the small Rue Daniel Milhaud, you cross the Rue Carnot and reach the Place Favier. Here you will find the Hôtel Mistral de Mondragon (no connection with Mistral the poet), a beautiful

Renaissance palace with an intimate and very elegant courtyard. The small rooms built around this display the collections of the Musée des Alpilles Pierre de Brun, a historical museum more interesting for its atmosphere and setting than for what it contains. Opposite the building, and entered from the Rue du Parage, is another, larger Renaissance palace, this one being originally in the possession of the infamous Sade family: inside is a small lapidary museum, exhibiting finds from both Glanum and SAINT-BLAISE.

Make your way back to the Rue Carnot, and turn left until you reach on the right-hand side the Rue Lucien Estrine. The Hôtel Estrine, half-way down this, has a grand baroque vestibule and is now a venue for important art exhibitions. At the far end of the street turn right and you will eventually come back to the Place de la République. On the way there you will pass on your left the Rue Hoche, where a plaque marks the birthplace of the famous astrologer Nostradamus.

On the southern edge of Saint-Rémy, on the Glanum road, stands the attractive fifteenth-century chapel of Notre-Dame-de-la-Pitié. This is now the centre of a Foundation dedicated to the painter and writer Mario Prassinos (1905–85). Prassinos lived at EYGALIÈRES, and wanted to decorate the chapel of the Penitents there with a series of monochrome panels. The Eygalières authorities had the good sense to turn his request down, a refusal considered by the local artists as an act of philistinism. The town of Saint-Rémy interceded, and offered not only to put these depressing works on permanent display in the chapel of Notre-Dame-de-la-Pitié, but also to set up in the town a museum in his memory. The museum (which is spread over four buildings in Saint-Rémy) owns a large number of Prassinos's works, and will provide you with as much information on him as you are ever likely to need. His paintings are all colourless and suggestive mainly of writhing tree trunks; far more interesting are his rambling but imaginative autobiographical writings, which can be bought in the chapel.

The small square on the southern side of the chapel has a statue in its centre to Gounod, who composed here his operatic version of Mistral's *Miréio*. Just before reaching Glanum, a signpost to the left points to Saint-Paul-de-Mausole, the psychiatric hospital where Van Gogh was confined in 1888 and which is now named after him (see page 170). Visitors cannot see the hospital itself, but can admire the delightful romanesque chapel and cloister attached to it.

The approach to Glanum is marked by the two outstanding Roman monuments known as 'Les Antiques' (see pages 48–9); beyond, enveloped in a field of the Alpilles, is the recently excavated site of Glanum (see pages 49–50). Outside the site there is a map marking the route by foot from here to Les Baux, one of the most magnificent walks you can do in Provence (about three hours). This path (follow the yellow arrows) begins by climbing a small hill and then descends to a small lake, which makes a fine picnic spot. Two kilometres from here you start climbing up to the ridge of the Alpilles and follow this all the way to LES BAUX, enjoying wonderful views on either side.

Two kilometres west of Saint-Rémy, off the D99 to TARASCON, is the eighteenth-century Château de Roussan. Approached from a straight narrow lane shaded by poplars, this building is surrounded by a wooded garden dotted with fountains and statues. The place, which seems so far from the busy, nearby main road, is how you might imagine the enchanted mansion in Alain-Fournier's *Le Grand Meaulnes*. It belonged originally to a descendant of Nostradamus, and is now a small family-run hotel with a perfectly preserved eighteenth-century interior. [3A]

SAINT-SAUVEUR-SUR-TINÉE, twenty-eight kilometres further down the Tinée valley from SAINT-ÉTIENNE-DE-TINÉE, is another little-spoilt Alpine community with many old buildings. The fifteenth-century church of Saint-Sauveur, set in a tiny square off the main road, has a late romanesque bell-tower and three seventeenth-century canvases with striking baroque frames. [2E]

SAINT-TRINIT, see SAULT.

SAINT-TROPEZ has such a reputation today as the playground of the young, rich and beautiful that it is easy to forget that the town has had a long and distinguished history. Originally the Greek trading post of Athenopolis, then renamed Heraclea Cacabaria by the Romans, Saint-Tropez acquired its present name in the fourth century A.D. in honour of a centurion of Nero's, who was beheaded for keeping his faith and whose truncated corpse miraculously landed near this town after sharing a boat with a cock and a dog. Every year, on 16 and 17 May, this cock and dog story is celebrated by a picturesque ceremony known as a *bravade*. In this a bust of Saint-Tropez is carried around the town, accompanied by men dressed in seventeenth-century costume and firing salvoes of bullets.

After being devastated by Saracen raids during the early Middle Ages, Saint-Tropez became a tiny self-governing republic in 1470 thanks to an offer made by a Genoese nobleman to repopulate the place on condition that it was exempt from taxes. It remained a republic until the seventeenth century and later slipped into obscurity, from which it was redeemed only by its being the home town of a celebrated eighteenth-century admiral, Pierre-André de Suffren, a man who thoroughly annoyed the English during the American War of Independence.

Saint-Tropez was still a quiet and completely unspoilt fishing village when the painter Paul Signac came here in 1892 and bought a villa behind the village (La Hune, on what is now the Rue Paul Signac). Thanks partly to him the place became a magnet for artists and writers, including the Fauves and Colette (see page 175). The widespread popularity of Saint-Tropez dates only from after 1957, when Roger Vadim made a film here starring the then unknown Brigitte Bardot, *And God Created Woman*.

Bardot and a number of other celebrities have stayed in Saint-Tropez to this day, though the lives they now lead here are far more private than they were before. Those who come to the town in expectation of glamour will find instead thousands of distinctly unglamorous tourists suffering from the same delusion. For all this, Saint-Tropez remains one of the liveliest, and certainly prettiest, of the Provençal coastal towns. It also boasts an outstanding art gallery.

This, the Musée de l'Annonciade, is beautifully housed in a sixteenth-century chapel right by the port. It contains paintings and sculptures of a uniformly high quality by nearly all the leading artists who have worked in Saint-Tropez, including Signac, Matisse, Derain, Van Dongen, Bonnard, Marquet and Dufy. An additional pleasure of this place is to be able to look out from the chapel's windows to the very port which features in so many of the landscapes on display.

From the Quai Suffren, directly in front of the museum, you should turn right into the Rue de la Citadelle and from here walk up through the old town to the well-preserved seventeenth-century citadel, which has an excellent panorama and a small naval museum.

By night Saint-Tropez offers a famed variety of attractions. Many of the town's bars and restaurants are situated by the port, but in many ways a more enjoyable place to spend an evening is the Place Carnot, a square lined with cafés. One of these is the Café des Arts, a place with a delightfully old-fashioned interior. This appearance is deceptive, for the café became in the 1960s the focal point of fashionable Saint-Tropez, and is still popularized by the remaining Bohemian elements in the town.

The Bay of Pampelonne, to the south-east of Saint-Tropez, has a sandy beach nearly four miles long. Nearly all this beach is parcelled into privately-run sectors, many of which are reached by winding, poorly signposted lanes leading off from the D93. The Plage de Tahiti on the northern end of the bay is the most famous of these sectors, but today it has a decadent character which has been likened to that of a late Roman orgy. To escape the crowds and to avoid paying for your swims, you should not turn off the D93 until you are past Cap Camarat and have begun climbing the Col de Collebasse. Just past the turning to Ramatuelle, you will reach a steep narrow road descending to the public beach of L'Escalet. The wooded stretch of the peninsula to the south of this beach is really only accessible by foot (a perilous non-asphalted road leads to the hamlet of La Bastide Blanche, but you are not allowed to leave your car there). The coastal path is one of the most beautiful and least spoilt in Provence, and the sandy beach at La Bastide Blanche (about an hour and a half's walk from L'Escalet) is a haven of peace. From here to Gigaro (another three hours' walk) there is nothing but wild wooded hillside plunging down to tiny rocky inlets.

Ramatuelle, a hill village high above the coast, is an attractive place which was once occupied by Saracens; the actor Gérard Philipe is buried in the church cemetery. To the north of Ramatuelle is the equally charming village of Gassin, which has one of the best situated restaurants in Provence, the Bello Visto. In between, on the highest point of the whole peninsula, are the ruined mills of Paillas, from where there is a remarkably extensive view of the coast from Sainte-Maxime to the Islands of Hyères (see HYÈRES). [5E]

LA SAINTE-BAUME: The wonderfully situated cave above the Sainte-Baume Massif where Mary Magdalene reputedly lived (see page 60) can be reached from two points along the D80 from Plan-d'Aups to

Nans-les-Pins: one is the large nineteenth-century pilgrims' hostel three kilometres to the east of Plan-d'Aups; the other is one kilometre further on, at the crossing with the D95. The wide forest paths from either point converge at the Oratory crossroads, where a path to the right climbs above the tree-level to a steep flight of steps carved into the rock and leading to the cave and adjoining buildings (a half-hour walk in all). To go from here to the top of the mountain – to the point where the Magdalene was daily transported by angels – you have to return to the Oratory crossroads, turn right until you reach the Pass of Saint-Pilon, then walk to your right along the ridge until you come to a small chapel (a thirty-five-minute walk from the cave). The walk nearly finished off Stendhal, but in fact the last stage along the ridge is fairly gentle, and is made lighter by the magnificent views on either side. [5C]

LES-SAINTES-MARIES-DE-LA-MER has been famous since early Christian times as the place where a remarkable group of saintly refugees from Palestine supposedly landed (see page 58). The three of them who decided to stay (Saints Mary Jacobé, Mary Salomé and Sarah) were buried locally, and the village became a major place of pilgrimage, the importance of which intensified after the remains of the saints were rediscovered during the reign of 'Good King René'. Saint Sarah, the black servant of the two Marys, has always been the patron saint of gypsies, who began attending the pilgrimage from the mid nineteenth century onwards, much to the delight of lovers of ethnography.

The village today is a very commercialized seaside resort and a centre for excursions around the Camargue. On 24 and 25 May, when the main pilgrimage is held, gypsies converge on the town from all over Europe both for traditional reasons and to profit from the presence of the equally large number of tourists. The occasion is certainly lively (see pages 88–9). At other times of the year, the main attraction of the place is the crenellated twelfth-century church where the Marys and Saint Sarah are buried, one of the finest examples of a fortified church in Provence. Near this, installed in the former nineteenth-century town hall, is a pleasantly old-fashioned museum named after that great mythologizer of the Camargue, the Marquis Folco de Baroncelli-Javon (see page 33).

The grave of the Marquis, a simple slab on a round plinth, lies in an isolated spot two kilometres to the west of the town, off the D38; horses graze by it. Four kilometres to the north of the town, off the D570, is the small and shoddy Musée du Boumian, where waxwork tableaux absurdly try to recreate the romantic Camargue life which the Marquis was aiming to preserve. Further north along the same road, at Ginès, is a Camargue Information Centre with a free slide show; next to this is a small aviary, gone somewhat to seed. By far the best place to find out about the history and life of the Camargue is the Musée Camarguais, situated twenty kilometres to the north of here, at Pont de Rousty, and beautifully installed in an old farm building; a signposted footpath (three kilometres long) leads from the museum to the marshes of the Camargue.

For special permission to visit the Zoological and Botanical Reserve in the centre of the Camargue, you have to apply (preferably in advance) to the Réserve Nationale at La Capelière on the eastern side of the Étang de Vaccarès. On the north-western side of this lake, at Méjanes, is another holiday centre owned by the *pastis*-merchant Paul Ricard. This mock-ranch has a scenic railway, and puts on bull-fights and equestrian displays; it is also one of numerous places throughout the Camargue that arrange excursions through the marshes on horseback in the company of a *gardian*. An easier and certainly cheaper way of glimpsing something of the area's extraordinary wildlife is to take a boat trip up the Petit Rhône from a landing stage near Baroncelli-Javon's tomb; you will see wild horses, bulls, and herons, and, if you come early in the summer, possibly flamingos as well.   [4A]

SAINTE-MAXIME is a friendly and unpretentious resort with a fine, sandy beach and an attractive, sheltered position on the Bay of Saint-Tropez. Though dating back to the Phoenicians, the place presents a largely modern aspect and has a town centre recently remodelled by the leading post-modernist architect, Ricardo Bofill.

The coast east towards Saint-Aygulf is dotted with tiny resorts and sandy coves. Ten kilometres inland from Sainte-Maxime along the D25 to Le Muy is the park of Saint-Donat, which has as its principal attraction a museum of phonographs and mechanical musical instruments. This large collection, displayed in an old Provençal farmhouse, is full of entertaining oddities such as a primitive eighteenth-century accordion, a nineteenth-century 'singing bird', and an early audio-visual apparatus for teaching foreign languages (a patheograph).

SALAGON: For this priory, see MANE.

SALON-DE-PROVENCE has been a busy market town and a major centre of olive oil production since the late Middle Ages. Its prosperity increased greatly in the sixteenth century with the construction of a nearby irrigation canal designed by a brilliant, locally born civic engineer, Adam de Craponne. The surroundings of present-day Salon are not very appealing, and the town itself was much damaged by an earthquake in 1909. None the less it has some important medieval and Renaissance buildings, and has been, since the late sixteenth century, a place of pilgrimage for lovers of that famous foreteller of doom, Nostradamus.

On the northern edge of Salon, outside the old quarter of the town, is the collegiate church of Saint-Laurent, which was built by Dominicans in 1344. This is an excellent example of the so-called 'Dominican gothic', a style which accords well with native Provençal tastes. It has the tall proportions of a northern gothic church, but is characterized by an overall austerity more typical of the romanesque and even has some round-arched windows. The interior, like that of all Dominican churches, is a vast aisleless hall. Michel de Nostredame, better known as Nostradamus, is buried in the fourth chapel on the left, where there is also a portrait of him by his son.

To see the house where Nostradamus lived in Salon, you have to enter the old town by the attractive Porte de l'Horloge and take the second turning to your left. The house, on the corner of the Place de Loge and the Rue Nostradamus, is now a small museum to him. Nostradamus, the son of a converted Jew, was born in Saint-Rémy in 1503 and began his career as a doctor. He soon distinguished himself by discovering successful remedies against the plague, but his refusal to disclose these was to lead eventually to his being expelled from his profession by his jealous colleagues. After an itinerant early life he married a Salon woman in 1547, and settled here. In 1555 he published his *Prophecies*, predictions about the future of the world that earned him immediate fame at the French court and an enormous amount of money. Because the style of these prophecies is so elliptical, they can be read in a whole variety of ways, and as such have provided constant employment for writers and charlatans up to the present day. Some claim that Nostradamus foresaw Napoleon and Hitler, while according to another interpretation of him, the world is on the verge of total catastrophe.

A catastrophe on a smaller scale is the large square immediately to the south of his house, under the rock of Puech. Badly shaken during the 1909 earthquake, this has recently been rebuilt in a bleak modern style which would have been depressing enough on the outskirts of Salon, but which in the centre of the town is a positive eyesore. The two remaining old buildings that lie, anachronistically, off it, are the fine romanesque church of Saint-Michel and – on the top of the Puech rock – the huge bulk of the Château de l'Empéri. The latter, begun in the tenth century, was originally the residence of the arch-bishops of Arles, who were the Lords of Salon from the tenth century up to the French annexation of Provence in the late fifteenth century. The castle has been rebuilt, remodelled and restored throughout his-tory, but its present appearance is due mainly to work carried out in the Renaissance. In the nineteenth century the castle was turned into a barracks, and today a large part of the building has been given over to a military museum, one of the finest in France and particularly im-pressive in its holdings of the Napoleonic era. [4B]

SANARY, a place with a long history but with little of architectural interest, is a pleasant fishing and sailing port which was much popu-larized by artists and writers in the 1930s. Aldous Huxley lived at the Villa Huley (*sic*) after 1930, and did a number of paintings of the area. Returning from a trip to Mexico in 1933, he found that Sanary had become a place of refuge to a crowd of German intellectuals headed by Thomas and Heinrich Mann. He described them as 'rather a dismal crew'. [5C]

SAORGE: Combining the little-spoilt beauty of LUCÉRAM with a position as spectacular as that of GOURDON, Saorge is in many ways the most exciting village in Provence.

Approached from the south along the N204, the village seems to hang above you on an almost vertical slope. It looks inaccessible, and in fact you have to drive on to the next village of Fontan before finding a road which will get you there. As you climb up from Fontan you pass one of the tunnels of the Nice to Turin railway, a sensational example of 1930s engineering which has recently been re-opened after having been partially destroyed in the Second World War. You leave your car on the north end of Saorge, which can only be crossed on foot. This long village is an almost intact complex of fifteenth- to seventeenth-century houses, coloured in pastel shades of ochre and blue. Remarkably, for Provence, the village has not been prettified, or invaded by artists, and in fact makes relatively few concessions to tourism: there are as yet no craft and souvenir shops.

In the middle of the village is the parish church, a fifteenth-century structure, the interior of which was redecorated in the eighteenth century with a striking baroque décor of stucco and painting. The seventeenth-century Franciscan church, on the eastern outskirts of the village, has a terrace with a wonderful view looking back on Saorge, which from here assumes the shape of a crescent. Below you is the isolated eleventh-century Sanctuary of the Madonna de Poggio, a remarkable building originally dependent on the abbey of Lérins (see CANNES), and a private property since the Revolution. It is dominated by its majestic *campanile* (rebuilt in 1516 in a romanesque style). [3F]

SAULT: The D942 from CARPENTRAS to Sault takes you the whole length of a splendid gorge cut by the river Nesque (a tributary of the Sorgue) into the calcareous rock of the Vaucluse plateau. Eleven kilometres before Sault, at the highest point of the road, is a belvedere looking across to the Cire rock, an immense cliff with a sheer 400-metre drop down to the river. The rock inspired some lines in Mistral's *Calendau*, and these are now recorded in a plinth at the belvedere; an extremely steep footpath descends from here down to the river, and would be very enjoyable were it not for the thought of having to climb back up it afterwards.

Sault stands on a rock at the end of the plateau. It is a tranquil and pleasant small town, which has a reputation among gourmets for producing some of the finest *charcuterie* in Provence (the Sault *saucisson* is particularly renowned). Seven kilometres to the east of Sault, off the D950, is the hamlet of Saint-Trinit, an almost deserted place with a most powerful atmosphere. The romanesque church here – originally a priory church dependent on the Benedictine abbey of

Saint-André at Villeneuve-lès-Avignon (see AVIGNON) – is a tall and noble building with exquisite ornamental details on the outside. [2B]

SAUVAN: For this castle, see MANE.

SÉGURET is a famed pretty village under the Dentelles de Mont-mirail. During the summer months the Atelier de Séguret runs a paint-ing course here, and during that period the village's over-restored streets are dotted with amateur painters attempting the most hack-neyed motifs. The view of the Rhône valley from the twelfth-century church of Saint-Denis is one which will greatly appeal to the wine-lover, for it embraces the vineyards of GIGONDAS and CHÂTEAUNEUF-DU-PAPE. Séguret itself is an Appellation Côtes-du-Rhône-Village, and the main street has several places where wine can be tasted. [2B]

SEILLANS: The name of this hill village is thought to be derived from the Provençal for 'pot of oil', a possible reference to the boiling liquid poured on the heads of Saracen invaders. Today the village specializes instead in bath oils and other aromatic products.

The charms of the place, with its views towards the Esterel and its steep paved streets leading up to the twelfth-century castle, were discovered in the last century by the likes of Alphonse Karr (see SAINT-RAPHAEL) and Gounod. The surrealist artist Max Ernst bought a house at the top of the village in 1962. Below the village, on the D19 to Fayence, is the isolated romanesque chapel of Notre-Dame-de-l'Ormeau, remarkable for its sixteenth-century altarpiece in polychromed wood. The work has traditionally been known as the 'forty-two years' on account of the long time which the anonymous artist (an Italian monk) must have taken to carve its multitude of figures. [4E]

SÉNANQUE: For this abbey, see GORDES.

SENEZ, a district capital in Roman times, became a bishopric in the fifth century and remained as such until the Revolution, despite vari-ous attempts to incorporate its diocese – one of the poorest in France – into those of VENCE and CASTELLANE. The former cathedral church of Notre-Dame-de-l'Assomption is the principal surviving monu-ment of this now tiny Alpine village: the building was begun in the late twelfth century but was heavily restored in the sixteenth century and again in the nineteenth.   [3D]

SÉRIGNAN-DU-COMTAT: On the outskirts of the small village of Sérignan, off the D976 towards ORANGE, is the L'Harmas J.-H. Fabre, the home of one of the most popular naturalists of the nineteenth century. Born in 1823 into a poor peasant family from Languedoc, Fabre was awarded a scholarship in 1840 to attend the École Normale in AVIGNON. In 1853 he obtained a teaching post at Avignon's Imperial College and he held this until 1865, when he was forced to resign after offending prudish parents and clergy by giving talks on such 'delicate' subjects as the fertilization of flowering plants. He moved subsequently to nearby Orange, where he soon published the first volume of his enormously successful *Souvenirs entomologiques*, a work which earned him the nickname of the 'Insects' Homer'. In 1879, thanks to financial support from his friend John Stuart Mill (see AVIGNON), he was able to buy this property at Sérignan, which he named L'Harmas after the old Provençal word for a plot of unculti-vated land. He lived here until his death in 1915, aged ninety-two, receiving in his old age visits from President Poincaré and Frédéric Mistral.

Inside the house you are shown Fabre's study, which has been kept exactly as it was in his day and even includes the satchel which he carried on his entomological excursions. The glass cabinets on the walls testify to the remarkable range of his interests. On top of these cabinets is Fabre's colossal herbarium, while underneath are diverse objects such as fossils, minerals, birds' nests, prehistoric flints, and even human remains found by the hearth of a cannibal tribe. On the ground floor is displayed a collection of Fabre's 700 painstakingly accurate watercolours of the fungi of the Vaucluse, works which Mistral was anxious to obtain for his Museon Arlaten in ARLES.

The large garden outside is a delight. Planted by Fabre himself, and filled with an amazing variety of plants, it deliberately has the look of a wilderness and invites exploration. Lost in the middle is a water-lily pond.   [2A]

SILVACANE: For this abbey, see LA ROQUE-D'ANTHÉRON.

SIMIANE-LA-ROTONDE: This remote, tranquil village is called 'La

Rotonde' after the strange 'rotunda' at the top of the village (the key can be had from the town hall). This hexagonal, cone-shaped building is thought generally to have been the keep of a castle built by Raimbaud de Simiane in the late twelfth century; but it has also been interpreted as a castle chapel, a mausoleum, and a combination of weapon-room, store-room, reception-room and state apartment. Whatever the function, it is one of the most unusual examples of romanesque architecture in Provence, and is at present being turned into a small museum. At the bottom of this steep village is the sixteenth-century church of Saint-Pierre, a former priory church attached to Saint-André at Villeneuve-lès-Avignon (see AVIGNON).   [3C]

SISTERON: At Sisteron the Durance valley narrows and is hemmed in by giant peaks which overshadow the town. Sisteron marks the northernmost boundary of the olive belt of Provence, and is a place with a strong Alpine character. Its beautiful situation and proximity to the high Alps make it a popular resort; it is also a small industrial centre, a lively market town, and a producer of jams, candied fruits, and an excellent nougat called *canteperdrix*.

The heavily fortified citadel rock which looms above the town is a reminder of Sisteron's important strategic position. The upper ramparts date from the twelfth century; the lower ones were put up in the late sixteenth century and soon afterwards reinforced by the great military engineer, Vauban. In 1944 German troops took refuge here and were bombed by the Americans from a great height, a blind attack which led to much senseless killing and destruction. The fifteenth-century chapel of Notre-Dame on top of the rock was totally destroyed and had to be rebuilt.

Fortunately much of the small but charming old town at the foot of the rock survived. Tall, tightly packed houses – some dating back to the thirteenth century – are contained within an animated pedestrian area. The former cathedral church of Notre-Dame-des-Pommiers is a romanesque structure influenced by Lombard architecture; at one time it formed part of a large episcopal complex.

The small road (the D3) which climbs up from Sisteron to Saint-Geniez passes through an impressive gorge known as the Défilé de Pierre-Écrite (the Gorge of the Written Stone), so-named after a Latin inscription here (indicated by a signpost) recording the conversion to

Christianity of Claudius Posthumus Dardanus. Saint Dardanus, as he later became, is supposed to have founded nearby the religious community of Théopolis, but of this no trace remains.   [2C]

SIVERGUES, a tiny, charming village high up on the northern slopes of the Grand Lubéron, was once a Vaudois, then a Protestant, place of refuge; today it has been reduced to a handful of houses and a small seventeenth-century church. The village is apparently the only one in the Vaucluse where the main road leading into it (the D113 from APT) is marked 'Attention, fin de route' (Caution, road ends). Beyond it is just a footpath, leading up to the ridge of the Grand Lubéron (about an hour's walk). If you turn left at the ridge and walk for a further hour and a half you will reach the Mourre Nègre, a television station placed on the highest point of the mountain. The television masts detract somewhat from the romantic beauty of the site, but the panorama extends on all sides and is very exciting.   [3B]

SOSPEL, though badly bombed in the Second World War, is a small Alpine town of great charm. The Bévéra river divides it in two, separating the main part of the town from the medieval suburb of Saint-Nicolas. The bridge which links the two districts together was partially ruined during the war but has been rebuilt exactly as it was; it is a delightful medieval construction with a tower in the middle which once served as a toll-gate. Both quarters of the town are full of old arcaded houses; the quiet traffic-free square of Saint-Michel in the 'Rive Droite' is particularly enchanting. The church of Saint-Michel, rising on steps above this arcaded square, has a thirteenth-century clock tower; the rest of the structure is sumptuously baroque.   [3F]

SUZETTE, see LE BARROUX.

TAMARIS, see TOULON.

TARADEAU, a village in the middle of a landscape of vineyards, is notable for the immensely tall twelfth-century tower which stands on the hill behind it. This tower, and the adjoining romanesque church of Saint-Martin, are all that is left of the medieval village of Taradeau, which was abandoned at the end of the fourteenth century.   [4D]

TARASCON, a former port on the Rhône opposite the Languedoc town of Beaucaire, was haunted at the beginning of this millennium by the amphibious, man-eating Tarasque, a composite of a lion and a crocodile. Fortunately this monster had latent Christian sentiments, and was easily made docile when Saint Martha held up a crucifix to it.

Saint Martha was buried at Tarascon, and the rediscovery of her body in the late twelfth century prompted the construction of the collegiate church dedicated to her. This became such a popular place of pilgrimage that in the thirteenth century, and again in the sixteenth, it had to be greatly enlarged. The south portal, though stripped of its sculptures in the Revolution, is the most notable survival of the romanesque structure. The nave, thought by many to be one of the most eloquent interpretations of the gothic style in Provence, has side chapels containing paintings by such important seventeenth-century French artists as Charles Van Loo and Mignard. The relics of Saint Martha are contained in the heavily restored twelfth-century crypt.

Fine though this church is, the greatest monument in Tarascon is its castle, one of the most harmonious and best preserved in the whole of France. Standing on a rock by the river and divided from the town by a wide moat, this imposing crenellated structure fulfils the most romantic notions of what a medieval castle should look like. It was built between 1400 and 1449 and served both as a castle and a palace. The most famous person associated with it was 'Good King René', who divided his time in Provence between AIX-EN-PROVENCE and Tarascon and is commemorated in the elegant courtyard of the castle's seigneurial lodge by a double portrait of himself and his wife, Jeanne de Laval. The castle was used as a prison from the eighteenth century up to 1926, and the interior is suitably bleak and little furnished: one room has remarkably neat graffiti by captive British sailors. The long tour which you are obliged to follow is partly relieved by the young guides, who delight in demonstrating the famed wit and stupidity of the Tarasconais (see below). Much is made of the 'ecologically sound toilets', in fact holes in the floor of projecting towers, from which excretions would drop directly into the river. From the terrace of the castle – the highpoint of the tour in more ways than one – prisoners were also thrown into the Rhône during the Revolution.

The town of Tarascon was bombed during the Second World War, and much of it was rebuilt. None the less there are a few interesting old buildings to the east of the church of Sainte-Marthe, including the cheerfully-decorated seventeenth-century town hall. In an eighteenth-century house at no. 39 Rue Proudhon is a well-known workshop specializing in block-printed fabrics. This industry was begun in Tarascon in the eighteenth century and revived in 1935; the old wooden blocks are still in use, and will be shown to you in the course of your visit.

On the Boulevard Itam on the north-eastern side of the town is Tarascon's most recent attraction, the House of Tartarin. Daudet's comic hero Tartarin – the subject of three of his novels – gave to Tarascon a reputation which extended well beyond France and made the Tarasconais the butt of many a joke. The Tarasconais were not at first pleased by this, but eventually came round to seeing the benefits which this reputation might bring to the local tourist industry. The figure of Tartarin is now included in the revived Tarasque procession (held on the last Sunday in June, see page 87), and in October 1985 this museum to him was opened.

The house has of course nothing to do with either Daudet or his fictional hero other than in that it dates from the late nineteenth century. Inside are souvenirs of Daudet, photographs of Tartarin in plays and films, and – on the ground floor – reconstructions of nine-teenth-century interiors with models of Tartarin dressed in some of the guises in which the great braggart took part in his extraordinary adventures. At present the 'Friends of Old Tarascon' are trying to recreate outside the museum the exotic garden of which Tartarin was so proud and to which hundreds of Tarasconais came on Sundays to admire the remarkable baobab tree.

It is impossible to come to Tarascon without wanting to visit Beaucaire on the other side of the river. The castle here – immortalized in the medieval romance, *Aucassin and Nicolette* – was destroyed by Richelieu in the early seventeenth century. Its ruins have been in-corporated into a beautiful garden with lovely views back towards Tarascon. At the foot of the castle are a number of attractive old buildings, most notably the extremely grand late seventeenth-century town hall.   [3A]

TENDE is the largest and northernmost of three villages in the upper Roya valley which belonged to Italy up to as late as 1947 (the other two are LA BRIGUE and Saint-Dalmas-de-Tende): when the rest of the County of Nice was handed over to Italy in 1860, Victor Emmanuel II insisted – against the wishes of most of the inhabitants – on keeping this remote district as his private hunting grounds.

Lying directly underneath what was once a near insurmountable mountain pass, Tende is a fascinating if rather bleak-looking place built up of tall old houses with rickety wooden balconies and grey-tiled roofs. All that is left of the fourteenth-century Lascaris castle (destroyed in 1692) is a tall sinister pillar of stones around which has been created the local cemetery. Lower down in the village is the sixteenth-century church of Notre-Dame-de-l'Assomption, with an attractive Renaissance portal executed in the green stone of the area; inside are some seventeenth-century wooden statuettes which once formed part of a triptych presented to the church by Charles-Emmanuel II of Savoy.

When Italy lost the district of Tende to Provence in 1947 it lost what is one of the great natural and archaeological wonders of Europe, the Valley of Marvels (see page 38). A visit to this valley and its 100,000 rock-carvings is an unforgettable experience, but requires a certain amount of effort. The tourist office at Tende provides detailed information both about access to the valley and about the availability of accommodation there. Jeep excursions are organized from both Tende and Saint-Dalmas-de-Tende. These take a full day, and are very expensive; their main advantage is that their drivers will point out to you the carvings, which otherwise are very difficult to find.

If you decide to go on foot, you should preferably allow at least two days: there are Alpine refuges at both 'Les Merveilles' and Fontanalbe, but it is important to book a place some time in advance, as they are often full. The walk is practical only between late June and late September, and the latter month is probably the best time, as the skies are at their clearest: always, in any case, bring with you protection against cold and rain, as storms develop very quickly here.

The best starting-off point for the walk is the Lac des Mesches, which is reached by driving up the D91 from Saint-Dalmas-de-Tende. Above this lake is a group of nineteenth-century mine buildings, which have recently been transformed by a former Renault worker from Nice into an ecological commune which gives crafts courses during the summer and autumn months; cheap and plentiful accommodation is also provided. An arduous uphill walk from here takes you to the

'Les Merveilles' refuge at the foot of the valley. A wild landscape of lakes and glistening rock stretches out in front of you. At the end of the valley (another two hours' walk) the path begins to climb again and becomes more difficult. Hardy tourists can continue into the valley of Fontanalbe on the other side, where there are also numerous carvings. Two kilometres beyond the refuge of Fontanalbe is the house where the British naturalist and archaeologist Clarence Bicknell (see page 38) lived and carried out his pioneering researches on the pre-historic art of the area. From here an asphalted road leads back to the Lac des Mesches. [2F]

LE THOR: This small market town, dating back to the early twelfth century, is famous for its white dessert grapes, which are sold all over France; a grape market is held every day from 1 August to 31 October. Nothing survives of the original fortifications, the impressive Douzabas Gate through which you enter the town from the main Avignon to Cavaillon road being only a fanciful nineteenth-century reconstruction. The romanesque church of Notre-Dame-du-Lac, with its classically-inspired ornamentation which greatly impressed Stendhal (see page 69), is charmingly set by a shaded river crossed by a medieval bridge.

Five kilometres west of the town, off the main Avignon road, is the nineteenth-century castle of Fontségugne, where the Félibrige movement was founded (see pages 105–6). [3B]

LE THORONET: The Cistercian Abbey of Le Thoronet is hidden among the forested hills of the Var, four and a half kilometres to the west of the village of Le Thoronet. Work was begun by the Cistercians around 1160, after they had abandoned a monastery which they had recently founded near TOURTOUR. All three of the surviving Cistercian abbeys of Provence – the others are Sénanque (see GORDES) and Silvacane (see LA ROQUE D'ANTHÉRON) – are characterized by their unity of style, but that of Le Thoronet is special in having been almost completely finished in the record time of just over forty years.

The monastery had entered a serious decline long before the Revolution, when it was abandoned and fell to ruins. Prosper Mérimée visited these ruins in 1834 and urged the state to purchase and restore them. Restoration work is still continuing. [4D]

TOULON, built around a deep natural harbour and sheltered by a ring of high hills, occupies a position which has always been praised by travellers. The town itself is the leading naval base of France, and is a sprawling commercial and industrial city, with many ugly buildings, dirty side-streets, and much of the sordid underworld which grows up around large ports. Yet it is also an exceptionally lively place, full of character and fascination. It has been unfairly neglected by tourists, though this has the advantage that the prices are among the cheapest on the coast.

A town of little importance in classical and medieval times, Toulon became a naval base shortly after Provence became attached to France in 1487. Louis XII built its first significant fortifications in 1512, but it was not until the middle of the next century that Toulon began to develop into the major town which it is today. Under Louis XIV the royal galleys were resited from Marseille to Toulon, the arsenal was expanded, and the military engineer Vauban was commissioned to improve and enlarge the port's fortifications. The plague of 1720 reduced the town's population from 26,000 to 17,000, but the place recovered with remarkable speed. Later that century the town revolted against the Revolutionary government and welcomed the English fleet. The young Napoleon defeated the fleet in 1793, and leapt to fame in consequence.

The town was badly damaged by Allied bombing during the Second World War, and its citadel and what little remained of its harbour-front were blown up by the Germans just before surrendering to the Allies. The modern blocks that were put up along the harbour in the 1950s are singularly grey and depressing.

The Naval Museum, at the eastern end of the harbour, has an important and well-displayed collection which includes excellent models of seventeenth-century galleys and a number of colourful figure-heads. Pierre Puget, a native of Toulon and one of the great baroque artists of France (see page 79), began his career as a decorator of galleys, and there are a number of studio carvings of his here which were intended to be placed on ships. The museum building is modern, but the elaborately carved baroque gateway which once served as the entrance to Louis XIV's arsenal has been attached to its main façade. Another, and more important, survival of baroque Toulon are Puget's two *Atlantes* which flanked the main door of the old town hall. The building, in the middle of the harbour, was completely destroyed

337

during the Second World War, but Puget's figures escaped damage by being taken off and hidden shortly before the outbreak of the war. Though attached now to the characterless civic building which replaced the seventeenth-century town hall, the struggling figures remain extraordinarily powerful works.

Behind the rows of modern blocks along Toulon's harbour lies much of the town's dirty but atmospheric old quarter. If you walk along the Cours Lafayette – a lively street with daily flower, fish and fruit and vegetable markets – you will reach at no. 63 a dilapidated eighteenth-century building housing the equally run-down Museum of Old Toulon, an interesting if ramshackle display of historical objects and paintings and sculptures by local artists, including minor works by Puget. The filthy and sombre cathedral behind this was altered and enlarged in the seventeenth century but has kept much of its romanesque and gothic interior. West of the cathedral is an attractive pedestrian quarter which runs south down to the harbour and north up to the Place des Trois Dauphins, a small square decorated by a delightful eighteenth-century fountain with dolphins.

The grand avenues and houses of nineteenth-century Toulon stretch to the west and north of here. In between the Place Victor Hugo and the Boulevard de Strasbourg is the majestic neo-classical opera house, the interior decoration of which rivals that of Garnier's Opéra at Monte-Carlo (see MONACO). The Boulevard de Strasbourg is the main thoroughfare of Toulon and, as you head west, turns into the Avenue General Leclerc. Off this stands another imposing nineteenth-century structure, this one built to house a library, a natural history museum and an art gallery. The art gallery (the Musée d'Art et d'Archéologie) is a very friendly institution, recently renovated with great style and boldness. Its policy has been to take Art out of the cloistered cobwebbed gloom in which it is so often found in French provincial museums, and to make it more widely accessible through challenging and imaginative displays. The gallery has works by Annibale Carracci, Puget and Rodin, and is particularly strong on contemporary art, to which it has recently devoted most of its purchasing funds. Sadly, lack of space allows only a fraction of the gallery's collections to be shown at any one time. Its loan exhibitions of modern art are among the most important put on in France outside Paris.

There are several places worth seeing outside the town centre. At the top of the peninsula on the eastern side of Toulon is the Tour Royale, a sturdy, well-preserved fortress which was built as part of Louis XII's harbour defences. This is now an annexe of the Naval Museum, and has a few cannons and figureheads displayed in a dark and sinister underground gallery: this Piranesi-like setting was once used as a prison. On the other side of the bay, guarding the western approaches of the town, is the Fort Balaguier, a fortress occupied by the English prior to Napoleon's attack; Napoleonic souvenirs are contained inside. South of here is the pleasant residential area of Tamaris, where George Sand frequently stayed. The Marine Institute in the middle of Tamaris is an amusing example of the neo-Moorish style; it was commissioned in the 1860s by Marius Michel ('Michel-Pacha'), a former engineer to the Sultan of Turkey (see page 152).

A very enjoyable funicular ride can be made up Mont Faron, the mountain which rises steeply up to the north of the town. At the top is a zoo, a museum devoted to the Liberation of Toulon by the Allies in August 1944, and – as you might expect – an outstanding view.   [5C]

LA TOUR-D'AIGUES: At the centre of this quiet market town is a magnificent gateway in the style of a triumphal arch. This is the most impressive surviving fragment of what was once the most visited and architecturally ambitious castle of Provence. It was built on medieval foundations between 1565 and 1577. This being Provence, 'the land of love', the man who commissioned the building, the Baron of Cental, is traditionally thought to have done so out of love for Marguerite de Valois (the future Queen Margot), whom he hoped would come and visit him here. The castle is for this reason sometimes referred to as 'the castle of love', but the story, sadly, is almost certainly apocryphal, as Marguerite would have been only eleven when the Baron first saw her.

The main architect responsible for the castle was an obscure Piedmontese called Ercole Nigra, who came to France aged only fourteen and was encouraged by the Baron to study all the finest examples of French Renaissance architecture. There was little in the building that was specifically Italian, the main source of inspiration being instead Lescot's Louvre in Paris.

Marguerite de Valois never visited the castle, but Catherine de Medici did, 'attracted by the great reputation of this house', as Nostradamus wrote in his diary entry for 6 July 1579. From then until the late eighteenth century almost every important visitor to Provence paid his respects to La Tour-d'Aigues. In 1780 the building was badly damaged by fire, and it was burnt down yet again in 1790 by a Revolutionary mob. After the Revolution the place was used as a quarry. The little that remains today has been well restored and, in the summer months, the courtyard is turned into a setting for plays and concerts.   [3C]

TOURTOUR: The name of this heavily restored show-piece of a village was once thought to refer to tortures carried out here in antiquity. Tourist brochures now prefer to think of the place as 'the village in the sky' on account of its picturesquely perched position on the edge of the wooded foothills of the Alps. Medieval castles guard two sides of the village, while in the main square are two splendid elms planted in 1638 to commemorate the birth of Louis XIV.   [4D]

TRANS-EN-PROVENCE, see DRAGUIGNAN.

LA TURBIE: The enormous Trophy which Augustus built on what is now the Upper Corniche celebrates the emperor's defeat of the last rebellious tribes of the Alps, and once marked the boundary between Italy and Gaul. Along with the Trophy of Adam-Klissi in Romania, it is the only such monument to have survived from the Roman world. The view from the Trophy's terrace down to the sea at Cap Martin, 1,300 feet below, is memorable.

The name of the small medieval village which grew up underneath the Trophy is a deformation of 'Tropea Augusti'. The Rue Comte-de-Cessole, which leads from the monument down into the village, follows the course of the ancient Via Julia Augusta. It is bordered by pretty medieval houses, one of which has a plaque recording some lines of Dante devoted to the Trophy.   [3F]

TOURRETTE-SUR-LOUP: The name of this fortified hill village near VENCE is derived from its three old towers. The place, though attractive, has been overrun by artists and craftsmen, and resembles today one huge craft shop (among the better shops are Paul Badié, for ceramics, and A. M. and J. Franson, for puppets). A curiosity inside the fifteenth-century parish church is a first-century Gallo-Roman altar (behind the High Altar) dedicated to Mercury.

VAISON-LA-ROMAINE is often called the 'Pompeii of France'. Its Roman ruins, dominated by the distant silhouette of Mont Ventoux, are more indicative than any others in Provence of what a Roman town once looked like (see pages 50–51).

Situated on the north side of the river Ouvèze, they are divided into two areas, the Quartier de la Villasse, and the Quartier de Puymin, the latter having a good, well-displayed museum, and a Roman theatre where a drama and music festival is held in July and August. In between the two areas is the large modern tourist office, in the basement of which is the excellent Maison du Vin. Vaison is on the edge of the Côtes-du-Rhône district, and in the Maison du Vin you can taste, buy and find out about a wide selection of the most important wines of the lower half of the Rhône valley.

Like many other important Roman settlements in Provence, Vaison was quick to embrace Christianity, and it became a bishopric from as early as the fourth century (it remained one until the Revolution). The former cathedral of Notre-Dame-de-Nazareth, situated to the west of the Quartier de la Villasse, was built originally around the sixth century, then rebuilt in the romanesque period after having been left in ruins by Frankish invasions. A special feature of this church is the apse, which has arcading supported on Roman columns, and a bishop's throne in front of which is the sarcophagus containing the relics of Saint Quenin, bishop of his native Vaison from 556 to 575. In the fine romanesque cloister is a small lapidary museum, with early Christian inscriptions and sarcophagi. One kilometre to the north of the church (off the D975) is the romanesque chapel of Saint-Quenin, which has a curious triangular apse with pagan carvings incorporated in it. Prosper Mérimée understandably mistook this structure for a pagan temple.

In the twelfth century Count Raymond of Toulouse built a castle on top of the rocky hill rising up on the southern side of the Ouvèze, and soon a small settlement grew up near it. For a while the population of Vaison was divided between the two banks of the river, but with the constant threat of invasion everyone eventually took refuge on the hill. The site of the Roman town lay abandoned until the nineteenth century, when the inhabitants of the upper town began moving down to the plain. The modern town developed around the Roman ruins, while the picturesque medieval town became ever more dilapidated and empty. Since the last war the houses have been restored and numerous artisans have moved in. A visit to this pretty medieval district should end with a climb to the castle, which, though closed and still in a poor state, offers wonderful views of the Ventoux. [2B]

VALLAURIS, today a lively small town set away from the main coastal roads, was in the early Middle Ages a seigniory of the Abbots of Lérins (see CANNES). Abandoned in the late fourteenth century, it was repopulated from the early sixteenth century mainly by Genoese immigrants. The main industry of the place has always been pottery, and it is said that this industry might even date back to Roman times. The industry declined early this century, but was revived after the last war by Picasso and is now more thriving than ever, at least in terms of the quantity of work produced. The Avenue Georges Clemenceau, and the many tiny streets leading off it, are packed with ceramic shops and studios. Traditionally the best of the studios is the Atelier Madoura, run today by Alain Ramié. The work of Alain's mother, Suzanne, was singled out by Picasso in the late 1940s as being by far the finest in the town, and since then the family workshop has been carrying out designs supplied by the artist. For information on the other studios that can be visited you should contact the Association Vallaurienne d'Expansion Céramique (A.V.E.C.) at 15 Rue Sicard.

Picasso first came to Vallauris in 1936, driving around the region with the beautiful Yugoslav photographer Dora Maar. He returned in 1947 with the new love of his life, Françoise Gilot, and settled here at the Villa La Galloise. They stayed until 1954, when Françoise walked out on him, saying that she did not want to spend the rest of her life with a historical monument. At Vallauris Picasso experimented with pottery for the first time, and executed a great many witty and very imaginative works in the medium (over 200 of these are displayed in the Musée Picasso at ANTIBES). For the main square of the town, he gave a bronze of a sullen-faced man inexplicably holding a struggling sheep. His greatest works in the town are to be seen in the castle chapel, off this same square.

The castle, originally a priory attached to the abbey of Lérins, was rebuilt in the sixteenth century and converted in recent times into a municipal museum. The chapel is a windowless barrel-vaulted room, against the walls of which Picasso attached with screws plywood panels representing the evils of war and the virtues of peace: the makeshift quality of the decoration and the dark simplicity of its setting help to increase its power. The main part of the museum is taken up by a display of ceramics from the biennial ceramics exhibitions which have been held in the town since 1966. The museum also has a small collection of contemporary paintings, most notably by Alberto Magnelli, an extremely original Italian artist associated with cubism, futurism and metaphysical painting. [4E]

VAUVENARGUES: The castle of Vauvenargues, an intimidatingly severe and powerful structure, sits under the shadow of Mont Sainte-Victoire. The outer defence wall was built in the fourteenth century, but the castle itself dates from the late sixteenth and early seventeenth centuries. In the eighteenth century the place belonged to the Marquis Luc de Chapiera de Vauvenargues, a famous writer and moralist who was born at AIX-EN-PROVENCE in 1715. Much of his short life was spent in Paris, where he won the respect and friendship of Voltaire but was misunderstood by the majority of his contemporaries. He died a desperate and lonely man at the age of thirty-two.

In 1958 the castle was bought by Picasso, who had begun to be tired of the crowds around his home at CANNES. In the enormous, echoing rooms of the castle, adorned with baroque fireplaces, Picasso left many decorations of his own, including, in one of the bathrooms, a mural of a piping Pan which was intended to serenade his third wife, Jacqueline Roque, in her bath. Picasso spent less and less time in Vauvenargues after purchasing a house at Mougins (see CANNES) in 1961, but he was buried in its garden. The castle is still in the possession of Picasso's heirs, but has remained empty since the suicide of Jacqueline in 1985. People who have tried visiting the place recently have been chased away by a large dog who even frightens the villagers. However, it now looks as if the castle is to become yet another museum to Picasso (for the latest information on this check with the tourist office at AIX-EN-PROVENCE). [4C]

VENASQUE, a small and very pretty village, stands high on a rock at the edge of the wild and wooded plateau of Ventoux. As a protection against barbaric raids, the bishopric of the exposed nearby town of CARPENTRAS made their base in Venasque from the sixth to the tenth centuries. During this period the village gave its name to the

'Comtat-Venaissin'. The first 'Bishop of Carpentras and Venasque' was Saint Siffrein, who founded a cathedral at Venasque and is buried in the church of Notre-Dame, which was built to replace the cathedral after the eleventh century. The oldest part of this building is the apse, which is similar in style to that of the church of Notre-Dame in VAISON-LA-ROMAINE. One of the treasures of the church is a powerful fifteenth-century *Crucifixion* of the Avignon School. Behind the church is the fascinating so-called 'Baptistery' (see pages 65–6). This small cruciform structure incorporating Roman columns was originally built at the same time as the cathedral, possibly on the foundations of a temple dedicated to Venus. The present building is generally thought to have been an eleventh-century reconstruction which might not have been a baptistery at all, but a funerary chapel. Even if this is true, the building is still one of the oldest and most unusual surviving structures from Christian Provence.

Immediately below the village, off the D4 to Carpentras, is the seventeenth-century chapel of Notre-Dame-de-Vie, which has a rare example of Merovingian carving: this, the tomb of Bohetius, Bishop of Carpentras and Venasque, dates from the early seventh century (see page 65).

Driving south from Venasque on the tiny D39, you will reach after four kilometres the attractive perched hamlet of Le Beaucet. From here the road leads into a small wooded valley, at the end of which is the Oratory of Saint-Gens. The popular pilgrimage which is made here each year on 16 May was a great inspiration to the young Mistral (see pages 87–8).   [3B]

VENCE, a Roman settlement, and then a bishopric from the fifth century to the Revolution, is today a sprawling and crowded inland resort. Its hillside setting and extremely attractive old town have made it popular this century with artists and writers, including D. H. Lawrence and Chagall, both of whom died here, in 1930 and 1986 respectively. The old town, partially surrounded by its medieval walls, boasts the beautiful Place Peyra on the other edge of the town – a shaded square marking the site of the Roman forum, and decorated by a nineteenth-century fountain. The former cathedral, in the centre of the old town, has some amusingly carved fifteenth-century choir stalls, and a baptistery decorated with a mosaic by Chagall representing *Moses Saved from the Waters*. The building itself dates back to the eleventh century, but its medieval parts were largely hidden when the church was unattractively remodelled during the baroque period.

The outstanding artistic monument of Vence is unquestionably the Chapel of the Rosary on the northern outskirts of the town, off the D2210 to Saint-Jeannet. The small chapel was completely designed and decorated by Matisse between 1949 and 1951, and was intended by him as a gift to the nuns of the adjacent Dominican convent, who had looked after him during an illness (see pages 181-2). Try to come here out of season, when you can appreciate to the full the atmosphere of serenity emanating from the chapel's moving and deceptively simple interior.   [3E]

LA VERNE: For this Charterhouse, see COLLOBRIÈRES.

VILLAGE DES BORIES, see GORDES.

VILLEFRANCHE, set in the wooded bay in between the NICE suburb of Mont Boron and SAINT-JEAN-CAP-FERRAT, has a lively fishing-port which was founded in the fourteenth century as a 'free port' (hence the name of the town). The small old town has changed surprisingly little since the eighteenth century, and has a seductive harbour-front lined with tall, Italianate houses painted red and ochre. Some of the dark and narrow streets behind this are vaulted, including the quaintly named Rue Obscure, where the townspeople hid from bombing during the last war.

The fourteenth-century harbourside chapel of Saint-Pierre, once used by fishermen for storing their nets, was completely covered in 1957 by insipid frescoes by Jean Cocteau. You cannot help feeling in front of works such as the *Homage to the Young Women of Villefranche* that the nets must have made a better use of the space; but at least the money you pay to enter the chapel goes to a retired fishermen's charity. If you are still in the mood for bad art, you can climb up to the citadel behind this. The citadel itself is an interesting and well-preserved sixteenth-century complex built by one Emmanuel Philibert of Savoy. Unfortunately parts of it now house a museum devoted to a contemporary local sculptor, Volti, who specializes in pretentious and ridiculous female nudes.

VILLENEUVE-LÈS-AVIGNON, see AVIGNON.

VILLENEUVE-LOUBET, a quiet village two kilometres off the bustling, ugly thoroughfare between NICE and ANTIBES, lies under the shadow of a fifteenth-century castle (founded in the twelfth century and heavily restored in the nineteenth) where Francis I once stayed. The great cook Auguste Escoffier was born in 1846 in a house off the Place de la Mairie. This building has now been turned into an evocative and rewarding museum devoted both to him and the art of cookery (see pages 203–4).   [4E]

Market-Days

The markets of Provence are among the best stocked and most colourful in France, and bring considerable animation to even the quietest towns or villages. I have listed below the market days of many of the places featured in the gazetteer. Generally these markets are held only in the mornings (up to about one o'clock), after which the crowds disperse to the surrounding cafés or bars.

AIX-EN-PROVENCE: Tuesday, Thursday, Saturday.

APT: Saturday.

ARLES: Saturday.

AVIGNON: daily (flea-market on Saturday).

BARBENTANE: daily (except Sunday).

BARCELONNETTE: Wednesday, Saturday.

BARJOLS: Tuesday, Thursday, Saturday.

LE BARROUX: daily (apricot market from 1 July to 1 August).

BEAULIEU: daily (citrus fruit, flowers, olive oil).

BOLLÈNE: Monday.

BONNIEUX: Saturday (daily during the asparagus seasons – from 1 April to 31 May, and from 15 August to 15 September).

BORMES-LES-MIMOSAS: (flea-market on 1st and 3rd Saturday of each month).

BRIGNOLES: Saturday.

CAGNES-SUR-MER: daily.

CARPENTRAS: daily (cherries in May; grapes, truffles, and game, Fridays in winter).

CASTELLANE: Wednesday, Saturday.

CAVAILLON: Monday.

CÉRESTE: every other Thursday.

CHÂTEAURENARD: Saturday.

COLLOBRIÈRES: Sunday.

COMPS-SUR-ARTUBY: Tuesday.

CUCURON: daily (melon and grapes on Tuesdays from 1 August to 3 November).

DIGNE: Wednesday, Saturday (lavender market from late August to early September).

DRAGUIGNAN: Wednesday, Saturday.

FONTVIEILLE: Monday, Friday (from May to October).

FORCALQUIER: Monday.

FRÉJUS: Wednesday, Saturday.

GORDES: Tuesday.

GRASSE: daily.

GRÉOUX-LES-BAINS: Thursday.

HYÈRES: 3rd Thursday of month.

L'ISLE-SUR-LA-SORGUE: Thursday, Sunday.

LE-LUC-EN-PROVENCE: Friday.

MAILLANE: Thursday.

MALAUCÈNE: Wednesday (fruit market daily from 15 April).

MANOSQUE: Saturday.

MARSEILLE: daily (*santon* market throughout December and January).

MARTIGUES: Thursday, Sunday.

MENTON: daily (flea-market on Friday).

MEYRARGUES: Wednesday.

MOUSTIERS-SAINTE-MARIE: Friday.

NICE: daily.

NOVES: Thursday.

OPPÈDE: Thursday.

PERNES-LES-FONTAINES: Saturday (daily in summer; renowned for asparagus).

PEYROLLES-EN-PROVENCE: Wednesday (daily from late April to June).

RIEZ: Wednesday, Saturday (truffle market, Wednesday and Saturday from 15 November to 31 March).

LA ROQUE-D'ANTHÉRON: Thursday.

ROUSSILLON: Wednesday.

SAINT-CHAMAS: Saturday.

SAINT-ÉTIENNE-DE-TINÉE: Sunday.

SAINT-MARTIN-VÉSUBIE: daily.

SAINT-MAXIMIN-LA-SAINTE-BAUME: daily.

SAINT-RAPHAEL: daily

SAINT-RÉMY: daily.

SAINT-TROPEZ: Tuesday, Saturday.

LES-SAINTES-MARIES-DE-LA-MER: Monday, Friday.

SALON-DE-PROVENCE: Wednesday.

SANARY: Wednesday.

SAULT: Wednesday.

SEILLANS: 1st Sunday in July.

SOSPEL: Tuesday, Thursday, Saturday.

TARASCON: Tuesday.

LE THOR: Wednesday, Saturday (daily grape market from 1 August to 31 October; asparagus market, Saturdays in April and May).

TOULON: daily (flea-market on Sunday).

LA TOUR-D'AIGUES: Tuesday.

VAISON-LA-ROMAINE: daily.

VALLAURIS: daily.

VENCE: daily.

Fêtes and Festivals

Most of the main tourist centres of Provence now organize cultural festivals during the summer months. A large selection of these festivals is included in the list below. A calendar of each year's events can be had from local tourist offices. With the major exception of the Avignon International Festival and the Cannes International Film Festival, tickets for these events can generally be had without difficulty and often on the day itself.

A cheaper and frequently more enjoyable form of summer entertainment in Provence is to attend a local fête (see pages 131–2 for a description of that of Lacoste). Though these occasions cannot be recommended for lovers of peace and sophisticated music, they provide a marvellous opportunity for meeting people, drinking and eating cheaply (often partaking of a communal *aïoli*), witnessing or even taking part in such activities as donkey-racing or bull-fighting, and, above all, dancing in the open air until the early hours of the morning. A fête has something to offer to all age groups, and is certainly ideal entertainment for those travelling with a family.

In addition to listing some of the better-known religious and folkloric events of the region, I have given below details concerning the local fêtes of almost all the places included in the gazetteer. These fêtes, though centred around a particular day of the year, are usually spread out over several days, each of which is characterized by different activities. You should note that further celebrations are generally put on for Christmas Eve (most notably candlelit masses and re-enactments of the Nativity) and 14 July (especially fireworks displays).

AIX-EN-PROVENCE: July/August, *Music Festival*.
ANSOUIS: 3rd Sunday in July, *local fête*.
ANTIBES: 2nd half of July, *International Jazz Festival* (Juan-les-Pins).
APT: last Sunday in August, *Fête de Sainte-Anne*.
ARLES: last Sunday in April, *Fête des Gardiens*; July, *Arles Festival* (photography, theatre, music, bull-fights).

AVIGNON: July/August, *International Festival* (theatre, dance and music).

BARBENTANE: last Sunday in August, *local fête* (with cycling races and bull-fights).

BARGEMON: 1st Sunday after 3 August, *local fête*.

BARJOLS: Sunday closest to 17 January, *Fête de Saint-Marcel* ('Grande Saint-Marcel', with traditional folk-dancing and singing, and the procession of the 'Boeuf', held every 4th year; see page 246).

LE BARROUX: 14–17 August, *local fête*.

LES BAUX: last Saturday in June, *Folklore Festival of Saint Jean*.

LE BEAUCET: 2nd Sunday in May, *pilgrimage to chapel of Saint-Gens* (see pages 87–8).

BEAULIEU: 14 July, *Folklore Festival*; 8 September, *local fête*.

BEAUMES-DE-VENISE: last Sunday in July, *local fête*.

BIOT: last Sunday in August, *local fête*.

BOLLÈNE: 1st Sunday in July, *local fête*.

BONNIEUX: 1st Sunday after 22 August, *local fête*.

BORMES-LES-MIMOSAS: 10 February, *'Grand Mimosa Parade'*.

BOULBON: 1 June, *blessing of wine bottles in chapel of Saint-Marcellin* (see page 251).

BREIL-SUR-ROYA: 15 August, *local fête*.

BRIGNOLES: 28 August, *Fête de Saint-Louis*.

LA BRIGUE: 15 August, *local fête*; 8 September, *fête, market-fair, and pilgrimage to chapel of Notre-Dame-des-Fontaines*.

CAGNES-SUR-MER: Easter, *International Flower Festival*; 29 June and 15 August, *local fêtes*; August and Sept., *Antique Dealers' Fair*.

CANNES: May, *International Film Festival*; 1 August, *Fête of the Fishermen*.

CARPENTRAS: July/August, *Music Festival* (in association with that of Vaison-la-Romaine); 14 July, *local fête*.

CASTELLANE: 31 January, *Fête des Pétardiers* (see page 259); last week in May, *local fête*.

CAVAILLON: 1st Monday in September, *local fête*.

CHÂTEAUNEUF-DU-PAPE: 25 April, *Fête of the Wine-growers* (blessing of the vines); 1st Sunday in July, *local fête*.

CHÂTEAURENARD: 1st week in July, *Fête de la Saint-Éloi* (with bull-fights); 1st Sunday in August, *Fête de la Madeleine*.

COMPS-SUR-ARTUBY: 7, 8 and 9 September, *local fête*.

CRESTET: 30 June, *local fête*.

CUCURON: 5 May and 1st Sunday in September, *local fêtes*.

DIGNE: 14 July, *local fête*; 1st Sunday in August, *lavender fête*, with floral procession.

ENTRECASTEAUX: 26 July and 1st Sunday in August, *local fêtes*.

ENTREVAUX: 24 June, *Fête de la Saint-Jean*, with colourful procession through streets; July/August, *Festival of Early Music*.

EYGALIÈRES: 9 and 11 August, *Fête de la Saint-Laurent* (with bulls and cavalcade).

ÈZE: 4 and 5 August, *local fête*.

FONTAINE-DE-VAUCLUSE: 2nd Sunday in July, *local fête*.

FONTVIEILLE: 1st Sunday in August, *local fête*.

FRÉJUS: 3rd Sunday after Easter, *bravade* (procession with drums and gun salute).

GANAGOBIE: Monday of Pentecost, *local fête*.

LA GARDE-FREINET: 5 August, *local fête*.

GIGONDAS: 1st Sunday in September, *local fête*.

GORDES: 1st half of August, *Theatre and Music Festival*; 3rd Sunday in September, *local fête*.

GOURDON: 5 May and 1st Sunday in August, *local fêtes*.

GRÉOUX-LES-BAINS: 6 and 7 July, *local fête*.

GRIMAUD: 15 August, *local fête*.

HYÈRES: 4 February, *local fête*.

L'ISLE-SUR-LA-SORGUE: last week in August, *local fête*.

LACOSTE: last Sunday in July, *local fête* (with donkey race along lower street of village).

LE LAVANDOU: 29 June, *Fête de la Saint-Jean*.

LE-LUC-EN-PROVENCE: 3rd Sunday in May, *cherry festival*; 1st Sunday in September, *local fête*.

LOURMARIN: 1st Sunday in May, *local fête*.

MANE: 1st Sunday after 10 August, *local fête*.

MAILLANE: 1st Sunday after 4 February, *Fête de la Sainte-Agathe* (offering of breast-shaped brioches in commemoration of the martyrdom of the saint); 3rd Sunday in July, *Fête de la Saint-Éloi*; 28 and 29 August, *Fête de Notre-Dame-de-Grâce*; 9 September, *Provençal mass and folklore festival honouring birth of Frédéric Mistral*.

MARTIGUES: 2nd half of July, *fortnight of popular festivities*, including music, street theatre, and free servings of fish and seafood.

MÉNERBES: 25 August, *local fête*.

MENTON: Mardi Gras, *lemon festival*; August, *Festival of Chamber Music*; 29 September, *local fête*.

MEYRARGUES: 25 August, *local fête*.

MIRABEAU: 1st Sunday in August, *local fête*.

MONACO: February, *International Television Festival*; April, *International Tennis Championships*; May, *Monaco Grand Prix*; July/-August, *International Fireworks Festival*; August/September, *World Amateur Theatre Festival*; November, *Monégasque National Fête*; December, *International Circus Festival*.

MOUSTIERS-SAINTE-MARIE: 8 September, *local fête* with torch-lit procession.

NICE: 25 March: '*Festin des Cougourdons*' (fête involving painted gourds filled with drink); fortnight preceding Lent, *Carnival*; April, *International Dog Show*, *Book Fair* and *Tennis Tournament*; May, *Spring Music Festival* given by Nice Philharmonic in Opera House, and *Fêtes des Maïs* (dancing and singing around a specially planted tree in the Cimiez gardens); 29 June, *Fishermen's Fête* (burning of old boat); July, *International Jazz and Folklore Festivals* (with Grand Jazz Parade through Cimiez gardens); October, *Autumn Music Festival* given by Nice Philharmonic in Opera House.

NOTRE-DAME-DE-LUMIÈRES: last Sunday in June, *local fête*; 15 August, 8 September, and 29 September, *pilgrimages to sanctuary* (see page 305).

ORANGE: last two weeks of July, *international music festival*.

OPPÈDE: Sunday before 15 August, *local fête*.

PERNES-LES-FONTAINES: 25 April and last week in August, *local fêtes*.

RAMATUELLE: last Sunday in August, *local fête*.

ROQUEBRUNE-CAP-MARTIN: night of Good Friday and afternoon of 5 August, *costumed procession recreating Christ's Passion* (see page 309); 1st week of August, *local fête*.

LA ROQUE-D'ANTHÉRON: last week in August, *Fête de la Saint-Louis*.

ROUSSILLON: last Sunday in July, *local fête*.

SAINT-CHAMAS: 1st Sunday in September, *local fête* (with bull-fights).

SAINT-ÉTIENNE-DE-TINÉE: 1st Sunday after 3 August, *local fête*.

SAINT-ÉTIENNE-LES-ORGUES: 15 August and the Sunday closest to 8 September, *pilgrimages to chapel of Notre-Dame-de-Lure* (see page 305).

SAINT-JEAN-CAP-FERRAT: 24 June, *local fête*.

SAINT-MARTIN-VÉSUBIE: last week in August, *local fête*.

SAINT-MAXIMIN-LA-SAINTE-BAUME: 22 July, *Fête de Sainte-Madeleine*; August, *Music Festival*.

SAINT-PANTALÉON: 1st Sunday in July, *local fête*.

SAINT-PAUL-DE-VENCE: July/August, *concerts of modern music* in Maeght Foundation.

SAINT-RAPHAEL: July, *International Festival of New Orleans Jazz*.

SAINT-RÉMY: 15 August, *Provençal Festival*.

SAINT-TROPEZ: 16–17 May, *Bravade de Saint-Tropez* (see page 320); 15 June, *bravade commemorating victory over Spanish fleet in 1637*.

LES-SAINTES-MARIES-DE-LA-MER: 24 and 25 May, *Gypsy pilgrimage* (see pages 88–9; other pilgrimages on weekend nearest 22 October and on 1st Sunday in September).

SALON-DE-PROVENCE: July/August, 'Nuits de l'Empéri' (theatre festival in château).

SANARY: 28 July, *local fête*.

SAORGE: 2nd Sunday in July, 3rd Sunday in August, *local fêtes*.

SÉGURET: 3rd week in August, *Provençal festival* (theatre, torch-lit procession, *bravades*).

SEILLANS: last Sunday in July, *local fête*.

SÉRIGNAN-DU-COMTAT: last Sunday in July, *local fête*.

SIMIANE-LA-ROTONDE: Sunday following 24 April, *local fête*.

SISTERON: last Sunday in July, *local fête*; July/August, 'Nuits de la Citadelle' (theatre, music).

SIVERGUES: 1st Sunday before 14 July, *Fête of Apt Rugby Team*.

SOSPEL: 15 August, *local fête*.

TARASCON: last Sunday in June, *Fête de la Tarasque* (see page 87).

TENDE: 1st Sunday after 20 August, *Fête du Traou* (dancing, tasting of *polenta*).

LE THOR: 15 August, *local fête* (with operetta performance out-of-doors).

TOULON: July, *Music Festival*.

TRANS-EN-PROVENCE: 1st Sunday after 15 August, *local fête*.

LA TOUR-D'AIGUES: last Sunday in July, *local fête*.

TOURTOUR: 4 September, *local fête*; 1st Sunday in August, *Folklore Festival*.

VAISON-LA-ROMAINE: July/August, *Festival of Dance, Music and Theatre*; 15 August, *local fête*.

VALLAURIS: 26 July and 29 August, *local fêtes*.

VAUVENARGUES: 24 April and 29 August, *local fêtes*.

VENCE: July, *International Music Festival*; 1st Sunday in August, *local fête*.

VENASQUE: 15 August, *local fête*.

VILLEFRANCHE: 29 September, *local fête*.

VILLENEUVE-LOUBET: 20–21 July, *Fête de la Saint-Éloi*.

Further Reading

GENERAL

In English

Percy Allen, *Impressions of Provence*, London, 1910.

John Ardagh, *The American Express Guide to the South of France*, London, 1983.

C. Bicknell, *Flowering Plants and Ferns of the Riviera and Neighbouring Mountains*, London, 1885.

A. N. Brangham, *The Naturalist's Riviera*, London, 1962.

Charlotte Dempster, *The Maritime Alps and their Seaboard*, London, 1885.

Carol Dix, *The Camargue*, London, 1975.

Ford Madox Ford, *Provence. From Minstrels to the Machine*, London, 1935.

Augustus Hare, *The Rivieras*, London, 1897.

John Hughes, *An Itinerary in Provence and the Rhône*, London, 1822.

Michael Jacobs, Paul Stirton, *The Traveller's Art Guide to France*, London, 1984.

Henry James, *A Little Tour in France*, Boston, 1885.

John Lough, *France Observed in the 17th century by British Travellers*, London, 1985.

Guy de Maupassant, *Afloat*, London, 1889 (*Sur l'Eau*, Paris, 1889).

C. Maxwell, *The English Traveller in France, 1698–1815*, London, 1922.

James Pope Hennessy, *Aspects of Provence*, London, 1952.

Tobias Smollett, *Travels Through France and Italy*, London, 1766.

Stendhal, *Travels in the South of France*, London, 1971 (*Journal d'un voyage dans le midi de France*, Paris, 1858).

G. K. Yeates, *Bird Life in Two Deltas*, London, 1946.

G. K. Yeates, *Flamingo City*, London, 1950.

Arthur Young, *Travels During the Years 1787, 1788, and 1789*, London, 1792.

In French

A.-M. Alauzen, *La Peinture en Provence du XIV siècle à nos jours*, Marseille, 1962.

Albert Babeau, *Les Voyageurs en France depuis la Renaissance jusqu'a la Révolution*, Paris, 1885.

Robert Bailly, *Dictionnaire des communes*, Vaucluse, Avignon, 1985.

E. Bénévent et al., *Visages de la Provence*, Paris, 1960.

F. Benoît, *La Provence et le Comtat-Venaissin. Arts et traditions populaires*, Avignon, 1975.

L. P. Bérenger, *Les Soirées provençales, ou lettres de M. Bérenger écrites à ses amis pendant ses voyages dans sa patrie* (3 vols.), Paris, 1786.

J. Boissieu, *Sentiers et randonnées de Provence*, Paris, 1977.

André Bouyala d'Arnaud, *La Provence des villages*, Paris, 1968.

René Bruni, *Lubéron*, Aix-en-Provence, 1984.

Jean-Paul Clébert, *Provence insolite*, Paris, 1958.

Jean-Paul Clébert, *Les Fêtes en Provence*, Avignon, 1982.

Jean-Paul Clébert, *Mémoire du Lubéron* (2 vols.), Paris, 1984.

Jean-Paul Clébert, *Guide de la Provence mystérieuse*, Paris, 1986.

B. Cousin, *Ex-Voto de Provence*, Paris, 1981.

M. Darluc, *Histoire naturelle de la Provence*, (3 vols.), Avignon, 1782–6.

R. Doré, *L'Art en Provence, dans le Comtat Venaissin et le Comté de Nice*, Paris, 1929.

D. Durandy, *Mon pays. Villages et paysages de la Riviera* (2 vols.), Paris, 1918.

François-Xavier Emmanuelli, *Histoire de la Provence*, Paris, 1980.

H.-P. Eydoux, *Promenades en Provence*, Paris, 1969.

Nicolas Claude Fabri de Peiresc, *Abregé de l'histoire de Provence, et autres textes inédits*, Avignon, 1982.

G. Gamet, *La Crèche provençale*, Marseille, 1984.

E. Garçin, *Lettres à Zoe sur la Provence*, Draguignan, 1841.

Garidel, *Histoire des plantes qui naissent aux environs d'Aix et dans plusieurs autres endroits de la Provence*, Aix, 1715.

Jean Giono, *Provence*, Paris, 1957.

Jean Giono, *Provence perdue*, Paris, 1967.

Pierre Julian, *Le Pélerinage littéraire du Mont Ventoux*, Carpentras, 1937.

Stéphen Liégeard, *La Côte d'Azur*, Paris, 1887.

A. Lunel, *J'ai vu vivre la Provence*, Paris, 1962.

J.-L. Massot, *Maisons rurales et vie paysanne en Provence*, Ivry, 1975.

Marie Mauron, *Quand la Provence nous est contée par ses plus grands poètes et chroniqueurs*, Paris, 1975.

Prosper Mérimée, *Notes d'un voyage dans le Midi de France*, Paris, 1835.

Aubin-Louis Millin, *Voyage dans les Départements du Midi de la France* (4 vols.), Paris, 1807–11.

Monuments Historiques, *Suivez le guide. Provence, Alpes, Côte d'Azur.*

Count Auguste Moszynski, *Voyage en Provence d'un gentilhomme polonais* (1784–5) (translated by F. Benoît), Marseille, 1930.

César de Nostredame, *L'Histoire et chronique de Provence*, Lyon, 1614.

Jean-Pierre Papon, *Histoire générale de Provence* (4 vols.), Paris, 1777–86.

Jean-Pierre Papon, *Voyage littéraire de Provence*, Paris, 1780.

Maurice Pézet, *Provence du souvenir*, Paris, 1983.

Quiqueran de Beaujeu, *La Provence louée*, Arles, 1551.

M. Rémy (ed.), *La Provence*, Paris, 1981.
H.-J. Reynaud, *Faïences anciennes de Provence*, Lausanne.
J.-L. Vaudoyer, *Les Peintres provençaux de Nicolas Froment à Paul Cézanne*, Paris, 1947.
A. Villard, *Art de Provence*, Paris, 1957.
Conte de Christophe de Villeneuve-Bargemont, *Statistiques du Département des Bouches-du-Rhône* (4 vols.), 1821–9.

PREHISTORY AND ANTIQUITY

In English

C. Bicknell, *The Prehistoric Rock Engravings in the Italian Maritime Alps*, Bordighera, 1902.
Theodore A. Cook. *Old Provence*, vol. 1, London, 1905.

In French

F. Benoît, *Recherches sur l'héllenisation du Midi de la Gaule*, Paris, 1965.
Jean-Paul Clébert, *Provence antique* (2 vols.), Paris, 1966–70.
Pierre Desaule, *Les Bories de Vaucluse*, Paris, 1976.
H. Rolland, *Fouilles de Saint-Blaise*, Paris, 1956.
H. Rolland, *Fouilles de Glanum*, Paris, 1958.
H. Rolland, *Le Mausolée de Glanum, Saint-Rémy de Provence*, Paris, 1969.

MIDDLE AGES

In English

A. Bonner, *Songs of the Troubadours*, London, 1973.
A. Borg, *Architectural Sculpture in Romanesque Provence*, Oxford, 1972.
Theodore A. Cook, *Old Provence*, vol. 2, London, 1905.
M. Gail, *Avignon in Flower (1309–1403)*, London, 1966.
A. Tomassello, *Music and Ritual at Papal Avignon*, London 1983.

In French

G. Barruol, *Provence romane* (2); *la Haute-Provence*, Paris, 1976.
Raymond Collier, *Monuments et art de Haute-Provence*, Digne, 1966.
R. Darbois, *Quand les papes régnaient en Avignon*, Paris, 1981.

M. Laclotte, *L' École d'Avignon*, Paris, 1983.

V. Lassalle, *Provence antique dans l'art roman provençal*, Paris, 1981.

Jean de Nostredame, *Les Vies des plus célèbres et anciens poètes provençaux*, Lyon, 1575.

J.-M. Rouquette, *Provence romane (1): la Provence rhodanienne*, Paris, 1974.

Charles Sterling, *Enguerrand Charonton, le peintre de la Pietà d'Avignon*, Paris, 1983.

L. Thevenson, *L'Art du Moyen Âge dans les Alpes méridionales*, Aix-en-Provence, 1985.

16th, 17th, AND 18th CENTURIES

In French

C. Astro, L. Thevenson, *La Peinture au XVIIème siècle dans les Alpes-Maritimes*, Aix-en-Provence, 1985.

Raymond Collier, *La Vie en Haute-Provence de 1600 à 1850*, Digne, 1972.

R. Duchêne, *Et la Provence devint français*, Paris, 1982.

H. Fauville, *La Coste, Sade en Provence*, Aix-en-Provence, 1984.

M.-H. Froeschlé-Chopard, *La Réligion populaire en Provence orientale au XVIIIème siècle*, Paris, 1980.

J.-J. Gloton, *Renaissance et baroque à Aix-en-Provence*, 1979.

L. Legré, *La Botanique en Provence au XVIème siècle* (5 vols.), Marseille, 1899–1901.

R. Moulinas, *L'Imprimerie, la librairie et la presse à Avignon au XVIIIème siècle*, Grenoble, 1974.

R. Moulinas, *Les Juifs du pape en France; les communautés d'Avignon et du Comtat-Venaissin aux XVIIème et XVIIIème siècles*, Toulouse, 1981.

G. Pradel, *Madame de Sévigné en Provence*, Montluçon, 1932.

M. Vovelle, *Les Métamorphoses de la fête en Provence de 1750 à 1820*, Paris, 1976.

M. Vovelle, *Piété baroque et déchristianisation en Provence au XVIIIème siècle*, Paris, 1973.

M. Vovelle, *De la cave au grenier*, Quebec, 1980.

19th CENTURY

In English

Maurice Agulhon, *The Republic in the Village. The People of the Var from the French Revolution to the Second Republic*, Cambridge, 1982.

A. Brown, *Wintering at Menton and the Riviera*, London, 1872.

Xan Fielding, *The Money Spinners*, London, 1977.

Charles Graves, *Royal Riviera*, London, 1957.

A. J. C. Hare, *A Winter at Mentone*, London, 1862.

C. James Haug, *Leisure and Urbanism in 19th century Nice*, Kansas, 1982.

P. Howarth, *When the Riviera was Ours*, London, 1977.

Tony Judt, *Socialism in Provence, 1871–1914. A Study in the Origins of the Modern French Left*, Cambridge, 1979.

J. M., *Thomas Robinson Woolfield's Life at Cannes, and Lord Brougham's First Arrival*, London, 1890.

Frédéric Mistral, *Memoirs of Mistral*, London, 1907.

R. Pickvance, *Van Gogh in Arles*, New York, 1984.

In French

Maurice Agulhon, *Histoire de Toulon*, Toulouse, 1980.

A. Alauzen, P. Ripert, *Monticelli. Sa vie et son oeuvre*, Paris, 1969.

D. Allary, N. Bine-Muller, *Rêveuse Riviera*, Paris, 1983 (a study of the *belle époque* architecture of the coast).

Horace Bertin, *Histoire anecdotique des cafés de Marseille*, Marseille, 1869.

Blanche Bianchi, *La Saison d'hiver à Cannes de 1870 à 1914*, Cannes, 1964.

Jean Boissieu, *Quand Marseille tenait les clés de l'orient*, Paris, 1982.

J. Charles-Roux, *J.-H. Fabre en Avignon*, Paris, 1913.

Jean-Paul Clébert, *La Provence de Mistral*, Aix-en-Provence, 1980.

V. Gaillard, *La Vie quotidienne des ouvriers provençaux au XIX siècle*, Paris, 1981.

R. Jouveau, *Histoire du Félibrige*, 1976.

L. Legré, *Le Poète Théodore Aubanel. Récit d'un témoin de sa vie*, Paris, 1984.

C. Mauclair, *Jules Chéret*, Paris, 1930.

Émile Ripert, *La Renaissance provençale; 1800–1860*, Paris, 1918.

20th CENTURY

In English

Geoffrey Bocca, *Bikini Beach, the Wicked Riviera as it Was and Is*, London, 1963.

B. Collier, *I Wore My Linen Trousers (on a Holiday in Provence)*, London, 1940.

David Dodge, *The Rich Man's Guide to the Riviera*, Boston, 1962.

E. Fearon, *Without My Yacht, How to be at Home in the South of France*, London, 1959.

E. Fearon, *The Marquis, the Mayonnaise, and Me*, London, 1961.

Lady Fortescue, *Perfume from Provence*, London, 1935.

Lady Fortescue, *Sunset House, More Perfume from Provence*, London, 1937.
P. Galante, Louis Sapin, *The Marseilles Mafia, The Truth Behind the World of Drug Trafficking*, London, 1979.
Charles Graves, *The Riviera Revisited*, London, 1948.
Graham Greene, *J'Accuse, The Dark Side of Nice*, London, 1982.
Madeleine Henrey, *Milou's Daughter*, London, 1955.
Marie Mauron, *Mount Peacock, or Progress in Provence*, Cambridge, 1934.
Albert Spaggiari, *The Sewers of Gold*, London, 1979.
R. T. Sussex, *Henri Bosco: A Study of the Novels*, London, 1966.
L. Wylie, *Village in the Vaucluse*, Harvard, 1977 (3rd edition).

In French

Francine Antonietto, *Le Mythe de la Provence dans les premiers romans de Jean Giono*, Aix-en-Provence, 1961.
Georges Berni, *Marcel Pagnol: sa vie, son oeuvre*, Aubagne, 1980.
André Raymond Castans, *Les Films de Marcel Pagnol*, Paris, 1982.
Jacques Chabot, *La Provence de Giono*, Aix-en-Provence, 1982.
Maurice Chevaly, *Giono à Manosque*, Marseille, 1986.
Jean-Paul Clébert, *Vivre en Provence, Lubéron, Pays d'Apt*, Aix-en-Provence, 1977.
C. Durandet, *Les Maquis de Provence*, Paris, 1974.
Marie Mauron, *Ces lointains si présents*, Paris, 1979.
François Morénas, *Le Cinéma ambulant de Provence*, Lyon, 1981.
Marcel Pagnol, *La Gloire de mon père*, Paris, 1957.
Marcel Pagnol, *Le Château de ma mère*, Paris, 1958.
Marcel Pagnol, *Le Temps des secrets*, Paris, 1960.
Georges Raillard, *La Provence de Bosco*, Aix-en-Provence, 1981.
Paul Ricard, *La Passion de créer*, Paris, 1983.

FOOD AND WINE

In English

Ludo Chardenon, *In Praise of Wild Herbs. Remedies and Recipes from Old Provence*, London, 1985.
Elizabeth David, *French Provincial Cooking*, London, 1960.
E. A. Herbodeau, P. Thalamas, *Georges-Auguste Escoffier*, London, 1955.
J. Livingstone-Learmonth, *Wines of the Rhône*, London, 1983.
Jacques Médecin, *Cuisine Niçoise. Recipes from a Mediterranean Kitchen*, Harmondsworth, 1983.
Claudia Roden, *Mediterranean Food*, London, 1987.

Waverley Root, *The Food of France*, London, 1958.
Roger Vergé, *Cuisine of the Sun*, London, 1979.

In French

R. Bailly, *Histoire du vin en Vaucluse*, Avignon, 1972.
R. Jouveau, *La Cuisine provençale de tradition populaire*, Berne, 1962.
J.-B. Reboul, *La Cuisinière provençale*, Marseille, 1895.
Lois Stouff, *Ravitaillement et Alimentation en Provence au XIV-XV siècles*, Paris, 1970.

Index